Scottish Planning Law

Scottish Planning Law

Third Edition

Raymond McMaster BSc (Hons), PG Dip, MRTPI

Alan Prior BSc (Hons), M.Litt, MRTPI

John Watchman LLB, Solicitor

Bloomsbury Professional

Bloomsbury Professional Limited, Maxwelton House, 41–43 Boltro Road, Haywards Heath, West Sussex, RH16 1BJ

Bloomsbury Professional, an imprint of Bloomsbury Publishing Plc

A CIP Catalogue record for this book is available from the British Library.

ISBN: 978 1 84592 779 0

Typeset by Phoenix Photosetting, Chatham, Kent
Printed in the United Kingdom by Hobbs the Printers Ltd, Totton, Hampshire

Preface

The planning landscape has changed considerably since 1999 when the last edition of this book was published. Back then we were only able to speculate about the changes that would result from devolution. There were no National Parks and no legal requirement for things like equalities impact and strategic environmental impact assessments. The full implications of Human Rights legislation were not yet fully understood. In the intervening period it seems that planning law and practice has been in a constant state of flux. For example, there have been several overhauls of national planning policy, both in content and organisation, the development planning system has been significantly reformed and major changes to domestic permitted development rights have been implemented. What was formerly called 'development control' is now known as development management and this area of planning law is almost unrecognisable compared with the system in 1999.

We have incorporated changes in the law up to June 2013 and also flagged some further impending legislative changes (such as those proposed for non-domestic permitted development rights).

Once more we must acknowledge our debt to the editorial board of, and contributors to, *Scottish Planning and Environmental Law* whose invaluable work helped us to cling on (barely) to the roller-coaster of planning law change. We would also like to thank Professor Angus McAllister and Deborah McMaster.

We have endeavoured to state the law as at 30 June 2013.

Contents

Table of Statutes

[*References are to paragraph number*]

Table of Statutory Instruments

[*References are to paragraph number*]

AMENDMENTS TO STATUTORY INSTRUMENTS

One of the most frequently quoted statutory instruments, the Permitted Development Order (PDO) has been affected by a number of amendment orders, which it would have been cumbersome to repeatedly quote in the text:

The Town and Country Planning (General Permitted Development) (Scotland)

Order 1992, SI/223 as amended by: SIs 1992/1078, 1992/2084, 1993/1036,

1994/1442, 1994/2586, 1994/3294, 1996/252, 1996/1266, 1996/3023,

1997/1871, 1997/3060, 1998/1226 and 2003/2155

SSIs 2001/266, 2004/32, 2006/270, 2007/209 and 2011/357

Table of Cases

[References are to paragraph number]

List of Abbreviations

Law reports

AC	Appeal Cases (Law Reports)
All ER	All England Reports
CA	Court of Appeal
CLY	Current Law Yearbook
Ch	Chancery (Law Reports)
Crim LR	Criminal Law Review
CSIH	Court of Session , Inner House
CSOH	Court of Session, Outer House
EG	Estates Gazette
EGCS	Estates Gazette Case Summaries
EGLR	Estates Gazette Law Reports
Env LR	Environmental Law Reports
EWCA	Court of Appeal (England & Wales)
EWHC	High Court (England & Wales)
GWD	Green's Weekly Digest
HL	House of Lords
JLS	Journal of the Law Society of Scotland
JPL	Journal of Planning and Environment Law
KB	Kings Bench (Law Reports)
LGR	Local Government Reports
LR	Law Reports
NPC	New Property Cases
OH	Outer House of Court of Session
PAD	Planning Appeal Decisions
P & CR	Property Planning and Compensation Reports
PLR	Planning Law Reports
QB	Queen's Bench (Law Reports)
RVR	Rating and Valuation Reporter
SC	Session Cases
SC (HL)	Session Cases (House of Lords)
SCCR	Scottish Criminal Case Reports
SCLR	Scottish Civil Law Reports
SLT	Scots Law Times
SPADS	Scottish Planning Appeal Decisions
SPEL	Scottish Planning and Environmental Law
SPLP	Scottish Planning Law and Practice
UKSC	UK Supreme Court

WLR	Weekly Law Reports

Other abbreviations

BAA	British Airports Authority
CAAD	Certificate of Appropriate Alternative Development
CARS	Conservation Area Regeneration Scheme
COSLA	Convention of Scottish Local Authorities
DETR	Department of Environment, Transport and the Regions
DOE	Department of the Environment
DMR	Development Management Regulations
DPEA	Directorate for Planning and Environmental Appeals
EC	European Community
ECHR	European Convention on Human Rights
EEC	European Economic Community
EIA	Environmental Impact Assessment
EIP	Examination in Public
ES	Environmental Statement
EU	European Union
HER	Historic Environment Record
HIE	Highlands and Islands Enterprise
HMSO	Her Majesty's Stationery Office (now TSO - see below)
HSC	Hazardous Substances Consent
IH	Inner House of the Court of Session
LEADER	Links Between Activities Developing the Rural Economy
LDP	Local Development Plan
LEC	Local Enterprise Company
MIR	Main Issues Report
MPA	Marine Protection Area
MSP	Member of the Scottish Parliament
NDPB	Non-Departmental Public Body
NPF	National Planning Framework
NPG	National Planning Guideline
NPPG	National Planning Policy Guideline
NSA	National Scenic Area
PAN	Planning Advice Note
PAS	Planning Aid for Scotland
PD	Permitted Development
PDO	Permitted Development Order
PLI	Public Local Inquiry
PPS	Plans Programmes and Strategies
PTA	Passenger Transport Authority

RSPB	Royal Society for the Protection of Birds
RTPI	Royal Town Planning Institute
SAC	Special Area of Conservation
SDD	Scottish Development Department
SDP	Strategic Development Plan
SDPA	Strategic Development Planning Authority
SEA	Strategic Environmental Assessment
SEDD	Scottish Executive Development Department
SEPA	Scottish Environment Protection Agency
SHEP	Scottish Historic Environment Policy
SG	Scottish Government
SI	Statutory Instrument
SMR	Sites and Monuments Record
SNH	Scottish Natural Heritage
SODD	Scottish Office Development Department
SOEnD	Scottish Office Environment Department
SOIRU	Scottish Office Inquiry Reporters Unit
SPA	Special Protection Area
SPG	Supplementary Planning Guidance
SPP	Scottish Planning Policy
SPSO	Scottish Public Services Ombudsman
SPTA	Strathclyde Passenger Transport Authority
SPZ	Simplified Planning Zone
SSI	Scottish Statutory Instrument
SSSI	Site of Special Scientific Interest
THI	Townscape Heritage Initiative
TPO	Tree Preservation Order
TSO	The Stationary Office
UCO	Use Classes Order
UNESCO	United Nations Educational Scientific and Cultural Organisation
WEPF	West Edinburgh Planning Framework
WHS	World Heritage Site
WWF	World Wide Fund for Nature

I The Planning System

Chapter 1

Introduction

1. THE PLANNING SYSTEM

1.1 The subject matter of this book is planning law, but we will not proceed very far in our understanding of this complex area without first gaining some appreciation of the planning system which the legal rules are designed to serve. Indeed the boundary between planning as such and planning law is not always a clear-cut one, and we will frequently find ourselves straying across that boundary in the course of the book.

1.2 Most people probably have some concept of what the planning system is about. They will know that someone who wants to carry out new development, eg erecting a building, will require planning permission, whether it is for a multi-storey office block or a modest bungalow. They may also see this system of development management in a negative light, as a major intrusion into the right of landowners to do what they want with their own property. However, there is also a very positive aspect to the planning function. When an individual's rights are curbed it is not at the whim of the decision makers, but for the benefit of the public as a whole. The remit of planning extends beyond mere management; it also has the function of protecting and improving the environment in which we all live.

What is planning?

1.3 It has been said that planning, as with much of public policy-making, is the art of achieving the possible, within a complex web of conflicting private, corporate and bureaucratic self interests.[1]

1 Bristow R, *Land-use Planning in Hong Kong: History, Policies and Procedures* (1984) Oxford University Press.

1.4 The Scottish Government provides the following description of planning on its website:

> The planning system is used to make decisions about the future development and use of land in our towns, cities and countryside. It considers where development should happen, where it should not

and how development affects its surroundings. The system balances different interests to make sure that land is used and developed in a way that creates high quality, sustainable places.[1]

1 www.scotland.gov.uk/Topics/Built-Environment/planning/National-Planning-Policy

2. EVOLUTION OF THE SYSTEM

1.5 The seeds of the modern planning system were planted and grew from the problems Britain's towns and cities faced in the nineteenth and early twentieth centuries. These were caused by the rapid urbanisation which followed the industrial revolution and are well documented.[1] Infrastructure could not cope with the rapid influx of people from the countryside seeking work in the new factories. The lack of housing led to severe overcrowding, and disease and poverty were endemic. Similar problems face cities in the developing world today.

1 See eg Gilg A W *Planning in Britain: understanding and evaluating the post-war system* Sage 2005; Ward S V *Planning and Urban Change*, 2nd edition, Sage 2004, Gordon (ed) *Perspectives of the Scottish City* (1985) Aberdeen University Press.

1.6 During the nineteenth century both national and local government slowly began to react to the problems with various public health and housing acts aimed at developing clean water supplies, efficient waste disposal, slum clearance and new house building. In Glasgow, for example, a city improvement trust was set up in 1870 to redevelop new housing in the area around the Saltmarket.

1.7 The Housing, Town Planning etc (Scotland) Act 1909, gave local authorities voluntary powers to produce town planning schemes for the promotion of new development. However, it was little used and subsequent legislation during the inter-war period (eg the Town and Country Planning (Scotland) Act 1932) was also relatively ineffective.

1.8 During the 1930s two further issues emerged relating to living conditions in the large cities. One was the rapid and uncontrolled spread of speculative house building into the countryside (ie 'suburbanisation'), and the consequent loss of agricultural land. Another (and related) issue became known as the 'regional problem',[1] ie that some regions were becoming increasingly prosperous (eg south-east England) while others were in serious economic decline (eg central Scotland). The rapid suburban developments around London were regarded as a symptom of that region's economic growth.

1 See Hall P and Tewdr-Jones M *Urban and Regional Planning* Routledge, 5th edition, (2011).

The modern system

1.9 The above matters were addressed in a number of Royal Commission reports notably that chaired by Montague Barlow.[1] After the 1939–45 war, the resulting recommendations were acted upon by the creation of a comprehensive and mandatory planning system. This was set up in Scotland by the Town and Country Planning (Scotland) Act 1947. (Similar provisions for England and Wales were contained in a separate Act.)

1 'Distribution of the Industrial Population' (1940) (Cmd 6153).

1.10 The planning system we have today stems largely from that 1947 Act (its current replacement being the Town and Country Planning (Scotland) Act 1997). It was an important part of the wide-ranging post-war programme of social legislation which also created the National Health Service, and nationalised industries such as British Coal.

1.11 The 1947 Act introduced the modern system of development management. Since it came into force (on 1 July 1948), almost all development has required planning permission, granted either by the relevant local authority or the Secretary of State (now the Scottish Ministers).

1.12 The same Act introduced the development plan system. Local authorities were given a duty to prepare documents setting out policies for land use and development in their area. They were then required to have regard to these development plans when taking decisions on applications for planning permission. Special controls were also introduced, including those for the protection of historic buildings and preservation of trees.

1.13 While many changes have been made over the years to the detailed operation of this system, it remains fundamentally the same as it was in 1948.

1.14 Since its inception in the late 1940s, planning has gone through a number of crisis periods, first in the late 1960s and early 1970s when problems caused by comprehensive redevelopment became apparent. Particularly unpopular was the demolition of many old buildings and their replacement by modern concrete structures and urban motorways. In response to this, development plans were made more flexible and public participation in planning became mandatory.[1]

1 Town and Country Planning (Scotland) Act 1969 (now re-enacted in the 1997 Act, Part II).

1.15 Planning once more came under close government scrutiny in the 1980s; along with other forms of market intervention.[1] This manifested itself in some relaxation of planning control, eg changes to the Use Classes Order [2] and the introduction of enterprise zones,[3] but the system survived largely intact. Indeed, legislative changes made in the early 1990s strengthened planning controls. For example, the introduction of a plan-led system of development management and the more effective enforcement measures introduced by the Planning and Compensation Act 1991.[4] Growing public concern about the need to protect the environment also reinforced the need for an effective planning system.

1 See eg Thornley *Urban Planning under Thatcherism* 2nd edition 1993.
2 See Chapter 4.
3 See Chapter 5.
4 Now incorporated in the 1997 Act; see Chapter 9.

1.16 More dramatic changes seemed to be on the way in 1994, when the government unexpectedly announced a major review of the Scottish planning system. Following an extensive consultation period, its plans were published in December 1995.[1] However, on closer inspection, the review did not result in a significant shake-up of the system. Much of what was carried out in the name of that review was going to happen anyway (eg consolidation of the planning legislation), and other review initiatives had more to do with fine-tuning or performance-auditing than with any fundamental transformation.

1 SODD 'Review of the Town and Country Planning System in Scotland: The Way Ahead', December 1995.

1.17 More significant was the re-organisation of local government, implemented in1996. The change from a two-tier system of regional and district councils to a unitary system encouraged a radical restructuring of council services, with many of the new authorities opting to create multi-disciplinary 'super-departments'. The planning function is now often found combined with many other services such as transport, environmental protection, estate management and economic development. Anecdotal evidence suggested that this marriage of disciplines initially brought tensions as; in some cases did the combination of former district and regional staff within the one authority. It is arguable that the status and identity of local authority planning services has never fully recovered from this. At least the Town and Country Planning (Scotland) Act 1997 provided a consolidation of earlier legislation dating from 1972.

1.18 The next radical change of the planning system came with the establishment of the Scottish Parliament in 1999. Scotland had its own planning legislation and separate land use planning system prior to devolution. However, Scottish statutory provisions and central government planning policies had largely mirrored those south of the border. New planning initiatives in England tended to be followed soon after by a tartan equivalent which was in substance at least similar but perhaps used slightly different terminology. Since devolution, however, there has been an increasing divergence between the Scottish and English planning systems. A good example of this has been the establishment of the statutory National Planning Framework for Scotland.

1.19 The Scottish Parliament and the Scottish Ministers have no power to make legislation or take (or fail to take) action that is incompatible with 'Convention rights'; or 'Community law'.[1] From the late 1990s onwards, the Human Rights Act 1998 heightened the awareness of the community generally and in particular public authorities regarding human rights issues. The actions of authorities were now more routinely considered with reference to the European Convention on Human Rights (ECHR), particularly as rights could be tested in domestic courts. This did not just apply in relation to tangible rights (such as those to enjoy property, home and family life) but it also affected decision making processes; in particular the need to comply with the ECHR right to a 'fair trial' under ECHR Article 6. Planning decision making processes came under judicial scrutiny in this regard with suggestions that, in a number of respects, the system of planning hearings and appeals did not give a fair hearing and so was not compliant with the ECHR. Scotland was first to see cases of this kind because the statute (the Scotland Act 1998) establishing the Scottish Parliament had incorporated the ECHR and so the Scottish Executive became answerable in our domestic courts as regards compliance with the ECHR before the rest of the UK. After a number of landmark cases, notable the *County Properties Ltd v The Scottish Ministers*[2] case in Scotland, it was held that the system was ECHR compliant in relation to the planning inquiry process at that time and in the decision regard was had to access to the courts (either through a statutory challenge or judicial review). We do not consider that the *County Properties* decision will be the last occasion on which our courts will be called upon to consider submissions about our planning system not being ECHR compliant and in particular about the planning system in Scotland not affording ECHR Article 6 guarantees.

1 See the Scotland Act 1998 (see s 29, 53 and 57(2) and 126(9)) and the Human Rights Act 1998 (see ss 1. 6 and 8 and Schedule 1).
2 2001 SLT 1125.

1.20 There had been a related debate for many years about the apparent one-sided process for determining planning applications. In particular, it had long been suggested that it was unfair that while a developer had the right to appeal a planning decision, third party objectors did not. The issues raised by Human Rights legislation added some potency to the case being made by supporters of third party rights of appeal.[1] In the event, there were to be no third party rights of appeal. Instead, the changes made by the Planning etc (Scotland) Act 2006 and related legislation provide a greater focus on public engagement earlier in the planning process, for example by requiring applicants for 'major developments' to engage in statutory pre-application consultation with communities. In tandem with this, the right for applicants to appeal to the Scottish Ministers was removed for all but the more significant and more controversial development proposals. Instead applicants now usually just have the right to require a planning authority (acting through its local review body) to undertake a review of the initial decision taken by an officer appointed by virtue of a scheme of delegation under s 43A(1) of the 1997 Act by the planning authority to determine the application. It is now normal for more planning application decisions to be delegated to planning officers of the relevant council (rather than be taken by the elected members) than previously was the case.

1 Notably in *Environmental Planning*, the 23rd report of the Royal Commission on Environmental Pollution, March 2002.

1.21 The first decade of the 21st century saw the arrival of e-planning which has made it much easier for applicants to lodge planning applications and for third parties to see what has been submitted and comment on it. It is also now much easier to check the planning history of sites.

1.22 In contrast to the reforms in England, the focus of planning modernisation since 2001, culminating in the 2006 Planning etc (Scotland) Act has been on reinforcing and updating the plan-led system. The starting-point was the *Review of Strategic Planning* in 2001, following an announcement of a review of the arrangements for strategic planning at the annual conference of the Royal Town Planning Institute in Scotland the previous year. The *Review* highlighted concerns about the operation of regional structure plans and proposed replacing these with new strategic plans for the four main cities. This was followed in 2003 by *Your Place, Your Plan*, a white paper on public involvement in planning. This included proposals for improving public consultation, such as transferring neighbour notification from applicants to councils, improving arrangements for advertising of planning applications, requiring planning authorities to give reasons for all planning decisions, and support for planning aid. The white paper also mooted general concerns about the lack of a third party right of appeal, but dropped this after consultation. The outcome of these and a raft of other consultations was the 2005 white paper *Modernising the Planning System*, which set out the Scottish Government's reform proposals ultimately included in the Planning etc (Scotland) Act 2006, the first primary planning legislation passed by the Scottish Parliament.

1.23 The purpose of the reforms was to deliver 'a fairer, more balanced system' (para 4.1). There were concerns: about significant delays in the approval and updating of development plans; that the planning system was bureaucratic, slow to respond to commercial and economic needs and unpredictable in its outcomes; that the system was overly complex, unresponsive to environmental or social concerns and lacked transparency. The reforms aimed to facilitate high quality appropriate development, protect heritage and environment and support sustainable economic growth. Hence the system needed to be fit for purpose, efficient, inclusive and sustainable. The subsequent reforms amended the 1997 Act to put the National Planning Framework onto a statutory footing, for the first time, established a statutory purpose for the NPF and development plans to promote sustainable development (though the reforms shied away from extending this statutory purpose to planning as a whole, in particular development management), and provided the basis for differential treatment of consultation on planning applications and appeals according to a new 'development hierarchy'. However, with plans from the previous system still subject to legal challenges in 2013 it remains to be seen whether the changes made achieve the desired objectives.

1.24 It is notable that each era of planning reform (or 'modernisation') has left intact the main principles of the 1947 Act which established the statutory planning system: the universal definition of 'development'; the requirement for a development plan for all parts of the country; the requirement for planning authorities to make decisions having regard to their development plans; the power to take enforcement action against unauthorised development and the right to challenge the decisions of planning authorities. The presumption has been that the basic system is sound, requiring only periodic adjustment in the face of contemporary agendas.

3. SOURCES OF PLANNING LAW

1.25 When we turn our attention to the law of planning, it may cause any lingering doubts about the health of the planning system to be seen in perspective. If volume of material is any guide to well-being, then the patient is certainly in a robust condition. As well as a substantial amount of primary legislation (fortunately, as we have noted, the much-amended Town and Country Planning (Scotland) Act 1972 has been consolidated and has then been supplemented by the provisions of the Planning etc (Scotland) Act 2006) there is a great deal of delegated legislation and a large body of case law. In any other legal area, particularly one extensively regulated by statute, the story would end there. But in the realm of planning we must also take account of a vast body of quasi-legal material which, though strictly not having the force of law is too influential to be ignored by the any researcher.

The legislative framework

Primary legislation

1.26 There are now three main statutes:

- Town and Country Planning (Scotland) Act 1997 ('the 1997 Act');
- Planning (Listed Buildings and Conservation Areas) (Scotland) Act 1997 ('the Listed Buildings Act');
- Planning (Hazardous Substances) (Scotland) Act 1997 ('the Hazardous Substances Act').

The first of these, the main legislative source, defines the scope of town and country planning and also covers the preparation of development plans,[1] the need for planning permission[2] and enforcement.[3] As their titles suggest, the other two acts deal separately with major areas of special planning control.[4]

1 See Chapter 3.
2 See Chapters 4–6.
3 See Chapter 9.
4 See Chapters 12–14.

European influence

1.27 A number of EC directives have had a substantial impact on planning law, especially in relation to the protection of the natural environment. These include the directives on bird habitat protection and the conservation of natural habitats and of wild flora and fauna,[1] and environmental assessment.[2] It is likely that this European influence will continue to grow in significance in years to come.

1 See Chapter 13.
2 See Chapter 15.

Subordinate legislation

1.28 A great deal of planning law exists in the form of secondary legislation, generally in the form of orders, regulations and directions issued by the Scottish Ministers under statutory powers. For example, under the 1997 Act[1] they can make a permitted development order specifying special categories of development (often minor in nature) that do not require an individual application for planning permission.[2] Where delegated legislation was passed prior to 1997 under earlier statutory powers that have been preserved in the 1997 Act, it continues in force as if it had been granted under the new act.[3]

1 Section 30.
2 Presently the Town and Country Planning (General Permitted Development) (Scotland) Order 1992 SI 1992/223 (as amended). See Chapter 5.
3 Planning (Consequential Provisions) (Scotland) Act 1997, s 2.

Directions

1.29 Most of the delegated legislation is published by TSO (formerly HMSO) and therefore easily available. However, there is an important exception in the case of directions made by the Scottish Ministers. These are generally issued along with circulars issued by the Scottish Government. Care is needed, therefore, as directions (unlike the circulars they accompany) *do* have legal force.

1.30 Some directions are issued under powers provided by primary legislation, such as that issued under s 13 of the Listed Buildings Act removing the requirement to notify certain classes of application for listed building consent to the Scottish Ministers.[1] Others derive from powers given by statutory instrument, eg the 2003 direction specifying the types of planning applications that have to be notified to the Scottish Ministers in order to safeguard airports and certain military installations.[2]

1 Issued with SDD Circular 17/1987 'New Provisions and Revised Guidance Related to Listed Buildings and Conservation Areas'; see Chapter 12.
2 The Town and Country Planning (Safeguarded Aerodromes, Technical Sites and Military Explosives Storage Areas) (Scotland) Direction 2003 issued with SEDD Circular 2/2003 'Safeguarding of Aerodromes, Technical Sites and Military Explosives Storage Areas'.

1.31 Many directions are made for small geographic areas at the instigation of the local planning authority and so are not even attached to any circular. For example, under Article 4 of the Permitted Development Order[1] local planning authorities may, subject to the approval of the Scottish Ministers, direct that specified classes of permitted development rights are removed in certain areas.[2]

1 SI 1992/223 (as amended).
2 See Chapter 5, pt 5.

Case law

1.32 There is a very large body of case law deriving partly from the fact that planning decisions, as in other areas of public administration, may be challenged in the courts on matters such as procedural correctness and the interpretation of legislation.[1] Also, the courts' normal function of statutory interpretation has been inflated by the legislators' omission to define certain key terms, eg the material considerations which a planning authority must take into account when deciding whether to grant planning permission.[2]

1 See Chapter 7.
2 See Chapter 6, pt 5.

English case law

1.33 We have already noted that the Scottish planning legislation, though separate, was very similar to that which applies south of the border. In fact many provisions were identical and so English case law, although not binding upon Scottish courts; is often highly persuasive. We will find, therefore, that a great many English cases will be referred to as a fruitful source of precedent. However, because there are a few significant differences in the legislation, English sources should always be treated with some caution.

Planning appeals

1.34 As we will see in due course,[1] some planning decisions can be appealed to the Scottish Ministers. At this stage the appeal can be on legal grounds or the planning merits of the case, or both. There is generally a further right of to make an application to the Court of Session on legal grounds only, and these decisions will of course form legal precedents in the normal way. Appeal decisions by the Scottish Ministers, on the other hand, do *not* form precedents. However, a great number of them are reported and can be very influential, especially in relation to points for which there is no court decision. In a book at this level, we have only thought it appropriate to refer to such appeal decisions occasionally.

1 See Chapter 7.

Scottish Government policy

1.35 We will see in Chapter 3 that the Scottish Government regularly produces a large number of policy documents, including circulars regarding the planning policies that should be adopted. They also provide comprehensive guidance on the interpretation of planning legislation, invariably accompanied by the proviso that such interpretation is of course properly the function of the courts. Some of these documents (eg The National Planning Framework) are statutory but most do not in the strict sense have the force of law. However, the roles of the Scottish Parliament in providing the legislative framework and planning policy framework and those of the Scottish Ministers and Scottish Government in the operation of the planning system is so dominant that the influence of policy documents is extremely significant and cannot be ignored.[1] We will therefore draw on them from time to time to supplement our account of the law.

1 See Chapter 3.

Chapter 2

The Structure and Operation of the Planning System

1. INTRODUCTION

2.1 In this chapter we outline how the planning system is organised in Scotland. We summarise the role and powers of the Scottish Parliament, the Scottish Government (formerly the Scottish Executive) and its Ministers, the planning authorities, and the main public agencies whose responsibilities impact on the Scottish planning system. Each of these aspects is explored in more detail in subsequent chapters.

2.2 It is the responsibility of the Scottish Ministers to oversee the effective functioning of the planning system in Scotland. The Scottish planning system operates mainly at local government level, but is supervised, co-ordinated and to a large extent directed by central government. Since the establishment of the Scottish Parliament in 1999, the Scottish planning system is a devolved responsibility of the Parliament and the Scottish Government. The main participants are the Scottish Parliament, the Scottish Government, the 32 local councils and two national park authorities (the planning authorities), but there are several other organisations which have roles relevant to planning. The roles of these various participants are illustrated in detail throughout the book, but here we provide an overview.

2. PLANNING AT NATIONAL LEVEL

Scottish Parliament

2.3 The Scottish Parliament comprises all 129 elected members (MSPs) and is the law-making body for devolved matters under the Scotland Act 1998. It considers proposed legislation and scrutinises the activities and policies of the Scottish Government through debates, parliamentary questions and the work of its committees. This includes responsibility for passing planning and other legislation in Scotland and for holding Scottish Ministers to account. The Planning etc (Scotland) Act 2006 was the first primary legislation for planning to be passed by the Parliament under its devolved powers. The Parliament operates through a number of committees which scrutinise legislation and conduct inquiries, including taking evidence from witnesses.

Scottish Government[1]

2.4 Since July 1999 planning has been a devolved responsibility of Scottish Ministers, along with most central government duties and powers. In exercising these powers, Scottish Ministers are answerable to the Scottish Parliament. At the time of writing, the planning system falls within the portfolio of the Cabinet Secretary for Finance, Employment and Sustainable Growth, assisted by a Minister for Local Government and Planning. The Scottish Government[2] (formerly the Scottish Executive) comprises the Scottish Ministers and their senior law officers (see below). Hereafter we use the term ***Scottish Ministers*** when we are referring to decisions of the devolved government of Scotland, since it is the Ministers who are accountable to Parliament for such decisions.

1 For further information on the role of the Scottish Government in the planning system see the Scottish Government website at www.scotland.gov.uk

2 As established by s 44 of the Scotland Act 1998, amended by s 12(1) of the Scotland Act 2012.

2.5 Most of the Scottish Ministers' powers, including those for planning, are exercised on their behalf by officials (civil servants). The administration of the Scottish Government is divided into a number of Directorates. The administration of the Scottish planning system falls within the responsibility of two Directorates: the Directorate for the Built Environment and the Directorate for Planning and Environmental Appeals. ***The Directorate for the Built Environment*** comprises five divisions which have responsibility for various aspects of the planning system including: planning legislation, performance of the planning system, e-planning, national and territorial planning, strategic environmental assessment, architecture and place. These divisions:

- maintain and develop planning legislation;
- provide advice and guidance to Ministers and planning authorities;
- prepare and monitor the implementation of the National Planning Framework;
- facilitate the dissemination of good practice in planning;
- promote good design of new development and place-making;
- lead and coordinate the implementation of e-planning; and
- undertake casework on specific planning issues.

2.6 The ***Directorate for Planning and Environmental Appeals***, as its name suggests, determines appeals against decisions made by planning authorities in Scotland (around 500 per annum). These are determined by professional ***Reporters*** (the equivalent of Planning Inspectors in England and Wales) appointed by Scottish Ministers. A small number of cases ('recalled' appeals) are decided by Ministers. The Directorate also deals with appeals made against decisions by the Scottish Environment Protection Agency (see below) in relation to the prevention and control of pollution, air and water quality, and waste management. As well as considering appeals against planning and environmental decisions, the Reporters of the Directorate also chair public local inquiries/examinations, including:

- 'examination' of strategic and local development plans prepared by planning authorities (see Chapter 3);
- applications for consent under the Electricity Act 1989;
- compulsory purchase and other statutory orders;
- core paths promoted by access authorities under the Land Reform (Scotland) Act 2003.

Government Agencies

2.7 In addition to the Scottish Government directorates, there are a number of government agencies whose remit bears on the operation of the planning system in Scotland. The main ones are as follows.

2.8 ***Historic Scotland*** is an executive agency[1] of the Scottish Government with responsibility for safeguarding the historic environment and promoting its understanding and enjoyment on behalf of Scottish Ministers. This includes protecting historic buildings, parks, gardens and landscapes, ancient monuments, and archaeological sites. The Agency is responsible to Scottish Ministers for maintaining the statutory schedule of monuments of national importance, the statutory list of buildings of architectural or historic interest, the inventory of gardens and designed landscapes, the inventory of historic battlefields and historic marine protected areas. Planning authorities must consult the Agency on any proposed development and plans that impact on the historic environment. In turn, the Agency provides financial assistance towards the conservation and protection of the historic environment and advises on its management (see Chapter 12 for further information on protection of the historic environment and Historic Scotland's role in this).

1 An 'executive agency' is a body established to carry out a specific executive function of government, but left as free as possible to manage within a policy and resources framework set by a government department.

2.9 ***Transport Scotland*** is an executive agency of the Scottish Government, directly accountable to Scottish Ministers. Its responsibilities include rail and trunk road networks, major public transport projects, coordinating the National Transport Strategy for Scotland, and local roads policy.

Other relevant organisations

2.10 There are a number of other relevant (including national) bodies with planning-related responsibilities. Most are appointed and funded by the Scottish Government to carry out various specialist activities, and through Ministers are answerable to the Scottish Parliament.

2.11 ***Scottish Water*** is a publicly-owned company, answerable to Scottish Ministers and the Scottish Parliament, responsible for providing water and waste water services to household customers and wholesale Licensed Providers across Scotland. It operates under a regulatory framework established by the Water Services etc. (Scotland) Act 2005. It is required to deliver the investment priorities of Scottish Ministers within the funding allowed by the Water Industry Commission for Scotland[1]. It therefore has a key role in supporting development. Its Board comprises a chair and non-executive members who are appointed by the Scottish Ministers, and executive members including the Chief Executive who are appointed by Scottish Water.

1 Sets charges and reports on costs and performance, and responsible for protecting public health by ensuring compliance with drinking water quality regulations.

2.12 The ***National Park authorities*** for ***Loch Lomond and the Trossachs*** and for the ***Cairngorms*** are non-departmental public bodies (NDPB),[1] established in 2002 and 2003 respectively, under the National Parks (Scotland) Act 2003. Each is funded by the Scottish Government and led by a Board, some of whom are elected and some appointed by Scottish Ministers and constituent local authorities. While the National Park Board for Loch Lomond and the Trossachs has full planning powers, the Board for the Cairngorms has responsibility only for the local development plan. While development management in the Cairngorms National Park remains with the constituent planning authorities, the Cairngorms National Park Authority board has powers to call-in planning applications which raise a planning issue of 'general significance' for the Park (see Chapter 13 for more information on National Parks).

1 NDPBs differ from executive agencies in that they are largely self-determining with greater independence, and are typically established under statute.

2.13 The ***Scottish Environment Protection Agency*** *(SEPA)* is a non-departmental public body, established under the Environment Act 1995, funded by the Scottish Government and accountable to the Scottish Parliament through Scottish Ministers. As Scotland's environmental regulator its responsibilities in relation to planning include regulating: activities that may pollute water or the air; the storage, transport, treatment and disposal of waste; activities that may contaminate land. As a non-departmental public body SEPA has a Board of Directors, supported by a management team led by a Chief Executive. SEPA is a key agency[1] under the Planning etc (Scotland) Act 2006, providing formal environmental advice on development plans and planning applications. Many of SEPA's responsibilities overlap with those of the planning system, for example SEPA is an important statutory consultee for many types of planning proposal, while some areas of planning control (for example over the development of polluting industries) have been relaxed in recent years because the Government believes that SEPA's powers offer sufficient protection for the environment.

1 'Key agencies' are bodies specified by Scottish Ministers with a duty to cooperate with planning authorities in the preparation of Strategic and Local Development Plans.

2.14 ***Scottish Natural Heritage*** *(SNH)* is a non-departmental public body, established under the Natural Heritage (Scotland) Act 1991, funded by the Scottish Government and accountable to the Scottish Parliament through Scottish Ministers. It provides advice on conservation and enhancement of the natural heritage to Scottish Government and its agencies, local authorities, developers, land managers and others. Like SEPA it is a key agency providing formal advice on development plans and planning applications. Chapter 13 includes more information on the management of Scotland's landscape and natural heritage.

2.15 SNH has a wide range of powers, including to: (a) designate sites and areas to protect habitats and wildlife (eg Sites of Special Scientific Interest (SSSIs)); (b) negotiate management and access agreements; (c) purchase, own, lease or manage land either alone or in partnership; (d) fund special projects; (e) conduct and commission research; (f) provide advice to the government and others on aspects of the natural heritage; and (g) comment to relevant local planning authorities on policies concerning the use of land and sea and on particular planning applications.

2.16 ***Scottish Enterprise*** (covering lowland Scotland) and ***Highland and Islands Enterprise*** (HIE) are non-departmental public bodies, funded by the Scottish Government to promote economic development and training, both directly and through the network of Local Enterprise Companies (LECs) which they supervise and fund. Scottish Enterprise and HIE are key agencies within their respective geographical areas. Many of the activities of LECs are relevant to planning, particularly property development, urban regeneration, land renewal and environmental improvements. Each LEC has to produce a business plan for its area, elements of which are similar to local authorities' development plans, especially in terms of setting priorities for new property development and environmental improvement

2.17 ***Architecture and Design Scotland*** (previously the Royal Fine Art Commission for Scotland) is an executive non-departmental public body of the Scottish Government established to promote appreciation of and high standards in place-making, architecture and planning. This includes being consulted by planning authorities on major planning applications and offering guidance and advice in response.

2.18 The ***Scottish Public Services Ombudsman*** (SPSO) was established in 2002 through amalgamation of three previous offices for the national health service, local government, and housing associations. It is the final stage for handling most complaints from individuals about public services in Scotland, including alleged maladministration by planning authorities. It investigates complaints once the complainant has exhausted the complaints procedures of the organisation concerned. If maladministration is found, the SPSO may make recommendations to the organisation concerned to redress the problems identified. As a last resort, the SPSO may notify the Scottish Parliament of a failure by an organisation to provide redress.

2.19 ***Planning Aid for Scotland*** (PAS) is a voluntary charitable organisation established in 1993 which gives information, advice and training about planning matters to individuals and community groups who cannot afford to pay for the services of a private planning consultant. Planning advice is provided by a network of professionally-qualified volunteers. PAS receives funding from a wide range of organisations, including the Scottish Government, the Royal Town Planning Institute, and local authorities.

2.20 The ***Royal Town Planning Institute*** (RTPI) is the professional body, established by royal charter, which governs the professional standards of planning practitioners throughout the UK. The object of its charter is to advance the 'art and science of town and country planning' in all its aspects for the benefit of the public. Its royal charter gives it a number of powers, including the operation of a code of professional conduct for those practising town planning and the setting of educational standards for entry to the profession. The RTPI also lobbies government on planning matters. In recognition of the independence of the Scottish planning system from the rest of the UK, RTPI Scotland has delegated powers to run RTPI affairs in Scotland and has had an office in Edinburgh since 1995.

Planning Powers of Scottish Ministers

2.21 The powers of Scottish Ministers under the Planning Acts and related legislation have a ubiquitous presence throughout the planning system. The main powers are summarised below.

Delegated legislation

2.22 The powers of delegated legislation give Scottish Ministers strong control of planning in Scotland. Through them Scottish Ministers can dictate the cut-off point between matters which will be dealt with nationally and those which can be left to planning authorities. They can also prescribe the procedures which planning authorities must use, eg in dealing with planning applications. Delegated legislation can also be used to implement government policy. For instance, the amendment made to the 1992 Development Procedure Order[1] to give community councils the status of statutory consultees was part of government policy to widen public participation in the planning process.

1 SI 1992/224 (as amended).

Appeals

2.23 Sections 17 and 19 of the Planning etc (Scotland) Act 2006 made significant changes to the operation of the planning appeals system in Scotland. Previously all appeals against the decisions of local planning authorities on a wide range of planning matters (eg the refusal of planning permission or other consents, and enforcement action) were made to Scottish Ministers through the Directorate for Planning and Environmental Appeals (see above). The decisions of Ministers were final, except on points of law. In practice, almost all appeal cases were actually decided by the Directorate's Reporters because most decisions were delegated.

2.24 The changes to the planning appeals system introduced in the 2006 Act included the removal of the automatic right of appeal to

Scottish Ministers.[1] Instead, an applicant's right of appeal is determined according to who made the decision on the planning application (or failed to make the decision within the statutory timescale, known as 'deemed refusal'). The 2006 Act introduced Local Review Bodies and statutory schemes of delegation for local authorities[2]. This required local authorities to specify the types of planning decisions to be made by their officials, and the types that would remain for decision by councillors. For decisions made by officials, the appeal is to a Local Review Body comprising of councillors. For decisions made by a committee of councillors, the appeal is to Scottish Ministers through the Directorate for Planning and Environmental Appeals, as previously. The Act also provided powers for Ministers to change the statutory period for making decisions on planning applications from a universal two months to four months in the case of 'major' applications (see Chapter 6) and reduced the statutory period for making an appeal in all cases from six to three months. The purpose of these changes was to ensure that decisions on local planning issues were made by the local planning authority, rather than by central government, and to speed up the appeals process.

1 Part 3 s 19 amended ss 47, 237, 239, 267 and 269 of the *Town and Country Planning (Scotland) Act 1997.*

2 Town and Country Planning (Schemes of Delegation and Local Review Procedure) (Scotland) Regulations 2008, explained in SG Circular 7/2009 *Schemes of Delegation and Local Reviews.*

2.25 A small number of appeals against other decisions are not affected by these changes because they are made under other legislation. This includes appeals in relation Listed Building Consent, Conservation Area Consent (see Chapter 12), and hazardous substances consent (see Chapter 14).

Call-in of planning applications

2.26 While all planning applications are submitted in the first instance to the relevant planning authority (Council or National Park Authority), the Scottish Ministers have a general power to call-in any planning application for their own decision. Under s 46 of the 1997 Act, Planning authorities are required to notify the Scottish Ministers where they propose to grant permission for certain categories of planning application. SG Circular 3/2009 *Notification of Planning Applications* also sets out the circumstances in which Scottish Ministers may call in a planning application for their own decision.

Designation of Strategic Planning Authority Areas and Approval of Strategic Development Plans

2.27 The Planning etc (Scotland) Act 2006 introduced important changes to the requirement for national coverage of development plans. For each of the four largest city regions of Scotland, a *strategic development plan* is required (for an area designated by Scottish Ministers) in addition to the local development plan covering the territory of each individual planning authority. Part II of the 1997 Town and Country Planning (Scotland) Act (as amended by the 2006 Act) gives Scottish Ministers powers to (a) designate the boundary for which a strategic development plan shall be prepared, and (b) approve such development plans and their associated *development plan schemes* (see Chapter 3).

2.28 Where representations have been made to a planning authority about a strategic development plan, and these remain unresolved after a defined period, the planning authority must submit the plan to Scottish Ministers for examination by a Reporter (or team of Reporters). Scottish Ministers are empowered under the Planning Acts to approve (with or without modifications) or reject the proposed strategic development plan. The decision of Ministers can be challenged in the Scottish courts by an 'aggrieved person' to the approval of the plan on a point of law.

2.29 At the time of writing, the Scottish Ministers' Reporters had issued their examination reports on (and the Scottish Ministers had approved) three (of the four) Strategic Development Plans[1], namely:

- Glasgow and the Clyde Valley ('GCVSDP');
- Dundee, Perth, Angus and North Fife (TAYplan); and
- Edinburgh and South-East Scotland (SESplan).

In all three examinations the Reporters requested additional information about a number of matters but considered that they did not need to hold any public hearing or inquiry sessions. So, strategic development planning by correspondence appears to be the Scottish Ministers' preferred option to date.

1 The Aberdeen City and Shire Strategic Development Plan was submitted to the Scottish Ministers for examination in July 2013.

Local Development Plans

2.30 Planning authorities have a duty to prepare local development plans. While Scottish Ministers do not approve these plans, they have responsibility for appointing a Reporter (or team of Reporters) to carry out an examination of a plan where objections remain unresolved. Where a Reporter concludes that there were shortcomings in public consultation during the preparation of the plan, the relevant planning authority must be notified, who may then make representations to Scottish Ministers. Ministers may then require further steps to be taken by the planning authority to address shortcomings in the preparation of the plan, or direct the Reporter to proceed with the examination. The Act also requires Scottish Ministers to be consulted on a proposed *development plan scheme* and the proposed *action programme* for implementation of the plan (see Chapter 3).

2.31 On behalf of Scottish Ministers, the Scottish Government's Directorate for the Built Environment monitors the implementation of the new provisions in the 2006 Act to ensure these are being met.

Default Powers

2.32 The 1997 Act (as amended) gives Scottish Ministers a number of default powers regarding the preparation of development plans including the powers to direct:

- one authority to appoint an employee as manager of a strategic development plan, and other constituent authorities to appoint assistants;
- a planning authority to submit a report on its failure to replace its local development plan within the statutory five year period; and
- a planning authority to consider modifying its local development plan, or for Scottish Ministers to approve the plan themselves.

Historic buildings, conservation areas and ancient monuments

2.33 Under s 1 of the Planning (Listed Buildings and Conservation Areas) (Scotland) Act 1997, the Scottish Ministers are responsible for preparing lists of buildings which are of architectural or historic interest. A similar duty relates to scheduled ancient monuments under the Ancient Monuments and Archaeological Areas Act 1979. Once given these designations such buildings are afforded special protection, and proposed works will usually require Ministerial approval (see Chapter 12). Whilst ***Conservation Areas*** are normally designated by local authorities, Scottish Ministers also have powers to deal with them. In all conservation areas consent is needed for demolition of all buildings listed and unlisted. In reality, most of this work is carried out on Scottish Ministers' behalf by the staff of Historic Scotland.

National Planning Policy

2.34 Scottish Government planning policies are set out in the National Planning Framework, Scottish Planning Policy and other national policies (such as 'Designing Streets – A Policy Statement for Scotland') and Circulars. The Scottish Government also issues Planning Advice Notes (see below). Policy, guidance and advice issued by Scottish Ministers are material considerations in planning decisions.

2.35 The 2006 Act requires Scottish Ministers to prepare and keep up to date a National Planning Framework ('NPF'). The NPF is a strategy for the development of Scotland's urban and rural areas over a 20-year period. A key purpose is to identify key strategic infrastructure needs for the future development of the country. Since the NPF is prepared by Scottish Ministers and approved by the Scottish Parliament, these designated 'national' developments are regarded as having planning permission in principle, and planning authorities are required to take the NPF into account in their development plan and development management decisions. The NPF is supported by an action programme which sets out how the national developments and other key components of the plan will be implemented, when and by whom, and a participation statement. As with strategic and local development plans, it is also subject to strategic environmental assessment. The 2006 Act introduced a requirement that functions relating to the preparation of the NPF by Scottish Ministers and development plans by local and national park authorities must be so exercised with the object of contributing to sustainable development.

2.36 The consolidated ***Scottish Planning Policy*** (SPP) sets out Scottish Ministers' view of the purpose of the planning system, its core principles, statutory guidance on the requirement for sustainable development under s 3E of the 2006 Act, concise subject planning policies, with implications for development planning and development management, and Government expectations for what the planning system should deliver in terms of its outcomes.

2.37 ***Circulars*** contain guidance on policy implementation through legislative or procedural change. Like the NPF and SPP, they can be material considerations in planning decisions. The Scottish Government provides guidance and advice on planning matters in a variety of forms including: ***Planning Advice Notes*** (eg PANs on design statements, enforcement), Guides (eg on compulsory purchase, community engagement), letters from the Chief Planner of the Built Environment Directorate (eg affordable housing policies), design guidance, and specific advice documents (eg development viability).

3. PLANNING AT LOCAL LEVEL

Local Government

2.38 The Scottish planning system is primarily operated by the 32 unitary councils and two National Park Authorities[1]. This system replaced a two-tier system of regional and district councils in April 1996. Under that system, planning responsibilities had been split between the two levels but since 1996 each council is the all-purpose planning authority for its area. The main planning powers and duties of planning authorities under the 1997 Act as amended by the Planning etc (Scotland) Act 2006 are:

- preparation and review of Local Development Plans;
- preparation and review of Strategic Development Plans (in the four designated Strategic Development Plan Areas);
- statutory requirement to promote sustainable development through the development plan;
- development management (ie taking decisions on applications for planning permission, but also including the power to revoke or modify an existing permission, and to require the submission of an environmental assessment to accompany an application for planning permission);
- Local Review Board to consider appeals against delegated decisions;
- planning enforcement;
- tree protection;
- advertisement control (including 'fly posting');
- acquisition of land for planning purposes;
- control and review of mineral workings and planning permissions for mineral operations, including the ability to revoke or suspend permission;
- ability to enter into planning obligations with land owners;
- promotion of Simplified Planning Zones;
- serving of Notices in respect of land 'adversely affecting the amenity of a neighbourhood';
- promotion of Article 4 Directions removing permitted development rights; and
- powers to require discontinuance of existing uses.

1 For a map showing the boundaries of the 32 Councils and the two National Park authorities see the Scottish Government Planning website at www.scotland.gov.uk/Topics/Built-Environment/planning/Local-Planning

2.39 The main powers under the *Planning (Listed Buildings and Conservation Areas) (Scotland) Act 1997* are:

- dealing with applications for Listed Building Consent;
- protection of Listed/historic buildings;
- designation of Conservation Areas;
- protection and enhancement of Conservation Areas; and
- enforcement of listed building and conservation area controls.

2.40 The main powers under the *Planning (Hazardous Substances) (Scotland) Act 1997* are:

- dealing with applications for Hazardous Substances Consent;
- variation or revocation of existing consents; and
- enforcement of hazardous substances control.

2.41 Most planning authorities make arrangements to delegate decisions to committees, sub-committees and officers of the council, and planning is no exception. Many authorities have separate committees for matters of planning policy (such as approving and reviewing the development plan) and for determining applications for planning permission. All councils are required to have a statutory scheme of delegation specifying the categories of planning application to be decided by professionally qualified officers of the council (see above).

2.42 Whereas in the past it was fairly easy to identify which council department dealt with planning, it has become more difficult in recent years as council responsibilities are grouped into larger departments whose remit covers several functions. It is common, for example, to find planning grouped with economic development and roads/transport.

Community Councils

2.43 The *Local Government (Scotland) Act 1973* provides for the election of community councils, voluntary bodies which have no statutory powers. Instead, they are given a general purpose of ascertaining, co-ordinating and expressing the views of the communities which they represent to the local authority and other public bodies.

2.44 In the past, it was common for local authorities to use community councils to help obtain local views on planning matters. This arrangement was first put on to a statutory footing in 1996, when community councils were given the legal right to be consulted on planning applications affecting their area. This was done through an amendment to the Town and Country Planning (General Development Procedure) (Scotland) Order 1992 to include community councils on the list of 'statutory consultees'.

4. SUMMARY

2.45 Planning legislation gives extensive powers of oversight to government Ministers in the operation of the Scottish planning system. Most of the management of the system occurs at local government level. The Planning etc (Scotland) Act 2006 provided new and revised powers and obligations (including the promotion of sustainable development through the development plan) intended to deliver a modernised planning system. This includes new types of development plan, new procedures for determining planning applications, and extended powers of enforcement. Consolidated planning policy seeks a more integrated plan-led approach to planning in Scotland, with more effective involvement of associated agencies and public bodies.

2.46 Audit Scotland assists the Auditor General and the Accounts Commission to ensure that public money is spent properly, efficiently and effectively. In its 2011 report[1] on performance to date in modernising the Scottish planning system it found that:

1) modernisation has significantly changed the way the planning system works at national, regional and local levels;
2) the Scottish Government, key agencies and planning authorities are working better together; however, more progress is needed to realise the full potential of modernisation;
3) Strategic and Local Development Plans are essential in achieving a plan-led system but progress in establishing these has been slower than expected;
4) while expectations for the time taken to process planning applications are not being met, users are generally satisfied with the planning system;
5) Councils have limited information about the costs of processing planning applications; this limits their ability to understand and reduce these costs; the Scottish Government sets planning fees but these are not based on accurate cost information.

It recommended that the Scottish Government should:

a) consider replacing the four-month timescale for deciding major applications and work with planning authorities to agree a new way of assessing performance for these applications as part of a new performance measurement framework for development management;

b) consider including a measure of performance of the planning system in Scotland's national performance framework;

c) clarify what activities planning fees cover, taking account of new activities that were introduced by modernisation and created additional costs for planning authorities.

It recommended that Councils and national park authorities should:

a) review their schemes of delegation to ensure the decision-making process is as efficient as possible;

b) ensure processes are in place to enable and support better and more creative engagement with community councils and the wider community;

c) use a project management approach for considering and determining major applications and agree key milestone stages and dates with applicants and key stakeholders;

d) continue to work together, and with the Scottish Government, to develop a new comprehensive performance measurement framework that clearly links planning activities with national outcomes.

1 *Modernising the Planning System*, Audit Scotland, September 2011.

Chapter 3

Planning policy

1. INTRODUCTION

3.1 Much planning practice involves trying to influence the activities of for instance developers and the private, public and third sectors. This is done, to a great extent, through the operation of planning policies which indicate, in advance, what the relevant planning authority's response will be to various proposals. Policies may state what the authority's priorities are for different types of development. They can be prepared on a locational basis by specifying, for example, areas where development will not be allowed save in exceptional circumstances (eg green belt), or identifying sites where certain types of development will be encouraged.

3.2 Policies can also be more general in nature, such as those restricting changes of use from shops to public houses in tenement properties. Others indicate design standards, such as the number of parking spaces needed for different types of development. What might be called 'positive' policies can also be identified. These give indications where authorities will take direct action, by carrying out environmental improvements for example.

3.3 Planning policy statements can be found at both national and local levels of government. This chapter looks, in turn, at the various documents involved at each level.

2. STRATEGIC ENVIRONMENTAL ASSESSMENT (SEA)

3.4 Before looking at the various planning policy documents in detail, it would be useful to highlight the requirement for SEA which applies to many policy statements and plans.

3.5 SEA originates from a European Directive[1] which has been implemented in Scotland via the Environmental Assessment (Scotland) Act 2005. Under this legislation all public bodies and some private companies which operate in a public character have to assess, consult and monitor the likely impacts of their plans, programmes and strategies (often referred to as PPS) on the environment through the process known as Strategic Environmental Assessment (SEA).

1 Directive 2001/42/EC, 'on the assessment of the effects of certain plans and programmes on the environment'.

3.6 There are some exceptions to the requirement for an SEA. Plans dealing with national defence, civil emergencies, budgets and finance are exempt. There are also a limited number of plans identified in the 2005 Act[1] which can be pre-screened as not requiring an SEA if they are shown to have no or minimal environmental impact.

1 Section 5(4).

3.7 SEA has three main elements which are:

- Systematic assessment and monitoring of the significant environmental effects of a proposed public sector strategy, plan or programme. This is set out in an Environmental Report and the SEA requirement also applies to modifications and updates to existing plans. The authority has to advertise that it has embarked on the SEA process and this is normally linked with statutory notices about the preparation of the plan being assessed.
- Formal consultation on the assessment should take place with Scottish Natural Heritage (SNH), Scottish Environment Protection Agency (SEPA), Historic Scotland and the public. Although there is no legal requirement to do so, it makes sense for the Environmental Report to be prepared and published alongside the proposed plan that is being assessed. For example when a Main Issues Report (MIR) has to be published and consulted on at an early stage in the plan preparation process the Environmental Report will also be published and consulted on at this stage. If changes are made to the plan that is being assessed as it makes its way through the preparation process it may be necessary to also revisit the SEA.
- Once a new strategy, plan or programme has been adopted, the authority that prepared it has to publish a public statement about how opinions expressed through the SEA process have been taken into account, highlighting the alternatives that were considered and explaining why the one selected has been chosen.

3.8 The introduction of SEA has meant that when preparing new plans authorities have to take care to adhere not only to the statutory process required for producing the plan itself but also to the SEA legal requirements running in parallel to that. Failure to do so could lead to the authority's plan being open to legal challenge.

3. NATIONAL PLANNING POLICY

3.9 We made the point in Chapter 2 that planning is primarily a local government function which is strongly directed by central government. This is especially true of planning policy. Central government wants local authority policies, decisions on planning applications and even the ways in which the planning system is operated, to reflect its views of national development priorities. It also expects the planning system as a whole to help deliver a range of Scottish Government objectives including for example on transport, housing and the economy.

3.10 National planning policy can take various forms. It may be site-specific (eg by identifying sites for national developments such as the Grangemouth Freight Hub).[1] It may be prescriptive without being site-specific, such as the policy that local authorities should ensure that at least a five-year effective supply of land for private house building is maintained in their areas at all times.[2] It may set out the criteria against which local authorities should judge planning applications for certain types of development.[3] Alternatively, it may be of a more general nature, such as the purpose and objectives set out for the planning system in SPP.[4]

1 National Planning Framework for Scotland 2 (NPF2) (2009).
2 Scottish Planning Policy (SPP), para 72 (2010).
3 See for example policy on new retail development in SPP paras 61–65 (2010).
4 SPP paras 3–9 (2010).

3.11 The Scottish Government's national planning policies are contained in several different documents. These are the National Planning Framework (NPF), the Scottish Planning Policy (SPP), Designing Streets, Circulars and, at the time of writing Designing Places and West Edinburgh Planning Framework. In due course Designing Places will be replaced by the Architecture and Place Policy. The NPF is the only one of these that has to be produced by law. The SPP contains the advice on sustainable development that the Scottish Ministers are empowered to give under the 1997 Act.[1] Beyond that, the SPP and other documents are non-statutory but still carry considerable weight within the planning system. For example, as we shall see in Chapter 6 planning authorities must by law take into account all 'material considerations' when deciding whether or not to grant planning permission for a proposed development and these considerations include national planning policy statements. To this list we should add Planning Advice Notes, Design Advice and Web advice on planning matters. While the Scottish Government does not identify these as part of its national policy statements, the advice and guidance that they contain is nevertheless extremely important and local planning authorities ignore it at their peril. We shall consider each of these in detail below.

1 Section 3E(3).

National Planning Framework (NPF)

3.12 The 1997 Act requires the Scottish Ministers to prepare a spatial plan called the National Planning Framework (NPF).[1] This has to set to set out in broad terms how the Ministers consider that the development and use of land could and should occur in Scotland. It must include a spatial development strategy and an indication of the Scottish Ministers' development priorities. It may also include an account of matters that the Scottish Ministers consider affect development, designate specific developments or classes of development as 'national developments' and contain any other material considered appropriate. National developments need to be those of strategic importance to the development of Scotland and, if included, the Scottish Ministers must justify this. The NPF sits at the top of the statutory development plan hierarchy in Scotland and is intended to guide the strategic and local development plans that have to be prepared by local planning authorities. As with most other plans produced by the Scottish Government and local authorities, a Strategic Environmental Assessment (SEA) of the NPF has to be conducted in tandem with its preparation[2] as do assessments or appraisals of its impact on habitats, equalities and carbon emissions.

1 Section 3A.
2 As required by the Environmental Assessment (Scotland) Act 2005. See Part 2 above.

3.13 The 1997 Act requires the Scottish Ministers to carry out consultations when preparing a new or updated NPF. To this end the Ministers have to publish a participation statement setting out who will be consulted, when and how. The participation statement also needs to describe the steps that are to be taken to involve the public at large in the preparation or review.[1]

1 1997 Act, s 3A(10).

3.14 Once they have prepared a proposed new or revised NPF, the Scottish Ministers must lay this before the Scottish Parliament for 60 days. They then have to take into account any Parliamentary resolutions or reports about the NPF made during that period.[1] Once they have done so, the final version of the NPF must again be laid before the Scottish Parliament accompanied by two other reports. One of these reports has to demonstrate that the Ministers have met or exceeded the extent of consultation set out in their participation statement. The second has to explain how the Ministers have responded to any Parliamentary resolutions or reports and highlight changes made to the NPF as a result.[2]

1 1997 Act, s 3B.
2 Ibid, s 3C.

3.15 The NPF needs to be kept under review and every five years a revised version should be produced or the Scottish Ministers have to give reasons why it is not to be updated. The first NPF (now known as NPF1) was a non-statutory policy document published in 2004. NPF2 was the first to be prepared under the current statutory requirements and was published in 2009. In September 2012, the Minister for Local Government and Planning announced to the Scottish Parliament that work had commenced on NPF3. The Minister said that NPF3 will set out the Scottish Government's development priorities for the next 20–30 years with a focus on supporting economic recovery and growth and the transition to a low-carbon economy. A participation statement was published at the same time and this included a project timetable aimed at achieving the Scottish Government's target of publishing NPF3 by 25 June 2014.[1] The Main Issues Report (MIR) and Draft Framework (entitled *Ambition-Opportunity-Place*) was published on 30 April 2013. A 12 week public consultation period then followed. The proposed Framework was due to be put to the Scottish Parliament for the 60 day period (see para 3.9 above) later in 2013. A number of related supporting documents were published shortly after the MIR and these were an updated Participation Statement, Strategic Environmental Assessment (joint with the new draft SPP), Habitats Regulations Appraisal, Business and Regulatory Impact Assessment, Equalities Impact Assessment and a Report of Analysis of national developments.

1 Scottish Government 'National Planning Framework 3: A Plan for Scotland – Ambition Opportunity Place' (2012).

Scottish Planning Policy (SPP)

3.16 The SPP is a statement of policy on nationally important land use planning matters. It sets out the Scottish Government's view on the purpose of planning and sets objectives, core principles and outcomes. It contains statutory advice on sustainable development. It also provides policies on the operation of Development Planning, Development Management and community engagement. Last but not least, it sets out Scottish Government policy in relation to various topics such as housing, the historic environment and surface coal mining, and outlines the implications of these for local authority development plans and handling of planning applications.

3.17 Prior to the publication of the current SPP, national policy was set out in numerous separate SPPs and National Planning Policy Guidelines (NPPGs) each dealing with a specific topic. Those older more specialised policy statements were superseded when the current consolidated SPP was published in 2010.

3.18 In September 2012 the Minister for Local Government and Planning announced to the Scottish Parliament that the SPP would be comprehensively reviewed and updated alongside the review of the National Planning Framework (NPF). The aim would be to publish a new SPP by the end of 2013. As well as general updating, the review would seek to focus on sustainable economic development and improved 'placemaking'. A participation statement[1] was issued by the Scottish Government setting out how it would consult on the SPP review and also outlining the other assessments and appraisals that would need to be conducted with it. These are the same as those required to accompany the NPF review (see para 3.15 above). A consultative draft of the new SPP was published on 30 April 2013 and was followed by a 12-week public consultation period.

1 Scottish Government 'Scottish Planning Policy: Participation Statement' (2012).

Designing Places

3.19 'Designing places'[1] was developed in response to concerns about the design quality of many modern developments, particularly the common failing of looking and feeling as if they could be anywhere. For example, in the year 2000 the then Scottish Planning Minister, Sam Galbraith, had asked the question 'where are the conservation areas of tomorrow?' It was considered that part of the problem had been a lack of a general statement setting out national aspirations for design and the role of the planning system in delivering these. Designing Places is intended to be that statement. It makes clear that design is a material consideration in the determination of planning applications, identifies a number of general principles that characterise good design and sets out a framework for achieving that with new development. That framework includes advice on design policies in development plans and supplementary planning guidance (SPG). It identifies specific types of SPG and where these are appropriate as follows: urban design frameworks (for areas of change), development briefs (for significant sites), master plans (for sites where a degree of certainty is possible), design guides (for sensitive areas or on specific topics) and design codes (where a degree of prescription is appropriate). It gives advice on how local authority development management teams with suitably qualified staff can promote better design using appropriate policy documents. Designing Places is due to be replaced by the new SPP at the end of 2013 and a new Architecture and Place Policy.

1 Scottish Executive 'Designing Places: A Policy Statement for Scotland' (2001).

Designing Streets

3.20 Traditionally, the design of streets was based on meeting technical standards defined by highways engineers. 'Designing Streets'[1] represents an attempt to move away from that towards a design-led approach which focuses on creating attractive places which prioritise the needs of people rather than traffic movements. While local authorities can produce their own policy documents on these matters, they should be consistent with the policies in 'Designing Streets'.

1 Scottish Government 'Design Streets: A Policy Statement for Scotland' (2010).

Circulars

3.21 The use of circulars is of course not confined to planning; they are used in many kinds of public administration. Planning circulars are used to give guidance on the implications of legislative or procedural changes. As we have already seen, circulars may even be used to issue legislation because, when the Scottish Ministers issue a new direction, it will usually be attached to a circular.[1] As most changes in the law or planning procedures are designed to implement aspects of government policy, circulars also set out the policy background to the changes.

1 See eg SG Circular 3/2009 'Notification of Planning Applications' which includes the Town and Country Planning (Notification of Applications) (Scotland) Direction 2009.

3.22 As well as introducing legislative changes, circulars are sometimes used to explain the implications of important court decisions.[1] This can present a problem when the view of the courts on what is lawful differs from government policy. For example, the Scottish Government's policy in Planning Circular 3/2012 *Planning Obligations and Good Neighbour Agreements* about when it is legitimate to use a planning obligation,[2] is considerably narrower than the legal position defined by the courts.[3]

1 Eg SODD Circular 4/1998 'The Use of Conditions in Planning Permissions'.
2 Under s 75 of the 1997 Act; see Chapter 8.
3 *Good v Epping Forest District Council* [1994] 1 WLR 376 CA; [1994] JPL 372; *Tesco Stores Ltd v Secretary of State for the Environment and Others* [1995] 2 PLR 72, [1995] 2 EGLR 147.

3.23 The Scottish Government maintains a list of extant circulars with copies of each on its website. It should also be noted that Historic Scotland produces its own circulars from time to time on aspects of planning law, policy and practice relating to the historic environment.[1]

1 See Chapter 12.

West Edinburgh Planning Framework

3.24 While, as its name suggests, the West Edinburgh Planning Framework (WEPF) deals with a specific part of Scotland[1], it has the status of national planning policy. Originally produced in 2003, the current WEPF was published in 2008. It was developed by a steering group with representatives from the Scottish Government, Edinburgh City and West Lothian Councils, and Scottish Enterprise. It was produced because of the importance that the Scottish Government attaches to West Edinburgh as a driver for the Scottish economy. WEPF includes a range of new developments including new transport infrastructure, relocation of the Royal Highland Centre to create a new national showground, an international business gateway and land safeguarding for future airport expansion. The implementation of these is to be supported by the local planning authorities, for example by reserving land for the airport in statutory development plans, and other agencies.

1 West Edinburgh is defined for the purposes of the WEPF as the area encompassing the A8 Corridor from Gogar to Newbridge interchanges including the Airport and land between the Airport and the A8 as well as land south of the A8 from the City Bypass through to the Ratho Station area.

Planning advice notes and other guidance

3.25 Planning advice notes (PANs) were originally issued in the mid-1970s to give technical advice to the authorities who were preparing regional reports; these were the responsibility of the now-defunct regional councils, and only one round of regional reports was ever produced, following the local government reorganisation of 1976. Since the publication of this early series PANs have been developed to give advice on good practice and other relevant information. This continues to be the case and there are currently around 30 extant PANs. These cover a wide range of issues including community engagement, archaeology and, affordable housing and land audits. In addition to PANs, Scottish Government advice can be found in design guidance (eg on charrettes), specific advice documents/sheets (eg on habitats regulations appraisal) online guidance (eg on renewables), guides (eg to environmental impact regulations) and even letters from the Chief Planner (eg providing an effective supply of land for housing). However, the letters from the Chief Planner are to be withdrawn once the new SPP is approved at the end of 2013.

Status of Scottish Government policy statements

3.26 Under the 1997 Act, planning authorities must take the NPF into account when preparing their own statutory development plans and also when dealing with planning applications for national developments. It also requires them to have regard to the Scottish Ministers' guidance on sustainable development (currently in SPP) when exercising any of their planning functions.[1] The other policy and advice documents issued by the Scottish Ministers have limited direct force in law but their influence is so great that they almost approach that status. For example, the courts have confirmed that government policy statements are material considerations to be taken into account in the determination of planning applications.[2] In 1992, the failure of the then Secretary of State for Scotland to take into account his own guidance contained in PAN 38 (about housing land allocations) led to the quashing of his decision to approve an update of the Strathclyde Structure Plan.[3]

1 1997 Act, s 2E(3).
2 See Chapter 6.
3 *Scottish House Builders Association v Secretary of State for Scotland* 1995 SCLR 1039; (1995) 52 SPEL 109.

3.27 Where relevant, therefore, planning authorities must take government policy statements into account when preparing development plans and in taking decisions on planning applications. They must also be taken into account by reporters, the officials appointed by the Scottish Ministers to determine appeals and carry out examinations of local authorities' proposed development plans. If any planning authority fails to take into account any relevant national policy, its decision could be overturned by the courts, as was seen in the *Scottish Housebuilders Association* case.[1]

1 1995 SCLR 1039; (1995) 52 SPEL 109.

3.28 When taking into account national policy, it is important that a planning authority does not misinterpret its meaning as to do so could open its decision to legal challenge.[1] However, the Supreme Court has held that an error in interpretation of policy is only material where there is a real possibility that the determination might otherwise have been different.[2]

1 For an example of a recent successful challenge, see *Manydown Co Ltd v Basingstoke and Deane BC* [2012] EWHC 977(Admin); [2012] JPL 1188.
2 *Tesco Stores Ltd v Dundee City Council* [2012] UKSC 13; [2012] PTSR 983.

3.29 Whilst national policies must be correctly understood and given proper consideration, they do not have to be slavishly adhered to. In *ELS Wholesale (Wolverhampton) Ltd and Crownbrae Ltd v Secretary of State for the Environment and Cheltenham Borough Council*,[1] it was held that the wording of a circular was not to be applied as if it were a statutory provision. The House of Lords made it clear that the weight to be attached to government policy is a matter for the decision-maker.[2] Planning authorities may legitimately choose to attach greater weight to other planning considerations and thus take decisions which are not in line with government policy.

1 [1987] JPL 844.
2 *Tesco Stores v Secretary of State for the Environment* [1995] 2 All ER 636.

3.30 However, there are good practical reasons why government guidance is usually followed. As we saw in Chapter 2, the Scottish Ministers have considerable planning powers, notably to approve and modify strategic development plans, stop the adoption of local development plans that they consider to be unsatisfactory, call in planning applications and make appeal decisions.[1] Any strategic planning authority which prepared a strategic development plan deemed to be at odds with national policy, therefore, would be likely to find this modified once submitted to the Scottish Ministers for approval. If councils refuse planning permission for development which government policy would support, their decisions are likely to be overturned by the Scottish Ministers on appeal, and they may even have to pay the appellant's costs. It is also possible for the Scottish Ministers to call in a planning application before the local authority has had the chance to refuse it as was seen with the *Trump International Golf Links Scotland* application for development at the Menie Estate, Aberdeenshire, in 2007. On the other hand, if a Council wishes to grant planning permission for development that is contrary to national policy, it may also find that the application is called in by the Scottish Ministers and refused eg in the case of Perth and Kinross Council's proposed demolition of the Perth City Hall in 2012.

1 See Chapters 2, 6 and 7.

Legal Challenge

3.31 The courts have been willing to consider challenges to the legality of government policy statements.[1] To be successful the challenge would have to show that the content of the policy statement contained errors of law or was wholly unreasonable. The Courts have also made clear that no policy can be set in stone, they are always open to reconsideration in the light of changing circumstances. An attempt by the UK government to stand by a policy in favour of a third runway at Heathrow Airport was open to challenge, therefore, because that policy had been established before important alterations to climate change policy.[2]

1 *Scottish Old People's Welfare Council* 1987 SLT 179 and *Gillick v West Norfolk and Wisbech Area Health Authority* [1986] AC 112.

2 *R. (on the application of Hillingdon LBC) v Secretary of State for Transport* [2010] EWHC 626 (Admin); [2010] JPL 976.

4. LOCAL AUTHORITY POLICY: GENERAL

3.32 Ever since the creation of a comprehensive planning system in 1948, local planning authorities have been required to prepare planning policies for the use and development of land in their area and set these out in a development plan. While the term 'development plan' has survived since then, the format of plans and the process for producing them have been subject to regular change down the years. The current arrangements date from amendments made to the 1997 Act in 2006[1] which introduced a new system containing three main elements which are Strategic Development Plans (SDP), Local Development Plans (LDP) and Statutory Supplementary Guidance. This system is designed to gradually replace the previous two-tier set up of Structure Plans and Local Plans. As we shall see later in this chapter, authorities can also produce non-statutory planning policy statements. The previous development plans remain in force until replaced by a new style one. New development planning regulations governing the new system and defining transitional arrangements came into force in February 2009.[2] At the same time, the Scottish Ministers issued a new circular setting out their policy on how the new development planning regime should operate.[3] The primary responsibility for the operation of the development plan system lies with local, national park and strategic planning authorities. However, as we shall see below, the Scottish Ministers are also heavily involved.

1 Town and Country Planning (Scotland) Act 1997, Part II as substituted by the Planning etc. (Scotland) Act 2006 Pt 2 s 2.

2 The Town and Country Planning (Development Planning) (Scotland) Regulations 2008 together with The Town and Country Planning (Grounds for declining to follow recommendations) (Scotland) Regulations 2009 and The Planning etc. (Scotland) Act 2006 (Development Planning) (Saving, Transitional and Consequential Provisions) Order 2008.

3 SG Circular 1/2009 'Development Planning'.

3.33 The Government's aims for the revised system are that development plans should set out ambitious long term visions for their area, be kept up to date and provide a sound policy framework for dealing with planning applications efficiently and with some certainty. One of the criticisms of the previous development planning system had been that plans took too long to prepare and replace. The resulting lack of up-to-date plans posed difficulties for development management decisions, especially as these are intended to be plan-led. The new system is meant to speed things up and this is partly to be achieved by streamlining the plan preparation process. Good project management was also to be encouraged eg through the publication of annual development plan schemes setting project timetables, and the plans themselves were to be succinct. However, to date the new approach does not appear to be much faster than its predecessor and by 2012 the Scottish Government was again consulting on possible measures to tackle this issue, in particular in relation to the examination process.

3.34 Despite their name, local development plans are not confined to proposals for local authority developments. In fact, they are designed to influence and guide all development activity, especially that of the private sector.

Status of Development Plans

3.35 Prior to 1994, planning authorities, when determining planning applications, were legally obliged to have equal regard to the relevant provisions of the development plan, and to 'any other material considerations'.[1] This gave considerable discretion to authorities to grant approval for developments that were contrary to their development plan. Furthermore, many developers effectively ignored development plans when submitting planning applications, especially during the 1980s, and government advice encouraged this, particularly in England.[2] During that time, large numbers of planning application decisions were made by the Secretary of State on appeal, rather than by local authorities.[3]

1 1972 Act, s 26(1) (still, for no immediately obvious reason, preserved in s 37(2) of the 1997 Act).
2 See especially DOE Circular 14/1985 'Development and Employment'.
3 See eg Robinson 'U-turn that surprised an industry' (1991) Financial Times, 1 November.

3.36 In 1994, the emphasis changed. Ever since then authorities have been required by law to determine planning applications (and make other planning decisions) in accordance with the development plan 'unless material considerations indicate otherwise'.[1] This reflects the policy of successive governments since 1994 that the planning system should be 'plan-led' and it certainly means that the development plan is now taken very seriously when considering planning applications. However, it does not mean that every proposal in accordance with a plan has to be approved or that all those contrary to a plan must be refused. All decisions on planning applications still involve a balancing act between the relevant development plan policies and other material considerations, as they always have done. Provided the planning authority is satisfied that other material considerations outweigh plan policy, it is still possible for it to grant permission for a development that is contrary to the plan.[2] However, in reaching such a decision, it is important that the authority acknowledges the statutory priority given to development plan policy when weighing this against other material considerations.[3] Sometimes different policies in a development plan may not be in complete harmony with one another. Where that is the case it is for the planning authority to decide which of those policies should be given greater weight when making a decision.[4]

1 1997 Act, s 25.
2 *City of Edinburgh Council v Secretary of State for Scotland and Revival Properties Limited* 1998 SLT 120.
3 *South Northamptonshire Council v Secretary of State for Communities and Local Government* [2013] EWHC 11 (Admin).
4 *R. (on the application of Cummins) v Camden LBC* [2001] EWHC Admin 1116.

Development Plan Schemes

3.37 Under the 1997 Act[1] each Strategic Development Plan Authority (SDPA) has to prepare a Development Plan Scheme at least annually as do all local and national park authorities regarding the preparation of their Local Development Plans (LDP). The scheme has to set out the authority's programme for preparing its SDP or LDP as the case may be and explain what will be involved at each stage in the process. It should also contain a participation statement indicating when, how and with whom consultation on the plan will take place, and the authority's proposals for public involvement in the plan preparation process. The Scottish Government expects each authority to include innovative approaches to participation which address the particular needs, characteristics and issues of its area. However, there is no need for the authority to consult on its participation statement nor on the development plan scheme as a whole. The Development Planning Regulations[2] require that schemes contain a timetable and specify the month when the authority proposes to publish its next Main Issues Report (see below), its proposed plan and when it will submit its plan to the Scottish Ministers. Each time the authority adopts a new scheme it has to send two copies to the Scottish Ministers, publish it (including electronically) and make copies available in local public libraries.

1 Town and Country Planning (Scotland) Act 1997 s 20B.
2 The Town and Country Planning (Development Planning) (Scotland) Regulations 2008 reg 24.

Habitats Assessments[1]

3.38 If a development plan is likely to affect a site designated (or proposed to be designated) as a European Site,[2] then before the relevant authority can submit its plan for approval or adoption it must conduct a habitats assessment.[3] If, having conducted that assessment, the authority is satisfied that the plan will not adversely affect the integrity of the protected site, then it is able to proceed to adopt its plan. However, if the assessment shows that there will be an adverse impact it may only adopt the plan if what is proposed is of overriding public interest and there are no alternatives for achieving this. It must also notify the Scottish Ministers and carry out measures that will compensate for the adverse impact on the protected habitat or species affected. See Chapter 13 for further discussion of the provisions of the Habitats Regulations.

1 See SG Circular 1/2009 'Development Planning Appendix 1: The Habitats Regulations' (2010); Scottish Natural Heritage *Habitats Regulation Appraisal of Plans: Guidance for Plan-Making Bodies in Scotland* (2010).
2 Under The Conservation (Natural Habitats &c) Regulations 1994.
3 The Conservation (Natural Habitats &c) Regulations 1994, Part IVA, regs 85A – E, inserted by The Conservation (Natural Habitats, &c) Amendment (Scotland) Regulations 2007 following the decision of the European Court of Justice in *Commission of the European Communities v United Kingdom of Great Britain and Northern Ireland*, Case C 6/04 in the second chamber of the European Court of Justice, judgment 20 October 2005.

Equalities Impact Assessment

3.39 The Equality Act 2010[1] places a duty on public authorities to pay due regard to the need to promote equality between all groups in society when exercising their functions. As a result, when preparing their development plans, authorities need to ensure that the policies and proposals they contain do not lead to discrimination against any particular groups in society and, at the same time, promote equality of opportunity. Authorities address this by conducting and publishing an equalities assessment alongside their development plan.

1 Section 149.

5. LOCAL AUTHORITY POLICY: STRATEGIC DEVELOPMENT PLANS

Purpose and content

3.40 As their name suggests, Strategic Development Plans (SDP) are largely strategic documents. While they can include policies and proposals for specific sites, detailed site-specific matters are normally left to Local Development Plans (LDP) to address. The 1997 Act[1] states that SDPs should contain:

- A ***vision statement***, which should be a broad statement of how development could and should occur in the area. It should also look at the factors which might affect that development, such as population distribution, transport infrastructure, major land uses and the area's social and economic characteristics;
- A ***spatial strategy*** setting out broadly based proposals as to the development and use of land;
- An analysis of the relationship between the plan's vision statement and spatial strategy, and development and land use proposals in neighbouring local authority areas;
- Other matters that may be prescribed by the Scottish Ministers and anything else that the SDPA thinks should be included.

In addition to these requirements, the Development Planning Regulations[2] provide that all SDPs must contain a map or diagram describing the plan's spatial strategy and any other illustrative material that the strategic development plan authority considers necessary.

1 Section 7.
2 Town and Country Planning (Development Planning) (Scotland) Regulations 2008, reg 2.

3.41 Circular 1/2009[1] expands on the above statutory requirements by outlining Scottish Government policy on their implementation. SDPs are expected to be 'concise visionary documents' setting clear parameters for LDPs and decisions on strategic infrastructure investment. The Vision Statement should set the context for the spatial strategy by providing a realistic view of what the plan area could be like 20 years hence. The spatial strategy should incorporate the 'headline changes' sought by the plan. It should include a 'locational strategy' for new development up to 12 years from the plan approval date and a broader indication of the scale and direction of growth up to year 20. It should be specific enough to limit the options available for LDPs to those that would have more or less the same impact on strategic infrastructure and green space networks (eg green belt).

The Government expects the main SDP topics to be: land for housing, business, shopping and waste management development; strategic infrastructure (eg transport and water supply); and, strategic green space (including green belts). While largely intended to be strategic, SDPs can be site-specific especially where there are no realistic alternative sites.

1 SG Circular 1/2009 'Development Planning'.

SDP preparation and review

3.42 SDPs are not required for all parts of Scotland. They are only produced by those groups of local authorities that the Scottish Ministers have designated to work jointly as a Strategic Development Plan Authority (SDPA).[1] At present there are only four such groups and these are based around the cities of Aberdeen (Aberdeen City & Shire),[2] Dundee/Perth (TAYplan),[3] Edinburgh (SESplan)[4] and Glasgow (Glasgow & The Clyde Valley).[5] An employee of one of the constituent authorities has to be appointed as the Strategic Development Manager and they have to be supported by other employees from the same group of authorities[6] along with other employees. Once designated, the SDPA has three months in which to propose to the Scottish Ministers the boundary of the area for which its SDP is to be produced. If there is any disagreement between the constituent local authorities as to what the boundary should be, alternative proposals can be submitted. Ultimately, it is for the Scottish Ministers to approve the SDP boundary and in doing so they can modify its extent or even choose a different boundary. Once the boundary is approved the area within it becomes a SDP area for which the SDPA must produce a SDP when the Scottish Ministers require it to. Once the SDP is approved by the Scottish Ministers, the SDPA must keep it under review and submit a new proposed SDP to the Scottish Ministers within four years.[7] The boundaries of the SDP areas also have to be kept under review. For example the area of the Tayplan SDP is to be reduced because of an alteration to the Cairngorms National Park Area.[8]

1 1997 Act, s 4.
2 Designated under The Strategic Development Planning Authority Designation (No. 2) (Scotland) Order 2008.
3 Ibid, (No. 3) Order 2008.
4 Ibid, (No. 4) Order 2008.
5 Ibid, (No. 1) Order 2008.
6 1997 Act, s 4(3).
7 Ibid, s10(8).
8 SG Circular 1/2013 'Strategic Development Plan Areas'.

Factors that must be taken into account

3.43 SDPs have to be prepared or reviewed with the objective of contributing to sustainable development and have regard to any statutory guidance on sustainable development published by the Scottish Ministers.[1] They have to be properly integrated with other statutory plans and strategies affecting the development and use of land[2] (eg the National Planning Framework, Regional Transport Strategy, River Basin Management Plan, Local Housing Strategy and the National Waste Management Plan). The SDPA also has to take into account the resources available for implementing SDP policies and proposals. It should consider the relationship with any SDPs prepared for areas neighbouring its own. Any approved or finalised flood risk management plans affecting the area should be considered as should any national or regional marine plans relating to any part of the Scottish Marine Area adjoining the SDP area. Any issues arising out of the EC Directive on the control of major accident hazards involving hazardous substances also need to be addressed. Doing so requires consideration of the need in the long term to maintain appropriate distances between establishments covered by the Directive and residential areas, buildings and areas of public use, major transport routes as far as possible, recreational areas and areas of particular natural sensitivity or interest.

1 1997 Act, s 3.
2 1997 Act, s 8(1) and Town and Country Planning (Development Planning) (Scotland) Regulations 2008, reg 3.

Monitoring Statement[1]

3.44 One of the first tasks that the SDPA must undertake is to establish an evidence base for its SDP by gathering data concerning physical, economic, social and environmental characteristics of the plan area. The subsequent monitoring of this and of the impact of any existing plan policies and proposals must be evidenced through a monitoring statement which has to be published at the same time as the Main Issues Report (see below).

1 1997 Act, ss 4(9) and 4(10).

Main Issues Report[1]

3.45 Before preparing a SDP, the SDPA must first produce a Main Issues Report (MIR) for the purpose of 'facilitating and informing their work'.[2] This should contain general proposals for development in the SDP area, including specific proposals for where development should (and should not) be carried out. It should also include one or more reasonable alternative(s). The generation of alternatives is especially important in relation to the Strategic Environmental Assessment that is likely to be running alongside the development plan process (see Part 2 above). The MIR needs to provide sufficient information to enable interested parties to readily understand what is proposed and make meaningful representations. If any of the proposals involve a departure from the SDPA's current spatial strategy then this should be flagged.

1 1997 Act, s9 and Town and Country Planning (Development Planning) (Scotland) Regulations 2008, reg 4.
2 1997 Act, s 9(1).

3.46 While preparing its MIR and prior to its publication, the SDPA needs to consult with key agencies, adjoining planning authorities and the Scottish Ministers. Key agencies are defined in the Development Planning Regulations.[1] Scottish Natural Heritage, Scottish Environment Protection Agency and Scottish Water are identified as key agencies for all SDP areas. Health Boards, Regional Transport Partnerships, Scottish Enterprise, Highland and Islands Enterprise and the Crofters Commission have this role only with those SDPs (if any) which cover at least part of their geographic area of responsibility. In addition to this Circular 1/2009 makes clear that Historic Scotland, The Forestry Commission and Transport Scotland should be treated as if they were key agencies. The purpose of these consultations is to ensure that the SDPA can fully take into account the policies and strategies of those other authorities and agencies when preparing their MIRs.

1 Town and Country Planning (Development Planning) (Scotland) Regulations 2008, reg 28.

MIR Publication and Consultation

3.47 Once the SDPA has prepared its MIR it has to publicise this in line with the minimum requirements prescribed in the Development Planning Regulations.[1] A notice must be published in one or more local newspapers and on the internet, advising that the MIR has been prepared and indicating where and when it can be viewed. The notice should give a brief description of the content and purpose of the MIR. It should also provide details about how further information can be obtained. Finally, it should state that representations may be made and explain how, to whom and by when these should be submitted. A notice containing all of this information must also be served on key agencies, adjoining planning authorities and all Community Councils within the SDP area.

1 The Town and Country Planning (Development Planning) (Scotland) Regulations 2008, reg 5.

3.48 A copy of the MIR has to be published on the internet and also made available for inspection at an office of each of the constituent planning authorities and in all public libraries in the plan area. The SDPA has to send copies of the MIR and Monitoring Statement to the Scottish Ministers.

3.49 The MIR is intended to provide an important focus for wider public engagement with the SDP process and so SDPAs need to do more than simply advertise it. The 1997 Act requires authorities to 'secure that people who may be expected to want to comment on the main issues report are made aware that they can do so, and are given such an opportunity'. Circular 1/2009 makes clear that Scottish Ministers expect SDPAs to have already carefully considered, through their participation statements (see para 3.37 above), the best ways of securing such engagement. It also explains that the MIR can be viewed as a progress report issued in the course of an ongoing process of engagement lasting throughout the plan period. At the MIR stage the SDPA's thinking should have started to focus on options and so the approach should be to seek public responses to those options. However, the SDPA should not yet have reached a firm view on its preferred strategy and its approach should be genuinely open and not one of defending proposals. In view of all this, the Scottish Government expects MIRs to be engaging documents that encourage the public to read and respond to.

Environmental Report

3.50 As with many other government policy documents, SDPs will normally have to be the subject of a Strategic Environmental Assessment (SEA).[1] PAN 1/2010[2] makes clear that the SEA process should be integrated with SDP preparation and engagement. To this end, an Environmental Report and a non-technical summary should be published at the same time as the MIR. The statutory consultation and public engagement requirements for SEA should be harmonised with those for the SDP. Following consultation and evolution of the SDP itself, the SEA and Environmental Report may need to be revisited at later stages if new options or proposals emerge. Detailed advice on the relationship between the Development Planning and SEA processes can be found in PAN 1/2010.[3]

1 Environmental Assessment (Scotland) Act 2005, s 1. See Part 2 above.
2 SG Planning Advice Note 1/2010 'Strategic Environmental Assessment of Development Plans'.
3 Ibid, Part 4.

Proposed SDP

3.51 Once the consultation period for the MIR has been completed, the SDPA must move to prepare its proposed SDP and, in doing so, take into account representations received during that period. It also has to consult with the Scottish Ministers. The proposed SDP should be the SDPA's settled view on the final content of its plan and not a 'test the water' exercise.[1] Controversial issues should already have been aired at the MIR stage.

1 Circular 1/2009, para 55.

3.52 The SDPA has to place a notice in a local newspaper and on the internet advising that it has prepared its proposed SDP and explaining where copies of the plan can be inspected (including on the internet). The notice should specify the date by which representations have to be made and how they should be submitted. The minimum period for making representations is six weeks. A copy of this notice has to be served on key agencies, neighbouring planning authorities, Community Councils and persons who commented on the MIR. A copy of the proposed plan has to be made available for inspection at an office of each of the planning authorities in the SDP area and should also be provided to key agencies and neighbouring planning authorities.

Modifications

3.53 After the period for making representations has expired, the SDPA has to decide whether or not to modify its plan prior to submitting it to the Scottish Ministers for approval. The 1997 Act provides that there are only three possible justifications for making modification. These are issues that have arisen through representations timeously received, matters raised in consultations (eg with the key agencies) and minor drafting or technical matters. If the SDPA decides to make changes then the proposed plan as modified has to be advertised in the same way as for a MIR (see above) and further representations sought. However, the SDPA can only modify its proposed plan if the alterations involved do not change the underlying plan strategy. If the changes would alter the underlying strategy then the SDPA has to prepare and publish a new proposed SDP.[1]

1 1997 Act, s 10(4).

Submission to the Scottish Ministers

3.54 If the SDPA decides not to modify its proposed plan, or has done so and completed the necessary publication requirements, it has to submit the plan to the Scottish Ministers. The plan has to be accompanied with a note on representations received and of whether and to what extent these have been reflected in the plan. In addition to this, the SDPA has to submit a report outlining the extent to which the consultation and wider public engagement activities have complied with the participation statement contained in its current Development Plan Scheme (see para 3.37 above). It also has to submit a copy of its proposed action programme for the plan. Finally, Circular 1/2009 suggests that it would be sensible for the SDPA to submit at this time the other documents that will be required for an examination into the plan. These are: the summary of any unresolved issues; copies of unresolved representations; the Environmental Report; opinions received about the Environmental Report; the Monitoring Statement; a report of any completed Habitats Appraisal of the plan; and the participation statement that was current when the proposed plan was published.

Alternative Proposals[1]

3.55 Each SDPA is made up of several different local authorities and they may not always agree on the content of their SDP. In order to address this potential problem, the 1997 Act provides that the plan can contain alternative proposals favoured by different individual authorities from the SDPA. A statement explaining the reasoning behind each alternative has to accompany the plan in such circumstances.

1 1997 Act, s 11.

Notification of Submission to the Scottish Ministers

3.56 Under the Development Plan Regulations[1] the SDPA has to publish a notice in at least one local newspaper and on the internet stating that the plan has been submitted to the Scottish Ministers, give the date it was submitted and set out details of when and where the plan may be inspected (including on the internet). Copies of this notice have to be sent to the key agencies and people who submitted representations about the plan. As with the MIR and Proposed Plan, copies have to be made available for inspection in the planning office of each local authority in the SDPA area, public libraries and on the internet.

1 Town and Country Planning (Development Planning) (Scotland) Regulations 2008, reg 7.

Examination

3.57 Examinations are intended to enable independent testing of unresolved issues affecting the proposed SDP. An examination has to be held in the following circumstances:[1]

- There are unresolved representations (ie representations which have not been withdrawn and have not been taken into account in modifications to the plan);
- The plan contains alternative proposals because of disagreement between the local authorities that make up the SDPA (see para 3.55 above);
- The Scottish Ministers consider that there are other issues which require examination.

The examination is conducted by a person appointed by the Scottish Ministers. This will normally be a reporter (supported by other reporters) from the Directorate for Planning and Environmental Appeals (DPEA) and the Scottish Ministers have to notify the SDPA once they have appointed one. They also have to advertise the appointment in a local newspaper and notify everyone who made a representation that has not been resolved. However, unlike with the previous development plan system, objectors whose issues remain unresolved have no right to be heard. It is for the appointed person to decide how the examination will be conducted and whether any further information or submissions are required. The SDPA has to advertise the appointment by placing notices in local libraries.

1 1997 Act, s 12(1).

Examination Scope and Procedure

3.58 Examinations are designed to be very different from the public local inquiries that were associated with the previous development plan system. Their scope is limited to unresolved representations, consideration of any alternative proposals and any other issues that the Scottish Ministers require to have examined. With regard to unresolved representations the focus is to be on the issues these raise rather than each individual representation. To assist with this the SDPA has to submit a summary of unresolved issues. A form for completing the summary is contained in the Development Planning Regulations.[1] This should number and list the representations and give the names of those who have made them. It should group them into a smaller number of issues and summarise each of these. The SDPA's reasons for not modifying the plan in response to the representations made, relevant to each issue, should also be set out using no more than 800 words per issue.

1 Town and Country Planning (Development Planning) (Scotland) Regulations 2008, Sch 4.

3.59 An important principle of the examination system is that the appointed person should at the outset be given all the information that is likely to be needed to reach conclusions and make recommendations about the issues at hand. Within 14 days of being notified of the appointment, the SDPA must submit all of the documents specified in the Development Planning Regulations[1] to the person appointed. In practice, these will already have been submitted to the Scottish Ministers along with the proposed SDP. Any other supporting productions must also be lodged within those 14 days. DPEA has published practical guidance about the examination process which is available on its website.[2]

1 Town and Country Planning (Development Planning) (Scotland) Regulations 2008, reg 20.

2 SG Directorate for Planning and Environmental Appeals 'Development Plan Examinations: Practical Guidance for Planning Authorities' (2011) and 'Development Plan Examinations – guidance note for people who submitted representations' (2012).

3.60 Before the substance of outstanding issues can be examined, the 1997 Act requires the person appointed to assess whether the consultations carried out by the SDPA conform to what it said it would do in its participation statement. This assessment is expected to be based on the available written evidence ie the participation statement, the SDPA's report on conformity with this and any unresolved representations that relate to issues about participation. If this assessment shows that the actions of the SDPA do not conform then the examination will be halted. The person appointed then has to produce a report for the Scottish Ministers giving reasons and recommending further steps that the SDPA should undertake to consult or involve the wider public. A copy is given to the SDPA which has 4 weeks to respond with its own representations to the Scottish Ministers. After that period has elapsed, if the Scottish Ministers consider that there is no need for further consultation activities then the examination may continue. However, if they do consider further action is needed they will direct the SDPA to carry these out. Once the SDPA does so the process is effectively back to the proposed plan stage and the steps required from that stage have to be followed all over again. The Scottish Ministers expect that this procedure will be used very rarely[1] which is just as well since having to do so would deal a serious blow to plan progress. Nevertheless, the fact that these provisions are contained in the 1997

Act emphasises the importance attached to participation as part of the development plan process.

1 Circular 1/2009, para 88.

3.61 If the person appointed is satisfied that the SDPA has conformed to its participation statement the examination of outstanding issues can then begin. It is for the person appointed to decide what form the examination should take. However, the Scottish Ministers expect that it will be largely based on an assessment of the written submissions made at the outset. The person appointed can decide to seek more information from any party on one or more issues if the information before them is insufficient to allow a properly informed examination. Again the Scottish Ministers expect that this information will normally be sought in writing. Where the person appointed decides that they wish to hear oral submissions this should normally be organised on an informal hearing basis but if necessary they can require a formal public inquiry. However, from experience to date it appears that SDP examinations are being conducted entirely by correspondence despite concerns expressed about the robustness of this approach.[1]

1 See Watchman, J 'Strategic Development Plan examinations' (2013) 157 SPEL 53.

3.62 Whatever combination of possible methods are used, the Scottish Ministers expect that the examination will be concerned primarily with the appropriateness and sufficiency of the content of the proposed plan. The person appointed should only consider other approaches if what is proposed in the plan is 'clearly insufficient or inappropriate' (Circular 1/2009 at para 78). In other words they are not required to make the plan 'as good as it can be' but just to address any areas where it is not adequate. However, as with the method being used to conduct examinations, there have also been concerns expressed about this approach. In one case (SESplan) the reporters were concerned that the SDP as submitted was inconsistent with national policy on housing land requirements and so was neither sufficient nor appropriate. They also concluded that the issue of housing land requirement could not properly be resolved through the examination process and so recommended that a requirement for the preparation of supplementary guidance was introduced to the plan to enable the deficiencies to be addressed.

3.63 Examinations are organised and administered by the Scottish Ministers, not the SDPA. The costs incurred by the Scottish Ministers or the appointed person in conducting the examination are, however, shared equally between the SDPA and the Scottish Ministers.[1]

1 Town and Country Planning (Development Planning) (Scotland) Regulations, reg 23.

Post Examination Procedure

3.64 Once the examination has been completed, the appointed person prepares a report for the Scottish Ministers giving reasoned conclusions and recommendations. The report must also contain the appointed person's assessment of the conformity of the SDPA's actions with its participation statement. The Scottish Ministers expect the report to include conclusions and recommendations for each of the issues identified at the start of the examination process but not on each individual representation. As well as submitting their report to the Scottish Ministers, the appointed person also has to publish it (including electronically) and notify the parties who made unresolved representations that the report has been published and submitted. They should also send a copy of the report to the SDPA.

Approval or Rejection by the Scottish Ministers

3.65 Once the Scottish Ministers have the proposed SDP and the report from the examination (if one was required) they can then decide whether or not to approve the plan. In approving the SDP they may do so in whole or part. They can also modify the plan but the procedure for doing so varies depending on whether or not an examination was held. Modification is straightforward in cases where an examination has been held as the Scottish Ministers can simply modify the plan and state their reasons for doing so as part of their approval. However, if no examination was needed they must first publicise their proposed modifications giving reasons and invite representations allowing a period of at least six weeks for these to be lodged. They also have to consult with the SDPA, key agencies and anyone else they consider appropriate.

3.66 Approval is given in the form of a written instrument from the Scottish Ministers. In practice this is a letter to the SDPA informing it of the decision. Where the Ministers have made modifications to the plan the letter gives the reasons for these and specifies what they are in an annex. There is no need for them to give detailed reasons for approving those parts of the plan that they have approved without modification.[1] Once this approval is issued the proposed SDP (as modified) is constituted as the Strategic Development Plan for the area from the date on the letter.

1 *Uprichard v Scottish Ministers (and another)* [2013] UKSC 21; 2013 WL 1741990.

3.67 The Scottish Ministers' decision to approve the SDP is final subject only to a statutory challenge[1] to the Court of Session on a point of law by a person aggrieved which must be made within six weeks of plan publication.

1 1997 Act, s 238.

Steps Required Following Scottish Ministers' Approval

3.68 As soon as possible after the approval of the SDP, the SDPA must send two copies of the approved version to the Scottish Ministers. It also has to publish the plan (which includes on the internet) and place a copy in local libraries. Finally, it has to advertise the publication in a local newspaper and send notices of this to all parties who made representations to the SDP.[1]

1 1997 Act, s 14.

3.69 In line with the requirements of the Environmental Assessment (Scotland) Act 2005,[1] the SDPA must publish a SEA Post Adoption Statement as soon as reasonably practicable after approval of the SDP. This has to explain how environmental considerations have been integrated into the approved SDP. It should set out how the Environmental Report, representations and consultations have been taken into account. An explanation should be given of the reasonable alternatives that were considered in preparing the SDP strategy and why, in the light of this, the approved strategy has been adopted. It is important that the rejected alternatives are given the same depth of consideration as the preferred option as failure to so could leave the plan open to legal challenge.[2] Finally, the statement should set out how the significant environmental effects of SDP implementation will be monitored.

1 Section 18.
2 *Heard v Broadland DC* [2012] EWHC 344 (Admin); [2012] EnvLR 23.

3.70 A copy each of the statement, the approved SDP and of the final version of the Environmental Report have to be made available for inspection free of charge at the principal offices of the SDPA. The SDPA also has to place a notice in a local newspaper giving details of the statement, the plan it relates to and of where it can be inspected. Copies of that notice, the Post Adoption Statement and related documents, have to be available on the SDPA's website. Finally, the SDPA has to inform the consultation authorities[1] of the SDP's approval and provide them with copies of the statement and related documents.

1 These are the Scottish Ministers, Scottish Natural Heritage (SNH) and Scottish Environment Protection Agency (SEPA).

3.71 Within three months of the date of SDP approval the SDPA must adopt and publish the final version of its Action Programme. This should list all of the actions required to deliver the policies and proposals in the SDP. It should identify who is responsible for implementing those actions and by when. Prior to its adoption the SDPA needs to have consulted with the Scottish Ministers, key agencies and any other party identified against an action in the programme. Two copies have to be sent to the Scottish Ministers and a copy placed in local libraries. The action programme also has to be published electronically. Thereafter, it has to be kept under review and, updated and republished biannually.

6. LOCAL AUTHORITY POLICY: LOCAL DEVELOPMENT PLAN (LDP)

3.72 Unlike Strategic Development Plans, which have to be approved by the Scottish Ministers, the responsibility for both the preparation and the final approval of Local Development Plan (LDP) lies with the local planning authority for the relevant area. A LDP comes into force when the local authority adopts it by resolution.[1] The plan is then described as being the constituted Local Development Plan.

1 1997 Act, s 20(1).

3.73 Authorities have to prepare and keep under review LDPs for all parts of their area[1] but they are given freedom to fulfil this requirement in various ways. If they want they can prepare different plans for different parts of their area, or different topics can be dealt with in different plans for the same part of their district.[2] However, the approach that tends to be followed is the preparation of one district-wide LDP.

1 1997 Act, s 16(1)(a)(ii).
2 Ibid, ss 16(3) and 16(4).

3.74 Neighbouring councils can, if they wish, work together to prepare a joint LDP extending to parts of each of their districts.[1]

1 1997 Act, s 16(5).

Purpose and content

3.75 The 1997 Act states that a LDP is a plan setting out the authority's detailed proposals for the use and development of land.[1] The Act refers to this as a 'spatial strategy'. The plan should contain a map or maps (to be known as the 'Proposals Map') which describe and illustrate spatially the policies and proposals of the local development plan.[2] It should be possible, therefore, to use the proposals map as a way of working out how the plan affects any property lying within the area. The 1997 Act also requires the planning authority to include a schedule of any land it owns that is affected by policies or proposals in the plan[3] and any other content (including illustrations) that it considers appropriate.[4] Finally, LDPs for areas outside of a SDP area have to contain what the 1997 Act refers to as a 'vision statement'.[5] This is a broad statement of the authority's views on how the development of land could and should occur and as to the matters which might be expected to affect that development. These matters are similar to those that have to be examined for the vision statement required for SDPs and include: the principal physical, economic, social and environmental characteristics of the district; the main land uses; population size, composition and distribution; the supply and use of transport and other infrastructure; and, any changes which the planning authority considers may occur with any of these matters.

1 1997 Act s 15(1)(a).
2 1997 Act s 15(4) and Town and Country Planning (Development Planning) (Scotland) Regulations 2008, reg 8(1).
3 1997 Act s 15(3).
4 Ibid, s 15(1)(c).
5 Ibid, s 15(2).

3.76 Circular 1/2009 sets out in detail Scottish Ministers' expectations on the form and content of LDPs in practice. They expect them to be concise map-based documents that make specific and significant proposals for up to 10 years from the date of plan adoption. The vision statement that has to be included in plans outside SDP areas should give a broad indication of the scale and location of new development and growth for up to 20 years. Local authorities are encouraged not to include minor proposals and detailed policies in their LDP. Provided an appropriate context is given in the plan, these should instead be set out in supplementary guidance documents (see Part 6 below). The proposals map can be made up of a number of separate sheets, thus allowing for the use of insets and different scales for different parts of the plan area. This advice is especially helpful for LDPs covering districts that combine urban areas with a large rural hinterland (eg see the proposals map for the Perth and Kinross LDP). With regard to the schedule that has to be included identifying all local authority owned land, it is stated that the Scottish Ministers intend this provision to apply to policies, proposals or views relating to specific built developments on specific sites, and not to broad policy designations.

Preparation and Review

3.77 The 1997 Act requires local authorities (including the two National Park authorities) to prepare a LDP 'as soon as practicable' after the coming into force of s2 of the Planning Etc (Scotland) Act 2006.[1] This was the legislation that established the new development plan system by making amendments to the 1997 Act. In practice, implementation of this new system required new regulations which did not come into force until 28 February 2009.[2] At that time some authorities were in the process of preparing old style local plans (or alterations to those) which were close to being adopted. In order to avoid that work being lost, transitional arrangements were put in place to allow those authorities to complete and adopt those plans and alterations prior to starting the new system. However, in some cases those old style plans were not finally adopted until late 2012[3] despite having been processed through the new plan approval system.

1 1997 Act, s16(1).
2 Town and Country Planning (Development Planning) (Scotland) Regulations 2008.
3 Eg Fife Council's *Dunfermline and West Fife Local Plan* was adopted in November 2012. At the time of writing that plan is subject to a pending legal challenge in the Court of Session.

3.78 LDPs prepared within a SDP area have to be consistent with that SDP.[1] This implies that within those areas the SDP process needs to be completed before LDPs can be prepared. However, the Scottish Ministers expect that LDPs should be adopted no later than two years after the approval of the relevant SDP. To achieve this it is necessary for some 'twin tracking' of preparation work for SDPs and LDPs and this is acceptable provided the LDP is not submitted to the Scottish Ministers prior to approval of the SDP.[2] However, with there now being a legal requirement to produce new SDPs every four years and new LDPs every five years, it is not inconceivable that the two levels of plans could get out of sync in future. This was not an uncommon problem with the previous development plan system of structure and local plans.

1 1997 Act, s 16(6).
2 SG Circular 1/2009 'Development Planning'.

3.79 Once a local authority has adopted a LDP it is required to keep it under review and prepare a new version every 5 years or whenever required to do so by the Scottish Ministers.[1]

1 1997 Act, s 16(1).

3.80 In preparing their LDP, authorities must have regard to the National Planning Framework[1] and also to the statutory objective of contributing to sustainable development.[2] They must include policies requiring all developments in the area to be designed in a way which ensures that all new buildings avoid a specified and rising proportion of the projected greenhouse gas emissions from their use, calculated on the basis of the approved design and plans for the specific development, through the installation and operation of low and zero-carbon generating technologies.[3]

1 1997 Act, s 16(a).
2 Ibid, s 3E.
3 Ibid, s 3F.

3.81 The Development Planning Regulations[1] contain a long list of other matters that the authority must take into account when preparing a LDP. This list is similar to the one we discussed above for preparing SDPs. However, when preparing a LDP it is also necessary that the authority considers any other local development plan it has prepared for a different purpose within its area. It also has to take LDPs in adjoining local authority areas into account. Those authorities whose areas border with England[2] have to consider the development plans produced by neighbouring planning authorities lying south of the border.

1 Reg 10.
2 Dumfries and Galloway Council and Scottish Borders Council.

Monitoring Statement

3.82 The gathering and then maintenance of an evidence base for monitoring purposes is the first step required in preparing a LDP. In particular this evidence should look at changes in the main physical, social, economic and environmental characteristics of the plan area. It should also be used to measure the impact of the policies and proposals in existing plans. A report based on this data called the Monitoring Statement should be published at the same time as the Major Issues Report (see below). The method of publication is basically the same as that for a SDP Monitoring Report. The evidence produced should eventually form part of the justification for the policies and proposals contained in the LDP.

Call for Sites

3.83 As part of the gathering of evidence required for planning purposes and prior to publication of its MIR, the authority will issue a call for development sites. This is an opportunity for land owners to put forward sites for allocation in the plan in the hope that these may be accepted and become available for new development. Bids for inclusion normally have to be made on a form provided by the planning authority and by a date specified in the call.

Major Issues Report (MIR)

3.84 The purpose, content, means of publication, consultation and wider public engagement requirements of the MIR for a LDP are essentially the same as that for the MIR of a SDP. One additional requirement is that the planning authority has to consult the other local planning authorities within the same SDP area (where that applies).

Environmental Report

3.85 Like SDPs, LDPs will normally require to be the subject of a Strategic Environmental Assessment (SEA). An Environmental Report from this assessment has to be published alongside the MIR. Its purpose, content, and method of publication are the same as those for a SDP as are the consultation and wider public engagement requirements.

Proposed Local Development Plan

3.86 Again, the purpose and procedures involved at this stage are broadly similar to those for a proposed SDP. However, for a proposed LDP the authority must also notify the owners, lessees and occupiers of any premises situated on land which the plan specifically proposes to be developed if what is proposed is likely to affect the amenity or use of that land. The same requirement applies to neighbouring land (within 20 metres of the proposal site). Authorities have to use the notice contained in Schedule 2 of the Development Planning Regulations. For each site three notices need to be served with one addressed to 'the owner' and the others addressed to 'the lessee' and 'the occupier' respectively, rather than named individuals. A map has to be attached to the notice showing the location of the site in question.

3.87 Circular 1/2009 recommends that representations by stakeholders and the general public should be concise (no more than 2,000 words plus any limited supporting productions). It also recommends that those submitting representations should fully explain the issues that they wish to be considered as there is no automatic opportunity for them to expand on their representation later in the process. The circular suggests that in view of this, authorities may wish to extend the period for submitting representations from the statutory minimum of six weeks to 12 weeks to give parties more time to properly formulate their representation.

Modifications

3.88 An authority can decide to modify its proposed LDP but only in response to representations timeously received, statutory consultations or on minor technical/drafting grounds. However, as with SDPs, if the changes being considered are necessary and would alter the underlying strategy of the plan then the authority cannot modify it. It has to prepare and publish a new LDP instead.

3.89 Provided any modifications are of a minor nature these can be made to the proposed plan without any further procedural requirement and the authority can move to submit its proposed plan to the Scottish Ministers. However, if the planning authority decides to make modifications which remove or significantly alter any policies in the published proposed plan, or would introduce new polices or proposals, then it has to publish the plan with those modifications. These are known as 'notifiable modifications' because if the authority wishes to make these it has to go back and carry out the same steps as were required to publish and advertise the original version of the proposed plan. In addition, the owners, occupiers and lessees of any premises on land that is affected by the modifications have to be notified using the form in Schedule 3 of the Development Planning Regulations. Once the six week period for representations has expired, the council can, if it wishes, make further modifications or submit the modified plan to the Scottish Ministers. If it wishes to make further modifications then again it may only do so if these arise from representations received or are required for technical/drafting reasons. The authority also has to carry out the above publication requirements all over again.

3.90 In practice, authorities are not encouraged to make modifications. This is because the Scottish Ministers are concerned that considerable delay could be caused if notifiable modifications were made as a matter of course. Circular 1/2009 advises that the modification provisions should only be used where an authority is minded to make significant changes to its plan. It also points out that changes can be made to the plan at the examination stage if the Reporter recommends this. As a result, it encourages authorities to flag changes that they would be happy for the Reporter to recommend following the examination. From experience to date it seems that authorities are following this advice rather than risking delay to the process by making their own modifications.

3.91 Another possible source of delay at the proposed plan stage is if an authority tries to negotiate withdrawal of representations prior to submitting the plan to the Scottish Ministers. Authorities might find this tempting because successful negotiations could reduce the number of unresolved representations that need to be examined, or even remove the need for an examination altogether. However, Circular 1/2009 makes clear that such negotiations are not encouraged because of the delay they can cause. Again experience to date suggests that authorities are largely following this advice.

Submission to the Scottish Ministers

3.92 Once the proposed plan stage is completed the authority has to submit its plan to the Scottish Ministers. If there are unresolved representations it must also submit a request that the Scottish Ministers appoint a person to conduct an examination of the plan. An action programme and report on conformity with the authority's consultation statement should be submitted with the plan. The requirements in relation to those documents are similar to those for SDPs. As with SDPs it is also suggested that it is good practice to lodge at this time copies of the documents required for an examination.

3.93 The authority has to advertise that the plan has been submitted to Ministers by placing a notice in a local newspaper giving the date it was submitted and explaining where copies can be examined. If there are no outstanding representations (and therefore no need to request an examination) the notice should also indicate that the authority intends to adopt the plan. Copies of the plan should be made available at the planning offices of the authority, in local libraries and on the internet.

Examination

3.94 An examination has to be held when a proposed LDP is submitted to the Scottish Ministers and there are unresolved representations.[1] Normally, unresolved representations will be flagged by the local authority asking the Scottish Ministers to appoint somebody to conduct an examination. However, it is possible that there might be disagreement about whether representations have actually been resolved. In order to address this problem the Scottish Ministers have the power to decide that there are unresolved representations and so appoint somebody to exam the plan anyway. The examination is normally conducted by a Reporter from the Directorate for Planning and Environmental Appeals (DPEA) and the process is essentially the same as that for SDP examinations.

An important difference is that the output from the examination will be a report to the planning authority not the Scottish Ministers. Also, the costs of the examination have to be met by the local authority[2] and not shared with the Scottish Ministers as is the case with SDP examinations.

1 1997 Act, s 19.

2 Town and Country Planning (Development Planning) (Scotland) Regulations 2008, reg 23.

Post Examination Procedure

3.95 Once the examination is completed the appointed person has to prepare and submit a report to the local planning authority and publish it electronically. The report should give reasoned conclusions and recommendations for all of the unresolved issues identified at the start of the examination but not for each individual representation. It should also provide an assessment of the authority's conformity with its participation statement. The appointed person has to notify all those who made unresolved representations that the report has been submitted to the local authority and has been published electronically. The report's recommendations are more or less binding on the local authority. If the report recommends that modifications be made to the plan, the authority can only decide not to implement these on the limited grounds set out in the Town and Country Planning (Grounds for Declining to Follow Recommendations) (Scotland) Regulations 2009 or based on a justification contained in the 1997 Act.

3.96 The justification from the 1997 Act relates to Strategic Environmental Assessment (SEA). If the report recommends that significant modifications be made to the LDP it may be necessary for the authority to conduct an assessment of those as part of its SEA of the plan. If this shows that the plan as modified would produce an unacceptable environmental impact then the authority can refuse to make that modification.[1]

1 1997 Act, s 19(11).

3.97 The grounds in the Town and Country Planning (Grounds for Declining to Follow Recommendations) (Scotland) Regulations 2009 are that the recommendations: are based on conclusions that could not reasonably be reached on the evidence considered at the examination; would make the plan inconsistent with the National Planning Framework, or with any SDP or National Park Plan[1] for the same area; or would make the plan incompatible with Part IVA of the Conservation (Natural Habitats &c) Regulations 1994.

1 Prepared under National Parks (Scotland) Act 2000, s 12(7)(a).

3.98 Circular 1/2009 makes clear that the ground relating to unreasonable conclusions is intended only to apply to a situation where the appointed person has made a clear mistake, eg a factual error. It is not meant to apply where the appointed person has reached a different planning judgment from the one favoured by the planning authority. The ground relating to the Habitats Regulations is only relevant where a recommended modification to the plan might have a significant effect on a European Site (see Chapter 13). In those circumstances the authority would have to first carry out an appropriate assessment before making the modification. It is possible that the assessment might then show that the recommended modification would cause unjustifiable harm to the European Site and so should not be made.

3.99 In making the required modifications to its plan, the authority can make other necessary changes of its own. However the need for these must arise directly from the Reporter's recommendations. For example, as a result of making a recommended modification, it may be necessary to alter terminology, factual information and cross references elsewhere in the plan. The authority cannot introduce other unconnected new material to the plan at this stage.

3.100 Having made the modifications (if any) it wishes to make, the authority can at last move to adopt its plan. To do so it first needs to publish the modified plan and the modifications. The requirements for doing so are similar to those at earlier stages in the process. It also has to advertise its intention to adopt the plan by placing a notice in a local newspaper. Copies of the modifications and of the revised plan have to be made available for inspection at the planning authority's offices, local libraries and on the internet. A notice has to be placed in a local newspaper advising where these can be inspected and also stating that the authority proposes to adopt the plan. The authority must also notify all parties who made representations prior to the examination stage that the plan has now been published in the form which the authority intends to adopt.

Submission to the Scottish Ministers

3.101 While a LDP does not normally need to be approved by the Scottish Ministers, the law still requires that it be submitted to them before it can be adopted. The local authority has three months from the date it received the examination report to submit the plan. It is during that three-month period that it has to carry out any assessments required, make modifications (if any) and publish the plan it intends to adopt.

3.102 Along with the plan that it wishes to adopt, the authority must submit copies of the examination report, any modifications made following the examination, the public notice advertising its intention to adopt and any environmental assessment carried out to the plan as modified. If the authority has decided not to implement any of the recommendations contained in the examination report, it must also submit a statement setting out its reasons for this.

Adoption

3.103 Unless the Scottish Ministers direct otherwise, the authority can proceed to adopt its plan 28 days after submitting it to them. Once it does so the plan becomes the constituted LDP for the area and the authority must publish it using the same methods as for the proposed plan.[1] Also, as with earlier stages in the process, the authority has to place a notice in a local paper advertising that the constituted plan has now been adopted and notify parties who made representations of this. Two copies of the constituted LDP have to be sent to the Scottish Ministers.

1 See para 3.86 above.

3.104 In line with the requirements of the Environmental Assessment (Scotland) Act 2005, the planning authority must publish a SEA Post Adoption Statement as soon as reasonably practicable after constitution of the LDP. This has to explain how environmental considerations have been integrated into the adopted plan. It should set out how the environmental report, representations and consultations have been taken into account. An explanation should be given of the reasonable alternatives that were considered in preparing the LDP and why, in the light of this, the approved approach has been adopted. Finally, the statement should set out how the significant environmental effects of LDP implementation will be monitored.

3.105 Within three months of adoption the authority has to publish its action programme and thereafter keep it under review and publish an updated version biannually.[1]

1 1997 Act, s 20A.

Intervention by the Scottish Ministers

3.106 During the 28 day period described in para 3.103 above, if there is something about the plan that the Scottish Ministers wish to consider further or if they are unhappy with the plan they have the power to delay or stop the authority proceeding to adopt it. There are several steps they can take. First, they can extend the 28 day period to give them more time to consider the plan.[1] Second, they can direct the authority to consider making modifications to the plan as specified in the direction.[2] Where they issue such a direction then the authority cannot adopt the plan until it has made the modifications required or the Scottish Ministers withdraw the direction. Finally, the Ministers can direct that the plan has to be approved by them, in effect taking over responsibility for it.[3]

1 1997 Act, s 20(4).
2 Ibid, s 20(5).
3 Ibid, s 20(6).

7. LOCAL AUTHORITY POLICY: SUPPLEMENTARY GUIDANCE

3.107 It has long been the practice of planning authorities to produce detailed policy guidance on specific planning topics and to publish this in documents separately from their development plans. These can include, for example, planning briefs for significant development sites, detailed policies on shop-front alterations in historic town centres and technical guidelines for assessing the suitability of housing proposals in the countryside. If all of this material had to be included within SDPs or LDPs, then these would become extremely long and unwieldy documents. It is also likely that the time required to complete the statutory development plan process would be considerably increased. Given the Scottish Ministers' desire to see succinct and up-to-date development plans in place throughout Scotland, it is simply not an option for authorities to include all of their planning policies and guidance in their development plans.

3.108 All supplementary guidance issued by planning authorities has to meet the requirements set out in the 1997 Act[1] and the Development Planning Regulations.[2] In particular, these require that the scope of such documents is to be limited to providing more detailed information, policy and advice on matters which a SDP or LDP says such guidance is to be produced for. An example of this would be where a LDP allocates a major site for new housing and states that the development of this is to be in accordance with a masterplan that will be prepared for the site. Once adopted by the local authority, the masterplan is then a supplementary guidance document linked with the LDP and becomes part of the statutory development plan for the area.

1 Section 22.
2 Reg 27.

3.109 Circular 1/2009 gives further advice on the kinds of issues that the Scottish Ministers expect to see addressed through supplementary guidance. These include development briefs, forestry strategies, aquaculture framework documents and detailed methodologies for calculating developer contributions. Matters which the Circular says should only be addressed within the SDP or LDP itself include departures from national policy, green belt boundaries and development proposals of more than local impact.

Procedure for producing new Supplementary Guidance

3.110 When preparing a new supplementary guidance document the authority must publicise its proposals and seek representations by a specified date. In doing so, the authority has to make sure that anybody who is likely to want to comment on the proposed guidance gets the opportunity to do so. It also has to take into account any representations received during the period allowed for making these. Once this process is complete the authority has to submit its proposed supplementary guidance document to the Scottish Ministers. It also needs to submit a statement describing the steps it took to publicise the proposals, outlining any representations received and explaining the extent to which these have been taken into account. The Scottish Ministers then have 28 days from the date of submission to satisfy themselves with the content of the proposed guidance and about how it was produced. If that period expires without them taking any action then the authority can adopt and publish its guidance.

3.111 If the Scottish Ministers wish to intervene in the process leading to adoption then there are three measures they can use. The first is to issue a direction extending the above 28 day period to give them more time to consider how to respond. The second is to issue a notice to the planning authority requiring it to make specified modifications to the guidance. The third is to issue a direction preventing the authority from adopting and issuing the guidance.

3.112 Authorities do not need to wait until a SDP or LDP has been constituted before starting on supplementary guidance. Circular 1/2009 makes clear that they can prepare it alongside the related SDP or LDP and in practice this is what most authorities do. A clear advantage of this is that the necessary consultation can be included with that required for the SDP or LDP.

Existing Supplementary Guidance

3.113 When a new development plan is constituted, the supplementary guidance associated with its predecessor falls. However, many of those guidance documents will still be up-to-date, relevant and useful. It would be a bureaucratic nightmare if all of these had to go back through the preparation process required under s22 of the 1997 Act. To avoid this authorities are able to readopt supplementary guidance by linking it with the new SDP or LDP and ensuring that consultation on the plan includes consideration of the existing supplementary guidance that the authority proposes to readopt.

Strategic Environmental Assessment of Supplementary Guidance

3.114 Where the authority proposes to prepare and adopt supplementary guidance after approval/adoption of the SDP or LDP to which it relates, then a SEA may be required. This is despite the 'parent' plan itself having gone through a SEA. However, in cases where the authority believes that the supplementary guidance will have no or minimal impact then it may be exempt. In order to reach that conclusion it has to use the screening process set out in the Environmental Assessment (Scotland) Act 2005.[1] The Scottish Ministers advise that such an exemption may apply in cases where the guidance involves minor modifications to the parent plan or relates to a small area at local level.[2] It is also possible that supplementary guidance could be exempt where its scope and content has been sufficiently outlined in the parent plan and so has already been subject to SEA in that context. As long as the content of the final guidance turns out as anticipated, it may be possible to screen it out on the ground of duplication. PAN 1/2010 gives advice on how authorities can minimise the amount of additional work that will be required to conduct a SEA in cases where one is needed for new supplementary guidance.[3]

1 Section 8.
2 SG Planning Advice Note 1/2010 'Strategic Environmental Assessment of Development Plans', para 4.53.
3 Ibid, para 4.55.

Non-Statutory Planning Guidance

3.115 It is possible for planning authorities to prepare and publish planning policy guidance without having to go through the procedures described above.[1] However, they may only do so for matters that have not been flagged in a SDP or LDP as being something for which supplementary guidance is to be produced. Once published, such policies do not form part of the development plan and therefore carry less weight in the planning process (eg when determining applications for planning permission) as those produced under the statutory requirements. It should also be noted that in certain cases this form of non-statutory guidance may need to be the subject of a SEA before it can be adopted by the planning authority.[2]

1 1997 Act, s 22(9).
2 Environmental Assessment (Scotland) Act 2005, s 5(4).

II General Planning Control

Chapter 4

Meaning of development

1. GENERAL

4.1 From Chapter 6 onwards we will be looking in some detail at the subject of development management, in particular at the procedures for obtaining planning permission and also the ways in which breaches of planning law or planning permission may result in a planning authority taking enforcement action. But first we must define our terms: we cannot talk about development management unless we first establish what is legally meant by the term 'development'. It will therefore be our task in this chapter first to formulate and then further examine such a definition.

4.2 It might seem at first that our task ends there, but it only takes us halfway. While it is true to say that if a project or activity falls outwith our definition of development, then it is outwith development management: it does not require planning permission and will not usually be subject to planning enforcement action. But the converse is not true. Everything falling within the definition of development does not automatically become subject to development management: if it did, planning authorities would be much busier places than they are now. In fact they are spared from having to concern themselves with many matters which, although in strict terms they amount to development, are not usually subject to individual scrutiny, perhaps because they are relatively minor (such as a small extension to a house), or perhaps because they are being carried out by a public body (such as a local authority) which can proceed with its development activities without another public authority looking over its shoulder. Permitted development rights and other exemptions will be examined in Chapter 5.

4.3 It should be made clear at the outset that even where an activity does as a mater of law amount to development, or does not require planning permission, it does not necessarily mean it is exempt from legal regulation. Planning control looks at an activity from its own particular perspective, but the would-be developer is also subject to other legal requirements or restrictions from different sources, eg title condition restrictions. For example, as we will see shortly, an internal alteration to a building does not amount to development and (unless it is a listed building) would not normally be subject to planning control. However (perhaps because of safety considerations) it might still require a building warrant. Even within the realm of planning, we will see later that there are certain special planning controls (eg those relating to listed buildings or environmental assessment) that extend beyond the definition of development.

Definition of development

4.4 The statutory definition of development is contained in s 26 of the Town and Country Planning (Scotland) Act 1997. See also Figure 4.1. The essence of the formula is to be found in sub-section 1, which classifies development under two main headings:

FIGURE 4.1 MEANING OF DEVELOPMENT (1997 ACT s 26)

Building, engineering, mining or other operations

OR

A material change in the use of any buildings or other land

EXCLUDING

- Internal alterations (unless the Scottish Ministers by order include mezzanine floors as 'development' – see below)
- Road and sewage works etc by relevant public authorities or statutory undertakers
- Incidental use within curtilage of a dwellinghouse
- Agriculture & forestry use
- Changes of use within same class of Use Classes Order
- Demolition described in a direction given by the Scottish Ministers to a planning authority (currently there is no direction – see para 4.81 below)

BUT INCLUDING

- Irrigation or drainage for agriculture or any other water management project
- By order of the Scottish Ministers works to the interior of a building which have the effect of increasing gross floor space by a specified amount (see internal alterations above)
- Subdivision of a dwellinghouse
- Extension of a refuse deposit
- Marine fish farms (out to 12 nautical miles)
- Some advertisements

1. the carrying out of building, engineering, mining or other operations in, on, over or under land; or
2. the making of any material change in the use of any buildings or other land.[1]

Recently the courts in considering whether the installation of mobile poultry breeding units was 'development' concluded that in deciding whether works are development the definition of development can, and should be, interpreted broadly so as to include, wherever possible, projects which require a EIA under the EIA Directive, or development which requires EIA under EIA Regulations. Otherwise the EIA Directive will not be effectively implemented into UK law.[2]

1 See also definition of 'use' – 1997 Act, s 277(1).
2 *R (Save Woolley Valley Action Group Ltd) v Bath and North East Somerset Council* [2012] EWHC 2161 (Admin).

4.5 We see immediately that what most people would think of as development (something that results in a physical change to land or an existing building) is found within the first part of the definition. However, the second part of the sub-section shows us that the boundaries of development extend some way beyond this basic concept: even *where there is no physical change at all* development may occur if a property comes to be used in a way that differs from the way it was used before, eg where a shop is used as an office. In many cases an activity will amount to development on both counts, eg if a factory building is erected on agricultural land. The essential point is that only one of the above two aspects needs to be present to be caught within the definition.

4.6 Section 26 goes on to elaborate upon this basic formula, mainly by identifying certain more specific aspects that amount to development and others that do not.[1] But before we look at these, we will first examine more closely the ingredients of our basic definition. In most cases (fortunately) it is obvious what amounts to a building, engineering or a mining operation; however, it is the marginal cases that cause the problems, and so we must briefly see what guidance there is from statute and case law to help focus on what is encompassed by the definition. Such statutory help as we have derives mainly from the interpretation section[2] of the 1997 Act.

1 See parts 5 and 6 below.
2 Section 277.

4.7 It will be necessary to discuss the concept of a material change in the use of any buildings or any other land at a little more length, not only to consider the Use Classes Order but also a number of difficult issues that arise in connection with this aspect of development.[1]

1 See parts 3 and 4 below.

2. 'OPERATIONS' TO LAND OR BUILDINGS

Building operations

4.8 For the purposes of the 1997 Act, 'building operations' are defined as including:

(a) demolition of buildings;
(b) rebuilding;
(c) structural alterations of or additions to buildings; and
(d) other operations normally undertaken by a person carrying on business as a builder.[1]

1 Town and Country Planning (Scotland) Act 1997, s 26(4).

4.9 Although demolition is stated to be a building operation, we will see later that certain kinds of demolition are permitted development for which no planning application is necessary.[1]

1 See paras 4.81 and 5.65 below.

4.10 It should also be noted that the above definition is a little open-ended: building operations are said to 'include' the above matters, but are not necessarily confined to them.

4.11 Most importantly, however, we see that the definition is somewhat dependent upon the meaning of the word 'building'; fortunately, the 1997 Act is also able to help us there: '"building" includes any structure or erection, and any part of a building, as so defined, but does not include plant or machinery comprised in a building'.[1]

1 1997 Act, s 277(1).

4.12 The inclusion of the phrase 'structure or erection' has led to the definition embracing things that we would not normally think of as a building. For example, in *Barvis Ltd v Secretary of State for the Environment*[1] it was held that an 89-foot tower crane that ran on a steel track fixed in concrete was a 'structure or erection' and therefore a building for the purpose of the planning legislation. It has also been held that the construction of a 38-foot steel-hulled yacht in the backyard of a house amounted to the erection of a building.[2] In *R v Ealing London Borough Council ex p Zainduddin*[3] a partially-completed building which lacked a roof was held nevertheless to fall within the definition. On the other hand, in *James v Brecon County Council*[4] it was held that six fairground swing boats which could be dismantled in about an hour were not capable of being considered a 'building' in this sense.[5] As always, it is a matter of fact and degree according to the circumstances of the case.

1 (1971) 22 P&CR 710.
2 *Corporation of the City of Noarlunga v Fraser* [1988] CLY 3488.
3 [1994] EGCS 130.
4 (1963) 15 P&CR 20.
5 See also *Thanet District Council and Host Group* [1986] 1 PAD 364.

4.13 Some guidance can also be obtained from other areas of law, though these are not completely authoritative in a planning law context. In *Cardiff Rating Authority v Guest Keen Baldwin's Iron & Steel Co Ltd*,[1] it was disputed whether certain items fell within the category of 'building or structure' for rating purposes. Four factors were suggested as guidelines: (1) whether the object was of substantial size; (2) whether it would be constructed on site rather than being brought on to the site ready-made; (3) whether it had some degree of permanence and could only be removed by being pulled down or taken to pieces; and (4) whether it was physically attached to the land.[2] In *R v Swansea City Council ex p Elitestone Ltd*[3] a number of wooden chalet-type dwellings were held to be buildings, even though they were owned by licensees rather than the landowner. Their degree of permanence was a material factor, and also their size. The *Cardiff* case was referred to with approval.

1 [1949] 1 KB 385 at 402 per Jenkins J.
2 For a more detailed discussion of planning case law, see Rowan Robinson *Scottish Planning Law and Procedure* (2001), paras 5.08 – 5.20.
3 (1993) 66 P&CR 422.

Engineering operations

4.14 For 'engineering operations' the 1997 Act only gives us a very incomplete definition: 'engineering operations' includes the formation or laying out of means of access to roads'.[1] Also stated to be an engineering operation is the placing or assembly of any equipment tank in any part of any waters including waters out to 12 nautical miles for the purpose of fish farming.[2]

1 1997 Act, s 277(1).
2 Ibid, ss 26(6), 26AA and 275. See also the Water Environment and Water Services (Scotland) Act 2003, s 24; Town and Country Planning (Marine Fish Farming) (Scotland) Regulations 2007 (SSI 2007 No 175); Town and Country Planning (Marine Fish Farming) (Scotland) Order 2007 (SSI 2007 No 268); Town and Country Planning (Scotland) Act 1997 (National Parks) (Marine Fish Farming) Direction 2007; and SEDD Circular 1/2007 'Planning Controls for Marine Fish Farming'. See paras 5.50 – 5.52 below regarding permitted development rights for fish farming.

4.15 Obviously engineering operations are not confined to these two activities, and so we have to look to case law to amplify our definition. In one English case, engineering operations have been defined (somewhat circularly) as 'operations of a kind normally undertaken by, or calling for the skills of, an engineer'.[1] Examples of activities that have been held to fall within the definition of engineering operations include bridge building, drilling of exploratory bore holes, turf stripping, substantial infilling, laying tarmac and hardstanding for vehicles and even installation of a fuel storage tank.[2]

1 *Fayrewood Fish Farms Ltd v Secretary of State for the Environment* [1984] JPL 267.
2 See Rowan Robinson *Scottish Planning Law and Procedure* (2001), paras 5.21– .23.

Mining operations

4.16 For 'mining operations' we have no comprehensive statutory definition; however, if we assume that they mean the extraction of minerals from the ground either by underground working, quarrying or surface working, then our main task is to determine what is meant by the term 'minerals': 'minerals' includes all substances of a kind ordinarily worked for removal by underground or surface working'.[1]

1 1997 Act, s 277(1).

4.17 Our definition is further supplemented by the following:

'For the purposes of this Act mining operations include –

(a) the removal of material of any description –
  (i) from a mineral-working deposit;
  (ii) from a deposit of pulverised fuel ash or other furnace ash or clinker; or
  (iii) from a deposit of iron, steel or other metallic slags; and
(b) the extraction of minerals from a disused railway embankment.'[1]

1 1997 Act, s 26(5).

4.18 It is clear, however, that the above addition is not intended to be comprehensive or exclusive and only adds to the fringes of our definition.

Other operations

4.19 The case law does not reveal any clear examples falling within this category. It has been suggested that it might embrace excavation and levelling works not included in mining or engineering operations or the deposit of materials other than refuse.[1]

1 Rowan Robinson *Scottish Planning Law and Procedure* (2001), paras 5.27 and 5.28.

3. MATERIAL CHANGE IN THE USE OF BUILDINGS OR OTHER LAND: USE CLASSES ORDER

4.20 We saw above that, even where no operations had occurred to physically change land or a building, development could still take place if there was a material change in the use of buildings or other land, ie where the property came to be used in a way that differst from its previous use. The 1997 Act does not define what is meant by a material change of use, and in marginal cases it is often necessary to fall back on case law to settle the matter; it is usually said that what amounts to a material change in the use of buildings or other land is a matter of fact and degree in each individual case. For instance the use of a property for holiday letting may, or may not, be a material change in the use of the property depending upon the facts and circumstance of the particular case.[1]

1 *Moore v Secretary of State for Communities and Local Government* [2012] EWCA Civ 1202.

4.21 In practice, however, we can usually tell when a material change in the use of buildings or other land has taken place by referring to a statutory instrument generally known for short as the *Use Classes Order*, the most recent version being the Town and Country Planning (Use Classes) (Scotland) Order 1997.[1] The Use Classes Order lists, fairly comprehensively, the various ways in which land or property may be used and divides them into 11 classes or categories as follows:[2]

Class 1:	Shops
Class 2:	Financial, professional and other services
Class 3:	Food and drink
Class 4:	Business
Class 5:	General industrial
Class 6:	Storage or distribution
Class 7:	Hotels and hostels
Class 8:	Residential institutions
Class 9:	Houses
Class 10:	Non-residential institutions
Class 11:	Assembly and leisure

1 SI 1997/3061 (as amended by SI 1998/1196 and SSI 1999 No 1).
2 Ibid, Schedule. For the full text of the Use Classes Order see Appendix.

4.22 In addition, certain stated uses are specifically excluded from all classes as being *sui generis* (one of a kind), namely use as (a) a theatre; (b) an amusement arcade or centre or funfair; (c) a petrol filling station; (d) a motor vehicle showroom; (e) a taxi or vehicle hire business; (f) a scrapyard, or yard for the breaking of motor vehicles; (g) the storage or distribution of minerals; (h) a public house; (i) work registrable under the Alkali etc Works Regulation Act 1906 (as amended); (j) a hot food take-away or (k) a waste disposal installation for the incineration, chemical treatment or landfill of waste to which Directive 91/689/EEC applies. Other uses, though not specifically stated, are also effectively *sui generis* because they are omitted from the order entirely (eg residential flats or some licensed hotels).

4.23 The Use Classes Order therefore provides a useful framework which in most cases helps us determine easily when a material change of use has taken place, as this will normally be the result of a change from one class to another or of a change to or from one of the excluded uses. However, strictly speaking, that is *not* what the Use Classes Order says, nor is it the Order's stated purpose. Article 3(1) of the Order reads as follows:

> 'Subject to the provisions of this Order, where a building or other land is used for a purpose in any class specified in the Schedule to this Order, the use of that building or that other land for any other purpose in the same class shall not be taken to involve development of the land.'

(The same principle applies when only part of the building or land is used for another purpose within the same class,[1] eg if a bookshop sublet part of its space to a retailer of DVDs).

1 1997 Act, s 26(2)(f).

4.24 In other words, the Use Classes Order is *negative* in effect: it provides that where a change is within the same class (ie where both the existing use and the proposed new use fall within the same class of the Order) no development has taken place. It does *not* say that a change from one class to another *does* involve development, ie that a material change of use has taken place, though in the vast majority of cases this will be so.[1]

1 See *Palisade Investment v Secretary of State for the Environment and Another* (1995) 69 P&CR 638 per Glidewell LJ at pp 643–4.

4.25 Although a change from one class of the Use Classes Order to another will normally amount to development, a planning application will not be required in certain specified cases, eg where the change is being made to a use that is less sensitive than the former one as regards amenity or environmental considerations. These cases (although technically falling within the definition of development) are included within the categories of permitted development.[1]

1 See paras 5.28 to 5.35 below.

4.26 Finally, although the Use Classes Order is very comprehensive in its scope, it does not succeed in listing absolutely every way in which land or buildings may be used.[1] And so, for this and other issues (considered below) relating to material change of use, it will still often be necessary to refer to the case law and to consider certain principles that have emerged from it.

1 Eg an egg-packing station: see *Kuxhays & Wenban v Secretary of State for the Environment and Lewes District Council* [1986] JPL 675, CA.

4.27 But first it will be appropriate for us to look in more detail at the various classes stated in the Schedule of the Use Classes Order:

Class 1: Shops

4.28 As well as the retail sale of goods, class 1 includes a number of other uses to which the traditional style of shop unit may be put, eg as a post office, travel agency, hairdressing salon, funeral parlour or launderette/dry cleaners. The determining factor is that the activity carried out is principally for visiting members of the public. A hot food take-away (though not the sale of cold food) is excluded, being one of the excluded or *sui generis* uses; however, government policy has indicated that a 'sandwich bar does not cease to be in the shops class merely because it also sells hot drinks, or if a few customers eat on the premises.'[1] Use as a car showroom is also a *sui generis* use, falling outwith class 1. It has been held in England that their equivalent of class 1 includes auction rooms[2] and also the supply of pharmaceuticals (including national health and private prescriptions) from within a supermarket,[3] but not a warehouse shopping club with restricted membership.[4]

1 SODD Circular 1/1998 'The Town and Country Planning (Use Classes) (Scotland) Order 1997', para 13.
2 *R v Kensington and Chelsea Royal London Borough Council ex p Europa Foods Ltd* [1996] NPC 4, [1996] EGCS 5.
3 *R v Maldon District Council ex p Pattani* [1998] EGCS 135.
4 *R v Thurrock Borough Council and Another ex p Tesco Stores* [1993] 3 PLR 114, [1993] EGCS 176.

4.29 There is no necessity for the activity in question to take place in a building designed as a traditional shop unit. However, in relation to the equivalent class in the English Use Classes Order, it has been held that only uses taking place within buildings are included and not where retail sales are taking place on open land.[1] Some doubt has been cast as to whether this interpretation is a true reflection of the legislators' intention, particularly as a definition confining a shop to a building, which appeared in earlier versions of the Use Classes Order, was subsequently dropped, the current English and Scottish orders containing no definition at all.[2]

1 *Cawley v Secretary of State for the Environment and Vale Royal District Council* [1990] 2 PLR 90.
2 See C Lockhart-Mummery *Is a Garden Centre a Shop?* [1996] JPL 725.

Class 2: Financial, professional and other services

4.30 At one time office uses were in a single class of their own, but are now split between class 2 and class 4 (business; see para 4.33 below). Class 2 contains those office uses which it is appropriate to find in a shopping area and where the services are provided principally to visiting members of the public. In some (though not all) cases a use in this class may be carried on in a unit designed as a shop unit. 'This class enables planning control to be maintained over proposals involving the conversion of shops for purposes other than for the retail sale of goods, while permitting free interchange within a wide range of service uses which the public expects to find in shopping areas, such as betting shops; the offices of lawyers, accountants and estate agents; health centres and surgeries of doctors, dentists and veterinary surgeons; where the services are provided principally to visiting members of the public.'[1] Banks and building societies also normally come under this class, and in *Palisade Investments v Secretary of State for the Environment and Another*[2] it was held that a *bureau de change* (where sterling was exchanged for travellers' cheques or foreign currency) provided a financial service falling within the equivalent class of the English Use Classes Order.

1 SODD Circular 1/1998 'The Town and Country Planning (Use Classes) (Scotland) Order 1997', para 14.
2 (1995) 69 P&CR 638.

4.31 The statement of government intention quoted above should perhaps be reviewed and reconsidered in the light of the English Court of Appeal decision in *Kalra v Secretary of State for the Environment and Waltham Forest London Borough Council*,[1] where the issue was whether a solicitor's office fell within Class A2 or B1 (the English equivalents of Classes 2 and 4 respectively). It was held that Mr Kalra's proposed business did qualify as class A2, but that a solicitor's office could conceivably fall under either class, depending on the particular nature of the legal business being carried out. It was a question of fact depending upon the circumstances of the case:

> 'Mr Kalra ... describes his ambitions as being 'a poor man's lawyer' for the Indian ethnic community whose languages he speaks. He does not intend to do conveyancing or commercial work and, having seen and heard him, there seems to me to be no reason to doubt the genuineness of his expressed aspirations nor the modesty of them. Nor is there reason to doubt that the segment of the community which he seeks to serve requires user friendly, cheap and convenient access to legal advice and so to justice. If Mr Kalra does not qualify in the eyes of the law as an A2 use then it is hard to see how or why any solicitor would so qualify.'[2]

The fact that Mr Kalra would normally see clients by appointment did not preclude the provision of legal services principally to visiting members of the public: the same applied, for example, to hairdressers, an A1 (class 1) use. This case shows that it is not possible to say in the case of solicitors (and possibly other professionals) that their business will always fall within class 2: within the range of specialist services that may fall under a particular professional category, some may not be provided principally to visiting members of the public. It should be noted that there is a difference in wording between the English and Scottish Use Classes Orders, which may have the effect of narrowing further the range of class 2 uses in Scotland. The proviso that the services in question should be appropriate to a shopping area applies in the Scottish Use Classes Order to the whole of class 2, whereas in the English order the criterion of 'appropriate to provide in a shopping area' is confined to the third category of services (including a bookmakers) other than financial services or professional services. Mr Kalra's business did not have to pass the test of being appropriate to a shopping area, as it would have had to in Scotland.

1 (1996) 72 P&CR 423.
2 Per Henry LJ at p 429.

Class 3: Food and drink

4.32 Class 3 comprises uses where food or drink is sold for consumption on the premises. It therefore includes restaurants, cafes and snack bars, but not public house use or hot food take-away use which both fall within the excluded uses. (It is interesting to note that in England public houses *are* included within the equivalent food and drink class, possibly reflecting a perception that English pubs are more civilised places than their Scottish counterparts). Hot food take-away use was formerly included within class 3, but was moved out of that class by the present Use Classes Order:

> 'This is because hot food take-away shops raise somewhat different environmental issues, such as litter, noise, longer opening hours and extra traffic and pedestrian activity, from those raised by other Class 3 uses. This does not mean that a restaurant whose trade is primarily in-house dining but which has a minor take-away cannot be in Class 3. Where take-away is a minor component of the business and will not affect environmental amenity it should be treated as *de minimus* (sic), ie as not requiring planning consent.'[1]

In other words, the takeaway will be an ancillary rather than the primary use.[2] Cold food for consumption off the premises may be sold from shops falling within class 1.

1 SODD Circular 1/1998 'The Town and Country Planning (Use Classses) (Scotland) Order 1997', para 16.
2 See paras 4.52 to 4.55 below.

Class 4: Business

4.33 Class 4 includes not only those office uses not encompassed within class 2, but also research laboratories and light industrial uses that can be carried on in a residential area without causing a nuisance that would harm the area's amenity; the factors that would create such a nuisance are stated as being 'noise, vibration, smell, fumes, smoke, soot, ash, dust or grit'. This categorisation reflects the increase in recent years of uses (such as computer research and development, micro-engineering and biotechnology) which could be carried on in a residential area with environmental consequences no more significant than for an office use. In many cases, therefore, there can be a change from an office to a light industrial use (or vice versa) without the need for planning permission, as the change would fall within class 4. It is always possible, however, that any such light industrial use could, with development, intensify to such a degree that a nuisance was created that affected the residential amenity. This might be enough to take it out of class 4 into class 5, so that a material change of use had occurred and planning permission would then be required.[1] The existence of the residential amenity test does not imply that a class 4 use needs actually to be situated in a residential area.[2]

1 See SODD Circular 1/1998 'The Town and Coiuntry Planning (Use Classes) (Scotland) Order 1997', para 19 see also *Blight & White v Secretary of State for the Environment* [1992] EGCS 94 and paras 4.48ff below.
2 SODD Circular 1/1998 'The Town and Country Planning (Use Classes) (Scotland) Order 1997', para 18.

Class 5: General industrial

4.34 Any industrial process that does not fall within class 4 will come under class 5. The 1998 Use Classes Order for the first time dropped the 4 (formerly 5) special industrial uses which had remained virtually unchanged since 1948, and which covered various types of heavy industry or other processes likely to have an adverse affect on amenity or the environment, including the processing of metal and other inorganic materials, of chemical products and of various types of organic material. Many of the industries involved have declined over the years, while at the same time there has been much new environmental legislation designed to exercise control in these and other areas.[1] While it is undeniable that the special industrial classes had become somewhat anachronistic, it is difficult not to mourn a little the passing of Special Industrial Group E, whose opening accurately conveyed the spirit of the whole:

'(a) boiling blood, chitterlings, nettlings or soap;
(b) boiling, burning, grinding or steaming bones;
(c) boiling or cleaning tripe;
(d) breeding maggots from putrescible animal matter'.[2]

Perhaps the decline of traditional British industries has its compensations.

1 See eg the Environmental Protection Act 1990; see also Chapters 14 (hazardous substances) and 15 (environmental assessment).
2 Town and Country Planning (Use Classes) (Scotland) Order 1989, SI 1989/147, Schedule, Class 10.

4.35 More serious concerns about the abolition of the special industrial use classes have been expressed by the RTPI and some planning authorities. Not all of the special industrial uses are out of date, nor are all of their planning implications necessarily dealt with by alternative controls. It can be difficult to find suitable sites for certain specialised uses such as small chemical works or pet food factories. Once such a use was established in a particular site, it was formerly possible for the planning authority to reserve future uses of that site for similarly problematic cases by refusing permission for a change to a use falling within the old general industrial class or one of the other special industrial classes. Now the planning authority will be powerless to prevent a change to a more innocuous industrial use within the new class 5, even though that use could have been suitably located elsewhere without difficulty.

Class 6: Storage or distribution

4.36 Class 6 relates to a use for storage or as a distribution centre. This class has been kept separate from the business and general industrial uses (classes 4 and 5) because of the higher level of lorry and van movements likely to be associated with either of these activities, which would be more harmful to the amenity of a residential area. Retail warehouses whose main purpose is to sell goods directly to the public will generally fall within class 1: shops.[1] In *Crawley Borough Council v Hickmet*,[2] it was held that the use of a site for parking the cars of business and holiday passengers flying out of Gatwick Airport was not commercial storage but merely parking, even though some of the vehicles might be left overnight or longer. '(S)torage really takes place where something is put away for a period of time because it is not needed … or its use is not contemplated in the short term.'[3]

1 SODD Circular 1/1998 'The Town and Country Planning (Use Classes) (Scotland) Order 1997', para 32.
2 [1998] JPL 210, CA.
3 Ibid, per Otton LJ.

Class 7: Hotels and hostels

4.37 Class 7 covers use as a hotel, boarding house or guest house, except for the limited bed and breakfast use now allowed under Class 9 (see below). It also includes hostels where no significant element of care is provided. (For the definition of care, see para 4.38 below). Premises with a liquor licence are excluded, except where the drink is only served to residents or persons having a meal; as we saw above public houses fall under the *sui generis* excluded classes and, by their specific exclusion here, the same effectively applies to licensed hotels if they allow visiting members of the public to buy alcoholic drink without having a meal.

Class 8: Residential institutions

4.38 Class 8 includes hospitals, nursing homes (including hospices and maternity homes), boarding schools and residential colleges. A use will fall under this class rather than class 7 if an element of care is involved. 'Care' is defined as 'personal care including the provision of appropriate help with physical and social needs or support; and … includes medical care and treatment'.[1]

1 Town and Country Planning (Use Classes) (Scotland) Order 1997, SI 1997/3061, art 2.

Class 9: Houses

4.39 Class 9 includes only houses and specifically does *not* include flats. To be included within this class a house must be occupied by either a single person, people living together as a family or by not more than five residents living together. In the last case, the residents must be living together communally as a single household (eg a group of students sharing the premises); if the residents occupy different parts of the house as separate, self-contained units, this would be a material change of use requiring planning permission.[1] Such small residential groups of unrelated people are specifically included within this class even where care is provided; thus uses which one would otherwise expect to fall within class 8 (residential institutions) will instead be included within class 9, provided that the number of residents does not exceed five. It is not necessary for people providing care to live in the property and, if any of them do, their number will not be included within the limit of five.[2]

1 SODD Circular 1/1998 'The Town and Country Planning (Use Classes) (Scotland) Order 1997', para 36. See also paras 4.85 and 4.86 below and SODD Circular 7/1998 'The Town and Country Planning (Use Classes) (Scotland) Amendment Order 1998'. See also SG Circular 2/2012 'Houses in Multiple Occupation: Guidance on Planning Control and Licensing'.

2 *R v Bromley London Borough Council, ex p Sinclair* [1991] 3 PLR 60.

4.40 The purpose of this provision is to facilitate, by providing more certainty over the planning position, the integration within the community of vulnerable people in small group homes. Often there can be misunderstanding of and opposition to such projects, and so the above policy will be made easier if such groups can be set up in an existing house without the necessity of obtaining planning permission.

4.41 The 1997 Use Classes Order extends Class 9 to include limited use as a bed and breakfast or guest house. As the relevant Scottish Office circular explains:[1]

> 'The use is permitted for this purpose of a maximum of one bedroom where the house has less than 4 bedrooms and a maximum of 2 bedrooms where the house has 4 or more bedrooms. This will allow householders to earn an income from accommodating paying guests on a small scale, without significant adverse effects on the surrounding area.'

If the above limits are exceeded, planning permission will be required for a change to class 7. For the avoidance of doubt, it is specifically made clear that this limited bed and breakfast/guest house exemption applies only to houses and *not* to flats.[2]

1 SODD Circular 1/1998 'The Town and Country Planning (Use Classes) (Scotland) Order 1997', para 37.

2 Town and Country Planning (Use Classes) (Scotland) Amendment Order 1998, SI 1998/1196 and SODD Circular 7/1998 'The Town and Country Planning (Use Classes) (Scotland) Amendment Order 1998'.

4.42 Where part of a house is used for business purposes, planning permission will not normally be needed where the business activity does not change the overall character of its use as a residence.[1]

1 SODD Circular 1/1998 'The Town and Country Planning (Use Classes) (Scotland) Order 1997', para 38; but see also paras 4.71 and 4.72 below.

Class 10: Non-residential institutions

4.43 Class 10 includes a number of disparate uses where buildings are visited by members of the public on a non-residential basis, eg crèches, day nurseries, educational establishments, art galleries and museums, libraries, and churches. Also included are day centres, defined as 'non-residential premises which are used for social purposes, recreation, rehabilitation or occupational training and at which care is also provided'.[1]

1 SI 1997/3061.

Class 11: Assembly and leisure

4.44 Class 11 includes uses such as cinemas, dance halls and concert halls, casinos and bingo halls, as well as most outdoor and indoor sports activities. Specifically excluded are sports and recreation involving the use of motorised vehicles or firearms. Also excluded (because they are listed in the Order among the *sui generis* excluded uses) are theatres, amusement arcades or centres, funfairs and public houses.[1]

1 SI 1997/3061; see also para 4.22 above.

4. MATERIAL CHANGE OF USE: OTHER RELEVANT FACTORS

4.45 In determining whether or not a material change of use has taken place, the Use Classes Order is a useful first point of reference. However, it will not always be enough to determine the matter in any particular case. For example, the Use Classes Order is not comprehensive, in that it does not include all possible uses of land or buildings; this may be because an unusual type of use has been overlooked or (more likely) because a sensitive category of use (eg flats) has been deliberately omitted so that changes involving them can be kept within planning control and subject to the discretion of planning authorities. Also, in determining whether a material change of use has taken place, certain other issues may arise that cannot be resolved by simple reference to a list of categories. For example, just how significant must a change be to be regarded as 'material'? Or what if a property is put to more than one use? Will a change in any of these uses be material or only if there is a main or predominant use that has been changed? What if the same person occupies two or more properties, which may be near one another and used in conjunction? Is the materiality of any change to be decided within the context of all the units of occupation taken together, or with regard to each unit in isolation? To resolve these (and other) issues we need to look outwith the legislation, mainly to the case law.

Meaning of 'material'

4.46 Whether or not a change of use is material is usually stated to be a matter of fact and degree depending upon the circumstances of the individual case. In other words, there is no hard and fast rule and each case has to be considered on its own particular merits. It has also been said that, while a change in kind of use is always material, a change in the *degree* of use will only be material if it is very marked.[1] An example of a change in kind would be a change from shop to office; an example of a change in degree, a change from the occupancy of a dwellinghouse by a single family to a house in multiple occupancy. In general one has to consider the differences between a property's current use and its proposed use and whether those differences (such as patterns of arrivals and departures (including those brought about by a change in operating hours), traffic generation and impacts such as on-street parking and other impacts on amenity) are such that those differences in impacts would amount to a material change in use of the property. It may be for instance that the impacts of a proposed use are such that the proposed uses can no longer be properly classified as being a Class 4 (Business) use because the proposed use cannot be 'carried on in any residential area without detriment to the amenity of that area by reason of noise, vibration, smell, fumes smoke, soot, ash, dust or grit.'

1 Rowan Robinson *Scottish Planning Law and Procedure* (2001), para 5.74.

4.47 Whether or not a change in kind of use has occurred is therefore a question of fact, and usually it can be settled by reference to the Use Classes Order. As we saw above, the Use Classes Order does not actually say that a change between classes will be a material change of use, only that a change within a class is not development. However, it is difficult to think of an example of a change of class (eg shop to business use, or residential to office use) that would not be a change in kind and therefore be material; likewise a change to or from a use not included within the order (eg a flat) or one of the excluded uses (eg a public house) would also usually be a change in kind.

Intensification

4.48 Even where there has been no change in the kind of use, a change in the degree of use can also be material provided that it is sufficiently marked. The principle usually applied here is that of *intensification*, where the type of use has not altered but it has grown in scale; for example a residential use where the number of residents has increased, an industrial use where the manufacturing output has grown, or a leisure use where more members of the public are catered for or the hours of activity have been extended. Only where the intensification is considerable will it be considered material.

4.49 In fact, due to the operation of the Use Classes Order, the principle of intensification is somewhat limited in scope. Even where a use has intensified, provided that the original and the new degree of activity remain within the same class of the Use Classes Order, there can, by definition, be no development.[1] For example, in *Brooks and Burton Ltd v Secretary of State for the Environment*[2] a company purchased land on which there was an established business for the manufacture of concrete blocks for garden use. A business expansion included the manufacture of blocks for general building as well as ornamental use, their output rose from less than 300,000 to 1,200,000 blocks a year and traffic to and from the site increased considerably. It was held that although (theoretically) such intensification was sufficiently great to be a material change of use, both the earlier and the intensified degree of activity fell within class 4 (general industrial)[3] of the Use Classes Order then current in England. The intensification alone did not amount to a breach of planning control.

1 See para 4.23 above.

2 [1978] 1 All ER 733, CA; see also *Emma Hotels v Secretary of State for the Environment* [1981] JPL 283.

3 The equivalent of class 5 of the current Scottish Use Classes Order: see paras 4.34ff above.

4.50 On the other hand, if a use is sufficiently intensified the result may be a change in class; for example, a household that took in lodgers might come within class 9 (houses), provided that the total number of residents did not exceed five, but if the number was increased beyond that limit, there would be a move to class 7 (hotels and hostels). In other words, the change in degree would be sufficiently marked to amount to a change in kind. There *would* be a material change of use, but it would not depend on the principle of intensification.

4.51 The principle mainly applies where the use is one not included within the Use Classes Order, or is one of the *sui generis* uses which have been specifically excluded in terms of the Order.[1] For example, in the case of several people sharing a flat (eg students) a material change of use could occur if the number of people sharing increased by a critical amount; this is in fact a sensitive issue in some university cities and towns, and quite a small increase in flat sharers can lead to enforcement action from the planning authority. Another possible example might be a car showroom, or a taxi business, where the number of vehicles involved had increased considerably.[2] In *Forest of Dean District Council v Secretary of State for the Environment*[3] it was held that a change in the use of static caravans from holiday caravans to a permanent residential use might amount to a material change of use if the change resulted in more vehicular and pedestrian traffic. It appears that an intensification of use can only amount to a material change in the use of any buildings or other land where the intensification is significant from a planning perspective, for instance an increase in traffic generated, and the impacts of that additional traffic, change the planning context to such a degree that the intensified use amounts to a material change of use.

1 See para 4.22 above.
2 See also *Lilo Blum v Secretary of State for the Environment & Richmond London Borough Council* [1987] JPL 278.
3 [1995] JPL 937.

Multiple uses

4.52 Where a property is put to a new use without the existing use or uses being discontinued, this may still amount to a material change of use, provided that the old and new uses are distinct and on an equal or comparable scale. For example, if the operators of a petrol filling station were to start repairing vehicles while still continuing to sell petrol; this could be a material change requiring planning permission. However, it is often possible to distinguish between a principal or predominant use and another use (or other uses) that are subsidiary, ie between a *primary* and *ancillary* use or uses of a property. In such a case it is only the primary use that is taken into account: if that primary use changes, there may be a material change of use, but the introduction of a new ancillary use will not amount to development.[1] For example, in *Borough of Restormel v Secretary of State for the Environment*[2] a caravan was parked on hotel grounds to provide sleeping accommodation for two waitresses during the summer season. The caravan was not capable of being used as a separate living unit, having no kitchen arrangements and no bathing or washing facilities. It was held that the use of the caravan was ancillary to the main hotel use.

1 See Use Classes Order 1997, SI 1997/3061, art 3(3).
2 [1982] JPL 785.

4.53 In *Alexandra Transport Company Ltd v Secretary of State for Scotland*[1] a quarry became used as a refuse tip. It was argued that no development had occurred because the quarry had always been used for the disposal of quarry waste. It was held that the latter had been ancillary to the use as a quarry and that there had now been a change in the primary use from quarry to refuse tip, which did amount to development. Likewise, if an ancillary use grows so that it becomes comparable in scale to, or even ousts, the primary use, then that will also amount to a material change of use. In *Jillings v Secretary of State for the Environment and the Broads Authority*[2] the appellant had planning permission to use land and buildings for hiring out boats for sailing on the Norfolk Broads, but not for the ancillary use of manufacturing boats for sale on the premises. It was held that the manufacturing use had grown so as to become a primary use of the land together with the hire business, and so there had been a material change of use. However, although in such a case the use, to the extent that it has grown, will be unlawful and can be stopped by enforcement action from the planning authority; it will remain lawful in its more modest, ancillary form. For example, in *Mansi v Elstree Rural District Council*[3] a group of glasshouses was used primarily as a plant nursery, though one of the glasshouses was also used for the retail sale of nursery produce. The latter use was later intensified until the glasshouse in question became primarily a shop which also sold articles imported from elsewhere, and the court agreed that a material change of use had occurred. However, it was held that the planning authority was not entitled to stop all sales. The original, limited retail use could continue, and could even intensify provided that it did not grow to a level that would no longer be ancillary to the horticultural use.

1 1974 SLT 81. See also Young, E 'When is a Use Ancillary to Another?' 1988 SLT 237.
2 [1984] JPL 32.
3 (1964) 16 P&CR 153; see also *R v Harfield* [1993] JPL 914.

4.54 It has been argued that for a use to be ancillary it must derive in some way from the main use, so that a use which is quite distinct (such as an amusement machine in a shop) may not be ancillary, even if it remains on a much smaller scale than the main use.[1]

1 See SPADS nos A4621, A4715 and A5630, discussed in (1984) 13 SPLP 86 and (1986) 18 SPLP 56.

4.55 It has been held in appeals to the Secretary of State that the use of a room in a doctor's surgery as a pharmacy mainly selling medicine prescribed on the premises was ancillary to the surgery use,[1] and that a disco for which admission was charged was ancillary to the use as a public house.[2] It should be emphasised, however, that it remains a matter of fact and degree, and that a significant increase in the scale of either of these ancillary uses could have amounted to a material change of use.[3]

1 *Hounslow London Borough Council v Gossain* (1989) 4 PAD 216.
2 *Shepway District Council v South Coast Leisure* (1988) 3 PAD 178.
3 See also *Walsall Borough Council v Cassidy Reproductions and J & LK Cassidy* (1986) 1 PAD 386; *Allen v Secretary of State for the Environment and Reigate & Banstead Borough Council* [1990] 1 PLR 25.

The planning unit

4.56 The concept of the planning unit has evolved to deal with situations where two or more adjacent or nearby properties are occupied by the same person; alternatively, a single property may be subdivided and (although used by a single occupier) different parts may be put to separate uses. The sort of problem that can arise here regarding a material change of use is perhaps best explained by an illustration.

4.57 A company, Wholegrain Bakeries, occupies two adjacent buildings, one large and one small. The large building is used as a bakery and the small building is used to sell the produce of the bakery to the public. The retail use is ancillary to the main use as a bakery. Then the company begins to extend the scope of the retail sales in the small building to include food bought from elsewhere, so that the building comes to be used as a general grocer's shop. Has a material change of use taken place? It might well depend on what is considered to be the 'planning unit', ie the area to be taken into consideration when deciding whether a material change of use has taken place. If the planning unit is taken as both buildings together (ie the whole unit of occupation) then it could be argued that a material change of use has taken place, since the retail use has so increased in scope that it can no longer be considered as ancillary to the bakery use. On the other hand, if the planning unit is taken to be the smaller building on its own, then it could be argued that no material change of use has taken place at all, since that building has always been used exclusively for retail purposes and therefore there has been no change in the kind of use taking place.

4.58 Like so many issues, there is no hard and fast rule for identifying the planning unit in any particular case: once more it is a matter of fact and degree depending upon the individual circumstances. However, three useful, indicative, criteria for determining the planning unit were formulated by Bridge J in *Burdle v Secretary of State for the Environment*:[1]

(1) the whole unit of occupation should be considered whenever it was possible to recognise a single main purpose of the occupier's use of land to which secondary activities were incidental or ancillary;

(2) the entire unit of occupation might aptly be considered when the occupier carries on a variety of activities and it is impossible to say that one was incidental or ancillary to another, which was well settled for a composite use with component activities fluctuating in their intensity from time to time but with the different activities not confined in separate and physically distinct areas of land; and

(3) where separate and distinct areas within a single unit of occupation were occupied for substantially different and unrelated purposes, each area used for a different main purpose (together with its incidental and ancillary activities) was to be considered as a separate planning unit.

1 [1972] 1 WLR 1207 at 1212.

4.59 This approach was later approved by the English Court of Appeal[1] and has generally been accepted in subsequent cases.

1 *Jennings Motors Ltd v Secretary of State for the Environment* [1982] QB 541.

4.60 There is therefore a presumption that the planning unit is the unit of occupation, although this may be displaced (in terms of the third rule) where the site in question is subdivided into areas devoted to quite separate types of activity. For example in *David W Barling Ltd v Secretary of State for the Environment and Swale District Council*[1] land adjacent to a dwellinghouse and in the same ownership was fenced off and used to store materials for a building contractor's business. It was held that the fencing off of the land gave it an independent existence and an independent use thereby creating a separate planning unit. Where a property comprises a number of separately occupied units (eg a block of flats or a shopping centre) each individual unit will normally be a separate planning unit.[2] However, in situations where a larger area has become established as a planning unit and is only subdivided later (eg a piece of farmland that is divided up and used for separate industrial purposes) the position is not entirely clear.[3]

1 [1980] JPL 594.

2 *Johnston v Secretary of State for the Environment* (1974) 28 P&CR 424; *Church Commissioners for England v Secretary of State for the Environment* (1996) 71 P&CR 73.

3 See *Small and DWS Car Breakers et al v Secretary of State for the Environment and Chelmsford Borough Council* [1993] JPL 923.

4.61 Also, it cannot be assumed that there will be a single unit of occupation in every case where two or more separate properties are used by the same occupier for a similar purpose. If the physical separation between the properties is sufficiently great there may be different units of occupation and therefore different planning units, as in a case where the buildings in question were 150 yards distant from and on the other side of a major road from a hotel in the same occupation.[1] In other words, a distinction can be made between the situation where physically separate properties nevertheless form a recognisable group and one where there is a substantial geographical separation; only in the former case will there be a single planning unit.[2]

1 *Duffy v Secretary of State for the Environment and Westminster London Borough Council* [1981] JPL 811; see also *Swinbank v Secretary of State for the Environment and Darlington Borough Council* [1987] JPL 781; *Fuller v Secretary of State for the Environment and Dover District Council* [1988] 01 EG 55.

2 For a particularly problematical example, see *Thames Heliports plc v London Borough of Tower Hamlets* (1997) 74 P&CR 164 (referred to in para 5.36 below). See also *Ralls v Secretary of State for the Environment* [1997] EWHC (Admin) 198.

4.62 It will be gathered from the terminology used that it is *occupation* and not ownership that is crucial in determining the unit of occupation. If the situation regarding occupation changes, then this may result in a change of planning unit. For example if two adjacent properties which were formerly separately occupied became occupied by the same person, then this might result in the merger of two planning units into one; conversely, if part of a planning unit came into separate occupation from the rest for a separate purpose, this could create two separate planning units. Such a change might result in a material change of use, but not necessarily so; for example, if a shop tenant acquired the tenancy of an adjoining shop for a business expansion, there would be no departure from class 1 of the Use Classes Order.[1]

1 For a fuller discussion of this topic, see Rowan Robinson Scottish Planning Law and Procedure (2001), paras 5.63 – 5.70; see also *Rawlins v Secretary of State for the Environment and Gregory* (1990) 60 P&CR 413; *Hertsmere Borough Council v Secretary of State for the Environment and Percy* [1991] JPL 552; *Uttlesford District Council v Secretary of State for the Environment and White* [1992] JPL 171.

4.63 Finally, it should be noted that some confusion has been created in the past by the use in some of the cases of the term 'planning unit' in a quite different sense. It has sometimes been taken to mean not the physical area to be considered when deciding whether a material change of use has taken place, but the period of time during which a given area is put to a particular use; when a new 'planning unit' is created in this sense of the phrase, it means that the existing use rights (those attached to the old 'planning unit') have been extinguished. The judicially preferred phrase for this concept is now a 'new chapter in planning history'.[1] It will therefore be convenient hereafter to confine our use of the phrase 'planning unit' to the sense we have been discussing above.

1 *Jennings Motors Ltd v Secretary of State for the Environment* [1982] QB 541; *South Staffordshire District Council v Secretary of State for the Environment and Bickford* [1987] JPL 635; see also paras 6.106–6.108 below.

5. MEANING OF DEVELOPMENT: SPECIFIC EXCLUSIONS

4.64 Section 26(2) of the Town and Country Planning (Scotland) Act 1997 lists a number of operations and uses of land that, for the avoidance of doubt, should not be taken to involve development. This of course means that carrying out any of these operations or uses would normally be exempt from planning control and would, therefore, not require planning permission. Some of these categories are relatively minor, or of a specialised nature, and therefore not unexpected; others, however, (like the exclusion of agriculture and forestry) are quite significant.

Internal alterations

4.65 This is defined as:

the carrying out of works for the maintenance, improvement or other alteration of any building being works which:

(i) affect only the interior of the building; or
(ii) do not materially affect the external appearance of the building.

However, any internal alterations that were sufficiently extensive to amount to rebuilding (eg the gutting and replacement of the building's interior, so that only the external shell was preserved) *would* fall within the definition of development.[1] In *Street v Essex County Council*[2] 'repairs' were carried out, after which the only part of the original structure still standing consisted of two walls which enclosed the original kitchen: it was held that development had taken place. As noted above the internal alterations exception doe not apply where the internal alterations have the effect of increasing the gross floor space of the building by an amount or percentage specified in an order made by the Scottish Ministers.[3]

1 Rowan Robinson *Scottish Planning Law and Procedure* (2001), para 5.14.
2 (1965) 193 EG 537; see also *Hughes v Secretary of State for the Environment and Another* [1994] EGCS 86.
3 1997 Act, s 26(2AA).

4.66 The exclusion also does not apply where the internal works are 'for the alteration of a building by providing additional space in it underground'.[1] Development will therefore occur (for example) if a cellar is extended to form a new basement, even if the result is not visible from outside the building.

1 1997 Act, s 26(2)(a).

4.67 It will be noted that this exclusion also applies to external alterations if they do not materially affect the external appearance of the building. Not surprisingly, the line between those external alterations which are not material and those which are can be difficult to draw. It has been held that the placing of floodlights on a building does not materially affect its appearance.[1] A cash-dispensing machine may or may not materially affect the exterior of a building, depending upon the extent to which the character of the building has been affected.[2] Some external alterations, although technically development, qualify as permitted development and may not require a planning application, eg painting or stonecleaning of a building.

1 *Kensington & Chelsea London Borough Council v CG Hotels* (1980) 41 P&CR 40; but see also *Westminster City Council v Verjee* (1992) 7 PAD 572.
2 SPADS no A6957, discussed in (1987) 22 SPLP 88 and (1988) 23 SPLP 26.

4.68 In *Burroughs Day v Bristol City Council*[1] Deputy Judge Mr Richard Southwell gave the most thorough exposition to date of the criteria for determining whether an alteration will materially affect the external appearance of a building:

'(1) What must be affected is the "external appearance", not "the exterior". The use of the word "appearance" means that it is not sufficient for the external surface of a building to be affected by the proposed alteration. The alteration must be one which affects the way in which the exterior of the building is or can be seen by an observer outside the building.

(2) … In my judgement, all roof alterations which can be seen from any vantage point on the ground or in or on any neighbouring building or buildings would be capable of affecting the "external appearance" of the building in question. It is not necessary to consider the position if a roof alteration were visible only from the air…

(3) The external appearance must be "materially" affected. This involves a judgement as to the degree to which the particular alteration affects the external appearance. The effect must be more than *de minimis*…

Whether the effect of an alteration is 'material' or not must, in my judgement, depend in part on the degree of visibility. A change to the front wall of a building or the front of the roof which is visible from the street is much more likely to be 'material', than a similar change which can be seen only from the top of much taller buildings.

(4) …"Materiality" must in every case take into account the nature of the particular building which it is proposed to alter. It is obvious that what is not a material alteration to the external appearance of a factory, eg a Coca-Cola factory, may be a material alteration to the external appearance of an 18th-century house whether or not it is listed or in a conservation area.

(5) …(T)he effect on the external appearance must be judged for its materiality in relation to the building as a whole, and not by reference to a part of the building taken in isolation.'[2]

The proposed alterations in that case would not have been visible from any street or from the windows of any building nearby, apart from the top two floors of one office building. Otherwise it would only have been visible from the air. Even though the building was listed and situated in a conservation area, it was held that the proposals would not have materially affected the external appearance of the building.[3]

1 [1996] 19 EG 126.

2 Per Deputy Judge Richard Southwell at 129–30.

3 In fact listed building consent was refused in this case, but in order to determine the plaintiffs' entitlement to compensation for the refusal, it was necessary to decide whether their proposals would have amounted to development.

Road and sewage works etc

4.69 Maintenance and improvement work on roads by the local roads authority, if carried on within the road boundaries, does not constitute development. The same applies to works by a local authority or statutory undertaker[1] 'for the purpose of inspecting, repairing or renewing any sewers, mains, pipes, cables or other apparatus, including the breaking open of any road or other land for that purpose'.[2] The purpose of these provisions is self-evident: it should not be necessary for public authorities always to have to seek permission to carry out their statutory duties, even if these involve the sort of activity that would normally count as development. In some cases these will come within the category of permitted development;[3] in the cases mentioned here, they are excluded from the definition of development altogether.

1 These are the words of the 1997 Act, though local authorities have not had responsibilities for sewage since 1996.

2 1997 Act, s 26(2)(b), (c).

3 See paras 5.12 and 5.59 below.

Use within the curtilage of a dwellinghouse

4.70 The full version of this exclusion is 'the use of any buildings or other land within the curtilage of a dwellinghouse for any purpose incidental to the enjoyment of the dwellinghouse as such'.[1] There is no definition of 'curtilage' in the 1997 Act, but case law yields the following:

> '[G]round which is used for the comfortable enjoyment of a house or other building may be regarded in law as being within the curtilage of that house or building and thereby as an integral part of the same, although it has not been marked off or enclosed in any way. It is enough that it serves the purposes of the house or building in some necessary or reasonably useful way.'[2]

In *McAlpine v Secretary of State for the Environment*[3] it was held that a swimming pool and tennis court constructed on an open grassed area beyond the formal garden of a large country house were outwith the curtilage of the dwelling. The judge (Nigel Macleod) after a useful review of the case law[4] identified the following three main criteria from the authorities:

(i) that the curtilage is constrained to a small area about a building;
(ii) that an intimate association with land which is undoubtedly within the curtilage is required in order to make the land under consideration part and parcel of that undoubted curtilage land; and
(iii) that it is not necessary for there to be physical enclosure of that land which is within the curtilage, but the land in question at least needs to be regarded in law as part of one enclosure with the house.

1 1997 Act, s 26(2)(d).
2 *Sinclair-Lockhart's Trustees v Central Land Board* 1951 SC 258 per Lord Mackintosh, 1951 SLT 121; approved in *Paul v Ayrshire County Council* 1964 SC 116, 1964 SLT 207. See also Watchman, P & Young, E 'The Meaning of "Curtilage"' 1990 SLT 77.
3 [1995]1 PLR 16.
4 Including *Sinclair-Lockhart's Trustees* (see note 2 above); *Dyer v Dorset County Council* [1989] QB 346; [1988] 3 WLR 213 and *Methuen-Campbell v Walters* [1979] QB 525; [1979] 1 All ER 606.

4.71 The sort of thing normally considered to be 'within the curtilage' of a dwellinghouse would be garden ground adjoining the house and outbuildings erected on that ground, such as garden huts, greenhouses, garages etc. However, we can see from the above definition that the land need not be enclosed and may sometimes be within the curtilage even if not within the garden area, eg a garage erected at the other side of a back lane. The parking of a car or caravan would normally be allowed, but not the parking of a commercial vehicle, and any use of land or buildings within the curtilage of a dwellinghouse for any substantial commercial purpose is likely to be considered a material change of use.[1] In deciding whether the use of a building is incidental to that of a dwellinghouse, the building's size is relevant but not conclusive.[2] Nor, if the additional use is substantial, need it be commercial in nature to amount to a material change of use, for example where a large number of dogs were kept in a cottage.[3] If an outbuilding, such as a garage, is used as living accommodation, this will be considered a use within the curtilage provided that it forms an integral part of the dwellinghouse as accomodation for a single family.[4] Where part of a house is used for business purposes (eg someone working from home), this will not amount to development provided that the overall character of the house as a residence has not been changed.[5] However, if a sufficiently large proportion of the house is devoted to a commercial use, this may take it outwith the definition of a dwellinghouse for the purposes of the planning legislation (see below); in such a case the business use could no longer be considered a use within the curtilage of a dwellinghouse, and development *would* have occurred.

1 See Rowan Robinson *Scottish Planning Law and Procedure* (2001), para 5.141.
2 *Emin v Secretary of State for the Environment* (1989) 58 P&CR 416.
3 *Wallington v Secretary of State for Wales* [1991] 1 PLR 87, CA; see also *James v Secretary of State for the Environment and Chichester District Council* (1990) 61 P&CR 234.
4 *Uttlesford District Council v Secretary of State for the Environment and White* [1992] JPL 171; see also *Whitehead v Secretary of State for the Environment and Mole Valley District Council* [1992] JPL 561. For Scottish authority see *City of Glasgow District Council v Secretary of State for Scotland* 1997 SCLR 711.
5 SODD Circular 1/1998 'The Town and Country Planning (Use Classes) (Scotland) Order 1997', para 38; see also para 4.42 above (Class 9 of the Use Classes Order).

Definition of 'dwellinghouse'

4.72 The 1997 Act does not give us a definition of 'dwellinghouse', but there is some help from case law. One of the main considerations is that there should be a building providing facilities for daily private domestic existence, and the use to which the building is actually put (in the case in question a holiday chalet) is not conclusive, nor is frequency of use always relevant.[1] In *Prosser v Sharp*[2] the respondent and the respondent's family slept in a caravan, adjacent to which was a wooden building comprising two rooms, which had been renovated and connected to gas, water and cesspool drainage, and which (apart from sleeping accommodation) was used for general living purposes. It was held that the building was not a dwellinghouse, and so the caravan could not be within its curtilage and had therefore to be removed. Even a building which bears all the physical characteristics of a dwellinghouse in the normal sense may cease to be one for the purposes of the planning legislation if the residential use is combined with a sufficiently substantial commercial use.[3]

1 *Gravesham Borough Council v Secretary of State for the Environment* (1984) 47 P&CR 142; see also *Moore v Secretary of State for the Environment* (1998) Times, 18 February, *CA and Magnohard Ltd v Cadogan* [2012] EWCA Civ. 594.
2 (1985) 274 EG 1249.
3 *Scurlock v Secretary of State for Wales and Another* (1977) 33 P&CR 202 (part usage as an estate agent's office); *Deitsch and Deitsch v Secretary of State for the Environment and Richmond-upon-Thames LBC* [1993] JPL 579 (part usage as a solicitor's office); see also para 5.18 below.

4.73 It should be noted that the present exclusion relates to the *use* of land and of buildings already erected there. The actual *erection* of a garage or other outhouse is a building operation and strictly speaking qualifies as development on that account; however, unless such a proposed building is large, or to be located in a sensitive position in relation to an adjoining road, it is likely to qualify as permitted development and not require a planning application.[1]

1 See paras 5.24ff below.

Agriculture and forestry

4.74 The most substantial and probably the most surprising exclusion from the definition of development is 'the use of any land for the purposes of agriculture or forestry (including afforestation) and the use for any of those purposes of any building occupied together with land so used' other than the carrying out or irrigation or drainage for agriculture or any other water management project for that purpose.[1] This simply means that not only farming, but also the cutting down and planting of trees, even on a large scale, does not amount to development and so falls outwith the system of development management. (Note, however, that the felling of trees will often require a felling licence from the Forestry Commission).[2] Also excluded from the development management system are the use of farm buildings and other buildings used in connection with these purposes; furthermore the actual erection of such buildings, provided that they are incidental to agriculture or forestry and within specified limits, will normally qualify as permitted development and not require a planning application.[3]

1 1997 Act, ss 26(2)(e) and 26(2A).
2 See para 4.78 and Chapter 13, part 3 below.
3 See paras 5.38ff below.

Definition of agriculture

4.75 The 1997 Act provides us with a wide list of activities that qualify as 'agriculture';[1] this includes everything we would normally think of as agriculture, ie most arable, pastoral and livestock-rearing activities. At the fringes, this definition has been held to include the use of land for the grazing of horses,[2] and for the keeping of allotments,[3] as well as the sale of bees bred on site (though not the manufacture of hives).[4] The definition has been held to exclude the installation of an egg-vending machine,[5] the breeding and training of horses for show-jumping,[6] the keeping of animals in transit[7] and cheese processing on a significant scale.[8] Even where the agricultural activity takes place entirely within a building or buildings (for example, in a case involving fox farming), this still counts as the use of 'land' for the purpose of agriculture and falls within the exemption.[9] In *Powell v Secretary of State for the Environment and Maidstone Borough Council*[10] the appellant bred rabbits whose droppings were converted by worms into compost for sale. The next proposed stage of this ingenious exercise in sustainable development was to feed surplus worms to tank-raised salmon and use the nutrient-rich water from the fish tanks for the hydroponic production of tomatoes and strawberries. It was held that the breeding of rabbits for meat was an agricultural use but that the vermiculture (the use of worms to produce compost) was not, being more akin to an industrial process. Planning permission was therefore required and was refused. It was not necessary for the court to determine the legal status of the other two proposed activities. However, the fruit and vegetable production can probably be safely assumed to be agricultural, though fish farming in inland waters has been defined as involving engineering operations.[11]

1 1997 Act, s 277(1).
2 *Sykes v Secretary of State for the Environment* (1980) 42 P&CR 19.
3 *Crowborough Parish Council v Secretary of State for the Environment* (1980) 43 P&CR 229.
4 *Tandridge District Council v Homewood & the Honey Farm* (1986) 1 PAD 410.
5 *Hidderley v Warwickshire County Council* (1963) 14 P&CR 134.
6 *Belmont Farm Ltd v Minister of Housing and Local Government* (1962) 13 P&CR 417.
7 *Warnock v Secretary of State for the Environment* [1980] JPL 590.
8 *Salvatore Cumbo v Secretary of State for the Environment and Dacorum Borough Council* [1992] JPL 366.
9 *North Warwickshire Borough Council v Secretary of State for the Environment* (1985) 50 P&CR 47.
10 [1993] JPL 455.
11 1997 Act, s 26(6); see para 4.14 above.

Definition of forestry

4.76 We are given no statutory definition of forestry apart from the fact (noted above) that forestry includes afforestation. In *Farleyer Estate v Secretary of State for Scotland*[1] the court quoted with approval part of a dictionary entry in *The New Oxford English Dictionary*: 'The science and art of forming and cultivating forests, management of growing timber'. It also adopted the following dictum taken from a rating case:[2] '... forestry, use of lands as woodlands, does not cease when the timber is grown, but may well include operations necessary to render the timber marketable or disposable to profitable use as timber'.

1 1992 SCLR 364.
2 *Assessor for the County of Midlothian v Buccleuch Estates Ltd* 1962 SC 453 at 462 per Lord Patrick.

4.77 As a result, use of a site 1,500 metres from the plantations, for storage of timber and as a transfer area, was held to fall within the definition of forestry and thus outwith development control.[1]

1 For comment on this case, see Brian Thompson *Not Seeing the Wood for the Trees?* (1992) 36 SPLP 54.

Tree protection

4.78 Although the general rule is that felling trees is outwith planning control, there are several important exceptions to this: (a) where the planning authority has placed a tree preservation order upon a tree or group of trees, making it an offence to cut down or otherwise damage them without permission; (b) where it has been made a condition of a planning permission that a tree or trees within the relevant site should be preserved; and (c) where the tree or trees are in a conservation area. Furthermore, many trees which are not protected within the planning system, may nevertheless require a felling licence from the Forestry Commission before they can be cut down. Each of these special cases will be considered in more detail later in this book.[1]

1 See Chapter 13, part 3 below.

Afforestation

4.79 The widespread planting of trees on bare land is a radical change of land use with considerable implications for amenity, recreation and the environment. Although this remains outwith the definition of development, most afforestation is dependent upon grants from the Forestry Commission, which includes planning authorities among its list of consultees. Such a grant may also be dependent upon the obtaining of an environmental assessment.[1] Afforestation is therefore subject to a measure of public control, though there is growing opinion that this control should be greater.[2]

1 See Chapter 15, part 3 below.
2 See Sandy Mather *Afforestation in Scotland* (1988) 23 SPLP 4 and *Afforestation and Planning* (1989) 26 SPLP 4.

Use within the same class of the Use Classes Order

4.80 As we have already seen, where the existing use and the proposed use fall within the same class of the Town and Country Planning (Use Classes) (Scotland) Order 1997, there is no development. The present sub-section of the 1997 Act provides the Secretary of State with the delegated power to make the Order.[1]

1 1997 Act, s 26(2)(f); see also part 3 above.

Demolition

4.81 We saw above that demolition was stated to be a building operation which ought to bring it within the definition of development.[1] However, the Scottish Ministers are empowered to direct that certain categories of demolition shall not involve development.[2] The Town and Country Planning (Demolition which is not Development) (Scotland) Revocation Direction 2011 revoked the Town and Country Planning (Demolition which is not Development) (Scotland) Direction 2001. The revocation of the 2001 Direction has the effect that the demolition of any building will be development for the purposes of the Town and Country Planning (Scotland) Act 1997. Class 70 of Schedule 1 to the Town and Country Planning (General Permitted Development) (Scotland) Order 1992 grants planning permission for the complete demolition of buildings, subject to certain limitations and conditions (including requirements for prior approval). Other classes of the 1992 Order grant planning permission for partial demolition required to carry out development permitted by that class.[3] The demolition of listed buildings, buildings in conservation areas and buildings which are scheduled monuments are all given special protection elsewhere in the planning legislation and permission for their demolition is required.[4]

1 See para 4.8 above.
2 1997 Act, s 26(2)(g).

3 See the Town and Country Planning (Demolition which is not Development) (Scotland) Revocation Direction 2011 and SG Circular 4/2011 'The Town and Country Planning (Demolition which is not Development) (Scotland) Revocation Direction 2011. See also para 5.65 – 5.68 below.
4 See Chapter 12 below.

6. DEVELOPMENT: SPECIFIC INCLUSIONS

4.82 Section 26 of the 1997 Act continues to refine the definition of development by declaring that certain other matters *do* amount to development.

Irrigation or drainage for agriculture or another water management project

4.83 The carrying out of irrigation of drainage for agriculture or of any other water management project for that purpose is declared to be development.[1] However water management projects are included as Class 18A in Schedule 1 to the Town and Country Planning (General Permitted Development) (Scotland) Order 1992, and this provides exemption from the need to obtain planning permission. Finally, the Town and Country Planning (Environmental Impact Assessment) (Scotland) Regulations 2011[2] includes the sorts of development projects requiring to undergo an environmental impact assessment, and therefore not entitled to deemed planning permission under the 1992 Order. The projects affected are those water management projects for agriculture, including drainage projects, but excluding irrigation projects; where the area of the works exceeds one hectare.

1 1997 Act, s 26(2A).
2 SSI 2011 No 139.

Increasing the internal gross floor space of a building

4.84 The Scottish Ministers are empowered to make a development order bringing with the definition of 'development' works to the interior of a building which have the effect of increasing the gross floor space by a specified amount (including percentage)[1] and, in turn, amend the general position regarding internal alterations being a specific exclusion from 'development'. Given the current economic climate the Scottish Ministers have decided not to introduce these additional controls on the retail and property sectors. The work on bringing forward an order about mezzanine floors has been postponed until further notice.[2]

1 1997 Act, ss 26(2AA) and s 26(2AB).
2 See Chapter 9, part 14.

Subdivision of a dwellinghouse

4.85 'The use as two or more separate dwellinghouses of any building previously used as a single dwellinghouse involves a material change in the use of the building and of each part of it which is so used'.[1] Multiple occupancy alone is not enough; for example if several people shared a house, having separate bedrooms but making common use of the living room, kitchen and bathroom, that would not be a material change of use. If there was some kind of internal physical reconstruction to separate the various units; that would greatly strengthen the argument that development had taken place. However, even in the absence of any such physical reconstruction, development may still occur: the main factor is that the units should be self-contained and occupied by different people, without shared facilities. As with so many parts of our definition of development, there is some blurring at the borders: once more it is a matter of fact and degree to be decided in each particular case.[2]

1 1997 Act, s 26(3)(a).
2 For discussion of the main principles involved here, see *Ealing Borough Council v Ryan* [1965] 2 QB 486.

4.86 An obvious example falling within this category is where a large dwellinghouse is subdivided into flats. Provided that any alterations remained internal, this would not qualify as development by virtue of being a building operation.[1] However, under the present sub-section, it undoubtedly *would* so qualify as a material change of use.

1 See para 4.65 above.

Refuse deposits

4.87 'The deposit of refuse or waste materials on land involves a material change in its use, notwithstanding that the land is comprised in a site already used for that purpose, if –

(i) the superficial area of the deposit is extended; or
(ii) the height of the deposit is extended and exceeds the level of the land adjoining the site.'[1]

This means that even where planning permission has already been obtained to use land as a refuse tip (or it is otherwise being used lawfully), a fresh permission may be required if the tipping is no longer contained within the original boundaries.

1 1997 Act, s 26(3)(b).

4.88 The best example of this is where a former quarry is used for the deposit of refuse.[1] As long as the refuse is contained out of sight below ground level, the effect on the environment and local amenity may be slight. However, if the quarry becomes full so that the refuse spills over the side into a wider area and/or begins to protrude above the adjoining skyline, then it becomes a different matter. By making such an overspill qualify as development, the present provision makes sure that the planning authority has another opportunity to exercise control over the situation.

1 See *Alexandra Transport Company Ltd v Secretary of State for Scotland* 1974 SLT 81.

Fish farming

4.89 The placing or assembling of any equipment in defined waters for the purpose of fish farming is included within the meaning of 'development'.[1]

1 See para 4.14 above and see paras 5.50–5.52 below for permitted development rights.

Advertisements

4.90 The erection of an advertisement hoarding is a building or other operation falling within the first strand of our definition of development.[1] In addition, the 1997 Act explicitly declares it to be a material change of use to display adverts on the exterior of a building not normally used for that purpose.[2] However, adverts do not need planning permission in the normal way, but generally require instead a special consent under the provisions of the Town and Country Planning (Control of Advertisements) (Scotland) Regulations 1984[3] which will be considered later.[4] There are exceptions in the case of certain minor types of advert which are totally exempt from planning control or have deemed consent; in the latter case, no permission is required for them, but the planning authority has the right to ask for them to be removed if this is thought desirable on grounds of amenity.

1 See para 4.4 above.
2 1997 Act, s 26(7).
3 SI 1984/467.
4 See Chapter 14, part 2 below.

Chapter 5

Permitted development and other exemptions

1. INTRODUCTION

5.1 In Chapter 4 we examined the definition of development and established that types of activity which do not fall within that definition are therefore outwith planning control. However, the converse is not true. If everything qualifying as development in terms of our definition required an individual permission, planning departments would be unable to deal with the flood of applications and the country would be faced with something of a bureaucratic nightmare.

5.2 Thankfully, not all development requires an individual application for planning permission. In some cases planning permission is not a legal requirement at all. In others (and the distinction is theoretical rather than practical) permission is deemed to have been granted. But the most common exceptions are developments for which planning permission is required, but is granted in advance, thereby making an individual application unnecessary. This is achieved by either: (a) a special development order; (b) a general development order (creating categories of what is known as permitted development); (c) a simplified planning zone scheme; or (d) an enterprise zone scheme. The last three of these automatically create planning permissions for large categories of development, either on the basis of the type of development involved, or because of the area in which it is situated.

5.3 The reasoning behind these exceptions varies and will be dealt with as we go along. In some cases it is due to the special status of the developer (eg in the case of development by local authorities), in others it is because the development is fairly minor (eg an extension to a dwellinghouse). In other cases it is a device for encouraging development in a particular area ie simplified planning zones or enterprise zones but these have fallen out of favour in Scotland. While the power to designate them still exists, the Lanarkshire Enterprise Zone was the last one created in Scotland and it expired in 2011.

2. DEVELOPMENT NOT REQUIRING PLANNING PERMISSION

5.4 The 1997 Act provides that a number of specific developments do not need planning permission.[1] Some of these are rather obscure transitional provisions, which no longer need concern us. However, two are worth noting: (1) where a temporary planning permission has expired, planning permission is not required to resume the previous normal lawful use;[2] where an enforcement notice has been served in respect of an unlawful development, planning permission is not required to use the land for the purpose for which it could lawfully have been used prior to the unlawful development.[3]

1 See s 28 and Sch 2.
2 Ibid, s 28(2).
3 Ibid, s 28(4).

3. PERMISSION DEEMED TO HAVE BEEN GRANTED

5.5 There are two main situations in which planning permission is deemed to have been granted.

Development involved in the display of certain adverts.

5.6 Where consent has been granted to display an advert in accordance with the relevant regulations[1] planning permission is deemed to be granted for any development of land involved (such as the erection of hoardings).[2] We will be considering further the special controls which are exercised over adverts in Chapter 14.

1 Town and Country Planning (Control of Advertisements) (Scotland) Regulations 1984, SI 1984/467 (as amended).
2 1997 Act s 184.

Development with government authorisation

5.7 Where the authorisation of a government department is required for development by local authorities or statutory undertakers, that department has power to deem that planning permission has been granted by issuing a direction to that effect.[1] The need for government authorisation may be imposed directly by legislation, or in some cases indirectly eg where borrowing money to pay for a development needs the approval of a government department.[2] In granting consent under the Electricity Act 1989[3] for major schemes such as large scale power generation projects and power transmission lines, the Scottish Ministers can direct that planning permission is deemed to be granted.[4] The same applies to projects authorised by the Scottish Ministers under the Transport and Works (Scotland) Act 2007 and the Flood Risk Management (Scotland) Act 2009.[5] A number of major projects have been approved through these routes in recent years including large wind farms and the Beauly to Denny high voltage power line.

1 1997 Act, s 57.
2 Ibid, s 57(4)(d).
3 Sections 36 & 37.
4 1997 Act, s 57(2).
5 Ibid, ss 57(2A) & 57(2B).

4. PERMITTED DEVELOPMENT

Special Development Orders

5.8 The 1997 Act[1] gives the Scottish Ministers power to grant, by statutory instrument, planning permission in advance for a specific type (or types) of development on a specific site or types of site or for specific categories of development. This is known as a *special development order*. As with other planning consents, planning permission may be granted either unconditionally or subject to conditions.[2]

1 Section 30(2)(b).
2 1997 Act, s 31.

The General Permitted Development Order (PDO)

5.9 The Scottish Ministers also have power to grant advance planning permissions on a general basis for any category of development.[1] This is done by a *general development order*, and at any one time there is normally just one such order in force, granting permission throughout Scotland for a broad range of mainly minor and non-contentious types of development. The current order is the Town and Country Planning (General Permitted Development) (Scotland) Order 1992[2], known for short as the 'Permitted Development Order' or 'PDO'.[2] In 2012 a number of significant changes were made[3] to those parts of the PDO dealing with 'householder' developments such as house extensions and garden sheds. At the time of writing the PDO provisions for non-domestic works are under review and consultation papers outlining possible changes were published in 2011 and 2012.[4] The 2012 consultation paper included a draft amendment order and we will refer to the possible changes that may affect individual classes as we discuss them below.

1 1997 Act, s 30(2)(a).
2 SI 1992/223 (as amended).
3 By the Town and Country Planning (General Permitted Development) (Scotland) Amendment Order 2011 (SSI 2011 No 357).
4 Scottish Government *Consultation on Non-Domestic Elements of The Town and Country Planning (General Permitted Development) (Scotland) Order 1992* (2011) and Scottish Government *Consultation on the General Permitted Development Amendment Order 2012* (March 2012).

5.10 Superficially, there is a resemblance between activities falling outwith the definition of development (which we examined in the last chapter) and those which are permitted development under the PDO, in that both can normally go ahead without an individual application for planning permission being made to the planning authority. However, there is an important distinction; unlike activities which are not development, permitted development remains subject to planning control. This is because it is subject to conditions and limitations (see below), and also because permitted development rights can be selectively removed in specified geographical areas for certain types of development. The main method of doing the latter (Article 4 directions) is discussed later in this chapter.[1]

1 See Part 5 below.

Conditions and Limitations

5.11 As in the case of special development orders, the Scottish Ministers can impose conditions on development permitted by the PDO.[1] As well as imposing specific conditions to each class of permitted development, there are also a number of general limitations that apply to all categories. Nothing in the Order permits development contrary to any condition on an existing planning permission.[2] For example; permission may have been granted for the erection of a house subject to a condition that it could not subsequently be extended. In many circumstances house extensions are permitted development but the provisions of the Order would not apply in this case because of the condition. From *Dunoon Development Ltd v Secretary of State for the Environment*[3] it appears that a condition has to unequivocally exclude the operation of the Order to remove permitted development rights. However, in *Northampton BC v*

First Secretary of State[4] the court held that such conditions should be interpreted in a common sense manner taking into account the planning context rather than in the wholly legalistic way that a lawyer might interpret them.

1 1997 Act, s 31.
2 Town and Country Planning (General Permitted Development) (Scotland) Order 1992, SI 1992/223 (as amended) art 3.
3 [1992] 2 PLR 128, CA.
4 [2005] EWHC 168 (Admin); [2005] JPL 1213; [2005] 7 EG 142 (CS).

5.12 Not surprisingly, permitted development rights only apply to a development which was lawful in the first place. For example, if a warehouse had changed use to a dwellinghouse without planning permission that property would not enjoy domestic permitted development rights until it had become immune from enforcement proceedings, ie at least four years after the change of use.[1] Permitted development rights can only be enjoyed by existing development and cannot be used to make changes to a new property which is still under construction.[2] With some limited exceptions (certain cases of permitted road repairs or development under local or private acts or orders), nothing in the Order authorises development which involves the formation, laying out, or widening of a means of access to a trunk or classified road or which obstructs the view of anyone using such a road. The Order also does not authorise the laying or construction of a notifiable pipeline (except by a public gas transporter as set out in class 39 of the PDO). Development involving the demolition of a complete building is not permitted except where authorised by Part 23 of the PDO. No development authorised by the PDO which is likely to have a significant effect on a European Site for the conservation of natural habitats can be begun without the written approval of the planning authority.[3]

1 See Chapter 9.
2 *R (on the application of Townsley) v Secretary of State for Communities and Local Government* [2009] EWHC 3522 (Admin).
3 Conservation (Natural Habitats, &c) Regulations 1994, SI 1994/2716, regs 60–63; see also Chapter 13.

5.13 With some exceptions (eg certain drainage works) the PDO does not permit any development that requires an Environmental Impact Assessment (EIA).[1] This means all developments listed in Schedules 1 of the Environmental Impact Assessment (Scotland) Regulations 2011 and those listed in Schedule 2 where the planning authority has adopted a screening opinion that the particular proposal is an EIA development[2] or the Scottish Ministers have issued a screening direction to that effect (see Chapter 15). We explain below that in some cases development which is permitted by the PDO may be subject to the need for the prior approval of the planning authority eg in relation to the design of agricultural buildings. It is possible that the issue of whether an EIA will be required may also arise at the prior approval stage even where the planning authority has already adopted a screening opinion that, in principle, the proposal is not an EIA development. This might happen if the proposed size or design of the structures involved raises issues of environmental impact which had not been envisaged earlier. In such circumstances a further screening opinion may be needed and if this indicates that the development requires an EIA then the development no longer enjoys permitted development status. If the developer still wants to go ahead they will first need to apply for planning permission (see Chapter 6) and also submit an Environmental Statement (see Chapter 15).

1 Town and Country Planning (General Permitted Development) (Scotland) Order 1992, art 3(8).

2 An EIA development is one which is either: a Schedule 1 development; or, a Schedule 2 development likely to have significant effects on the environment by virtue of factors such as its nature, size or location (Town and Country Planning (Environmental Impact Assessment) (Scotland) Regulations 2011, reg 2).

5.14 Schedule 1 to the PDO sets out the various forms of development permitted by Article 3 of the Order. These are divided into 36 'parts', (see Figure 5.1) which are further subdivided into 'classes' of permitted development. We only have space to look in detail at the most important parts and classes, but the others will be considered briefly. When disputes have arisen about whether a particular development falls within one of the permitted development classes the courts have generally been reluctant to rule on the matter, considering it a matter of fact and degree to be decided by the planning authority or by the Scottish Ministers on appeal.[1] This may account for the sparsity of case authority in this area. And where there is a change to the categories of permitted development as a result of an amendment to the Permitted Development Order (something which happens regularly), the position will be governed by the law in force when the development *commences* rather than when it is completed.[2] Otherwise, the change in the Permitted Development Order would have the effect of revoking a permission which the developer had already begun to implement.

1 See eg *Cotswold District Council v Secretary of State for the Environment and Alexander* [1993] JPL 1026.

2 *R J Williams Le Roi v Secretary of State for the Environment and Salisbury District Council* [1993] JPL 1033.

FIGURE 5.1 PERMITTED DEVELOPMENT (PDO parts 1–32)

1	Development within the curtilage of a dwellinghouse – extensions, outbuildings, satellite dishes etc.
1ZA	Development to a building containing a flat – limited alterations to the external appearance.
1A	Installation of domestic microgeneration equipment.
1B	Installation of non-domestic microgeneration equipment.
2	Minor operations – gates, walls, painting, stonecleaning etc.
3	Changes of use – non-contentious changes of use class.
4	Temporary buildings and uses.
5	Caravan sites.
6	Agricultural buildings and operations.
6A	Fish farming.
7	Forestry buildings and operations.
8	Industrial and warehouse development.
9	Repairs to private roads and ways.
10	Repairs to services.
11	Development under local or private acts or orders.
12	Development by local authorities.
13	Development by statutory undertakers.
14	Aviation development.
15–17&19	Mineral developments.
20–21	Telecommunications developments – satellite and mobile phone antennae etc.
22	Development of amusement parks.
23	Demolition of buildings.
24	Toll road facilities.
25	Closed circuit television cameras.
25A	Temporary protection of poultry and other birds.
26	Development by the Scottish Ministers as Roads. Authority.
27–30	Developments by the Crown.
31	Development for national security purposes
32	Ancient monuments.

Prior Approval

5.15 For some classes of permitted development, the order grants planning permission for the erection, extension or alteration of buildings or other structures subject to the possibility that the planning authority's prior approval may be required for the siting, design or external appearance of these. Examples include agricultural buildings (class 18), forestry buildings (class 22) and domestic air source heat pumps (class 6H). Prior approval may also be required for the demolition of a whole building (in terms of the method to be used and any site restoration) (Class 70). Prior approval operates in two stages. Firstly the developer has to apply for a 'determination' from the planning authority as to whether its prior approval will be required. There is a standard fee that has to be paid for this.[1] The application has to include a written description of the proposed development including of the materials to be used and a plan showing the site location. If the planning authority does not respond within 28 days or if it says that its prior approval is not required the developer can go ahead with the work. However, they must do so within either 3 or 5 years (depending on the relevant class of permitted development relied upon) and in accordance with the plans submitted to the planning authority. If the planning authority determines that its prior approval is required then work cannot go ahead until a design has been approved and this may require the submission of additional information. In such circumstances the principle of the erection, extension or alteration is not in contention, simply the siting, design or external appearance.[2] Once approved the developer again has either 3 or 5 years in which to implement the development. Where a development proceeds without the authority's prior approval this breach cannot be remedied with a retrospective prior approval application,[3] an application for full planning permission will be needed. On the other hand, where prior approval is granted, the permitted development right to which it relates is crystallised. This means that if there is a material change in circumstances after prior approval but before the permitted development is implemented, the development given prior approval remains permitted. For example, in *R. (on the application of Orange Personal Communications Services Ltd) v Islington LBC*[4] prior approval was given for a telecommunications development. However, before this was implemented the area in which the development site lay was designated as a conservation area. Ordinarily, the type of development involved was not permitted in a conservation area. Nevertheless, the court held that because of the prior approval, this particular development was still permitted. As a result the planning authority could not take enforcement action against the developer.

1 The Town and Country Planning (Fees for Applications and Deemed Applications) (Scotland) Regulations 2004 as amended, most recently by Town and Country Planning

(Fees for Applications and Deemed Applications) (Scotland) Amendment Regulations 2013.

2 See for example *R. (on the application of Murrell) v Secretary of State for Communities and Local Government* [2010] EWCA Civ 1367; [2012] 1 P&CR 6.

3 *Airwave MMO2 Ltd v First Secretary of State* [2005] EWHC 1701 (Admin); [2006] JPL 362.

4 [2005] EWHC 963 (Admin); [2006] 1 P&CR 12.

Part 1: Development within the curtilage of a dwellinghouse

5.16 This part relates to alterations to a dwelling-house (eg extensions or dormer windows) or minor developments within its garden area. (We saw from our definition in the last chapter that the 'curtilage' is not necessarily confined within the garden boundaries, though it usually will be.)[1]

1 See Chapter 4.

5.17 In terms of the number of applications and enquiries received by planning departments, this is probably the aspect of development management work which they encounter most often. It is also the area of planning law which the average person is most likely to come across at some time in their life. With this in mind, the Scottish Government has produced a circular that provides a relatively easy-to-follow guide to the subject.[1]

1 SG Circular 1/2012 'Guidance on Householder Permitted Development Rights'.

5.18 The intention of this part of the PDO is to strike a balance between maintaining the rights of individuals to do what they want with their property while, at the same time, safeguarding residential amenity, especially in conservation areas and around listed buildings.

5.19 What we have attempted to do here is to outline the general content of this part of the PDO, as well as draw attention to some important principles that might otherwise become lost in the detail.

5.20 In order to make sense of the details of domestic permitted development rights, it is first necessary to define some of the main terms used. These are as follows:

Principal elevation: This is used to describe the 'front' of the house. This is important because extensions, alterations and outbuildings are normally only permitted if they are to the side or back of a house and not if they are in to the front. The PDO definition of principal elevation is 'the elevation of the original dwellinghouse which by virtue of its design or setting, or both, is the principal elevation' and in most cases it will be obvious where this is (eg it will contain the main door, have windows and face a road). However, where it is not obvious the factors to be taken into account include the location of the main outside door, windows, relationship to a road, boundary treatment and architectural ornamentation. Circular 1/2012[1] includes drawings of different situations to help explain the concept. Once the principal elevation has been identified it is usually then straightforward to identify the rear and side elevations.

1 SG Circular 1/2012 'Guidance on Householder Permitted Development Rights'.

Fronting a road: It is important to be clear what this means because permitted development rights to the front or side of a house are significantly restricted if those elevations front a road and this can even affect parts of the rear garden area. 'Fronts' means facing onto a road and other factors to take into account are the angle of the house to the road, the distance between the house and road and the size of any intervening land. For example, where a house elevation is more than 30 metres away from a road this will not normally count as fronting that road. Circular 1/2012 includes a number of drawings to help explain in more detail how this concept is to be applied.

Front and rear curtilages: This is basically a way of describing and defining the front and rear garden areas. The front curtilage is the land to the front of the principal elevation. The rear curtilage is the remaining land around the original dwellinghouse. This concept is important when calculating the maximum amount of curtilage ground that can be built on under the PDO.

Site Coverage: This relates to the maximum amount of land that can be built on within the curtilage. It is normally calculated against the rear curtilage of the original house and the effect is cumulative. Every time an extension is built or a garden shed erected, this will use up some of the total site coverage allowance. The aim is to ensure that the total curtilage area built on is never more than the same size as the original house. If the primary elevation does not front a road then the front curtilage is added to the total for site coverage purposes.

Original or existing dwellinghouse: The original dwellinghouse is that which was originally built and the planning permission for its erection will define what that is. If the house was built before the introduction of the modern planning system then the original house is as it was on 1 July 1948 (ie the date after which it became necessary to obtain planning permission for new development). The existing dwellinghouse is as at the date any new development is to be carried out. In other words it includes any extensions and alterations carried out since it was first built (or since 1 July 1948 for older houses) but does not include any outbuildings.

Enlargement: This means any development increasing the internal volume of the original dwellinghouse. Surprisingly, this includes a canopy or roof without walls but not a balcony. This means that a car port or a rear covered seating area attached to the house counts as an enlargement. The total amount of ground covered by enlargements cannot be more than the area covered by the original dwellinghouse.

Height: Many developments permitted under Part 1 of the PDO are restricted in terms of height. This has to be measured against the lowest part of the natural ground surface immediately adjacent to the new building or structure. Any attempt to get to build higher by first adding to the natural ground level does not count. Maximum height is also calculated with reference to the exterior of a building not the internal ceiling height.

Footprint: This refers to the total amount of ground taken up by a building and so will be greater than the internal floor area.

5.21 There are 11 separate classes of permitted development within Part 1 and we will now look at each in some detail:

Class 1A. Any enlargement of a dwellinghouse by way of a single storey ground floor extension, including any alteration to the roof required for the purpose of the enlargement: Ground level single storey extensions are permitted provided they are not in a conservation area and also as long as they do not breach a number of restrictions relating to height, size, position and closeness to the site boundary. These restrictions are that the eaves height must not exceed three metres and the total height must not be over four metres. The total area of ground covered by the house once extended must not be more than twice the area of the original house. No part of the extension can be in front of the principal elevation of the house or any side elevation that fronts a road. The extension cannot cover more than 50 per cent of either the front or rear curtilage. Finally, no part of the extension should come within 1 metre of the curtilage boundary and cannot extend more than four metres from the part of the existing dwellinghouse's rear wall nearest that boundary (three metres in the case of a terraced house).

Class 1B Any enlargement of a dwellinghouse by way of a ground floor extension consisting of more than one storey, including any alteration to the roof required for the purpose of the enlargement: House extensions that are more than single storey in height are also permitted as long as they are not in a conservation area and do not extend beyond the principal elevation of the house or any side elevation fronting a road. They must also not exceed the height of the highest part of the existing dwellinghouse roof (excluding any chimney) or come within ten metres of the curtilage boundary. The area of ground covered by the house as extended must not be more than twice that of the existing house. The development must not cover more than 50 per cent of the existing rear and front curtilages respectively.

Class 1C. The erection, construction or alteration of any porch outside any external door of a dwellinghouse: As with house extensions porches are not permitted in a conservation area. Elsewhere, they are permitted provided they do not have a footprint of more than three sq metres, do not come nearer than two metres from a boundary between the curtilage and a road and are not more than three metres in height.

Class 1D. Any enlargement of a dwellinghouse by way of an addition or alteration to its roof: This class relates to the kinds of works that are normally needed to create new or extra space within the roof area of a house. While the internal works themselves are not subject to planning control, any resulting external changes to the roof (normally the formation of dormer windows) do need planning approval. However, such works are permitted by Class 1D of the PDO provided they are not in a conservation area and not on a roof plane forming part of: the principal elevation; any elevation fronting a road; or any elevation within ten metres of the curtilage boundary that it faces. The works cannot be higher than the highest part of the existing roof (excluding any chimney) or wider than half the width of the existing roof plane that it is located on. Finally, no part of the development can be within 0.3 metres of any edge of the roof plane.

Class 2A. The erection, construction or alteration of any access ramp outside an external door of a dwellinghouse: Ramps are not permitted within the curtilage of a listed building or in a conservation area. The maximum permitted height including any handrails, fences etc is 1.5 metres. The maximum permitted height of the access ramp surface is 0.4m.The maximum combined length of all ramp flights is five metres and the maximum combined length of flights and landings is nine metres

Class 2B. Any improvement, addition or other alteration to the external appearance of a dwellinghouse that is not an enlargement: This class effectively creates a one metre 'bubble' around the walls and roof of a house within which a number of different developments can take place without the need to apply for planning permission. These include satellite dishes, installation of solar roof panels, replacing windows, or fixing cladding to the walls. Once again, this class does not apply in a conservation area and the development must be completely external ie it cannot increase the internal volume of the house (even in the form of a canopy such as a car port). All of the development must be within one metre of the wall or roof. Certain works are excluded because they are covered by other permitted development classes eg fixing, to a wall, a CCTV camera or a flue for certain heating systems. Wind turbines, balconies and roof terraces or platforms are totally excluded.

Class 3A. The provision within the curtilage of a dwellinghouse of a building for any purpose incidental to the enjoyment of that dwellinghouse or the alteration, maintenance or improvement of such a building: This covers the types of outbuildings commonly found in domestic gardens eg garages, greenhouses, sheds and summer houses. These are permitted development provided no part of the building lies to the front of the principal elevation wall or any elevation wall fronting a road. In other words they normally need to be located in the back garden. The eaves height cannot be more than three metres high and no part of the building can exceed four metres. No part of a building that comes within 1 metre of the curtilage boundary can be higher than 2.5 metres. The area of ground covered by the building cannot be more than 50 per cent of the total front and rear curtilage. If the building is to be located in a conservation area then it cannot have a footprint of more than four square metres. The building cannot be used as a separate dwellinghouse and can only be used as something connected with residential use eg for parking a car, storing bicycles, gardening equipment, a child's playhouse or for hobbies.

Class 3B. The carrying out of any building, engineering, installation or other operation within the curtilage of a dwellinghouse for any purpose incidental to the enjoyment of that dwellinghouse: This class covers freestanding structures and works not covered by other permitted development classes. It includes things like swimming pools, flag poles, free standing solar panels, oil tanks and garden works. It does not apply in a conservation area. Structures cannot be more than three metres high and normally need to be located in a back garden as they cannot be placed in front of the principal elevation wall or any side elevation wall facing a road. They must not cover more than 50 per cent of the curtilage. As with all other classes in part 1 the purpose of the structure must be something connected with normal domestic activities. In *Croydon London Borough Council v Gladden*.[1] the Court of Appeal held that a large wooden replica of a spitfire aircraft could not reasonably be regarded as incidental to the enjoyment of a dwellinghouse. Unfortunately, the court's view was not sought regarding certain other items, including large replicas of a military tank and a rocket-type missile and, an inflatable figure of Winston Churchill.

1 (1994) 68 P&CR 300.

Class 3C. The provision within the curtilage of a dwellinghouse of a hard surface for any purpose incidental to the enjoyment of that dwellinghouse or the replacement in whole or in part of such a surface: Hard surfaced patios, paths, driveways etc. are normally permitted development provided they are not in a conservation area or the curtilage of a listed building. The only other restriction relates to the need to avoid possible flooding problems. With this in mind, any hardstanding that lies between the dwellinghouse and a road bounding the curtilage of the property needs to be made of porous materials or, if not, to have a system ensuring that water running off the hard surface is directed to a permeable or porous surface area within the curtilage.

Class 3D. The erection, construction, maintenance, improvement or alteration of any deck or other raised platform within the curtilage of a dwellinghouse for any purpose incidental to the enjoyment of that dwellinghouse: Decking is permitted provided the platform surface is not more than 0.5 metres high and any wall, fence, hand rail etc associated with it is no higher than 2.5 metres. It generally needs to be in the back garden ie not in front of the wall of the principal elevation or any elevation facing a road. If it lies within a conservation area or the curtilage of a listed building then the maximum footprint of the decking area is just 4 square metres.

Class 3E. The erection, construction, maintenance, improvement or alteration of any gate, fence, wall or other means of enclosure any part of which would be within or would bound the curtilage of a dwellinghouse: These are permitted except in a conservation area or, within or bounding the curtilage of a listed building. The maximum height of a new wall, fence, gate etc is normally two metres. However, if it fronts a road or projects beyond the line of the wall of the principal elevation or side elevation that is nearest a road it can only be up to one metre in height. If replacing an existing wall etc, then the replacement can be to the same height as the original even if this is higher than the above limits.

5.22 There are some important points to note in relation to Part 1:

(a) The above permitted development rights apply only to *dwellinghouses*, ie detached, semi-detached and terraced houses. They do *not* apply to *flats*. A flat is defined as 'a separate and self-contained set of premises whether or not on the same floor and forming part of a building from some other part of which it is divided horizontally'.[1] This means that not only are obvious examples of flatted accommodation excluded (eg tenement blocks), but also less obvious examples such as dwellings in four-in-a-block (or cottage flat) buildings. (Note, however, that Part 1ZA of the PDO gives flats some limited permitted development rights which we will consider below). A house which is partly used for a commercial purpose may cease to be considered a dwellinghouse for the purposes of the planning legislation, even though it is also still used as a residence, and this will have the effect of excluding the permitted development rights conferred by Part 1 of the Permitted Development Order.[2]

(b) While there is no need to apply for planning permission for a development permitted by the PDO there may be other consents that have to be obtained. Examples of the types of permission that might be needed include a building warrant and listed building consent. Householder should also check that the permitted development class that they are relying on has not been removed in their particular locality by an Article 4 direction (see Part 5 below).

(c) A householder cannot get round the permitted development restrictions by carrying out a development in stages, eg by building an extension that is within the permitted dimensions and later adding an 'extension to the extension'. As soon as any alteration to an extension (or other development) brings the combined size outwith the prescribed dimensions, it ceases to be permitted development. The same would apply if the alteration resulted in any part of the extension contravening the restrictions regarding location (eg proximity to curtilage boundary).

(d) In cases where there is any doubt about the extent of the curtilage of a dwellinghouse, the burden of proof is on the householder to show that they are entitled to the permitted development rights granted by Part 1.[3]

(e) It is important to be clear that any developments which have been excluded, eg because they exceed the size restrictions, or are in a conservation area etc, are not necessarily absolutely forbidden. They are only denied permitted development status, ie the householder is not entitled to carry them out without submitting a planning application to the planning authority. In many of these cases planning permission, if applied for, may well be granted.

1 Town and Country Planning (General Permitted Development) (Scotland) Order 1992, SI 1992/223, art 2(1).

2 See *Scurlock v Secretary of State for Wales and Another* (1976) 33 P&CR 202 (part use as an estate agent's office) and *Deitsch and Deitsch v Secretary of State for the Environment and Richmond-upon-Thames London Borough Council* [1993] JPL 579 (part use as a solicitor's office); see also para 4.72 above.

3 *Mohammed Asghar v Secretary of State for the Environment and Harrogate Borough Council* [1988] JPL 476.

Part 1ZA: Development to a building containing a flat

5.23 Residential flats used to have very few permitted development rights. That changed in 2012 with the introduction of revised domestic permitted development rights which included a new part of the PDO applying exclusively to flats. These are set out in Part 1ZA which contains just one class as follows.

Class 4A: Any improvement or other alteration to the external appearance of a dwelling situated within a building containing one or more flats: In essence this gives flats similar permitted development rights to those that houses enjoy under Class 2B above. Within a one metre 'bubble' around the building's external walls and roof, a number of different developments can take place without the need to apply for planning permission. These include installing satellite dishes, solar roof panels or fixing cladding to the walls. However, unlike for dwellinghouses, changes to the size of windows and doorways (and of their frames) are not permitted. As usual this class does not apply in a conservation area and the development must be completely external ie it cannot increase the internal volume of the building (even in the form of a canopy such as a car port). All of the development must be within 1 metre of the wall or roof. As with Class 2B, certain works are excluded because they are covered by other permitted development classes. Wind turbines, balconies and roof terraces or platforms are totally excluded. Residential flats also have permitted development rights under other parts of the PDO, ie for some microgeneration developments (Part 1A), erection or replacement of walls, fences, gates etc (Class 7) and fixing a CCTV camera to an external wall (Class 72).

Part 1A: Installation of domestic microgeneration equipment

5.24 This part relates solely to domestic property and applies to dwelling houses and flats. The types of development covered are associated with various types of renewable energy heat generation systems. There are six classes of development in Part 1A each dealing with a different system. There also used to be two classes covering solar power systems (Classes 6A and 6B) but these are now revoked. This is because permitted development rights relating to domestic solar power systems are now granted by Classes 2A and 3B (for dwellinghouses) and Class 4A (for residential flats).

Class 6C: The installation, alteration or replacement of a flue, forming part of a biomass heating system, on a dwellinghouse or building containing a flat: These are not permitted on the principal elevation if the house or flat is in a conservation area or world heritage site. The same is the case if the house is within an Air Quality Management Area.[1] The flue cannot protrude more than one metre above the highest part of the roof to which it is fixed (excluding any chimney).

Class 6D The installation, alteration or replacement of a ground source heat pump within the curtilage of a dwellinghouse or building containing a flat: There are no restrictions on this Class of permitted development.

Class 6E: The installation, alteration or replacement of a water source heat pump within the curtilage of a dwellinghouse or building containing a flat: There are also no restrictions on this Class.

Class 6F: The installation, alteration or replacement of a flue, forming part of a combined heat and power system, on a dwellinghouse or building containing a flat: This class of permitted development is subject to the same restrictions as those relating to flues for biomass heating systems (see Class 6C above).

Class 6G: The installation, alteration or replacement of a free standing wind turbine within the curtilage of a dwelling: In theory this class gives permitted development rights for domestic wind turbines (one per dwelling) but the restrictions are such there will be very few cases where these will actually be permitted. As a result, householders will normally need to apply for planning permission if they want to erect a wind turbine. Wind turbines are not permitted if they would be sited within 100 metres of the curtilage of another dwelling, which rules out most houses in built-up areas. They are also not permitted within the curtilage of a listed building or on land inside a world heritage site, conservation area, site of special scientific interest (SSSI) or of archaeological interest. They have to be sited to minimise impact on amenity, be used only to generate energy for domestic use and be removed as soon as practicable if no longer used. Even if all these restrictions and conditions can be met, the approval of the planning authority is still required for the design and size of the turbine. In addition, the planning authority must first be asked whether their prior approval is also needed for siting and external appearance. This process is mainly designed to safeguard aerodromes, radar technical sites, radio and television networks and National Scenic Areas (NSAs) as these could be affected by wind turbines. The procedures involved with prior approval are described at para 5.15 above. Where prior approval is given the development must be implemented within three years.

Class 6H: The installation, alteration or replacement of an air source heat pump within the curtilage of a dwelling: Similar restrictions to those that apply to wind turbines also apply to air source heat pumps and so in most cases an application for planning permission is likely to be required for this type of heat generation system.

1 Designated under Environment Act 1995, s 83(1).

Part 1B: Installation of non-domestic microgeneration equipment

5.25 As the title suggests, this part covers developments relating to renewable energy systems for non-residential property and there are five separate classes of these. *Class 6I* permits underground pipes for ground source heat pumps, water source heat pumps or both these systems, provided the total surface area under which the pipes are installed does not exceed 0.5 hectares. *Class 6J* deals with solar power systems attached to the roofs or walls of non-domestic buildings. *Class 6K* permits biomass generation through burning or anaerobic digestion on agricultural land and *Class 6L* makes similar provisions for biomass systems and storage on forestry land. Finally, *Class 6M* provides for the alteration or extension of an industrial building or warehouse by up to whichever is the greater of 25 per cent of the original floor area or 1000 sq metres for biomass burning operations. All three of the classes permitting biomass operations also permit the storage of biomass fuel.

5.26 Not surprisingly all of the classes in Part 1B are subject to a range of restrictions, limitations and conditions. These include limits on the total amount of energy or heat that can be generated – usually 50 Kilowatts of electricity or 45 kilowatts of thermal energy. There are various restrictions on height, in sensitive locations and, in the case of biomass developments, how close the development can be to most types of residential property. Biomass facilities on agricultural or forestry land have to first be notified to the local planning authority who will then decide whether or not their prior approval is require for the siting, design and external appearance of the development. The procedures involved with prior approval are described in para 5.15 above. Where prior approval is given the development must be implemented within three years.

Part 2: Sundry minor operations

5.27 Part 2 applies mainly to non-domestic property and currently deals with means of enclosure, accesses, stonecleaning and the painting of external walls. In 2012 the Scottish Government proposed adding a range of other works and we also look at those below.

Class 7: Gates, fences, walls etc: The erection, construction, maintenance, improvement or alteration of a gate, fence, wall or other means of enclosure is permitted development. This applies to residential flats and non-domestic property and mirrors the provisions concerning means of enclosure for dwellinghouses in Class 3E (see above). In *Prengate Properties Ltd v Secretary of State for the Environment*[1] it was held that a wall has to perform some function of enclosure in order to qualify. Permission does not apply within or surrounding the curtilage of a listed building. Other than that, the main limitations of this class relate to height. Any new wall, fence etc which is within 20 metres of a road is restricted to one metre in height above ground level. Further away from a road this limit is two metres. Alterations to an existing means of enclosure are restricted to the existing height or the above limits, whichever is the greater.

1 (1973) 25 P&CR 311. See also *Wycombe District Council v Secretary of State for the Environment and Trevor* [1995] JPL 223.

Proposed Classes 7A–H: A draft amendment order published by the Scottish Government in March 2012[1] proposes adding the following classes to Part 2. *Class 7A* would permit alterations and extensions to shops and financial services establishments. The provision of shopping trolley stores within the curtilage of a shop would be covered by *Class 7B*. Works to extend or alter buildings used as Hospitals, Universities, Colleges, Schools, Nurseries and Care Homes would be permitted by *Class 7C*. The other new classes would permit minor extensions of office buildings (*Class 7D*), electric vehicle charging points (*Classes 7E and 7F*), access ramps for non-domestic buildings (*Class 7G*), and pavement cafes (*Class 7H*).

1 Scottish Government Consultation on the General Permitted Development Amendment Order 2012 (March 2012).

Class 8 Accesses to roads: This class gives permitted development status to the formation and laying out and construction of any means of access required for any development granted permission by the PDO (other than by classes 3E and 7).[1] Accesses to trunk or classified roads are excluded.

1 But see *Shepherd v Secretary of State for the Environment* [1998] JPL 215.

Class 9 Stone cleaning and painting: This grants permission for stone cleaning and the exterior painting of buildings or works for non-domestic property. Painting is defined as 'any application of colour'.[1] These works are not permitted development in conservation areas or in relation to listed buildings. Permission is also excluded if the effect is to create an advertisement, announcement or direction.

1 PDO Sch 1, Part 2, class 9(3).

Part 3: Changes of use

5.28 We saw in Chapter 4 that under the Use Classes Order a change of use between classes of that Order normally amounts to a material change of use and is therefore development. However, it is not thought necessary to subject all such changes of use class to individual scrutiny by planning authorities through a planning application. For example, control by the planning authority might be desirable for a change to a use that is more environmentally sensitive or has more effect on amenity than the existing use, but less needed for a change in the opposite direction. Thus if a shop unit changes from use as a newsagents (use class 1) to a restaurant (use class 3) a planning application will be required, but if a restaurant changes to a newsagents it will be permitted development. Other changes of use class are permitted development for economic reasons, to allow more flexibility in changes between different commercial uses of property.

5.29 There are four classes, each permitting movements between certain use classes as defined in the Use Classes Order (see figure 5.2).[1] Obviously it is important to avoid confusion here between permitted development classes and use classes, especially as both orders label classes numerically. Perhaps the government should have considered using slightly different terminology or different labelling arrangements.

1 See Chapter 4.

FIGURE 5.2: PERMITTED CHANGES OF USE (PDO PART 3)

TO	**FROM**
CLASS 1	CLASSES 2, 3 or CAR SHOWROOM* or HOT FOOD TAKEAWAY
CLASS 2	CLASS 3 or HOT FOOD TAKEAWAY
CLASS 4	CLASSES 5 or 6
CLASS 6*	CLASSES 4 or 5

* Only for 235 sq metres or less

5.30 *Class 10* permits changes *to* use class 1 (shops) *from* use class 2 (financial, professional and other services), use class 3 (food and drink) and the *sui generis* uses of hot food takeaway and car showroom, though in the last case only where the floor area is not more than 235 square metres. This means that a change of use from, for example, a bank branch office (class 2) to a shop does not require planning permission. A change in the opposite direction is not, however, permitted development. Control is maintained over such changes in the interest of protecting the vitality of shopping centres by retaining retail uses rather than allowing uncontrolled introduction of non-retail 'blank frontages'.

5.31 *Class 11* permits a change *from* use class 3 (food and drink) and from hot food takeaways *to* use class 2 (financial, professional and other services). This means, for example, that it is possible to change the use of a cafe to a bank. This change is permitted development because use class 2 is seen as having a lesser effect on amenity than use class 3 and takeaways which may give off cooking smells and fumes. Accordingly, a move in the opposite direction is not permitted since it could result in an adverse affect on amenity.

5.32 *Class 12* grants permission for changes *to* use class 4 (business) *from* use class 5 (general industrial) and use class 6 (storage or distribution). A move *from* use class 4 *to* use class 5 is, however, not permitted development. The permitted changes are intended to allow the market, rather than the planning authorities, to decide to a large extent where office, industrial and warehousing development takes place.

5.33 Relaxation of control in this way is seen to be acceptable since only moves from uses with a greater environmental impact to those with a lesser one are permitted development. Use class 5 contains industrial uses which fail a residential amenity test,[1] whereas use class 4 includes industrial uses which pass that test.

1 See Chapter 4.

5.34 Because of the nature of vehicles likely to be needed to service warehouses, this use would also usually have a greater environmental impact than use class 4 uses. The impact of permitted development class 12 on local authority planning policies has been considerable. It is now more difficult for them to implement policies safeguarding land for industry or warehousing since, unless there are clear planning conditions restricting changes attached to the existing permission, the change of use of such sites to offices is permitted development.

5.35 *Class 13* permits changes *to* use class 6 (storage or distribution) *from* use class 4 (business) or use class 5 (general industrial) provided that the floor area is no greater than 235 square metres.

Part 4: Temporary buildings and uses

5.36 *Class 14* grants permission for the provision of temporary buildings, machinery etc subject to conditions that the buildings etc are removed when the operations for which they are required have ceased and the land in question is reinstated to its original condition. However, buildings etc. connected with minerals operations are excluded. *Class 15* grants permission for the use of land for any purpose (except as a caravan site or an open-air market) on not more than 28 days in any calendar year.[1] In deciding whether or not a use is temporary the determining factors are duration and reversion to the original use.[2] Physical changes to the land are not relevant unless these would prevent the site changing back to its original use. With the growth in farmers' markets, something which the Scottish Government wishes to encourage, it is proposed that open-air markets will be added to the temporary uses permitted by Class 15 in future.[3]

1 For problems relating to the calculation of the 28 day period see *Attorney-General's Reference No 1 of 1996* [1996] EGCS 164, *Thames Heliports plc v London Borough of Tower Hamlets* (1997) 74 P&CR 164.
2 *Ramsey v Secretary of State for the Environment, Transport and the Regions* [2002] EWCA Civ 118; [2002] JPL 1123.
3 Scottish Government *Consultation on the General Permitted Development Amendment Order 2012* (March 2012).

Part 5: Caravan sites

5.37 Part 5 grants permission for the use of land under certain circumstances specified in the Caravan Sites and Control of Development Act 1960 (*Class 16*). Permission is also granted for any development required by the conditions of a current site licence issued under that Act (*Class 17*). A draft amendment order published by the Scottish Ministers in March 2012 proposes adding the formation of a hardstanding area to Class 17.[1]

1 Scottish Government *Consultation on the General Permitted Development Amendment Order 2012* (March 2012).

Part 6: Agricultural buildings and operations

5.38 As we have already seen[1] the use of land for agriculture is largely exempt from planning control because it is not defined as development in the 1997 Act.[2] Building and other operations for agricultural purposes do, however, fall within the definition of development, although most have traditionally been permitted development.

1 See Chapter 4.
2 Section 26(2).

5.39 The 1992 PDO extended the scope of planning control over these matters compared with previous General Development Orders.

Under *Class 18* permitted development rights apply to: erecting, extending or altering buildings (other than dwellinghouses); forming or altering private roadways; and excavation or engineering operations. Permission is granted only for development which is 'requisite' for the purposes of agriculture on agricultural land comprised within an agricultural unit The word 'requisite' has caused problems of interpretation in the past. In *R v Secretary of State for the Environment ex parte Powis*[1] it was taken to mean 'reasonably necessary' for agriculture.[2]

1 [1981] 1 WLR 584.
2 See also *MacPherson v Secretary of State for Scotland* 1985 SLT 134.

5.40 The Scottish Government has proposed to remove permitted development rights for the creation of new access tracks under Class 18 because of concerns about the environmental damage caused by hill tracks. However, maintenance works on existing tracks would still be permitted provided these do not involve widening a track or changing it in a material way; for example changing from a chipped surface to tarmac would not be allowed.[1] The consultation findings noted that this proposal attracted strong support from environmental interest and strong opposition from rural interests.

1 Scottish Government *Consultation on the General Permitted Development Amendment Order 2012* (March 2012).

5.41 'Agricultural land' is defined as land used for agriculture for the purposes of a trade or business but does not include a house or garden. An 'agricultural unit' does, however, include the houses occupied by the farmer or farmworkers and any other buildings which are occupied for the purposes of agriculture as well as land occupied for agricultural purposes. The 'purposes of agriculture' include fertilising land and the maintenance, improvement or alteration of any buildings, structures or works required for agriculture. Fish farming is specifically excluded from the definitions of 'agricultural land' and 'agricultural unit'.[1]

1 For the definition of 'agriculture' see the 1997 Act, s 277(1); see also Chapter 4 above.

5.42 Whether or not land used for agriculture is so used for a trade or business, thereby qualifying as agricultural land entitled to permitted development rights, is a question of fact and degree and not a matter for the courts.[1] However from time to time they have indicated the relevant considerations to be taken account of in such a determination, and these were usefully gathered together in a Lands Tribunal decision:

> 'Firstly the primary meaning of trade or business is an occupation by which a person earns a living. Secondly it is not necessary that the trade or business be viable or profitable. Thirdly it is necessary

that the trade or business is actual rather than prospective. Fourthly relevant factors in determining whether there is an actual trade or business include (a) whether a full time job was held elsewhere and (b) whether the accounts showed that the activity was small scale and loss making. Upon such matters a judgement must be formed as to whether as a matter of fact the purpose of a particular activity is for the purposes of business.'[2]

1 *R v Sevenoaks District Council ex p Palley* [1995] JPL 915.
2 *Vaughan v Chelmsford Borough Council* [1997] RVR 139, per Rich J.

5.43 Permitted development status is denied if the development is on agricultural land amounting to less than 0.4 of a hectare in area. (In crofting areas only, namely the council areas for Argyll and Bute, Badenoch and Strathspey, Caithness, Inverness, Lochaber, Orkney Islands, Ross and Cromarty, Shetland Islands, Skye and Lochalsh, Sutherland and the Western Isles, land in separate parcels can contribute to the 0.4 hectare.) It is also denied where agricultural use takes place in combination with other uses.[1]

1 *R. (on the application of Lyons) v Secretary of State for Communities and Local Government* [2010] EWHC 3652 (Admin).

5.44 Any buildings, structures or works not designed for agricultural purposes are excluded. This is a long established principle. In *Belmont Farm Ltd v Minister of Housing and Local Government*[1] the test was seen to be one of physical appearance and layout and, therefore, an aircraft hanger would fail. Buildings, structures etc are also only permitted development within certain size and height limitations, and at certain locations. They are not permitted if they cover an area greater than 465 square metres, are over 12 metres high (over three metres if within three kilometres of the perimeter of an aerodrome) or are within 25 metres of a classified or trunk road. These limits are designed to ensure that the effects on the landscape and air traffic of large or tall buildings can be controlled.

1 (1962) 13 P&CR 417.5.49.

Protected buildings

5.45 For buildings housing potentially malodorous agricultural uses such as hen houses, piggeries or slurry stores, a planning application is needed for development within a *cordon sanitaire* of 400 metres of the curtilage of a 'protected building'. This is a building occupied by people, except one which forms part of a working farm.

Developments requiring notification

5.46 If the development involves the construction of a new building, a significant extension or alteration to an existing building, or engineering or excavation operations, then a prior notification regime is in force. This process involved is as outlined at para 5.15 above. (A 'significant' alteration or extension is defined as one which is either higher than the original building or exceeds its original cubic content by more than 10 per cent.)

5.47 It is a further condition of permission under class 18 that a 'significant' alteration or extension can only be carried out once in respect of a particular building.

5.48 Planning Advice Note 39 on farm and forestry buildings[1] gives advice on the siting and design issues relevant to these farm and forestry notification procedures. Annex C. to SOEnD Circular 5/1992 'The Town and Country Planning (General Permitted Development) (Scotland) Order 1992' gives advice on the procedures involved in prior notification.

1 SOEnD Planning Advice Note 39 'Farm and Forestry Buildings' (March 1993).

Water Management

Class 18A permits drainage and other water management works (excluding irrigation) for the purposes of agriculture. If a building is needed for these works then the same prior approval process applies as for Class 18

Mineral and peat extraction; land drainage

5.49 *Class 19* permits, subject to conditions, the extraction of minerals from land within an agricultural unit which are 'reasonably necessary' for agricultural use within that unit. *Class 20* permits the carrying out of works to maintain or improve watercourses and land drainage works and *Class 21* allows people to extract peat for their own domestic requirements.

Part 6A: Fish Farming

5.50 This part allows existing fish farms to carry out a range of operations or to make changes in the types of fish being farmed without the need to apply for planning permission. There are six separate classes. The first five deal with equipment and the other relates to the types of fish being farmed. *Class 21A* covers finfish pens[1] and allows, within the fish farm area, the replacement or relocation of existing pens and installation of new pens. The maximum area of surface water under which pens can be located is 15,000 square metres and in the case of replacement or new pens the maximum increase in surface water area allowed to have pens underneath is 10 per cent of the existing pens area or 1000 sq metres, whichever is the greater. The size of individual tanks and cages is restricted by an amount which depends on their shape. Those which are circular cannot have a circumference of more than 100 metres while tanks and cages of other shapes are restricted to a maximum area of 796 sq metres. There are conditions relating to the total amount of 'biomass' that can be contained within tanks at any one time and also requiring the removal of the permitted equipment in specified circumstances. The notification and prior approval system[2] applies to the size, design and colour of pens and, in the case of additional ones, their location. If prior approval is given then the operator must implement this within three years.

1 A finfish pen is defined as a 'tank or cage used for the purposes of fish farming other than for the breeding, rearing or keeping of shellfish (including any kind of sea urchin, crustacean or mollusc).'

2 See para 5.15 above.

5.51 Feeding barges are permitted by *Class 21B* while top nets and structures for supporting those nets up to a maximum height of 2.5 metres are covered by *Class 21C*. The temporary installation of any other equipment needed for fish farming is permitted by *Class 21D*, provided the equipment involved does not cover more the one per cent of the total surface area of the fish farm area and has not been present on the farm within the previous 12 months. *Class 21E* permits the placing or assembly of a long line for use in shellfish farming up to ten per cent of the surface water area covered by the original equipment and an absolute maximum of 500 sq metres. All these permitted developments must be within the existing farm area and the same notification and prior approval system that applies to Class 21A applies to all 4 of these classes.

5.52 Changes in the species of fish being farmed are permitted by *Class 21F*. These are limited to: a change to halibut from Atlantic salmon; from sea trout or rainbow trout to Atlantic salmon; and, to sea trout or rainbow trout from Atlantic Salmon.

Part 7: Forestry buildings and operations

5.53 *Class 22* gives permitted development status to forestry buildings and operations, similar to those permitted for agricultural purposes by *class 18*, and subject to similar conditions. As with new tracks for agricultural use, the Scottish Government has proposed to remove the right to create new forestry tracks under this class. It would still be possible to maintain existing tracks as long as they are not widened or changed in character.[1]

1 Scottish Government *Consultation on the General Permitted Development Amendment Order 2012* (March 2012).

Part 8: Industrial and warehouse development

5.54 A wide range of extensions, alterations, hard surface areas, and operations relating to industrial processes and warehousing is permitted in this part. *Class 23* permits extensions and alterations to industrial buildings and warehouses provided these are only for the purposes of the undertaking concerned. Developments are excluded where the extension or alteration is: higher than the original building; within five metres of the curtilage of the premises; would materially affect the external appearance of the undertaking concerned; or, would result in a loss of car parking or vehicle turning areas. The floor area of any building must not be increased by more than 1,000 square metres or 25 per cent of the original floor area, whichever is the greater.

5.55 *Class 24* allows, subject to conditions, the installation or replacement of plant and machinery and the installation, rearrangement or replacement of certain types of infrastructure required for the purposes of an industrial operation. In a recent case the court held that a metal fragmentiser (a kind of metal shredder often used by scrap yards) met the definition of industrial plant and machinery in the equivalent class in the English PDO.[1] *Class 25* authorises the creation of a hard surface within the curtilage of an industrial or warehouse undertaking. However, the Scottish Government is proposing that this right should be amended in order to address possible flooding concerns. The surfacing material would have to be porous or, if not, all water running off the surface would need to be directed to an area of permeable or porous surface elsewhere within the curtilage.[2] The deposit of waste material resulting from an industrial process (except from the winning or working of minerals) on any land comprised in a site which was used for that purpose on 1 July 1948 is permitted by *Class 26*.[3]

1 *Hertfordshire CC v Secretary of State for Communities and Local Government* [2012] EWHC 277 (Admin); [2012] JPL 836.

2 Scottish Government *Consultation on the General Permitted Development Amendment Order 2012* (March 2012).

3 See *Kent County Council v Secretary of State for the Environment and Another* [1997] EGCS 64.

Part 9: Repairs to private roads and ways

5.56 *Class 27* permits work required for the repair, maintenance or improvement of a private road as defined by s 151(1) of the Roads (Scotland) Act 1984. However, the Scottish Government is proposing that this class should be altered to make clear that it does not apply to the maintenance of tracks for agricultural or forestry use which are covered by Classes 18 and 22 respectively.[1]

1 Scottish Government Consultation on the General Permitted Development Amendment Order 2012 (March 2012).

Part 10: Repairs to services

5.57 *Class 28* permits the inspection, repair or replacement of services such as sewers, cables etc, subject to the condition that on completion of the work, or nine months after its commencement (whichever is sooner), the land be restored to its original condition or a condition acceptable to the planning authority. In *Doncaster Borough Council v Secretary of State for the Environment*[1] it was held that an open drain or ditch running along one boundary of the site in question qualified as a sewer for this purpose.

1 (1996) 72 P&CR D16.

Part 11: Development under local or private acts or orders

5.58 *Class 29* approves, subject in many cases to the prior approval of the planning authority, development authorised by a local or private Act of Parliament or of the Scottish Parliament, an order approved by both Houses of Parliament, or the Scottish Parliament, or any order made under s 14 or 16 of the Harbours Act 1964. This can often involve major development proposals such as roads or bridges. For example, the City of Edinburgh Council used private legislation to promote the Edinburgh Trams project.[1] Where the authorised project involves the erection, construction, alteration or extension of any building, bridge, aqueduct, pier or dam then the planning authority's prior approval is still required. This is also the case for any work involving the formation, laying out or alteration to any road used by vehicular traffic. However, the authority's power to refuse such application is limited to one or both of two grounds. These are that the development ought to and could reasonably be carried out elsewhere (dams are excluded from this) or that the design or external appearance would injure the amenity of the area and is reasonably capable of modification to avoid this injury. Because of concerns about the amenity impact of overhead power line equipment required for the Edinburgh Tram, the Edinburgh Tram Acts include provisions requiring the planning authority's prior approval for this.[2]

1 Edinburgh Tram (Line One) Act 2006 and Edinburgh Tram (Line Two) Act 2006.
2 Eg Edinburgh Tram (Line One) Act 2006, s 74(4).

Part 12: Development by local authorities

5.59 A wide range of development is granted through this part. *Class 30* allows local authorities to construct, maintain or improve any building (not exceeding 4 metres in height or 200 cubic metres capacity) which is required for any of their functions except those as a statutory undertaker. In *R. (on the application of Richards) v West Somerset Council*[1] it was held that this included constructing a bandstand. This class also permits development in the form of street furniture, such as bus shelters, lamp standards and refuse bins. *Class 31* permits roads authorities to carry out work required for, or incidental to, the maintenance of roads on land adjoining the boundary of an existing road. *Class 32* has been repealed. Under *Class 33* a planning authority is permitted to construct houses within its own district provided this conforms to an adopted local plan. This class also permits the planning authority to carry out any other development in its district, provided it does not cost more than £100,000 and does not involve a change of use or a so called 'bad neighbour' development.[2] A draft amendment Order published by the Scottish Ministers in March 2012 would increase the maximum permitted cost to £250,000 and permit the local authority to build residential flats as well as houses.[3]

1 [2008] EWHC 3215 (Admin).
2 See Chapter 6.
3 Scottish Government *Consultation on the General Permitted Development Amendment Order 2012* (March 2012).

Part 13: Development by statutory undertakers

5.60 This contains *Classes 34–43A* which grant permission, subject to conditions, for a wide range of activities by statutory undertakers: electricity, gas and railway undertakers; universal service providers (ie postal services); lighthouse, docks, ports and canal operators; road and tramway undertakers and sewage authorities. Gas and electricity undertakers may need the approval of the planning authority for the design and external appearance of any buildings erected solely for the protection of plant and machinery; in these cases, and in the case of development by sewage authorities, the procedure to be followed is as described in para 5.15 above.

Part 14: Aviation development

5.61 Development required for aviation as specified in *Classes 44–52* is permitted. This does not, however, include construction or extension of a runway. In addition, permission is subject in some cases to prior consultation with the planning authority (for example if what is proposed involves the erection of a new operational building).

Parts 15–17 and 19: Various mineral developments

5.62 Certain types of mineral development as defined in *Classes 53–66* are permitted and include, subject to conditions, mineral exploration (except for oil and gas), development ancillary to mining operations, various mining activities by the Coal Authority and its licensees, waste tipping at a mine and the removal of material from mineral working deposits. Part 18 (Waste tipping at a mine) was revoked in 2012.[1] Article 7 of the PDO gives the planning authority the power to direct that any of these classes is not to apply to a specific development proposal. For example, this could be because it is located in a national scenic area or the cumulative impact of the proposal would cause serious nuisance to the inhabitants of nearby housing, hospitals or schools. All of these classes are subject to the prior approval process[2] and if the planning authority wishes to serve a direction under Article 7 it must do so within 21 days of receiving an application under the prior approval regime. An Article 7 direction needs to be confirmed by the Scottish Ministers.

1 Under the Management of Extractive Waste (Scotland) Regulations 2010.
2 See para 5.15 above.

Parts 20 and 21: Telecommunications developments

5.63 Parts 20 and 21 cover the telecommunications developments specified in classes 67 and 68. *Class 67* deals with equipment needed for phone networks. This is generally not permitted in a: National Scenic Area; National Park; Natural Heritage Area; conservation area; historic garden or designed landscape; site of special scientific interest; European Site; scheduled monument; on a Category A listed building or, within the setting of such a building (except temporarily in an emergency). It can include an operator's equipment attached to a dwelling-house. Where the development involves a telephone call box the fact that this may have also have advertisements on it is not material as these are controlled under the advertisement regulations (see Chapter 14).[1] There are restrictions on matters such as height, position and volume. An operator cannot get round restrictions on size, volume etc by developing in stages. If they try to do this the planning authority is entitled to regard the combined works as a single development but must advise the operator that they are doing so.[2] A notification and prior approval system (see para 5.15 above) operates for developments involving one or more antenna or equipment housing. *Class 68* permits the fixing of up to four satellite dishes to non domestic buildings (provided no more than two of those dishes face a road) and there are restrictions relating to issues such as location, size and height.

1 Infocus Public Networks Ltd v Secretary of State for Communities and Local Government [2010] EWHC 3309 (Admin); [2011] JPL 1048.
2 *O2 (UK) Ltd v Secretary of State for Communities and Local Government* [2009] EWHC 522 (Admin).

Part 22: Development at amusement parks

5.64 Subject to various conditions to protect amenity, *Class 69* permits certain categories of development on land used as an amusement park.

Part 23: Demolition of buildings

5.65 We saw in Chapter 4 that demolition is a building operation and so is a form of development subject to planning control. However, *Class 70* permits the complete demolition of buildings subject to certain conditions and limitations, including the need for the prior approval of the planning authority. As with all other classes in the PDO, it is now clear that where the demolition concerned requires an Environmental Impact Assessment it is not permitted by the PDO. Demolition is subject to the prior approval regime[1] in relation to the method of demolition used and site restoration. Under Article 7A an additional requirement to notify neighbours of a prior approval application applies for demolition.

1 See para 5.15 above.

Exceptions

5.66 A developer may proceed without prior notification to the planning authority where demolition is urgently necessary in the interests of health or safety, provided that they give a written justification to the planning authority as soon as reasonably practicable. However, if the building was rendered unsafe or uninhabitable through the action or neglect of anyone having an interest in the land, the permitted development rights will not apply at all. In this situation, as well as any other where prior notice has not been given, the failure to give sufficient justification could lead to enforcement proceedings. Other exceptions to the need for notification include: (a) where permission for demolition has already been given as part of a planning permission for redevelopment; (b) where it is required under a planning obligation;[1] and (c) where it is required by an enforcement notice.[2]

1 See Chapter 8.
2 See Chapter 9.

Enforcement

5.67 The unlawful demolition of a building is subject to the usual enforcement proceedings, which may include a requirement to construct a replacement building or buildings.

5.68 Finally, it should be remembered that, irrespective of the planning situation, a building warrant from the local authority may be required for any demolition. Also, it cannot be emphasised too often that the demolition of listed buildings, buildings in conservation areas and scheduled monuments, although technically excluded from development, is subject to separate and even more stringent planning control.[1] Not only will permission always be required, but it will only be granted in exceptional circumstances.

1 See Chapter 12.

Part 24: Toll road facilities

5.69 *Class 71* grants permitted development rights for the provision of buildings, structures or other facilities reasonably required for the collection of tolls for a toll road. As usual, there are restrictions regarding size and location. Also, the prior approval regime applies to such development.[1]

1 See para 5.15 above.

Part 25: Closed circuit television cameras

5.70 *Class 72* grants permitted development rights for the installation, alteration or replacement on any building or other structure of a closed circuit television camera for security purposes. The number of cameras is limited to four on the same side of any building and to a total of 16 per building. There are also conditions relating to camera size, field of vision and positioning. A camera must also, so far as practicable, be sited so as to minimise its effect on the external appearance of the building or structure on which it is situated. These permitted development rights do not apply in conservation or national scenic areas.

Part 25A: Temporary protection of poultry and other captive birds

5.71 *Class 72A* was introduced in 2007 at the time of the 'bird flu' scare and permits, subject to restrictions and conditions, the erection, extension or alteration of buildings designed to protect poultry and captive birds from avian influenza. All buildings had to be removed and the land restored to its previous condition either by the relevant date (26 March 2009) or the date when no longer required to protect against avian influenza.

Part 26: Development by the Scottish Ministers as Roads Authority

5.72 *Class 74* permits the construction of new roads and improvement of existing roads by the Scottish Ministers. *Class 75* permits any other ancillary and incidental developments required in connection with the Scottish Ministers' exercise of their functions under the Roads (Scotland) Act 1984. There are no conditions, restrictions or limitations applied to these classes of permitted development.

Part 27: Development by the Crown

5.73 It used to be that the planning system did not apply to the Crown but that is no longer the case. However, a wide range of Crown developments are permitted by Parts 27-31 of the PDO. *Class 75* permits small ancillary buildings, equipment and works plus the erection of specified small structures such as lamp posts, kiosks, barriers, shelters and seats required for operational purposes. *Class 76* permits the extension or alteration of operational Crown buildings subject to various restrictions and limitations. *Class 77* covers the installation of additional plant and machinery, apparatus (such as pipes and cables) and private ways, private railways, sidings and conveyors. *Class 78* allows the creation of hard surfacing within the curtilage of an operational Crown building.

Part 28: Aviation development by the Crown

5.74 *Class 79* permits development related to services at an airbase (not including runways) on Crown land. *Classes 80 to 86* provide for a range of developments related to air traffic services within and outwith the perimeter of operational Crown airbases and also the temporary stationing of apparatus and equipment for conducting surveys and investigations.

Part 29: Crown railways, dockyards etc and lighthouses

5.75 Subject to certain limitations, *Class 87* permits development by or on behalf of the Crown on Crown land connected with the movement of traffic by rail but excluding the construction of railways, stations, bridges and hotels. However, it does allow the construction of buildings for a wide range of other uses provided these are contained wholly within a railway station; for example restaurants, offices, car parking, garages and petrol filling stations. *Class 88* covers shipping related developments by the Crown or its lessees on operational Crown land. It includes embarkation and discharge of military and civilian personnel, equipment and munitions from docks, harbours, piers and pontoons. It does not permit the construction of bridges or buildings not required for the handling of traffic. *Class 89* allows the Crown to spread material from dredging on any land provided that dredging was required for some kind of water transport undertaking. *Class 90* relates to lighthouse development, including alteration of existing lighthouses and the placing of buoys and beacons.

Part 30: Emergency development by the Crown

5.76 Under *Class 91* the Crown can carry out any development required to prevent an emergency or to control, reduce or mitigate its effects. The definition of what constitutes an emergency is wide and includes threat to life, human illness and injury, damage to property and disruption of communications and food supply. The Crown has to notify the planning authority as soon as practicable after beginning the development. After 6 months the emergency use has to stop and the site restored either to its original condition or to a standard agreed with the planning authority.

Part 31: Development for national security

5.77 This part covers the erection and installation of various types of equipment required for national security purposes. Fences, walls, gates and other means of enclosure up to 4.5 metres high are permitted by *Class 92*. CCTV and lighting equipment are the subject of *Class 93*. *Class 94* deals with electronic communication equipment and ancillary buildings which are subject to a wide range of limitations and conditions.

Part 32: Ancient monuments

5.78 Ancient monument status covers buildings, structure and sites of archaeological interest and this is a subject we look at in Chapter 12. *Class 95* permits the Scottish Ministers or agents acting on their behalf to carry out certain reinstatement, repair and maintenance works to an ancient monument and any other of their functions under the Ancient Monuments and Archaeological Areas Act 1979 that affect such a site.

5. ARTICLE 4 DIRECTIONS

Modification of permitted development rights

5.79 Under the PDO,[1] the Scottish Ministers or a planning authority may modify on a selective basis the provisions for permitted development. This may apply to any or all of the classes (or parts of any class) of permitted development (except classes 54 and 66) in a particular area, or even to a particular development.[2] In practice, directions are usually used to remove permitted development rights for specified types of development (eg window alterations) in conservation areas or other areas where authorities wish to safeguard amenity.[3]

1 Town and Country Planning (General Permitted Development) (Scotland) Order 1992, SI 1992/223 (as amended) art 4.
2 Ibid, art 4 (1)(a) and (b).
3 See Chapter 12.

5.80 Once an Article 4 direction comes into force, an individual planning permission is needed to carry out any of the types of development specified in the direction. However, it may be of some comfort to property owners who are affected in this way to note that no application fee is required.[1] In addition, compensation may be payable in certain limited circumstances.

1 Town and Country Planning (Fees for Applications and Deemed Applications) (Scotland) Regulations 2004, SSI 2004 No 219, as amended, most recently by Town and Country Planning (Fees for Applications and Deemed Application) (Scotland) Amendment Regulations 2013, SSI 2013 No 105); there is a limited exception in relation to some agricultural buildings and works.

Procedure for making a direction

5.81 Where a direction affects a particular site there is the usual requirement to notify anyone with an interest in the land; otherwise, it will be enough to place an advertisement in the Edinburgh Gazette and in a local newspaper.[1] The advertisement or notification will be carried out by the planning authority unless the Scottish Ministers see fit to do so instead. Nevertheless, it can be difficult to find out precisely where Article 4 directions are in force. In addition, although directions are commonly used in conservation areas the specific forms of development affected can vary from area to area. This problem is compounded by the changes made to permitted development classification by the 1992 PDO. Where directions made under the previous general development orders remain in force it can be difficult to match these with the current Order. The government has recommended that planning authorities review their existing directions to try to simplify the position by producing easy-to-follow guides.[2] It can also be difficult to find out about directions issued by the Scottish Ministers.[3]

1 PDO, art 5.
2 SOEnD Circular 5/1992 'The Town and Country Planning (General Permitted Development) (Scotland) Order 1992', para 36.
3 See Chapter 2.

5.82 Where an Article 4 direction is made by a planning authority, the Scottish Ministers' approval is required,[1] unless it relates to development affecting or within the curtilage of a listed building (and does not restrict development by statutory undertakers specified in Article 4(6)(b)).[2]

1 PDO, art 4(3).
2 Ibid, art 4(5).

5.83 An Article 4 direction may not be made in respect of development authorised by a local or private Act or order, or development by telecommunications code system operators or certain statutory undertakers (eg maintenance work in relation to the railway network, docks or aerodromes).[1] They also may not be made in respect of roads developments by the Scottish Ministers and certain permitted developments by the Crown (emergency and national security developments).[2] There is a special procedure for certain work related to mineral workings, where development is not permitted in any case without notifying the planning authority.[3]

1 PDO, art 4(2) and (6).
2 Ibid, art 6(aa).
3 Ibid, art 7.

5.84 An Article 4 direction may subsequently be cancelled either by the Scottish Ministers or (provided that it was made by it) by a planning authority; in the latter case, the Scottish Ministers' permission is *not* required.[1]

1 PDO, art 6.

Compensation[1]

5.85 The effect of an Article 4 direction is that a planning application will now be required for developments that previously did not require one. If such an application is refused or granted conditionally (ie for a proposal that was formally permitted development), the applicant is entitled to compensation.[2] The entitlement is the same as if a revocation order had been made under s 65 of the 1997 Act.[3]

1 1997 Act, ss 76, 77.
2 But see *Jones v Metropolitan Borough of Stockport* (1985) 50 P&CR 299, CA.
3 1997 Act, s 77(1); see Chapter 11 below.

5.86 Quite apart from the powers granted under Article 4, the Scottish Ministers are of course entitled to modify the PDO at any time by passing a further statutory instrument, eg by passing an amending order. This could have the effect of revoking or amending one or more of the classes of permitted development, not in the selective way achieved by an Article 4 direction, but generally, across the country. In other words, a class or classes of permitted development may be modified or entirely removed and, as a result, the need for planning permission may be reinstated for certain kinds of development. Surprisingly, if a planning application for a development falling under such a modified or discontinued class is subsequently refused or granted conditionally, this may also give rise to an entitlement to compensation, as if an Article 4 direction had been made.[1] This means that a compensation claim can arise, not just from the discriminatory application of Article 4, but also from a change in the general law. In such a case, however, the planning application which prompted the adverse decision must have been made within 12 months of the revocation or amendment.[2] Otherwise, compensation claims could be made at any time in respect of changes in the law that happened far in the past.

1 1997 Act, s 77(1).
2 Ibid, s 77(2).

6. SIMPLIFIED PLANNING ZONES

5.87 A simplified planning zone (SPZ) is a device which is intended to encourage development in certain areas by removing the need for developers to apply for planning permission. This is done by the granting of planning permission in advance for specified types of development within the area. Permission is granted by a SPZ scheme which could be regarded as a sort of permitted development order for the area. Like the PDO, the permission granted can be subject to conditions. Once adopted, the scheme lasts for ten years.

5.88 Simplified planning zones were introduced by the Housing and Planning Act 1986.[1] All planning authorities were given a duty to consider, as soon as practicable, whether it was desirable for SPZ schemes to be prepared for any parts of their district and, having done so, to keep this issue under review.[2] Planning authorities are also required to consider requests from anyone for the establishment of new SPZs or the alteration of existing ones.[3] If, as a result of such a request, the authority declines to promote a SPZ or does not reply within three months, the person who made it can insist that the authority refer the matter to the Scottish Ministers. If they agree that a SPZ should be prepared or altered, they can direct the planning authority to do so.

1 The relevant provisions are now incorporated in ss 49–54 and Sch 5 of the 1997 Act.
2 Ibid, s 50(1).
3 Ibid, Sch 5, para 3.

5.89 SPZs cannot be prepared for land which is contained within a site of special scientific interest, green belt, conservation area or national scenic area. They also cannot affect land in respect of which a nature conservation order or land management order made under Part 2 of the Nature Conservation (Scotland) Act 2004 has effect. The Scottish Ministers have the power to specify by order any other type of area that a SPZ cannot be prepared for. A planning authority may not include in a SPZ scheme any development that requires an environmental impact assessment or is likely to have a significant effect upon a European site for the conservation of natural habitats.[2]

1 1997 Act, s 54.
2 Town and Country Planning (Simplified Planning Zones) (Scotland) Regulations 1995, SI 1995/2043, reg 20; see also Chapters 13 and 15 below.

5.90 A SPZ scheme will consist of a map and written statement. The latter should be written in clear and unambiguous language since it is effectively a legal grant of planning permission. Any other illustrative material should be kept out of the written statement and confined to annexes.[1]

1 SDD Planning Advice Note 31 'Simplified Planning', para 21.

5.91 There are two possible approaches which may be adopted by the scheme. These are:

(a) *a use specific scheme*. This itemises the type of development permitted and the limits imposed. Those types of development which are omitted are excluded from the scheme and so require the submission of a planning application in the normal way; or

(b) *a general scheme*. This grants a general or wide permission and only lists the exceptions which are not permitted.

It is possible to include within the scheme sub-zones where different consents or restrictions apply. These may be needed, for example, if land within the zone is to be protected for open space or if housing near the zone might be adversely affected by certain types of industrial use.

5.92 Procedures for preparation and adoption of schemes are set out in detail in the 1997 Act[1] and in the Town and Country Planning (Simplified Planning Zones) (Scotland) Regulations 1995[2] and are similar to the procedures for the preparation and adoption of a development plan (see Chapter 3).

1 Sch 5.
2 SI 1995/2043.

5.93 Despite government encouragement, including extensive advice on the use, content and preparation of simplified planning zones,[1] and streamlining of procedures incorporated in the 1995 Regulations, SPZs have not proved popular with planning authorities, and very few have ever been designated.

1 See SDD Planning Advice Note 31 'Simplied Planning' and SDD Circular 18/1995 'Planning and Compensation Act 1991 Simplified Planning Zones'.

7. ENTERPRISE ZONES

5.94 Enterprise zones were introduced by the Local Government, Planning and Land Act 1980 as an experimental initiative to encourage the redevelopment of derelict areas by temporarily removing planning controls and giving relief from a variety of taxes such as rates and corporation tax. Five enterprise zones were established in Scotland at Clydebank, Tayside (Dundee and Arbroath), Invergordon, Inverclyde and Lanarkshire. While all of these zones have now been wound up, the 1997 Act still contains relevant planning provisions. The effects of enterprise zone designation in planning terms are very similar to those of a simplified planning zone in that planning permission is granted in advance for specified developments. The main difference is that the fiscal benefits which accompany enterprise zone status do not apply in a SPZ.

Chapter 6

Development Management

1. PLANNING APPLICATIONS

6.1 Having identified what types of development are subject to control, we now move on over the next few chapters to consider how that control operates in practice. If a project or activity falls within the definition of development and is not permitted development (or exempt for one of the other reasons considered in the last chapter), it must not proceed unless planning permission has first been obtained.[1] The process involved in obtaining that permission used to be called development control but is now described as development management. Applications for planning permission have to be submitted to the planning authority in whose area the proposed development lies. This normally means the relevant local council. The exception is for proposed development in the Loch Lomond and the Trossachs National Park area where planning applications have to be submitted to the national park authority instead. In a minority of cases, as we will see later, the final decision on the application may be made by the Scottish Ministers, for example if they decide to call in the application.[2] It is also possible for the Cairngorms National Park Authority to call in applications that were initially submitted to the relevant local council within that national park area.[3] However, the vast majority of planning application decisions are taken by the local planning authority. Useful information about the development management process is available on the Scottish Government's e-Planning website which can also be used to submit planning applications electronically for processing by the relevant local authority.[4]

1 Town and Country Planning (Scotland) Act 1997, s 28(1).
2 See Part 7 below.
3 Cairngorms National Park Designation, Transitional and Consequential Provisions (Scotland) Order 2003, Art 7.
4 https://eplanning.scotland.gov.uk

Planning Permission and Planning Permission in Principle

6.2 Before a development can proceed, approval will be required for all aspects of the development, including detailed specifications of any proposed building or other operations. In the case of a substantial development (eg a new office block or shopping centre) this will involve the developer in a fair amount of cost, particularly in the form of fees for the architects or other professionals involved in the design of the buildings etc. It would be unfortunate if a developer were to undertake such preliminary expense only to have their planning application refused, not because there was anything wrong with the design, but because the development was not acceptable in principle, ie that the planning authority did not want an office block or shopping centre, however wonderful, in that particular location.

6.3 It is therefore desirable that potential developers should have some way of testing the water before committing themselves to undue expense. One way of achieving this is to submit the planning application in stages. First they could submit an in principle application, without detailed specifications, to test the acceptability of their proposal. If that is turned down, their loss will be minimal. On the other hand, if it is accepted, they may then safely undertake the expense of obtaining more detailed technical studies and works (including designs) which will inform the detail of the proposed development. The 'in principle' permission will be subject to conditions which specify the detailed design matters that still require approval of the planning authority and only when those further approvals have been obtained can the development proceed. Where there is an 'in principle' approval, the planning authority has committed itself in principle to the development and may not refuse an application for approval of matters specified in conditions except on grounds specifically relating to those matters.[1]

1 *Lewis Thirkwell Ltd v Secretary of State for the Environment* [1978] JPL 844, (1978) 248 EG 685.

6.4 The ability to apply for an 'in principle' permission can also be very useful in the situation where an owner wants to sell land for development. In such a case it is very common for owners first to apply for planning permission in the hope that, by selling the property with the benefit of planning permission, they will be able to get a better price. However, they will not want to spend the time and incur the expense of drawing up detailed plans, and in any case the eventual developer is likely to have their own design ideas. An in principle application is therefore ideal for such an owner's needs. The new owner may follow up the in principle permission with an application for approval of the matters specified in conditions or, as often happens, go back to square one and submit an application for planning permission.

6.5 Where a proposed development consists of a material change of use only, without any building or other operations that qualify as development being involved, it will be treated as an application for planning permission. This is simply because an in principle application is not appropriate in such circumstances; there are no building or other operations that require approval, so there will be no plans or specifications that can be held back for submission at a later date.[1]

1 *Glacier Metal Co Ltd v London Borough of Hillingdon* (1975) 239 EG 573.

Application Procedure

6.6 The procedure required for planning applications is mainly set out in the Town and Country Planning (Development Management Procedure) (Scotland) Regulations 2013, often referred to as the DMR. SG Circular 3/2013 *Development Management Procedures* (which superseded SG Circular 4/2009 – see para 6.51 below) provides detailed advice on how the Scottish Ministers expect the development management system to operate in practice.[1] Between them, Scotland's planning authorities receive around 40,000 planning applications each year and over 90 per cent of these are approved.[2]

1 See also Scottish Planning Policy (SPP), Scottish Government (2010), paras 22–28. Note, however, that this policy document is due to be replaced at the end of 2013 and it appears that the new version will not contain a section dedicated to development management.
2 Scottish Government Planning Performance Statistics 2011/12.

Hierarchy of developments

6.7 The 1997 Act[1] sets a hierarchy containing three categories of development. These are 'National', 'Major' and 'Local' and, as we will explain below, the process that has to be followed when applying for planning permission varies depending on the category of development proposed. National developments are those identified in the National Planning Framework (see Chapter 3). The Major and Local development categories are defined in Regulations issued in 2009.[2] Generally speaking, these classify new development proposals on sites exceeding two hectares as Major. Development that falls within Schedule 1 of the Environmental Impact Assessment (Scotland) Regulations 2011[3] will also be Major. Other examples of Major developments include residential projects of 50 or more new houses, business/industry/distribution developments of 10,000 sq metres or more and some commercial schemes (eg retail) of 5,000 sq metres and above. Any development proposal that does not fall within the definition of National or

Major development is automatically classified as Local.[4] To this list we can usefully add householder developments as a sub-category of Local. There is a separate householder application form that should be used for this type of development and, as we shall highlight at various points in this chapter, some of the requirements of the application process are slightly less onerous than for other types of local development. Householder development is defined[5] as the carrying out of building, engineering or other operations:

(a) to improve, add to or alter an existing dwellinghouse;
(b) within the curtilage of a dwellinghouse for a purpose incidental to the enjoyment of that dwellinghouse; and
(c) to erect or construct a gate, fence or wall or other means of enclosure along a boundary of the curtilage of a dwellinghouse.

1 Section 26A.
2 The Town and Country Planning (Hierarchy of Developments) (Scotland) Regulations 2009 (SSI 2009 No 51).
3 SSI 2011 No 139. See also Chapter 15.
4 The Town and Country Planning (Hierarchy of Developments) (Scotland) Regulations 2009, reg 2(2).
5 The Town and Country Planning (Development Management Procedure) (Scotland) Regulations 2013 (SSI 2013 No 155), Reg. 3.

Pre-application consultation

6.8 There is often a great deal at stake when a planning application is submitted for new development. The developer will have already invested money and time preparing the project and so will be eager to get a positive decision as soon as possible. The local community may have serious concerns and fears about the impact of the development on their area and so could submit objections to the application and might even organise themselves against it. The planning authority may have a difficult balancing act to perform in deciding between potentially opposing planning objectives like supporting economic development and ensuring environmental conservation. It will also need to ensure that it follows due process and will want, if possible, to determine the application within the statutory time period. The potential for conflict and delay in such a decision making process is obvious. With so much at stake it is not surprising that particularly controversial planning applications sometimes end up in the Courts and even being reported on the national news (eg the *Trump International Golf Links Scotland* development at the Menie Estate in Aberdeenshire).

6.9 The Scottish Government believes that by encouraging early engagement between the various stakeholders in the development management process it will be possible to reduce conflict, improve the quality of new development and speed up decision-making. There are essentially two types of pre-application consultation. The first is where the developers voluntarily approach the planning authority for advice while preparing their scheme. The second is the statutory consultation with communities that is required for some types of development. We will now look at each of these in turn.

Non-Statutory Pre-application Consultation

6.10 The Scottish Government encourages developers and planning authorities to discuss the details of a proposed development prior to the submission of a planning application, especially for National and Major development. Such discussions may also include officials from the statutory bodies[1] that the planning authority will have to consult once the application is submitted, eg on matters such as roads, nature conservation, environmental health and flooding. As well as giving advice on the nature and design of the development itself, this type of pre-application consultation can also assist the developer to identify and prepare the additional information that they may need to be provide with their application, such as transport impact assessments and design and access statements.[2] It is also possible that a 'processing agreement' will be discussed at this stage and we will look at these in more detail later in this chapter. Non-statutory pre-application consultation can be very valuable for developers as it can help them to design a scheme which will have a greater chance of obtaining planning permission and with less chance of them having to make modifications to their proposals after submitting the application. Authorities are also keen to engage in such discussions as it can improve the quality of development and speed up decision-making. However, in the case of Local developments, they may offer only to conduct the consultation in writing as it would be far too time consuming for them to agree to meet with every potential applicant.

1 See para 6.55 below. For more information about what these organisations do see Chapter 2.
2 See para 6.21 below.

Statutory Pre-application Consultation[1]

6.11 There is a statutory requirement for developers to consult with local communities before submitting a planning application for certain types of development. This gives communities an opportunity to find out about what is proposed for their area and to tell developers what they think about it. The process runs in addition to the normal opportunity for making representations to the planning authority (once the planning application is submitted) and developers are under no obligation to take the views expressed into account. However, they may be able to use the exercise to gather useful information from the public. For example, a retail developer might ask those attending to complete a questionnaire about their shopping habits and this information may help in the preparation of a retail impact assessment to be submitted with the planning application. The types of development proposals that are subject to this process are those classified as either a National or Major development.[2] The 1997 Act requires the developer to first submit a 'proposal of application' notice to the local planning authority. This has to be done at least three months before the developer intends submitting their planning application. Copies of the notice have to be served on any Community Council whose area includes or adjoins all or part of the proposal site. This includes Community Councils in a neighbouring planning authority area.[3] The notice has to identify the site concerned, give a general description of the proposed development and give the prospective applicant's name and contact details. The reference to a 'general description' of the proposal is important. While this needs to be clear enough to enable meaningful consultation about the development proposed, it should also give enough scope for the scheme to evolve as a result of those consultations. If the description is too specific, however, then it may be necessary to start the process all over again, even for fairly minor changes.

1 1997 Act, s35B and Town and Country Planning (Development Management Procedures) (Scotland) Regulations 2013 (SSI 2013 No 155), regs 5–7.
2 Applications under s 42 of the 1997 Act are excluded (The Public Services Reform (Planning) (Pre-application consultation) (Scotland) Order 2013, SSI 2013 No 25).
3 SG Circular 3/2013 'Development Management Procedures'.

6.12 The 'proposal of application' notice has to explain how the applicant intends to carry out pre-application consultation. In particular, it should say when the consultation will take place, identify who will be consulted and describe the form it will take. It also has to state whether or not the planning authority has adopted a screening opinion (or the Scottish Ministers have made a Screening Direction) concerning the proposed development.[1] On receiving the proposal of application notice, the planning authority has 21 days to decide whether or not the consultation arrangements proposed are satisfactory. During that period it can, if necessary, issue a notice requiring the applicant to notify additional parties and/or carry out specific additional consultation activities.

1 Ie in relation to the Environmental Impact Assessment (Scotland) Regulations 2011. See Chapter 15.

6.13 The prospective applicant has to hold at least one public consultation event where members of the public can make comments. Ideally, this should be held at an accessible venue close to the proposed development site. They also have to publish a notice in a local newspaper advertising the event at least 7 days beforehand. The notice should describe the proposed development and explain where to find more information about it. It should also outline how and by when anybody wishing to make representations may do so. At the same time it should make clear that comments made at this stage will be going to the potential developer and that there will be opportunities later in the process to make representations directly to the planning authority.

6.14 Once the applicant has conducted the necessary consultations they have to prepare a 'pre-application consultation report' which is then submitted to the planning authority along with the planning application.[1] The statutory purpose of this report is to demonstrate that the developer has carried out the consultations prescribed by law plus any additional requirements that the planning authority has imposed in response to the proposal of application notice. If the planning authority is not satisfied that the report demonstrates these requirements have been met, then it must refuse to validate the related application and give the applicant reasons for this. However, in addition to this statutory compliance role, the report is also an opportunity for the developer to demonstrate how they have responded to community representations. For example, if they can show that changes have been made to the proposed development in order to address community concerns, the report is likely to flag this in the hope that it might help their case for planning permission.

1 1997 Act, s 35C.

6.15 The Scottish Government expects that statutory pre-application consultation will improve the quality of planning applications and, where possible, mitigate the negative impacts of development. It should also have the potential to address misunderstandings and give a means through which community issues can be aired and tackled. Ultimately this should lead to quicker decision making and a better standard of development. Guidance on methods of community engagement is given in PAN 3/2010.[1] Developers can also look to the National Standards for Community Engagement[2] and other models of good practice.[3] Mediation services might also be helpful in some circumstances.[4] Planning authorities should have details of relevant local representative organisations that developers may wish to consult. Planning Aid for Scotland (see Chapter 2) and private professional consultants can also be of assistance.

1 SG Planning Advice Note 3/2010 'Community Engagement'.
2 Communities Scotland National Standards for Community Engagement (2005); see also the work of the Scottish Community Development Centre www.scdc.org.uk
3 For example see RTPI Good Practice Note 1 'Guidelines on Effective Community Engagement and Consultation' (2005) and SP=EED, 'Scottish Planning = Effective Engagement and Delivery. A Practical Guide to Better Engagement in Planning in Scotland' Planning Aid for Scotland (2011).
4 See Scottish Government 'A Guide to the Use of Mediation in the Planning System in Scotland' (2009).

6.16 The above statutory pre-application consultations are not required for proposed Local developments. From a developer's perspective, therefore, there can be a significant saving in the time and effort involved if what they propose is classified as Local. While identifying which category a proposed development falls under is normally straightforward, this is not always the case. Understandably, if there is any doubt, developers will not want to commit the additional time and resources involved with a Major or National development application unless what they propose definitely falls into one of those categories. In order to address this difficulty, the 1997 Act provides a mechanism through which developers can establish definitively which development category a proposed development falls under.[1] This is done by serving a notice on the planning authority describing the proposed scheme and asking for its opinion on what category it falls under. The authority has 21 days to respond with its opinion or to request more information should it need this. If the authority issues an opinion that the proposal is not a National or Major development, then this is valid for 12 months. During that time the applicant can submit a planning application without having to carry out the statutory pre-application consultations, provided the scheme is materially the same as that described when seeking the opinion.

1 1997 Act, s 35A.

Processing Agreements

6.17 A 'processing agreement' is an agreed framework for the processing of an application or a related group of planning applications. There are no statutory provisions about processing agreements. A 'processing agreement' is simply a voluntary agreement between the developer, planning authority and statutory consultees. A 'processing agreement' is a useful project management tool. The main purpose is to set a clear timescale for determining the application with dates defined for the key stages in that process. The agreement will also establish what needs to be done to meet the targets set and who is responsible for doing that. It is possible that it may include the establishment of a project team. However, an agreement does not guarantee that permission will be granted. The major benefits should be establishing clear lines of communication between the stakeholders and certainty about when a decision will be reached. The Scottish Ministers expect processing agreements to be used with all applications for major development and also encourage their use for contentious local developments in small communities. They have published a template to help authorities and other stakeholders draw up such agreements.[1]

1 Prepared with assistance from City of Aberdeen and City of Edinburgh Councils and available to download on the Scottish Government website www.scotland.gov.uk

Submitting the Planning Application[1]

6.18 Planning applications have to be made using an application form.[2] The relevant form can be completed and submitted online using the national *eplanning* website.[3] Alternatively, for applicants who wish to submit their application in hard copy, paper forms can be obtained from local authority offices or downloaded and printed from either the eplanning website or the local planning authority's website. Applications can be for planning permission or permission in principle and the information that needs to be submitted varies depending which of these is sought. The detailed requirements regarding applications for planning permission are set out in Regulation 9 of the DMR. Those for 'in principle' applications are set out in Regulation 10. If the application is to renew an existing unimplemented planning permission that is about to lapse (known as a further application) then the requirements of Regulation 11 apply. Applications for the approval of conditions attached to an in principle planning permission are covered by Regulation 12.

1 Town and Country Planning (Development Management Procedure) (Scotland) Regulations 2013, regs 9–12.
2 Some authorities will accept a further application in the form of a letter.
3 https://eplanning.scotland.gov.uk

Notification of Owners and Agricultural Tenants[1]

6.19 Applicants do not need to own a site in order to apply for planning permission to develop it. While normally the applicant will be the owner, in cases where they are not (or they are a joint owner) they have to notify the owners (or the other owners) before submitting their application. In addition to this, if there are agricultural tenants on the land, these also have to be notified before the application is submitted. The notice to be served on owners and agricultural tenants has to be in the form set out in Schedule 1 of the DMR.[2] When submitting their planning application the applicants have to certify that these notifications have been made giving the names of the relevant parties and the address where each was served with the notice. Alternatively, if the applicants are the only owners they simply have to certify this and if there are no agricultural tenants on the land they just have to certify that too. Anyone who knowingly or recklessly makes a false declaration could be liable, on conviction, to a fine of up to £1,000. In addition, a failure to notify could put any grant of planning permission subject to a legal challenge if a materially affected party has been denied the opportunity to make representations to the planning authority prior to its making a decision.[3]

1 1997 Act, s 35.

2 Town and Country Planning (Development Management Procedure) (Scotland) Regulations 2013, reg 15.

3 *Macpherson v Edinburgh City Council* 2003 SLT 1112; 2003 GWD 7-183.

Planning permission[1]

6.20 An application for planning permission must give: a written description of the proposed development;[2] the postal address of the site concerned or, if it has no postal address, a description of the site location; and, the name and address of the applicant and their agent (if using one). The application has to be accompanied by a location plan showing the site boundary and neighbouring land and also plans and drawings showing the details of the proposed development.[3] If the applicant owns any neighbouring land this should also be identified on a map. A fee also needs to be submitted and the amount required will depend on the type and size of the proposed development as prescribed in the current fees regulations.[4] If the proposed development is classified as National or Major, a pre-application consultation report and, a design and access statement (see para 6.22 below) must be provided. In certain situations, a design statement (see para 6.21 below) also has to be provided with a development classified as Local, for example if the site is in the setting of a category A listed building, a conservation area, a National Scenic Area or an inscribed World Heritage Site. For applications to install an antenna for an electronic communication network an ICNIRP declaration has to be provided.[5]

1 Town and Country Planning (Development Management Procedure) (Scotland) Regulations 2013 (SSI 2013 No 155), regs 9 and 13.

2 It is important that the applicant provides an accutate description of the proposed development on the application form. In *Cumming v Secretary of State for Scotland* (1993 SLT 228) the application (and also a press advert) referred to the 'building of a roadside petrol station and service area'. The accompanying drawing, however, revealed that

two separate petrol stations were intended, one on each side of the road, as well as two restaurants, two car parks and a 40-bed lodge. Permission was granted, but was later reduced at the instance of the owner of a local inn, who had not objected to the application because he had not realised from the advert that his interest was affected.

3 SG Circular 3/2013 gives details about the types of plan and drawings that are normally required and the appropriate scales to use.

4 The Town and Country Planning (Fees for Applications and Deemed Applications) (Scotland) Regulations 2004 as amended, most recently by the Town and Country Planning (Fees for Applications and Deemed Applications) (Scotland) Amendment Regulations 2013 (SSI 2013 No 105). Advice on calculating planning application fees is available on the eplanning website and also from local planning authorities.

5 International Commission on Non-Ionising Radiation Protection. In essence this applies to the development of infrastructure to support mobile phone networks and the declaration confirms that the design complies with guidelines to protect health.

Design Statements and, Design and Access Statements

6.21 Applications for planning permission for certain local developments need to be accompanied with a Design Statement. This applies where the application site lies in a sensitive location eg a conservation area. The requirement does not apply to proposed alterations or extensions of existing buildings, householder developments within the curtilage of an existing house, development only involving a material change of use and engineering or mining operations. A Design Statement is a written statement about the design principles and concepts underpinning the proposed development. It should explain the approach taken to the design and how any design policies in the development plan have been considered. It should outline the steps taken to appraise the context of the development and show how the adopted design takes that context into account. Finally, it should explain what, if any, consultation has been carried out concerning the proposed design and give an account of how such consultation has influenced the proposal. PAN 68 *Design Statements* contains detailed advice on their preparation.[1]

1 SEDD, Planning Advice Note 68 'Design Statements'.

6.22 A Design and Access Statement has to be submitted with all applications for planning permission for development classified as National or Major. This is a Design Statement as outlined above but which also explains how issues relating to access to the development for disabled people have been addressed. This should include a description of how any accessible design features will be maintained. In addition to PAN 68, PAN 78 *Inclusive Design*[1] provides useful advice when preparing a Design and Access Statement.

1 SEDD Planning Advice Note 78 'Inclusive Design'.

Planning Permission in Principle

6.23 Applications for planning permission in principle have similar submission requirements. However, there is no need to supply detailed drawings and plans showing the proposed development nor for a design statement or a design and access statement. A description has to be given of the location of access points from a road to the development.

Approval of matters specified in conditions

6.24 Where planning permission in principle has been granted the permission will contain conditions specifying the detailed matters that still need approval before development can commence. These will relate to any work involving the alteration or construction of buildings, other structures, roads and landscaping. An application needs to be made to the planning authority giving the details required for each matter. The application needs to be in writing, identify the planning permission it relates to and describe the matter or matters concerned. It should also give the name and address of the applicant and of their agent (if any). Drawings and plans showing the details proposed need to be submitted with the application along with any fee required.[1]

1 Under the Town and Country Planning (Fees for Applications and Deemed Applications) (Scotland) Regulations 2004 as amended, most recently by the Town and Country Planning (Fees for Applications and Deemed Applications) (Scotland) Amendment Regulations 2013 (SSI 2013 No 105).

Further applications

6.25 All planning permissions are subject to a time limit for implementation and lapse if this passes without development commencing. However, it is possible to apply to renew an existing permission that has not yet been implemented provided this is done before it lapses. This is known as a 'further application' (see reg 11 of the Town and Country Planning (Development Management Procedure) (Scotland) Regulations 2013). If successful, it can buy the developer more time to implement their scheme or for the land owner to be able to market their site with the benefit of planning permission. A further application needs to identify the planning application to which it relates and give the name and address of the applicant and their agent. It needs to be accompanied by one of the certificates relating to ownership and agricultural tenants (see para 6.19 above) and the appropriate application fee. In cases where the application is for permission not to comply with time limit conditions on the existing consent (ie under s 42 of the 1997 Act), this must be made explicit.

Retrospective applications[1]

6.26 The normal situation is of course for planning applications to be made and permission obtained before a development commences. However, it is possible for an application to be made for a development that has already begun, or has even been completed. In such a case, the planning authority may grant permission retrospectively, as if the application had been made in the normal manner; needless to say, it may also refuse it, leaving the developer open to enforcement proceedings, and so this back-to-front way of proceeding is not generally recommended. However, if an unlawful development has taken place for any reason (perhaps because the developer did not realise that permission was necessary) a retrospective application may save the day. Also, if a planning authority becomes aware of an unlawful development in their area which they nevertheless find acceptable, it can serve a notice[2] on the owner requiring them to submit a retrospective application as an alternative to enforcement proceedings. A retrospective application may also be appropriate in cases where planning permission was obtained for a development for a limited period and that period has now expired, or where the development consists only of an unlawful material change of use, without any building or other operation having taken place.[3]

1 1997 Act, s 33.
2 Ibid, s 33A.
3 See Chapter 9 for a discussion of enforcement powers.

Alternative applications

6.27 It is also possible for two or more applications relating to the same property to be submitted in respect of different developments that may even be incompatible with each other.[1] However, if more than one permission is granted, the implementation of one of them will prevent the future implementation of any incompatible permission and may have the effect of extinguishing the latter.[2]

1 *Pilkington v Secretary of State for the Environment* [1973] 1 WLR 1527.
2 Ibid.

Duplicate applications

6.28 Duplicate applications occur where two or more identical applications are submitted, either simultaneously or within a short period of each other. This can be used as a tactic by developers to speed up the process of approval with major developments. If the planning authority does not make a decision within two or four months as the case may be, the developer can treat one of the applications as a deemed refusal and proceed with an appeal to the Scottish Ministers;[1] if the planning authority turns down the remaining application, the developer will have saved time by starting the appeal early. If the planning authority actually approves the duplicate application, that can be implemented immediately without waiting for the outcome of the appeal. While the legality of this procedure has been confirmed by the courts, it was also held that the planning authority was not entitled to make a decision if a duplicate application had proceeded sufficiently far in the appeal process ; the reason is that the outcome of the appeal may be a material consideration that the planning authority is bound to take into account when making its decision.[2] However, this will only apply if the second application is identical or substantially the same as the first. In *Henderson v Argyll and Bute Council and Gary & Rowena Groves*[3] while an appeal against refusal of planning permission was still pending, a substantially modified application for a much smaller development was made to and approved by the planning authority. It was held that the planning authority was entitled to do this.

1 See para Chapter 7 below.

2 *James Aitken & Sons (Meat Producers) Ltd v City of Edinburgh District Council* 1990 SLT 241; *Trusthouse Forte (UK) v Perth and Kinross District Council* 1990 SLT 737; see also (1989) 28 SPLP 76, (1990) 30 SPLP 33, 30 SPLP 47; and 'Duplicate Applications and Call-ins' by Bruce Smith (1996) 57 SPEL 88.

3 1998 SCLR 1.

Environmental Impact Assessment (EIA)[1]

6.29 When considering a planning application for development that is subject to the Environmental Impact Assessment Regulations,[2] the planning authority must take into account the outcome of that assessment before reaching its decision.[3] While there is no legal requirement for the applicant to submit an Environmental Statement (ES) along with their planning application, it clearly makes sense that they do so since the authority cannot determine the planning application without one. Where an ES will (or may) be required it is clearly advisable for the applicant to discuss this with the planning authority in pre-application consultation (see para 6.8 above). Where necessary, applicants will want to obtain a screening and/or scoping opinion from the planning authority prior to working up the details of their proposal. In that way the requirements of the EIA process can be harmonised with those of the application for planning permission

1 See Chapter 15.
2 The Town and Country Planning (Environmental Impact Assessment) (Scotland) Regulations 2011.
3 Ibid, Reg 3.

Declining to Determine an Application

6.30 If an application for planning permission is refused, it is possible that the developer will later submit a new application for the site which is the same as or substantially the same as that which has already been refused. This may be because there has been a change of circumstances (eg a new development plan) which makes it more likely that the application will be approved. However, it has not been unknown for developers to submit repeat applications in the hope that they will eventually wear down the planning system and get their way. Such applications may be considered undesirable because of the continuing uncertainty they can cause for affected neighbours and local communities. They also require the planning authority to devote time and resources to what may be a pointless exercise. In order to avoid these difficulties, the 1997 Act[1] gives planning authorities a discretionary power to refuse to determine repeat applications. This applies in a number of different situations but in each the authority has to be satisfied that there has been no significant change in the development plan or other material considerations since the previous application was determined. The first situation is where within the previous two years the Scottish Ministers have dismissed an appeal for a similar application (or refused permission having called in a similar application). The second is where the authority has refused more than one similar application within the previous two years and there has been no appeal to the Scottish Ministers. The other situations involve various permutations where appeals to the Scottish Ministers have been submitted but not yet determined. It is also worth noting that if an application has been submitted for a development that is subject to statutory pre-application consultation but the applicant has not complied with the requirements of that process,[2] it is mandatory that the planning authority decline to determine the planning application.[3]

1 1997 Act, s 39; see also *Noble Organisation Ltd v Falkirk District Council* 1993 SCLR 406, and comment in (1993) 39 SPEL 50.
2 See paras 6.11–6.16 above.
3 1997 Act, s 39(1A).

2. LOCAL AUTHORITY PROCESSING OF APPLICATIONS

Validation, Acknowledgement and Publicity

6.31 On receiving a planning application it is the planning authority's responsibility to check that it complies with the requirements of the DMR.[1] If what has been submitted does not comply, for example because there is information missing, then the authority cannot process it and must advise the applicant of what they need to submit to remedy this problem. Once what has been submitted meets all of the legal requirements, the authority must then validate the application. The validation date is when the clock starts running on the period for making a decision and is the date when the planning authority received all of the information required, not the date when it confirmed that this was the case. The authority should issue an acknowledgement to the applicant which explains the time period for reaching a decision. It should also inform them of their right to appeal to the Scottish Ministers or a Local Review Body if a decision is not reached by that date. The Scottish Ministers expect authorities to complete the administrative task of validation and acknowledgement within 5 working days of receipt of all of the information needed for an application to be valid.

1 Town and Country Planning (Development Management Procedure) (Scotland) Regulations 2013 (SSI 2013 No 155), regs 9–12, 14 & 17.

Neighbour Notification[1]

6.32 It used to be the case that the applicant had to identify and serve notices on neighbours prior to submitting their application but since 2009 this responsibility has transferred to the local authority. As soon as possible after it has validated an application, the planning authority has to notify all the owners, occupiers and lessees of land which neighbours the development site. Scottish Government guidance states that this should be done either by hand or first class post. Neighbouring land is defined as an area or plot of land which, or part of which, is conterminous with or within 20 metres of the boundary of the land (other than land forming part of a road) for which the development is proposed. Where there are premises on neighbouring land then three notices should be served, one addressed to "the owner" and the others to "the occupier" and "the lessee" respectively. The notice has to be dated, identify the applicant and their agent, describe the location and nature of the proposed development, give the reference number which the planning authority has assigned to the application, advise how more details can be inspected and explain how and by when representations can be made. The date for making representations will be not earlier than 21 days after the date on which the notice is sent. The notice should also advise how to find out more information about planning procedures. A location plan identifying the site should be attached to the notice. If statutory pre-application consultation has been undertaken, the notice should remind neighbours that any representations previously made would have been to the developer and that they should now be made to the planning authority. Neighbour notification is not required for further applications (see para 6.25 above). A failure to notify a neighbour with a notifiable interest may result in the subsequent planning permission being quashed by the court.[2] Anecdotal evidence suggests that in order to try to avoid the risk of judicial review, some developers are drawing up the notifications and passing them to the planning authority.[3]

1 Town and Country Planning (Development Management Procedure) (Scotland) Regulations 2013 (SSI 2013 No 155), reg.18.

2 *Lochore v Moray District Council* 1992 SLT 16; *Macpherson v Edinburgh City Council* 2003 SLT 1112; 2003 GWD 7-183.

3 Morton Fraser Solicitors' Website 'New Notification Requirements now in Place' 7 December 2009.

Press and Site Notices

6.33 In certain circumstances, the planning authority has to advertise the application by placing a notice in a local newspaper using the form set out in Schedule 4 of the DMR. This has to be done in the following circumstances:[1]

- There are no premises on neighbouring land and so it is not possible to serve neighbour notices (but this requirement no longer applies where the application is for a 'householder development' or the neighbouring land concerned is owned by the planning authority or the applicant).
- The applicant has certified under Regulation 15 that it has not been possible to identify all the owners or agricultural tenants of the land.
- The application is for development that is contrary to the development plan.
- The proposed development is one of those listed in Schedule 3 to the DMR. These are traditionally described as *bad neighbour* developments. They include the development of operations, uses or buildings which may adversely affect the amenity of an area because, for example, they bring crowds into a normally quite area or will be noisy or give off fumes. Other types of development specifically referred to include a scrap yard, new waste treatment

facilities and cinemas. A full copy of Schedule 3 is contained in an annex to this book.

1 Town and Country Planning (Development Management Procedure) (Scotland) Regulations 2013 (SSI 2013 No 155), reg 20.

6.34 The press notice has to contain similar information to that contained in the notice served on neighbours.[1] The date to be specified for submitting representations should be no less than 14 days from the date of publication. The applicant has to pay for the cost of placing the press advert and should be notified of this in writing.[2] They have 21 days from the date notified to pay the planning authority and the application cannot be determined until the applicant has done so. In cases where a notice advertises more than one application the costs can be shared between each applicant. It is common for councils to advertise a number of applications together in a single block advert on the same day each week (eg in the 'Evening Times' in Glasgow and the 'Evening News' in Edinburgh).

1 Town and Country Planning (Development Management Procedure) (Scotland) Regulations 2013 (SSI 2013 No 155), reg 20.
2 The Town and Country Planning (Charges for Publication of Notices) (Scotland) Regulations 2009 (SSI 2009 No 257).

6.35 Some planning applications have to be advertised in the press under other legislation. For example, the Planning (Listed Buildings and Conservation Areas) (Scotland) Act 1997 requires this for development proposals that could affect the character or appearance of a conservation area[1] or the setting of a listed building[2] (see Chapter 12). A notice also has to be placed on or near the site for at least 7 days. Where an application is for a development that requires an Environmental Impact Assessment, the authority must notify neighbours of the publication of the Environmental Statement (in the same way as the neighbour notices required for the planning application) and also place a notice in the Edinburgh Gazette and a local newspaper.[3]

1 Section 65.
2 Section 60.
3 The Town and Country Planning (Environmental Impact Assessment) (Scotland) Regulations 2011, regs 17 and 18.

Variation of Applications[1]

6.36 It is possible that an applicant may wish to make changes to their validated application before it has been determined. However, they can only do so if the planning authority agrees to this. In fact, proposed variations of this kind are often suggested to the applicant by the planning authority as solutions to problems with the proposed development. In view of this, the applicant would be well advised to consider making those changes if they want to get planning permission. When an application is varied in this way it is for the planning authority to decide whether and who to notify about this. If the authority decides that a proposed variation would substantially change the description of what is proposed then it is not possible to vary the existing application, a new one would need to be submitted. It is also possible to vary an application that has been called in by the Scottish Ministers provided they agree to allow the applicant to do that. It is not possible, however, to vary an application that is the subject of an appeal to the Scottish Ministers.

1 1997 Act, ss 32A and 32B.

Planning Register and Lists

Planning Register

6.37 Every planning authority must keep a register of applications, to be divided into two parts. Part I should contain copies of every application for planning permission and for approval of matters specified in conditions that have still to be decided, including copies of the plans and drawings. Part II should contain prescribed particulars relating to all applications which have already been decided. These particulars include copies of decision notices (including appeals), approved plans and drawings, any variations made to the permission and any s75 obligations linked to the permission (see Chapter 8). It should also contain a report of handling for each application (see para 6.83 below). Where an application relates to development requiring an Environmental Impact Assessment the register also has to contain prescribed information from that.[2] The register must be available for inspection by the public at all reasonable hours.[3] Most planning authorities now maintain a planning portal through which all of this information can be searched and viewed online.

1 1997 Act, s 36; Town and Country Planning (Development Management Procedure) (Scotland) Regulations 2013 (SSI 2013 No 155), reg 16 and Sch 2.

2 Town and Country Planning (Environmental Impact Assessment) (Scotland) Regulations 2011, reg 25(1).

3 1997 Act, s 36(4).

Weekly Lists[1]

6.38 In addition to maintaining the planning register described above, planning authorities also have to prepare and publish a list of all planning applications received by them in the previous week. For each application listed this should give a reference number, a description of the proposed development, the location, the name of the applicant, the name and address of any agent and the date by which representations should be submitted. This list has to be sent to all Community Councils within the planning authority's district and copies made available in local libraries and at the planning authority's offices. Most authorities also make the weekly lists available on their website.

1 Town and Country Planning (Development Management Procedure) (Scotland) Regulations 2013 (SSI 2013 No 155), reg 23.

List of Extant Applications[1]

6.39 As well as producing weekly lists and keeping a planning register, authorities also have to maintain an up to date list of extant planning applications and other live matters. This has to be divided into two sections. The first lists and gives information about all live planning applications in the authority's area. The second section lists and gives information about live notices of proposed applications, the consultation activities involved with each and the earliest date for each that a planning application can be submitted. The format for these lists is for the authority to decide but they must be published on the council's website. Copies have to be made available in local libraries and the planning authority's offices.

1 1997 Act, s 36A and Town and Country Planning (Development Management Procedure) (Scotland) Regulations 2013 (SSI 2013 No 155), reg 21.

3. PLANNING AUTHORITY CONSIDERATION OF APPLICATIONS

Further Information

6.40 Planning authorities have the power to require information from applicants that goes beyond the statutory minimum described above. For example, it might be necessary to produce an assessment of the likely impact that a proposed new retail development might have on the vitality and viability of existing shopping centres. Under Regulation 24[1] the authority can ask for any further particulars, documents, materials or evidence which it considers it requires to enable it to deal with the application. If this request is made after the application is submitted then this will add delay while the applicant secures the necessary information. For this reason it is advisable that applicants engage in pre-application consultation with the planning authority since these discussions should flag the need to produce this additional material enabling the applicant to provide it when submitting the application and so avoid this delay.

1 Town and Country Planning (Development Management Procedure) (Scotland) Regulations 2013 (SSI 2013 No 155).

Schemes of Delegation

6.41 Once the planning application has been validated the planning authority will appoint a case officer to handle it and, where required, that officer will prepare a report to the elected members of the council with recommendations on a decision. However, for most straightforward non-contentious applications the case officer, or their line manager, will actually be given the power to take the decision themselves. This allows the elected members to focus on the more difficult cases and so hopefully all planning applications can be determined more quickly. It also means that if the applicant subsequently decides to appeal to the Local Review Body there is a degree of separation between the initial decision and that of the planning authority's review body. The 1997 Act[1] requires planning authorities to prepare a scheme of delegation through which certain planning applications will normally be delegated to officers. The applications concerned are those seeking planning permission for local developments and for the approval of matters subject to a condition attached to an in principle permission for a local development. This legislation was introduced through the 2006 Act and is linked with the new arrangements for appeals against planning application decisions. In the past all applicants had the right to appeal to the Scottish Ministers if they were dissatisfied with the planning application decision. However, now when a decision relates to a local development and so has been (or could have been) delegated under planning legislation, the applicant will normally only have the right of appeal to a Local Review Body whose decision is final (subject to a Court of Session challenge on legal grounds). Traditionally, delegation was made under the Local Government (Scotland) Act 1973 and the circumstances in which it occurred varied from authority to authority. Authorities can still delegate decisions using this legislation but only for those applications that are not delegated under planning legislation. A common example of the type of application delegated in this way is for Major development that is consistent with the development plan and has not given rise to a significant number of objections.

1 Section 43A.

6.42 The Town and Country Planning (Schemes of Delegation and Local Review Procedure) (Scotland) Regulations 2013[1] set out the detailed requirements for schemes of delegation and further advice on how these should operate in practice is given in Circular 5//2013.[2] While it is largely for individual planning authorities to develop schemes that meet their needs, each must comply with certain requirements. It used to be the case that developments where the applicant is the planning authority, or an elected member of that authority, could not be delegated. Neither could applications for development on land owned by the authority or in which it has a financial interest. However, these restrictions were removed by the 2013 Regulations although it may take some time before this change is reflected in local authorities' published delegation schemes.

1 SSI 2013 No 157.
2 SG Circular 5/2013 'Schemes of Delegation and Local Reviews'.

6.43 The scheme should set out the classes of local development that can be determined by an appointed officer and, where relevant, outline the circumstances in which this will be possible. For example, decisions on local developments might normally be delegated but only provided there has not been a significant number of objections. The appropriate circumstances may differ depending on whether the decision is to approve or refuse. The scheme does not have to appoint individual officers; it need only outline the framework for taking such decisions. In practice, however, some authorities have identified named officers (eg in the case of Glasgow City Council) or specific posts (eg in the case of Perth and Kinross Council) appointed to determine applications. Once appointed the officer takes on most of the powers and responsibilities of the planning authority in determining the application.[1]

1 1997 Act, s 43A(5) and Town and Country Planning (Development Management Procedure) (Scotland) Regulations 2013 (SSI 2013 No 155), reg 29.

6.44 Authorities have to prepare a scheme of delegation every five years and cannot adopt this until it has been approved by the Scottish Ministers. The authority has to make its adopted scheme available for inspection at planning authority offices, local libraries and on the internet.

4. FACTORS TO BE TAKEN INTO ACCOUNT: THE DEVELOPMENT PLAN

6.45 Planning authorities have a great deal of discretion in deciding whether to approve or refuse a planning application. However, they have a statutory duty to take certain factors into account and must be able to show that they gave consideration to these, even if they eventually reached a contrary decision. We will now look at the main factors in some detail starting with the most important one which is the development plan. The planning authority's decision must be made 'in accordance with the (development) plan unless material considerations indicate otherwise'.[1] (What is meant by 'material considerations' will be discussed below). As we have already noted,[2] this recent provision represents a departure from the previous law, where the planning authority's obligation was to give equal regard to the development plan and other material considerations. The effect is to create a presumption that a planning authority will follow the development plan (ie the Strategic Development Plan, Local Development Plan and Supplementary Guidance) in making its decision, and gives it less scope than it had before to approve applications in respect of developments that are contrary to the development plan though such approvals are still possible if the other material considerations are strong enough to displace the presumption.[3]

1 1997 Act, s 25.
2 See Chapter 3.
3 *City of Edinburgh District Council v Secretary of State for Scotland and Revival Properties Ltd* 1997 SCLR 1112.

The Revival Properties case

6.46 The operation of s 25 was given thorough consideration by the House of Lords in *City of Edinburgh District Council v Secretary of State for Scotland and Revival Properties Ltd.*[1] A planning application for a food store and petrol station was contrary to the existing development plan, though in conformity with a new draft plan which had been finalised by the planning authority but not yet approved. The application was turned down by the planning authority, but upheld on appeal. It was held that the new draft plan was a material consideration which the reporter (who heard the appeal) could legitimately allow to outweigh the presumption in favour of the existing plan. Their Lordships confirmed that the system was still sufficiently flexible to allow departures from the plan when there was good enough reason, and that this was a matter of judgment for the decision-maker, the courts having only a very limited power to intervene. The process to be undertaken by the decision-maker was summarised by Lord Clyde:

> 'In the practical application of section [25] it will obviously be necessary for the decision-maker to consider the development plan, identify any provisions in it which are relevant to the question before him and make a proper interpretation of them. His decision

will be open to challenge if he fails to have regard to a policy in the development plan which is relevant to the application or fails properly to interpret it. He will also have to consider whether the development proposed in the application before him does or does not accord with the development plan. There may be some points in the plan which supports the proposal but there may be some considerations pointing in the opposite direction. He will require to assess all of these and then decide whether in the light of the whole plan the proposal does or does not accord with it. He will also have to identify all the other material considerations which are relevant to the application and to which he should have regard. He will then have to note which of them support the application and which of them do not, and he will have to assess the weight to be given to all these considerations. He will have to decide whether there are considerations of such weight as to indicate that the development plan should not be accorded the priority which the statute has given to it. And having weighed these considerations and determined these matters, he will require to form his opinion on the disposal of the application. If he fails to take account of some material consideration or takes account of some consideration which is irrelevant to the application, his decision will be open to challenge. But the assessment of the considerations can only be challenged on the ground that it is irrational or perverse'.[2]

A recent case has qualified this by making clear that the planning authority must acknowledge that the provisions of the development plan have priority when weighing these against other material considerations and failure to do so could lead to its decision being quashed.[3]

1 1997 SCLR 1112.
2 1997 SCLR 1112 at 1122.
3 *South Northamptonshire Council v Secretary of State for Communities and Local Government* [2013] EWHC 11 (Admin).

Interpretation of Development Plan

6.47 Quite separately from the issue of whether there are any material considerations that justify departure from the development plan, the preliminary question can arise as to whether or not a proposal is actually in accordance with the plan. The above passage from the *Revival Properties* case confirms that such interpretation of the development plan is a matter of law in which the courts have jurisdiction. However, from a recent Supreme Court[1] decision it is clear that development plan policies should not be read as if they are statutory or contractual provisions. Development plans tend to be worded in a way which requires judgment when being applied to specific circumstances and that judgment is a matter for the planning authority. An error by the planning authority in interpreting policies will be material only if there is a real possibility that the determination might otherwise have been different.

1 *Tesco Stores Ltd v Dundee City Council* [2012] UKSC 13.

6.48 As we have already seen, applications in respect of developments contrary to the development plan have to be the subject of a press advert.[1] In addition, if the departure is significant and the planning authority has an interest in the development, the Scottish Ministers have to be given an opportunity to call in the application if the planning authority is minded to grant permission.[2]

1 Town and Country Planning (Development Management Procedure) (Scotland) Regulations 2013 (SSI 2013 No 155), regs 20 and 39.
2 The Town and Country Planning (Notification of Applications) (Scotland) Direction 2009.

5. FACTORS TO BE TAKEN INTO ACCOUNT: MATERIAL CONSIDERATIONS

General

6.49 The presumption in favour of the development plan may be rebutted if material considerations indicate otherwise. 'Material considerations' are not given a statutory definition, although a number of them can be identified either directly or indirectly from statute, or from government policy statements. Otherwise it has been left to the courts to develop the meaning of the term, which they have been doing for many years. So much depends on the individual circumstances of each case that it is difficult to generalise; however, two broad criteria have emerged: (1) material considerations must be planning considerations, that is they must have consequences for the use and development of land; and (2) they must be relevant to the application in question.[1] In fact, in this context 'material' is synonymous with 'relevant'.[2]

1 *Stringer v Minister of Housing and Local Government* [1971] 1 All ER 65, [1970] 1 WLR 1281; see also *Westminster City Council v Great Portland Estates* [1985] AC 661, [1984] 3 WLR 1035.
2 *Fairclough Homes & Rayford Properties v Secretary of State for the Environment and Canterbury City Council* [1992] JPL 247.

6.50 Although identifying material considerations is a question of law which it is within the jurisdiction of the courts to decide, it is entirely within the discretion of the decision maker (ie the planning authority, national park authority or the Scottish Ministers as the case may be) to decide what weight should be given to a particular consideration.[1] As the considerations relevant to a particular case may of course not be compatible with each other, none can be binding on an authority and, depending on the circumstances, it may decide that one outweighs another, eg that financial considerations or need for a development outweigh environmental factors. However, the planning authority has a duty to at least take into account all material considerations and if it does not, or if it takes account of any irrelevant or non-material considerations, then the decision may be declared *ultra vires* by the court.[2] On the other hand, provided that a material consideration *has* been taken it into account, the decision maker is perfectly entitled to accord it no weight at all:

> 'If the planning authority ignores a material consideration because they have forgotten about it, or because they wrongly think that the law or departmental policy ... precludes them from taking it into account, then they have failed to have regard to a material consideration. But if the decision to give that consideration no weight is based on rational planning grounds, then the planning authority are entitled to ignore it.'[3]

In a case where negotiations with the planning authority were protracted over a number of years, during which the planning situation in the area changed, it was held that the time for taking material considerations into account was immediately prior to the decision being made.[4] However, there is no legal requirement in such cases for the application to be referred back to the planning committee before the decision notice is issued, although it may be prudent to do so if significant new material considerations have emerged since the committee's original resolution to grant permission subject to an agreement.[5]

1 *City of Edinburgh District Council v Secretary of State for Scotland and Revival Properties Ltd* 1997 SCLR 1112.
2 See Chapter 7.
3 *Tesco Stores Ltd v Secretary of State for the Environment* [1995] 2 All ER 636 HL, per Lord Hoffman at 661.
4 *John G Russell (Transport) Ltd v Strathkelvin District Council* 1992 SCLR 345.
5 *R (on the application of Kides) v South Cambridgeshire DC* [2002] EWCA Civ 1370; [2003] 1 P&CR 19.

6.51 As we will see over the succeeding pages, the sources of our list of material considerations are somewhat scattered and contain items whose inclusion is debatable. SG Circular 4/2009 (now withdrawn) helpfully provided a list of some material considerations as follows:

- Scottish Government policy, and UK Government policy on reserved matters
- The National Planning Framework
- Scottish Planning Policy, advice and circulars

- European policy
- A proposed strategic development plan, a proposed local development plan, or proposed supplementary guidance
- Guidance adopted by a Strategic Development Plan Authority or a planning authority that is not supplementary guidance adopted under s 22(1) of the 1997 Act
- National Park Plan
- The National Waste Management Plan
- Community plans
- The environmental impact of the proposal
- The design of the proposed development and its relationship to its surroundings
- Access, provision of infrastructure and planning history of the site
- Views of statutory and other consultees
- Legitimate public concern or support expressed on relevant planning matters

To this list we would add the following considerations (not an exhaustive list)

- Impact on the locality
- Impact on the natural environment
- Impact on the historic environment
- Amenity
- Compatibility with other uses in the area
- Desirability of retaining the existing use
- Effect of planning conditions on the development's acceptability
- Safety of the public and users of the development
- Public perception of a health and safety risk
- Immune use on part of the site
- 'Fall-back' position
- Development already in existence
- Possibility of antisocial behaviour
- Planning obligation terms (if material)
- Whether a grant of permission for one scheme would act as a disincentive to the development of another
- The planning authority's liability to pay compensation as a result of its decision
- The healthy eating concerns of having a proposed takeaway close to a school
- The fact that a proposal complies with some of the policies in a development plan
- Consistency in decisions, especially recent decisions on similar proposals in the same locality

Sometimes material

- Economic and financial considerations
- Availability of alternative sites
- Personal circumstances, eg hardship to applicant, educational needs
- Fears and concerns about crime
- Other legal controls, eg building control or criminal law

Considerations with a statutory basis

6.52 Although there is no statutory definition of material considerations as such, there are other matters which the 1997 Act, or other legislation, either states (or in some cases implies) should be taken into account. Although such matters are not always explicitly stated to be material considerations, there seems no doubt that it is proper to regard them as such.

National Planning Framework (NPF) and Scottish Ministers' Guidance on Sustainable Development

6.53 Until the changes introduced by the 2006 Act, all central government planning policy and advice statements were non-statutory documents. However, the NPF together with Ministers' advice on sustainable development (currently contained in SPP) are now statutory policy statements which local authority development plans have to conform. Given the primary importance of development plans in the development management system, it follows that the contents of the NPF and sustainable development guidance are material considerations.

Representations

6.54 The planning authority is bound to take into account any representations made to it within the prescribed time limit from anyone having a notifiable interest, or from anyone else.[1] However, where the content of those representations is not relevant to planning the planning authority will make clear that this is non-material and so will have no bearing on its decision. Examples of non-material considerations that are often cited in objections include loss of view and impact on property values. It is important, therefore, that those making representations ensure their grounds of objection are material considerations because, if not, they are wasting their time making the representation.

1 1997 Act, s 38(1).

Statutory Consultees

6.55 In a large number of cases, planning authorities are required to consult with certain specialist or otherwise interested parties (usually known as statutory consultees) where a proposed development may affect the interests of the party in question. The current list of consultees and the circumstances where they have to be consulted is mainly contained in the DMR[1] and is as follows:

(1) *Scottish Environment Protection Agency (SEPA)* (for developments materially increasing the risk of flood damage, or involving fish farming, mining, storage of mineral oils, sewage disposal (certain buildings only), rivers, cemeteries, refuse and waste deposits, and developments related to major accident hazards).
(2) *Scottish Natural Heritage (SNH)* (for developments affecting areas of special interest, non-domestic peat working and developments related to major accident hazards).
(3) *The Health and Safety Executive* (for certain developments in areas affected by hazardous substances and major accident hazards).
(4) The Scottish Ministers (in the cases noted at para 6.56 below).
(5) *The Community Council* (if any) (where it wishes or has agreed to be consulted, or the amenity of its area is likely to be affected).
(6) *The Coal Authority* (for certain types of development in areas of coal working).
(7) *Any adjoining planning authority* (if the development is likely to affect land in their district).
(8) *Network Rail Infrastructure Limited* (if the development could affect a railway level crossing or is within 10 metres of a railway line forming part of the national rail network).
(9) *The relevant Roads Authority* (if the development will result in increased traffic on, or will create an access to, a road for which the planning authority is not the roads authority eg a trunk, special or toll road).
(10) *The Theatres Trust* (if the development affects land on which there is a theatre).
(11) *Scottish Water* (if the development will materially change or increase the need for their services).
(12) *A district salmon fishery board* (where the proposed development is a fish farm).
(13) *The Crofting Commission* (if the development may adversely affect the continuing use of land for crofting).
(14) *Cairngorms National Park Authority* (if the development is likely to affect land within the Cairngorms National Park).

(15) *Airport or aerodrome operator* (where development is proposed within an area defined on a safeguarding map around airports, aerodromes and air traffic control equipment).[2]

(16) *The Secretary of State for Defence* (where development is proposed within an area safeguarded around military airfields or explosives storage areas[3] or where a marine fish farm development may affect a controlled site under the Protection of Military Remains Act 1986.

(17) *Sport Scotland* (where development would result in the loss, or prejudice the use, of an outdoor sports facility).

1 Town and Country Planning (Development Management Procedure) (Scotland) Regulations 2013, regs 25, 36, and Sch 5.

2 The Town and Country Planning (Safeguarding Aerodromes, Technical Sites and Military Explosives Storage Areas) (Scotland) Direction 2003.

3 Ibid.

6.56 Developments for which the Scottish Ministers must be consulted are those affecting trunk or special roads, a Royal Palace or Park, a historic garden or designed landscape, a scheduled monument or its setting, or a category A listed building or its setting. They must also be consulted about certain developments that may affect a historic battlefield, marine fish farm proposals and non-domestic peat working. The Scottish Ministers can also direct that other bodies have to be consulted in specific circumstances.

6.57 While planning authorities are required to consult with these authorities and to take their views into account, they do not necessarily need to agree with them. However, if a planning authority is still minded to grant permission where a statutory consultee has recommended refusal it has to first notify the Scottish Ministers who may decide to intervene by calling the application in. The same applies where the consultee has recommended that permission only be granted if certain conditions are attached and the planning authority intends to grant it without these.

6.58 In addition to the above statutory consultees, in any particular case a planning authority may be directed by the Scottish Ministers to consult, or may consult voluntarily, with any person or body not on the list. Where a consultation occurs, the planning authority must give the consultee 14 days' notice and must postpone its decision until after that period has elapsed. A consultation may be dispensed with if the consultee agrees to it in writing. A number of other consultations will generally be required if the proposed development is one which requires an environmental impact assessment.

Environmental Statement

6.59 Planning applications for developments that are subject to the Environmental Impact Assessment Regulations[1] cannot be determined without consideration of an Environmental Statement submitted as part of the planning application. This will normally be submitted along with the planning application. The content of that statement is a material consideration as are opinions expressed on the statement by statutory consultation bodies and other interested parties who will have been notified of its publication either directly or via a press advert.

1 Environmental Impact Assessment (Scotland) Regulations 2011.

Court decisions

6.60 Court decisions tend to explore the grey areas on the fringe of the material considerations concept. The following factors have been held to be normally or potentially material considerations depending on the circumstances of each case.

Non-statutory statements of government policy

6.61 We have already seen that the planning policy statements which the Scottish Ministers have to prepare by law are material considerations.[1] The courts have held that the numerous non-statutory planning policy documents issued by central government (see Chapter 3) are also material considerations[2] particularly in the form of circulars.[3] A Parliamentary answer by a minister can also be material.[4] However, a directive in a government circular cannot exclude another factor which is legally a material consideration.[5]

1 See para 6.53.
2 *Charnwood Borough Council v Secretary of State for the Environment* (1990) 60 P&CR 498.
3 *JA Pye (Oxford) Estates Ltd v Wychavon District Council* [1982] JPL 575.
4 *R v Secretary of State for the Environment ex p Surrey Heath Borough Council* (1988) 56 P&CR 250.
5 *Gransden & Falkbridge v Secretary of State for the Environment and Gillingham Borough Council* [1986] JPL 519.

Other legal controls

6.62 As we have remarked before, there are other legal controls of the use and development of land (eg building control and licensing control) that operate separately from planning control. The question has often arisen whether the fact that a matter is subject to such an alternative control can be taken as a material consideration, or whether that should be ignored by the planning authority and left to the appropriate other authority to deal with under its own legal powers. Case law and other opinion is not entirely consistent in this, and has failed to provide a clear ruling. In *North Tyneside Borough Council v Secretary of State for the Environment*[1] planning permission was refused for certain alterations to hotels as this would increase the accommodation available for alcohol consumption in an area which already had problems because of heavy drinking. Permission was granted by the Secretary of State on appeal, but the planning authority challenged his decision in court. It was held that the above consideration was a matter for the licensing law and criminal law to deal with, rather than planning control, and the permission was upheld. However, this decision seems incompatible with that in *Aberdeen District Council v Secretary of State for Scotland*[2] where it was held that the prospect of increased dropping of litter was a valid consideration in refusing permission to use a shop unit as a hot food takeaway. Even though litter was dealt with under the criminal law, it was also a planning issue because of its effect on residential amenity. This was echoed in a more recent Scottish case, *Di Ciacca v Scottish Ministers.*[3] The Court held that a planning authority could not lawfully disregard the material consideration of impact on residential amenity caused by the late night opening of a wine bar just because this matter also fell within the scope of licensing regulation. However, it also stated that the existence of another statutory regime might, in some circumstances, resolve the planning authority's concern about development impact and so allow it to grant permission. Some reconciliation of these opposing positions can perhaps be derived from *Gateshead Metropolitan Borough Council v Secretary of State for the Environment*[4] where it was held that, in the case of an overlap between planning and other legal controls, it is a matter of judgment for the decision-maker as to where one control ends and the other begins. In that particular case the environmental impact of emissions into the atmosphere and the existence of other legal controls over pollution were both held to be material considerations; as we have already seen, it is up to the decision-maker to decide what weight should respectively be accorded to these.[5]

1 [1989] JPL 196.
2 1992 SCLR 104.
3 2003 SLT 1031; 2003 GWD 13-449.
4 (1996) 71 P&CR 350, CA.
5 See para 6.46 above.

Economic and financial considerations

6.63 Although the case law is not always entirely consistent, the mere fact that a proposed development is not thought to be financially viable is not generally viewed as a material consideration that would justify refusal of planning permission.[1] Nor is the desire to grow a business a reason for granting permission.[2] However, if the economic or financial factors concerned also have planning implications, then it is well settled that they *will* be material considerations, eg where a building would be left derelict if a proposed development was not carried out,[3] where an otherwise undesirable office development at Covent Garden would finance improvements to the Royal Opera House,[4] or where the development of an open-cast coal mine by British Coal in an area of outstanding natural beauty would subsidise unprofitable deep mining elsewhere.[5] The economic impact of a proposed development in a particular area is also a material consideration.

1 *J Murphy & Sons Ltd v Secretary of State for the Environment* [1973] 1 WLR 560; *Walters v Secretary of State for Wales* (1979) 77 LGR 529.
2 *Jobson v Secretary of State for Communities and Local Government* [2010] EWHC 1602 (Admin).
3 *Sosmo Trust Ltd v Secretary of State for the Environment* [1983] JPL 806; *Brighton Borough Council v Secretary of State for the Environment* (1980) 39 P&CR 46.
4 *R v Westminster City Council, ex p Monahan* [1989] 1 PLR 36, CA.
5 *Northumberland County Council v Secretary of State for the Environment and British Coal Corporation* (1990) 59 P&CR 468.

Availability of alternatives[1]

6.64 The existence of a better site for a development is not normally a material consideration and there is no obligation on the decision-maker to 'root around' to find other sites.[2] The same is true about the possibility of a different development on a site subject to an application. However, the Courts have held that these considerations can be material in exceptional circumstances. No hard and fast rules have been set for what would constitute exceptional circumstances so this is a matter of fact and degree in each case. In *Greater London Council v Secretary of State for the Environment and London Docklands Corporation*[3] the court suggested four characteristics that would normally have to be present before alternative sites would have to be examined: (1) the presence of a clear public convenience (sic), or advantage, in the proposed development; (2) the existence of inevitable adverse effects to some section of the public; (3) the existence of an alternative site which had less, or no, such disadvantage; and (4) a limited provision, in the sense of only one or very few such permissions being able to be granted.

An example given more recently would be where the provisions of the development plan or other policy guidance make it relevant to consider other sites.[4] The possibility of a different development on the same site will only be relevant if there is a real possibility that the alternative will actually be carried out.[5]

1 See Stephen Whale The Importance of Alternative Proposals in Development Control J.P.L. 2004, Jul, 887-890.

2 *Rhodes v Minister of Housing and Local Government* [1963] 1 WLR 208.

3 [1986] JPL 193; see also *Vale of Glamorgan Borough Council v Secretary of State for Wales* [1986] JPL 198 and *R v Carlisle City Council and the Secretary of State for the Environment, ex p Cumbrian Co-operative Society Ltd* (1985) 276 EG 1161; *R. (on the application of J (a Child)) v North Warwickshire Borough Council* [2001] EWCA Civ 315; [2001] 2 PLR 59.

4 *Phillips v First Secretary of State* [2003] EWHC 2415 (Admin); [2003] 4 PLR 75.

5 *R. (on the application of Mount Cook Land Ltd) v Westminster City Council* [2003] EWCA Civ 1346.

6.65 When refusing a planning application because of the availability of alternative sites, it is not necessary for a planning authority to specify alternatives, especially if there are clear planning objections to development of the proposed site .[1]

1 *Trusthouse Forte Hotels Ltd v Secretary of State for the Environment* [1986] JPL 834.

Personal Circumstances

6.66 Since planning considerations relate to the use of land rather than to the identity or circumstances of the person or persons using it, the latter are not normally relevant considerations in a planning decision. However, an exception can sometimes be made to this rule, for example if an adverse planning decision will cause hardship to the applicant.[1] It has generally been held that personal circumstances carry less weight than other material considerations, only being decisive when the issues are finely balanced;[2] however, in one Scottish case personal circumstances (the need of a bank to extend into a rear courtyard area) were considered sufficiently material to override the adopted development plan policy. [3] In *Basildon DC v Secretary of State for the Environment, Transport and the Regions*[4] it was held that the educational needs of children in that case were material and that the decision maker was entitled to judge that this consideration outweighed green belt policy. In *Willis v Argyll and Bute Council*, the financial difficulties that a proposed development would cause an objector were held *not* to be a material consideration.[5] In another case, local residents' expressions of support for proposed extended opening hours for a hot food takeaway were held not to be material because an inspector had to take into account the potential impact on the amenity of adjoining residential properties and not the subjective views of the current inhabitants of those properties.[6]

1 *Great Portland Estates plc v Westminster City Council* [1985] AC 661; *Tameside Metropolitan Borough Council v Secretary of State for the Environment* [1984] JPL 180.
2 *General Education Ltd v Secretary of State for the Environment* [1993] JPL 243.
3 *City of Glasgow District Council v Secretary of State for Scotland and the Bank of Scotland* 1992 SCLR 964.
4 [2001] JPL.
5 [2010] CSOH 122; 2010 G.W.D. 31-633.
6 *Kuccuk v Wirral BC* [2010] EWHC 807 (Admin).

Precedent

6.67 Strictly speaking, planning authorities are not bound by precedent (except, of course, on points of law that have been decided in court). However, while they are theoretically free to treat similar applications in different ways, previous decisions are a material consideration.[1] Authorities have to be seen to be acting consistently so if they depart from a previous decision they need to give planning reasons for doing so.[2] This includes decisions on other sites, not just for the land affected by the application under consideration. In the recent case of *Fox Strategic Land & Property Ltd v Secretary of State for Communities and Local Government*[3] the Court of Appeal upheld a decision of the High Court to quash an inspector's decision on a planning appeal because of serious inconsistencies between that decision and one for another appeal on a different site in the same area. Although the inspector was entitled to reach a different decision his handling of the appeal was flawed because he had neither considered the other application nor given reasons for reaching a different decision.

1 *Spackman v Secretary of State for the Environment* [1977] 1 All ER 257.
2 *North Wiltshire DC v Secretary of State for the Environment* (1993) 65 P&CR137; *Dunster Properties Ltd v First Secretary of State* [2007] EWCA Civ 236; [2007] 2 P&CR 26.
3 [2012] EWCA Civ 1198; [2013] 1 P&CR 6.

6.68 Planning authorities are entitled to refuse planning permission because the grant would make it more difficult to resist similar applications in the future.[1] In such a case, although the application under consideration might be unexceptionable on its own, the cumulative effect of a number of similar developments might be undesirable, eg where the application was to build a house in an area without a public sewer.[2] Fear of creating a precedent will only be a material consideration if there is evidence (or it is obvious) that the fear is well-founded.[3]

1 *Collis Radio v Secretary of State for the Environment* (1975) 29 P&CR 390; *Lowrie v Secretary of State for Scotland* 1988 SCLR 614; *R v Secretary of State for the Environment ex p Collins* (1989) Times, 8 February.
2 *Lowrie* above.
3 *Poundstretcher Ltd v Secretary of State for the Environment and Liverpool City Council* [1989] JPL 90.

Planning obligation provisions

6.69 Planning obligations (or agreements), which are considered in detail in Chapter 8,[1] are either voluntary obligations or agreements between a landowner and the planning authority. A planning obligation is usually (though not always) linked to an application for planning permission and, because its terms will reflect the agreement which has been reached with the planning authority, it will usually facilitate the obtaining of that permission. It follows from this that the terms of the planning obligation will be taken into account by the planning authority in reaching its decision. However, this does not automatically make them material considerations: for this the terms have individually to pass a separate test, which was formulated by the House of Lords in *Tesco Stores v Secretary of State for the Environment.*[2]

1 See also 1997 Act, s 75.
2 [1995] 2 All ER 636, HL.

6.70 The Secretary of State had granted permission for a new supermarket to a rival developer instead of Tesco. Tesco argued that the minister had failed to take account of a material consideration, namely Tesco's offer to fund a new road through a planning obligation. It was established that the road would help to ease any traffic congestion caused by the building of a new supermarket, but that it was not absolutely necessary before such a development could go ahead. It was held that an offered planning obligation which has nothing to do with the proposed development cannot be a material consideration. However, if it is linked to the development (as Tesco's offer was) in a way that is more than *de minimis*, then it will be a material consideration. In spite of this, Tesco's appeal was dismissed because the Secretary of State *had* taken their offer of funding into account; and, as we saw above, it is entirely up to him as decision maker to determine what weight should be given to any material consideration or, having taken account of it, to accord it no weight at all.

6.71 The above means that a term in a planning obligation which is linked to a planning application will be a material consideration, provided that it passes the test of having at least a minimal connection with the proposed development. Conversely, if planning permission is granted in conjunction with an obligation containing terms which do not pass that test, that permission may be open to legal challenge as *ultra vires* on the ground that the planning authority has taken account of a consideration that is irrelevant or non-material. This means that the *Tesco* case has important implications regarding the legal scope of planning obligations, which we will consider further in Chapter 8.

Other material considerations

6.72 Other material considerations include amenity,[1] the compatibility of the proposed use with other uses in the area,[2] the desirability of retaining the existing use,[3] the safety of the public and of users of the development,[4] mis-statements made to the planning committee considering an application,[5] the local plan inspector's view about an appeal site,[6] the Secretary of State's decision in a duplicate application that has reached the inquiry stage,[7] sound insulation in a proposed conversion of houses into flats[8], whether there is a use on part of the site that is immune from enforcement[9], an existing permission (or 'fall back' situation) for a less desirable development[10], the fact that a building which is the subject of a retrospective application for permission is already in existence,[11] the healthy eating concerns about having a proposed takeaway close to a school,[12] and the fact that the proposed use could give rise to antisocial behaviour in the neighbourhood.[13] In *Newport Metropolitan Borough Council v Secretary of State for Wales*[14] it was held that the public perception of a risk to public health and safety from a proposed chemical waste treatment plant, even though this belief was unfounded, was a material consideration which could amount to a valid ground for the refusal of permission. However, in another case, it was held that public fears and concerns about crime could only be regarded as material if these were grounded on evidence of past activities and not simply assumptions based on the characteristics of the occupants or users of development.[15]

1 Eg from Town and Country Planning (Development Procedure Management) (Scotland) Regulations 2013 (SSI 2013 No 155), Sch. 3, para 8(b).

2 *Collis Radio Ltd v Secretary of State for the Environment* (1975) 29 P&CR 390; *Stringer v Minister of Housing and Local Government* [1970] 1 WLR 1281; *RMC Management Services Ltd v Secretary of State for the Environment* (1972) 222 EG 1593.

3 *Clyde & Co v Secretary of State for the Environment* [1977] 1 WLR 926; *London Residuary Body v Secretary of State for the Environment* (1989) Times, 18 August, CA; *Mitchell v Secretary of State for the Environment* [1994] 2 PLR 23, CA.

4 Eg from Town and Country Planning (Development Procedure Management) (Scotland) Regulations 2013 (SSI 2013 No 155), Sch. 5, para 3.

5 *R v Lewes District Council* [1991] COD 75.

6 *Barrow-in-Furness Borough Council v Secretary of State for the Environment and Russell* [1992] JPL 665.
7 *Trusthouse Forte (UK) Ltd v Perth & Kinross District Council and Flicks (Scotland) Ltd* 1990 SLT 737.
8 *Newham London Borough Council v Secretary of State for the Environment* (1987) 53 P&CR 98.
9 *John Kennelly Sales v Secretary of State for the Environment* [1994] 1 PLR 10.
10 *New Forest District Council v Secretary of State for the Environment and Shorefield Holidays Ltd* [1995] EGCS 136, (1995) SPEL 51:91.
11 *R v Leominster District Council ex p Pothecary* (1997) Times, November 18.
12 *R. (on the application of Copeland) v Tower Hamlets LBC* [2010] EWHC 1845 (Admin); [2011] JPL 40.
13 *West Midlands Probation Committee v Secretary of State for the Environment* (1997) Times, 1 December; *R v Broadlands District Council ex p Dove* [1998] NPC 7.
14 [1998] Env LR 174.
15 *Smith v First Secretary of State* [2005] EWCA Civ 859; [2006] JPL 386.

6.73 The planning authority's potential liability to pay compensation as a result of its decision was held to be material in *Health and Safety Executive v Wolverhampton City Council.*[1] Whether a grant of permission for one scheme would act as a disincentive to the development of another scheme supported by a development plan was deemed material in *R. (on the application of Estates and Agency Properties Ltd) v Barking and Dagenham LBC.*[2]

1 [2012] UKSC 34; [2012] 1 WLR 2264.
2 [2012] EWHC 3744 (Admin).

6.74 In one appeal to the Secretary of State it was decided that the emotional stress that would be caused to nearby elderly residents by the proximity of a proposed funeral parlour was a material consideration.[1]

1 *Bromsgrove District Council v Huxley Funeral Services* (1989) 4 PAD 117.

6. LOCAL PLANNING AUTHORITY DECISION

6.75 A planning authority may approve an application unconditionally, may grant approval subject to conditions or may refuse the application.[1] It may also approve only part of the application and refuse other parts, and different conditions can be imposed on different parts of the permission.

1 1997 Act, s 37(1).

6.76 The subject of planning conditions requires examination in a little depth and we will do that at the end of the chapter. Also, in the event of a refusal, or if the applicant is dissatisfied with any conditions imposed, a review of the decision can be required or, in some cases, an appeal to the Scottish Ministers may be made. In some circumstances the planning authority may be required to purchase the property. These topics will be examined further in the next chapter and in Chapter 10 respectively. For the moment we will confine ourselves to other aspects of the planning authority's decision-making process.

6.77 Unless an application is called in by the Scottish Ministers or the Cairngorms National Park Authority, there are three main ways in which the planning authority's decision may be made. The precise details vary from council to council but in general decisions may be taken as follows:

- By a planning officer under the authority's delegation scheme (normally local developments and non-controversial major developments).
- By the authority's planning committee or a sub-committee dedicated to determining planning applications (normally local and major developments that have attracted significant numbers of objections or raise issues that need to be considered by the elected members).
- By the full Council (all applications for national development and for any major development that would involve a significant departure from the development plan; a pre-determination hearing will also have been held in such cases).

Councillors' role

6.78 When elected members of the council are involved in taking decisions on planning applications they are acting in a quasi-judicial role and are bound by the Councillors' Code of Conduct.[1] It is important that they are completely impartial and take a decision based on their own judgment of the proposal taking into consideration only the development plan and other material considerations. If the applicant or objectors try to lobby them in favour or against the proposal, they should be careful not to give the impression that they have made up their mind ahead of the relevant council meeting to determine the application. If a member wants to argue against or in support of a proposed development in their ward they can do so but only if they take no part when the decision is made. However, where the final decision has to be made by the full Council, elected members who have already made their views known can still take a full part. Where a councillor has a personal vested interest in a development they should declare this and refrain from taking part in any of the decision making process. A planning decision could be quashed if councillors breach the terms of the code of conduct when making a decision, if they appear to have been biased or have taken into account non-material considerations. For example, in *R (on the application of Gardner) v Harrogate BC*[2] planning permission granted to a councillor who was a member of the Conservative Party was quashed because of the appearance of bias. The permission was for a house in an area of outstanding beauty and the planning officer had recommended refusal. The permission was granted on the casting vote of the committee chair who was also a member of the Conservative Party and a personal friend of the applicant. Councillors also have to take care when attending site visits as part of the decisions-making process. To help avoid this kind of problem authorities provide training to their elected members about their responsibilities when taking planning decisions.[3]

1 Standards Commission Scotland *The Councillors Code of Conduct* (3rd Edition) Scottish Government, 2010.
2 [2008] EWHC 2942 (Admin); [2009] JPL 872; see also *R v Sevenoaks ex p Terry* [1985] 3 All ER 226; [1984] JPL 420 and *Lothian Borders and Angus Cooperative Society Ltd v Scottish Borders Council* [1999] 2 PLR 19; 1999 GWD 6-316.
3 See eg The Improvement Service and TPS Planning Ltd. *The Planning System in Scotland: an introduction for elected members* (2011).

Pre-determination hearing[1]

6.79 For certain types of application, the planning authority has to hold a hearing before it reaches a decision. The applications concerned are those for major developments which would be a significant departure from the development plan and all national developments. Planning authorities can also choose to offer a hearing for other types of application if they wish. The hearing is an opportunity for applicants and those who have made representations to be heard by elected members of the council before a decision is made. The procedures involved are for each individual authority to decide. The planning authority's decision on an application that is subject to a pre-determination hearing has to be taken by the full council of the relevant local authority.[2]

1 1997 Act, s 38A.
2 Local Government (Scotland) Act 1973, s 56(6A).

Time period for reaching a decision[1]

6.80 The time within which planning authorities should determine applications varies according to the type of development involved. For national and major developments the period is 4 months. Local developments should be decided within 2 months unless the development is subject to an environmental assessment in which case it is also 4 months. Applications for approval of matters specified in conditions attached to a planning permission in principle should be determined within 2 months. These time periods run from the application validation date (see para 6.31 above) or, in the case of applications subject to an environmental impact assessment, the date when the Environment Statement was submitted (if this was later than the validation date). It is possible for authorities to extend these periods in agreement with the applicant. If an authority does not determine an application within the prescribed time period, the applicant then has the right to appeal to a local review body or, as the case may be, to the Scottish Ministers, as if the application had been refused. This is known as a deemed refusal. Where the applicant and authority have agreed to a longer period, this right to appeal on a deemed refusal starts from the expiry of the agreed time extension.

1 Town and Country Planning (Development Management Procedure) (Scotland) Regulations 2013 (SSI 2013 No 155), reg 26.

6.81 According to the Scottish Government, in the year 2011-12 only about 68 per cent of applications that should have been determined within two months met this target. The situation was even worse for major applications of which only 29 per cent had been determined within the statutory four month period. However, that performance was an improvement on the previous two years.[1]

1 Scottish Government Planning Performance Statistics 2011/12.

6.82 There is also a minimum time period within which decisions should be made.[1] This is normally 14 or 21 days and authorities cannot determine an application until those periods have expired. This is to give neighbours and other notified parties time to make representations before the decision is made.

1 Town and Country Planning (Development Management Procedure) (Scotland) Regulations 2013 (SSI 2013 No 155), reg 26(4).

Report of Handling

6.83 Planning authorities have to produce a report of handling for every planning application that they determine. The minimum contents of that report are prescribed by the DMR.[1] In effect; the report is an explanation of everything that the planning authority took into account in reaching its decision. It should give the number of representations received and summarise the main issues these raised. The statutory authorities consulted on the proposal should be identified and a summary given of their responses. In cases where assessments or statements have been required (eg a Design and Access Statement, an Environmental Statement or a report on flood risk) then the main issues raised by these should be summarised. Where the planning permission is linked with a planning obligation under s75 of the 1997 Act (see Chapter 8), this should be highlighted and the terms of that agreement outlined. Finally, where the Scottish Ministers have made directions[2] requiring the authority to provide them with information about the application, consider attaching conditions to the permission or restricting the grant of planning permission, this should be explained. The report of handling has to be included in Part II of the authority's planning register. In practice, the report of handling can be a very useful document. For planning applications that are delegated to officers it effectively takes the place of a report to the planning committee as it outlines the reasoning for the decision that the case officer has taken on behalf of the authority. As such it is the starting point for an applicant who wishes to appeal against that decision to the Local Review Body.

1 Town and Country Planning (Development Management Procedure) (Scotland) Regulations 2013 (SSI 2013 No 155), Sch. 2, para 4.
2 Ibid, regs 31 and 32.

Decision Notice

6.84 Once the authority has made its decision, it must issue a decision notice to the applicant or their agent (where they used one). As we explained above, the decision may be may be an unconditional or conditional approval or an outright refusal. The authority must give its reasons[1] for the decision and, where conditions are attached, reasons for each of these too. The date of the decision is the date shown on the decision notice issued to the applicant, not the date that the authority made its decision.[2] It is from that date that the time periods for implementing the permission, submitting applications for approval of matters specified by conditions imposed on the permission or exercising the right of appeal are calculated. However, in a case where, many years after a planning authority's decision to grant permission, no formal notification could be traced, it was held that planning permission could be presumed.[3]

1 1997 Act, s 43(1A).
2 Ibid, s 37(4).
3 *Calder Gravel v Kirklees Metropolitan Borough Council* [1990] 2 PLR 26.

6.85 The 1997 Act[1] and the DMR[2] prescribe the content of decision notices and also identify who else must be notified of the decision. The notice has to contain the application reference number, a description of the development (including any variations made after it was submitted) and identify the site with a postal address if possible. The notice should also identify the plans and drawings relating to the application as determined. If the authority has decided to apply time periods for implementing the permission that differ from the statutory periods then this should be specified. If this is not done then the statutory time periods apply by default (although in practice authorities often specify the statutory periods in the notice anyway). Where the application is linked with a Section 75 Obligation (see Chapter 8) then the notice should highlight this and explain where the terms of that agreement can be inspected. If the application has been approved subject to conditions or refused, details should be given on the applicant's right of appeal (see Chapter 7) and also to serve a purchase notice (see Chapter 10). Where an appeal would have to be made to the Scottish Ministers then Form 1 from Schedule 6 the DMR[3] should be used. Where the appeal would be to a Local Review Body, Form 2 should be used. The notice should also contain a statement about where to find out information about how to seek a local review of the decision or (if applicable) appeal to the Scottish Ministers. The authority has to notify every 'authority, person or body' who made written representations about the application and provided an address. The notice should advise them of the decision and of where a copy can be inspected.

1 Section 43(1A).
2 Town and Country Planning (Development Management Procedure) (Scotland) Regulations 2013 (SSI 2013 No 155), reg 28 and Sch 6.
3 Town and Country Planning (Development Management Procedure) (Scotland) Regulations 2013 (SSI 2013 No 155), reg 28(4).

6.86 When granting planning permission, the authority has to advise the applicant of the requirement for them to notify the planning authority once the development has been initiated. It makes sense for planning authorities to do this by including the relevant information in the decision notice. It is also good practice for the authority to advise the applicant at the same time of the need to serve a development completion notice and also, in certain cases, to display an on-site notice. We will look in more detail at these post permission requirements later in this chapter.

7. CALL IN OF APPLICATIONS

Scottish Ministers' power

6.87 As we saw in Chapter 2, the Scottish Ministers have the power to call in applications for planning permission for their determination, which means that they may take over from the planning authority the consideration of a planning application at first instance (as opposed to on appeal).[1] In such a case all the statutory provisions (for neighbour notification etc) apply equally, so far as appropriate. The applicant must also be notified by the planning authority that the application has been called in, informed of the reasons for this and advised that the Scottish Ministers decision will be final.[2]

1 1997 Act, s 46.
2 Town and Country Planning (Development Management Procedure) (Scotland) Regulations 2013 (SSI 2013 No 155), reg 35.

6.88 In practice, the statutory procedure of neighbour notification etc will have been carried out by the planning authority itself prior to the application being called in, which will normally only happen at a late stage in cases where the authority intends to grant approval. Since by this time the council will already have gone through the whole process of considering the application and of making its own decision, the procedure has some of the characteristics of an appeal, which is of course the Scottish Ministers' more usual role.[1]

1 See Chapter 7.

Notification of applications

6.89 Since the Scottish Ministers can only call in an application that they know about in the first place, the planning authority is required to notify them in circumstances that raise issues which are important enough for the Ministers to consider using their call-in powers.[1] Such notification is necessary only where the planning authority proposes to grant permission, and in many cases only where to do so would be against the advice of the Scottish Ministers or another statutory consultee:

1 Development in which the planning authority has an interest[2] and the proposed development would be significantly contrary to the development plan for the area.
2 Development to which a government agency has either recommended refusal and the planning authority intends to grant permission, or has recommended conditions and the planning authority does not intend attaching these. The types of development and government agency involved are:
   - Scottish Ministers (acting though Transport Scotland) for development affecting trunk or special roads;
   - The Health and Safety Executive for development in the vicinity of major hazards;
   - Scottish Natural Heritage for developments affecting sites which have been designated for the protection of the natural heritage;

- Historic Scotland for developments affecting Category A listed buildings or Scheduled Ancient Monuments;
- Scottish Environment Protection Agency for developments in areas at risk of flooding;
- Sport Scotland for development resulting in the loss or an adverse impact on outdoor sports facilities;
- The Secretary of State for Defence where a marine fish farm development may affect a controlled site under the Protection of Military Remains Act 1986.

3 Certain open cast coal developments, for example where the site boundary is within 500m of an existing community or sensitive establishment.

4 If a planning authority proposes to grant permission for the development of land forming the site of or in the neighbourhood of an aerodrome, technical site or military explosives storage area, against the advice of the consultee, or not to attach conditions which the consultee has advised, or to attach conditions which the consultee has advised against, it shall notify the Scottish Ministers, and in addition:
(a) both the Civil Aviation Authority and the consultee; or
(b) the Secretary of State for Defence
as the case may be.

1 The Town and Country Planning (Notification of Applications) (Scotland) Direction 2009 (see also SG Circular 3/2009 'Notification of Planning Applications' and SEDD Circular 2/2003 'Safeguarding of Aerodromes, Technical Sites and Miltary Explosives Storage Areas).

2 This applies where the planning authority is the applicant, the developer, has a financial interest in the development, is the landowner (in whole or part) or has some other interest in the development site.

6.90 The Scottish Ministers can call in any application, and not just in the circumstances listed above. It is possible, for example, that they can even decide to use their call in powers where the planning authority intends to refuse permission as occurred with the *Trump International Golf Links Scotland* development at the Menie Estate in Aberdeenshire in 2007. However, in practice call in powers are seldom used and only where an application raises issues that are significant enough to have implications at national level. In the words of Circular 3/2009

> Ministers will exercise this power very sparingly, recognising and respecting the important role of local authorities in making decisions on the future development of their areas. It is not the Scottish Government's role or intention to micro-manage planning authority decision-making.[1]

1 SG Circular 3/2009 'Notification of Planning Applications', para 5.

8. EFFECT AND DURATION OF PLANNING PERMISSIONS

Effect of permission

6.91 Section 44(1) of the Town and Country Planning (Scotland) Act 1997 provides that 'any grant of planning permission to develop land shall (except in so far as the permission otherwise provides) enure for the benefit of the land and of all persons for the time being interested in it'. ('Enure' means 'take effect'.) This simply means that planning permission (like the conditions in title deeds of property) 'runs with the land', ie it is not normally personal to the applicant but can be used by future owners, tenants or occupiers of the property. This is an important provision, as it is not always the applicant who implements a permission. For example, an owner of agricultural land before putting it up for sale may obtain planning permission (probably in principle only) for residential, commercial or industrial development in order to obtain a better price from purchasers interested in using the permission. Alternatively, developers may obtain their own permission, but then sell the development as a going concern once it is completed. And even where the original applicant implements the permission and continues to occupy the property, it is always possible that it will come up for sale in the future; and so the present provision ensures that future purchasers will inherit the existing use rights of the property and will be subject to the same ongoing conditions governing its use. It is possible, however, for the planning authority to grant a planning permission that is personal to an individual. This is likely to done to allow land or property to be put to a particular use by that person. Once someone else occupies the property the personal permission is no longer valid.

6.92 Where planning permission is granted for the erection of a building, it may specify the purposes for which the building may be used; failing that, it is implied that the building may be used for the purpose for which it was designed.[1] It has been held that the word 'designed' is not used here in its architectural sense, but means 'destined or intended'.[2]

1 1997 Act, s 44(2), (3).
2 *Wilson v West Sussex County Council* [1963] 2 QB 764, [1963] 2 WLR 669.

Interpretation of permission

6.93 There is a general rule in interpreting planning permissions that regard can only be given to the permission itself, ie that extrinsic evidence (documents other than the permission) cannot also be taken into account.[1] The reasoning behind this derives from the principle that we noted above, ie that planning permission runs with the land. If, therefore, a future owner or tenant wants to take advantage of a planning permission, it is not reasonable that their rights should partly depend upon documents (eg correspondence relating to the application) to which they may not have access. However, there have come to be recognised two exceptions to this rule: (1) where another document (eg a plan or the planning application itself) has been specifically incorporated into the planning permission by reference;[2] or (2) where the planning permission is so ambiguous that its validity is called into question.[3] In view of the fact that planning applications and the documents connected with them are now widely available to the public, including online, there is a growing trend towards allowing reference to the application, even where one of the above exceptions does not apply.[4]

1 *Miller-Mead v Minister of Housing and Local Government* [1963] 2 QB 196.
2 *Slough Estates Ltd v Slough Borough Council* [1971] AC 958; but see also *R v Secretary of State for the Environment ex p Slough Borough Council* [1995] EGCS 95, (1995) Times, May 24.
3 *Springfield Minerals Ltd v Secretary of State for Wales* [1995] EGCS 174, (1995) SPEL 53:13.
4 For a review of the case law in depth, see Watchman, P 'Interpreting Planning Permissions' (1990) 30 SPLP 40.

Duration of planning permission

6.94 Once planning permission has been granted there is no compulsion upon a developer or anyone else actually to carry out the development. However the permission will lapse unless it is implemented by work beginning on the development. The 1997 Act specifies maximum time periods for such work to begin. However, as we have already discussed above, it is open to the planning authority to apply its own time limits where it considers this appropriate and where that has happened this will be stated in the decision notice. If the decision notice does not say anything about a time period then the statutory ones apply by default. The statutory time periods are as follows:

- Where planning permission has been granted at the outset, the development must begin within three years of the granting of permission.[1]
- Where in principle planning permission has been obtained first, application for approval of the matters specified in conditions must all have been made within three years of the in principle approval[2] and the development itself must begin either within three years of the in principle approval or two years of the date

when all of the matters subject to condition have been approved, whichever is the later.[3]

1 1997 Act, s 58(1).
2 Or, where one of those applications for approval has been refused (or dismissed on appeal), within 6 months of that refusal if this is later than 3 years from the date of the in principle permission.
3 1997 Act, s 59(4).

Date when development begun[1]

6.95 In order to calculate the above time limits (as well as for other purposes) it is necessary to know what legally counts as a development having begun. In law, a planning permission is deemed to be implemented once a 'material operation' has taken place. In the case of operational development (eg building operations) it is when the operations are begun, in the case of a change of use, when the new use is instituted. If the development involves both operations and a change of use, it is begun at the earlier of these two times. A material operation includes any construction work for the erection of a building and also any demolition work on a building, but relatively minor operations also qualify, eg the digging of a trench to contain foundations or any operation laying out a road or part of a road.[2] This means that if a time limit is running out, only a very small effort is required by a developer to save the permission.

1 1997 Act, s 27.
2 Ibid, s 27(4).

6.96 There have been a number of case decisions on the meaning of 'specified operation' (which was defined in the earlier legislation in identical terms to that of 'material operation' in the 1997 Act).[1] In *Thayer v Secretary of State for the Environment*[2] all that had been done to implement the planning permission for the building of a house had been the removal of part of a hedge and some surface earth to provide highway access. It was held that this amounted to a specified operation; provided that the work was referable to the planning permission,[3] the degree or extent of the work (unless it was entirely trivial) was irrelevant. Other works to qualify as specified operations included stripping topsoil and making a temporary access road,[4] marking out an estate road with pegs,[5] and even digging a trench and immediately filling it in again.[6] However, in a case where no approval of reserved matters had been obtained, development following upon a grant of outline permission alone did not count as a specified operation.[7] As long as enough has been done for the development to have commenced, it is not necessary for the developer also to demonstrate their intention to complete the development.[8]

1 Town and Country Planning (Scotland) Act 1972, s 40(2), (3) (as amended) (now replaced by 1997 Act, s 27(4), (5)).
2 [1991] 3 PLR 104, CA.
3 *South Oxfordshire District Council v Secretary of State for the Environment* [1981] 1 WLR 1092.
4 *United Refineries v Essex County Council* [1978] JPL 110.
5 *Malvern Hills District Council v Secretary of State for the Environment* (1983) 46 P&CR 58, 262 EG 1190, CA.
6 *High Peak Borough Council v Secretary of State for the Environment and Courtdale Developments* [1981] JPL 366; see also *Spackman v Secretary of State for the Environment* [1977] 1 All ER 257.
7 *Oakimber v Elmbridge Borough Council and Surrey County Council* (1991) 62 P&CR 594, CA; but see *R v Flintshire CC ex. p. Somerfield Stores Ltd* [1998] PLCR 336.
8 *East Dunbartonshire Council v Secretary of State for Scotland and Mactaggart & Mickel Ltd* (1999) 71 SPEL 16.

Reapplications

6.97 As we discussed above (see para 6.25 above), at any time before a time limit has expired, the applicant can seek to renew the permission by reapplying to the planning authority. This is known as a 'further application'. There is of course no guarantee that the planning authority will grant permission again,[1] but if it does, the time limits will of course apply in relation to the new permission and thereby be extended. Where a reapplication is made, it is not necessary to resubmit the plans and other details of the development.

1 See *Nawar v Secretary of State for the Environment* [1995] EGCS 151, (1996) 53 SPEL 13.

Other necessary approvals

6.98 Once planning permission has been granted developers should be aware that this does not necessarily mean they can then go ahead with building operations or put an existing property to a new use. In many cases approvals under other legislation will be required first. For example, new buildings or alterations to existing ones will need a building warrant under the building regulations. A proposed change of use from a shop to a restaurant may need a licence from the local licensing board. It is also possible that planning approvals other than planning permission may also be needed. For example, a development involving alterations to the frontage of an existing shop in a listed building may also require listed building consent (see Chapter 12) and consent to display an advertisement (see Chapter 14). However, where other types of planning approval are required for a development these will normally be processed and determined in tandem with the application for planning permission.

9. IMPLEMENTING PERMISSION

Notification of initiation of development[1]

6.99 Where someone intends to start a development which has planning permission they have to inform the planning authority of the date work will start. There is no minimum period for serving the notice it just has to be done as 'as soon as practicable' before work starts. The notice should also give the date and reference number of the planning permission and state the full name and address of:

1 The person intending to carry out the development;
2 The landowner if they are a different person; and
3 Any site agent appointed for the development.

The purpose of the notice is to ensure the planning authority is aware that development is underway so it can then follow up on any suspensive conditions attached to the permission. These might include, for example, that a site contamination report should be submitted to the satisfaction of the planning authority before building begins. Another possibility might be that certain parts of the development (possibly the less profitable elements) have to be completed and available for occupation before other (possibly more lucrative) parts of the project. It is a breach of planning control[2] to begin work without first serving this notice and the applicant will have been advised of this in the decision notice that the planning authority issued at the time the permission was granted. While theoretically this could lead to enforcement action, The Scottish Government advises that an informal approach should be taken to resolving this. However, once the authority has found out that development has started without it being notified it will want to satisfy itself that more serious breaches of planning control, such as failure to comply with planning permission conditions have not occurred. If for some reason development does not start until after the date notified to the planning authority this is not a breach of planning control.

1 1997 Act, s 27A and Town and Country Planning (Development Management Procedure) (Scotland) Regulations 2013 (SSI 2013 No 155), reg 40.
2 1997 Act, s 123(1).

Display of site notice while development is carried out[1]

6.100 Developers of certain classes of development have to display a notice on site for the duration of construction. The developments involved are National, Major and so called *bad neighbour*[2] developments. The notice has to be in the form provided by the DMR,[3] be displayed in a prominent place at or in the vicinity of the site, easily visible to members of the public and printed on durable material. As well as providing information about the development and developer, the notice should also give the planning authority's contact details for enquiries and enforcement action.

1 1997 Act, s 27C and Town and Country Planning (Development Management Procedure) (Scotland) Regulations 2013 (SSI 2013 No 155), reg 41.
2 As defined in Town and Country Planning (Development Management Procedure) (Scotland) Regulations 20013 (SSI 2013 No 155), Sch. 3.
3 Town and Country Planning (Development Management Procedure) (Scotland) Regulations 2013 (SSI 2013 No 155), Sch 7.

Notification of completion of development[1]

6.101 Once the development has been completed, the person who carried it out must give a notice of that completion to the planning authority. As with a notice of initiation of development there is no time limit for doing so, it simply has to be done as soon as practicable after completion of the development. Failure to serve a completion notice is not normally a breach of planning control. However it may be in the case of phased developments as these are granted subject to a condition that the developer serve separate completion notices after completion of each phase (except the last).[2] Failure to comply with this would be a breach of condition and thus a breach of planning control subject to enforcement action. Once the last phase is completed the developer has to serve a final completion notice in the normal way.

1 1997 Act, s 27B.
2 Ibid, s 27B(2).

Completion notice (planning authority)[1]

6.102 It may be that a development is begun within the appropriate time limit, but that thereafter the developer is taking unduly long to complete it, or may even have abandoned it. It is obviously undesirable that the landscape should be blotted indefinitely by partially-completed developments, and so planning authorities are also given the power to remedy this type of situation. In such a case if the planning authority believes that the development will not be completed within a reasonable period, it may serve a completion notice stating a deadline for completion of the development. The period for completion must be at least 12 months, though it may be longer. The notice must be served on the owner and the occupier of the property, and on anyone else who may be affected by the notice. The notice will take effect only after it has been confirmed by the Scottish Ministers, who may change the deadline. The recipient of a notice may appeal against it to the Scottish Ministers within 28 days.[2]

1 1997 Act, ss 61, 62.
2 Ibid, s 62(3).

6.103 If the deadline in a completion notice expires without the development being completed, the planning permission will cease to have effect. This will render the partially-completed development unlawful and therefore subject to enforcement proceedings by the planning authority.[1]

1 See Chapter 9.

Variation of permission

6.104 If requested to do so by the grantee or by a person acting on their behalf, a planning authority may later vary any planning permission it has granted, if it appears to it that the variation sought is not material.[1] It is important to note that if the current owner of the site did not obtain the planning permission that person is unable to apply for a variation in this way unless the consent of the applicant is obtained. This means that if a developer purchases a site which already has planning permission and intends implementing that permission the developer would be well advised to secure, as part of the terms of purchase, the consent of the applicant to apply for any future non material-variations to the permission. If objections were received in relation to the original application, the authority may choose to notify the objectors of the proposed variation, or even advertise the variation in the local press (eg if the proposal relates to a conservation area). If neighbours are likely to be materially affected by a proposed change it would be prudent to notify them. In *Eriden Properties Ltd and others v Falkirk Council,*[2] the planning authority's approval of a 'non-material' variation was quashed by the Court because directly affected third parties had not been given the opportunity to make representations and, furthermore, the Court was of the view that the amendment concerned was clearly a material one and no reasonable planning authority could have considered otherwise.

1 1997 Act, s 64.
2 Court of Session 21 January 2003, (2003) 97 SPEL 70.

Revocation or modification of permission

6.105 A planning authority is entitled to change its mind about a grant of planning permission and has power to modify or revoke entirely permission for a development, not only where the development is uncompleted, but even where it has been completed and perhaps even been in existence for some time. In such a case, it is obviously not the fault of the owner and they will be entitled to compensation. This topic is sufficiently important to deserve a chapter to itself.[1]

1 See Chapter 11 below.

Loss of development or use rights

6.106 This is a complex area, which we only have space to touch upon briefly. It concerns not only the duration of planning permissions, but also the way in which use rights, not deriving from a planning permission, can be lost. The latter category includes uses which predate the planning legislation (ie that were begun prior to 1 July 1948) and uses which have become immune from enforcement proceedings through lapse of time.[1]

1 See Chapter 9.

6.107 As we saw above (and will explore in more depth in Chapter 11), the planning authority can, in certain circumstance, take legal steps to discontinue an existing use or revoke an existing planning permission. However, it is also possible to lose existing use or development rights without intervention by the authority. The ways in which this can happen (other than by expiry of the relevant time limit considered in the previous section) are by: (1) the implementation of a planning permission (which thereafter becomes 'spent');[1] (2) the implementation of an inconsistent planning permission;[2] (3) abandonment (ie if a use has ceased indefinitely);[3] and (4) extinguishment (ie by the carrying out of a new development on the site).[4]

1 *Cynon Valley Borough Council v Secretary of State for Wales* (1986) 280 EG 195.
2 *Pilkington v Secretary of State for the Environment* [1974] 1 All ER 283; see also *Hands v Kyle & Carrick District Council* 1988 SCLR 470.
3 *Hartley v Minister of Housing and Local Government* [1970] 1 QB 413, [1969] 3 All ER 1658. See also *William Tracey Ltd v Scottish Ministers* 2005 SLT 191; 2005 GWD 4-56.
4 *Petticoat Lane Rentals Ltd v Secretary of State for the Environment* [1971] 2 All ER 793.

6.108 Whether or not one of these criteria applies will often depend on how the development or use right came about (eg by planning permission or immunity from enforcement). In determining whether a use has been abandoned important factors include the physical condition of the building, the period of non use of the property, whether there has been any other use in the intervening period and evidence regarding the owner's intentions. The above is the barest outline of some of the main principles and readers seeking enlightenment on this difficult area should consult other sources.[1]

1 See Mungo Deans 'Loss of Rights to Use or Develop Land' (1990) 31 SPLP 68; see also the leading case of *Pioneer Aggregates (UK) Ltd v Secretary of State for the Environment* [1985] AC 132.

10. PLANNING CONDITIONS

6.109 We saw above that, although a planning permission can be granted unconditionally, it is normally granted subject to conditions. This is an area that can cause problems and on which there has been much discussion, in court and elsewhere.

The statutory provisions

6.110 Section 37 of the 1997 Act[1] provides that planning authorities may grant planning permission 'either unconditionally or subject to such conditions as they think fit'. This (on the face of it) appears to give planning authorities completely unfettered discretion regarding the type of planning conditions they may impose. Section 41 goes on to elaborate upon some of the types of condition that may be imposed:

(a) for regulating the development or use of any land under the control of the applicant (whether or not it is land in respect of which the application was made) or requiring the carrying out of works on any such land, so far as appears to the planning authority to be expedient for the purposes of or in connection with the development authorised by the permission;
(b) for requiring the removal of any buildings or works authorised by the permission, or the discontinuance of any use of land so authorised, at the end of a specified period, and the carrying out of any works required for the reinstatement of land at the end of that period.[2]

1 Section 37(1)(a).
2 Ibid, s 41(1).

6.111 This basically describes three types of condition: (1) one that regulates the development of land within the applicant's control; (2) one requiring the carrying out of works on such land; and (3) one requiring the reinstatement of land when permission has been granted for a limited period. It should be noted that heads (1) and (2) can relate to land other than the site which is the subject of the planning application, provided that such land is within the applicant's control. However, if that other land lies within the area of a different planning authority, that authority's approval is needed for the condition to be attached.[1] While the above are fairly typical examples of the sort of thing a planning condition is likely to be about, it is clear that they do not exhaust the possibilities with regard to planning conditions. To give only one example, it is clear from elsewhere in the 1997 Act that a planning condition may also be used to require the preservation of trees within the land being developed.[2] In any case, s 41 is stated to be without prejudice to the generality of s 37(1).[3]

1 1997 Act, s 41(2).
2 Ibid, s 159.
3 Ibid, s 41(1).

6.112 And so, as far as the legislation is concerned, it would appear that planning authorities virtually have *carte blanche* with regard to the imposition of conditions. One qualification is that when imposing conditions the authority must give reasons for doing so.[1] Another is that the dissatisfied applicant has the same right of appeal to a local review body or the Scottish Ministers against planning conditions as is the case with an outright refusal, and this certainly could have the effect of curbing the effects of any planning authority which was over-enthusiastic in the use of its power.

1 1997 Act s 43(1A).

Conditions relating to time limits on permissions[1]

6.113 We saw above that the 1997 Act imposes time limits within which a development must be begun (usually three years).[2] We also saw that the planning authority has the power to vary any of the time limits as it deems appropriate. This is simply another way of saying that, when granting permission, the planning authority has the power to direct that any time limit it considers appropriate will apply and if it does not do this, the statutory time limit will apply by default. Although this is not strictly speaking a condition subject to which the planning permission has been granted, in specified instances it has to be treated as such.[3] Consequently, it is possible for the applicant to require a review of, or appeal against, a time limit in the same way as they can for any other condition.

1 1997 Act, ss 58 & 59.
2 See paras 6.25 and 6.97 above.
3 1997 Act, ss 58(3) and 59(6).

Variation or removal of conditions[1]

6.114 An application may be made to the planning authority to have conditions which are attached to an existing planning permission either varied or removed altogether. The authority has the power to do either of the above or, if it considers that the original conditions should continue to apply, to refuse the application. However, in deciding whether or not to vary or remove a condition, the planning authority can only take into consideration the acceptability of any existing and proposed conditions, and are not entitled to re-consider whether or not the development is acceptable in principle.[2] The power to vary or remove conditions does not apply where the condition imposed a time limit for the development to begin, and that time limit has expired without the development having commenced;[3] however this exception does not extend to a condition imposing a time limit for an application for the approval of a matter specified in a condition and such a condition *can* be varied or removed by the planning authority after the relevant time limit has expired without an application having been made.[4]

1 1997 Act, s 42.
2 Ibid, s42 (2). See also *Allied London Property Investment v Secretary of State for the Environment* [1996] EGCS 52, (1996) Times, 28 March.
3 1997 Act, s 42(4).
4 *R v Secretary of State for the Environment, ex p Corby Borough Council* [1995] JPL 115.

Limits on planning authority's discretion: case law

6.115 Although the 1997 Act appears to give planning authorities almost unlimited discretion in the imposition of planning conditions, in practice this discretion is not quite as wide as it seems. When discussing planning appeals in the next chapter we will see that, although a local review body or the Scottish Ministers have the last word on the merits of the application, there is a limited right of appeal beyond that to the Court of Session on legal grounds.[1] One of these grounds is that the planning authority (or the Scottish Ministers, as the case may be) have acted *ultra vires* (ie outwith their legal powers). Over the years, this right has been used to challenge the legality of planning conditions on a number of occasions and a substantial body of case law has evolved. The result has been a number of rules regarding the nature of planning conditions that curtail somewhat the apparent discretion of planning authorities under the legislation. (The first three of these derive from the leading English case of *Newbury District Council v Secretary of State for the Environment*):[2]

1. Planning conditions must be for a planning purpose and not for any ulterior one.

2. Conditions must fairly and reasonably relate to the development permitted.
3. They must not be so unreasonable that no reasonable planning authority could have imposed them.
4. They must be capable of being given an intelligible meaning, otherwise they may be declared to be void from uncertainty. Merely being ambiguous is not enough to make a condition void.[3]
5. They must be necessary.[4]

1 See Chapter 7.

2 [1981] AC 578 at 599 per Viscount Dilhorne.

3 *Fawcett Properties Ltd v Buckingham County Council* [1961] AC 636; *Caledonian Terminal Investments Ltd v Edinburgh Corporation* 1970 SC 271, 1979 SLT 362; *David Lowe & Sons Ltd v Musselburgh Town Council* 1973 SC 130, 1974 SLT 5; *Aberdeen City Council v Secretary of State for Scotland* 1997 (GWD 33–1692 (1997) 64 SPEL 127 but see also *Eastwood District Council v Mactaggart & Mickel Ltd* 1992 SCLR 656.

4 *British Airports Authority v Secretary of State for Scotland* 1979 SLT 197; *South Lanarkshire Council v Secretary of State for Scotland* 1997 GWD 1–37, (1997) 60 SPEL 34.

The BAA Case

6.116 The application of several of these criteria is illustrated in the leading Scottish case of *British Airports Authority v Secretary of State for Scotland*.[1] This was an appeal against planning conditions imposed on the permissions granted to three separate applicants in respect of proposed developments at Aberdeen Airport. The context of this case was the greatly increased air traffic caused by North Sea oil developments in the 1970s. The planning authority was naturally concerned to minimise the nuisance caused by this, particularly in residential areas, and one of the ways in which it sought to tackle the problem was by the imposition of planning conditions. The conditions appealed against here (after modification by the then Secretary of State) related to (a) the restriction of operational hours to prevent night flying and (b) the restriction of permitted directions for take-off and landing.

1 1979 SLT 197.

6.117 The three appellants were British Airports Authority and two helicopter companies, British Airways Helicopters and Bristow Helicopters. The British Airports Authority application was in respect of several developments: a new aircraft apron, a new terminal building and car park, improved runway approach lighting and the improvement of an existing taxiway. British Airways Helicopters was proposing to erect a one-storey building to provide an office for its flight operations headquarters for the whole of the UK and accommodation for the ground training of personnel. The proposal of Bristow Helicopters was to build an extension to an existing terminal building. British Airports Authority was appealing against both of the conditions and the helicopter companies against the first one only (ie regarding operational hours).

6.118 In the appeal by British Airports Authority it was held that both conditions fairly and reasonably related to the development, as there was a relationship between the nature of the developments proposed and the increase in air traffic; the developments were, in fact, in response to that increase. As a result, the first condition (operational hours) was valid. However, the second condition (direction of take-off and landing) was held to be *ultra vires* on the ground that it was both unreasonable and unnecessary. It was unreasonable because only the Civil Aviation Authority had the power to control flight paths, making it outwith the power of the applicants to ensure compliance with the condition. It was unnecessary because the control of flight paths by the Civil Aviation Authority dealt with the problem, so that there was no need to deal with it elsewhere by the imposition of planning conditions.

6.119 In the appeals by the two helicopter companies it was held that the condition relating to operational hours was *ultra vires* in each case because it was unnecessary. Because the same condition had been validly imposed on the first appellants, British Airports Authority, that dealt with the situation for the whole airport, and so there was no need to impose it separately on companies operating there.

6.120 In the case of the British Airways Helicopters' appeal it was also held that the condition relating to operational hours did not fairly and reasonably relate to the development. The nature of the development (office headquarters serving the whole UK) was not directly related to the increase in air traffic at Aberdeen airport, and no helicopters took off or landed there.

Other case law

6.121 The case of *Birnie v Banff County Council*[1] provides another good example of a planning condition held to be *ultra vires* because it was unreasonable. The owners of a piece of ground were granted planning permission for the erection of a house, subject to a condition that an access lane be formed on other ground to the rear of their land which was not in their ownership. As in the BAA case, the condition was held to be unreasonable because it required the applicants to do something that was outwith their control: they could not compel the owners of the adjoining land to sell it to them or give them permission to use it.

1 1954 SLT (Sh Ct) 90; see, however, the position regarding Grampian conditions (see para 6.130 below and, more especially, Chapter 8).

6.122 A condition requiring the applicant to do something outwith their control is unreasonable because failure to adhere to a planning condition could lead to enforcement proceedings and to the applicant being fined. This would be unfair if compliance with the condition was outwith their power. This principle is in fact implicit in s 41(1) of the 1997 Act where it provides that a condition may regulate the development of or require works on land 'under the control of the applicant'. However, such a condition is only illegal if it is framed in a positive form, ie where is it imposing on the developer a positive obligation to do something, eg to carry out works. It is perfectly legal to impose a similar condition in negative form, eg that the planning permission will not be valid unless certain works are carried out. In such a case, it is not even necessary for the applicant to be the one who should carry them out, or for there to be a reasonable prospect that they will be carried out.[1] This is in fact an example of a 'Grampian' condition, a type of condition that we will describe more fully in Chapter 8.

1 *British Railways Board v Secretary of State for the Environment* [1993] 3 PLR 125, [1994] 02 EG 107; see also *Strathclyde Regional Council and Another v Secretary of State for Scotland and Elcomatic Ltd* 1996 SLT 579, (1996) 55 SPEL 51.

6.123 The first of the above rules (that the condition must be imposed for a planning purpose and not an ulterior one) is well illustrated in the English case of *R v Hillingdon London Borough Council ex parte Royco Homes Ltd*.[1] Here the applicants were granted permission for a housing development subject to a condition that a proportion of houses should be let to people on the council's waiting list for council houses. These would have been protected tenancies under the Rent Acts, giving the tenants security of tenure and the right to have a fair rent registered, and the developers would no doubt have found it more economic to sell all of the houses instead. The condition was held by the court to be *ultra vires*. The council was misusing its powers as planning authority to fulfil its duties as housing authority: the condition was imposed, not for a planning purpose, but for an ulterior one.

1 [1974] QB 720; see also *North East Fife District Council v Secretary of State for Scotland* 1990 SCLR 647.

Effect of ultra vires *declaration*

6.124 We also need to consider what effect it will have on the planning permission as a whole when a condition is declared *ultra vires*. Does the whole permission stand or fall along with the condition, or is the applicant left with a valid permission minus the condition that has been successfully challenged? It was held in the *British Airports Authority* case that the whole permission fell with the outlawed conditions, as they were not severable from the permission as a whole. The planning authority had to be given an opportunity to reconsider whether (knowing it was unable to impose that particular condition) it wanted to impose an alternative condition or conditions, or even grant permission at all.

6.125 The above shows that an applicant should be cautious about challenging conditions in court. They may well get the unconditional permission they want after a reapplication. On the other hand, they may not, and the result of their legal challenge may be to exchange a conditional permission for no permission at all. They should also keep similar considerations in mind before making an initial appeal to the local review body or Scottish Ministers. Although they, (unlike the court) *do* have the power to replace a conditional permission with an unconditional one, it is also open to them, should they think the planning merits justify it, to refuse permission altogether.

Unauthorised developments

6.126 Quite apart from the question of whether a planning condition is *ultra vires*, a condition can be unenforceable for the much more basic reason that the planning permission to which it is attached was never implemented. If this simply means that no development has occurred at all, then there is unlikely to be a problem. However, a more difficult situation can arise where a condition is imposed on a permission and the development takes place in a way which differs to a material extent from the terms of the permission. In *Handoll v Warner Goodman & Streat*[1] a dwelling-house was erected 90 feet west of the approved location. It was therefore in breach of planning control, but later became immune from enforcement under the 4 year rule. It was held that an agricultural occupancy condition attached to the planning permission could not be enforced because the planning permission had never been implemented. To avoid such a situation, planning authorities will therefore have to ensure that operational developments do not differ materially from the approved plans.[2]

1 [1995] 25 EG 157.
2 See SODD Circular 4/1998 'The Use of Conditions in Planning Permissions', Annex, para 28.

Central government policy

6.127 Current Scottish Government policy and advice on the use of conditions is contained in Circular 4/1998 *The Use of Conditions* *in Planning Permissions.*[1] Its general policy is that conditions should only be imposed where they are:

- necessary;
- relevant to planning;
- relevant to the development to be permitted
- enforceable;
- precise; and
- reasonable in all other respects.

In fact, as we saw above, a condition in breach of the first 3 or the last of these would be ultra vires in terms of the rules laid down by the courts. The remaining legal rule (that a condition should be sufficiently intelligible to avoid being declared void from uncertainty) is included within the above recommendations that a condition should be enforceable and precise, though the government advice goes beyond the strict legality of the situation; in fact it has been held that a condition is not ultra vires merely because it is difficult to enforce in practice.[2] However, few would disagree that it is good practice to avoid unenforceable conditions. To use the example given in the circular, a condition may be sufficiently precise and not otherwise *ultra vires*, but effectively be unenforceable because it is in practice difficult to prove, or even detect, an infringement. 'For example, a condition imposed for traffic reasons restricting the number of persons resident at any one time in a block of flats would be impracticable to monitor and pose severe difficulties in proving an infringement.'[3] In *Edinburgh City Council v Scottish Ministers*[4] a reporter's decision to grant listed building consent subject to conditions preventing a room being used as a bedroom, requiring the removal of net curtains from windows and seeking to control the height of a privet hedge was quashed because these were not matters that could be enforced through planning controls.

1 SODD Circular 4/1998 'The Use of Conditions in Planning Permissions' (1998). See also Scottish Planning Policy (2010), para 26.
2 *Bromsgrove District Council v Secretary of State for the Environment and AE Beckett & Sons (Development) Ltd* [1988] JPL 257.
3 SODD Circular 4/1998, Annex, para 26.
4 2002 SLT 1243; [2002] 4 PLR 54.

6.128 The circular gives further extensive advice on the best practice for the use of planning conditions. This includes consideration of how conditions can be employed to regulate noise, traffic and transport, design and landscape, and the development of contaminated sites, as well as the relevance of conditions to nature conservation, archaeological sites and developments involving an environmental impact assessment. However, planning conditions should not normally be used to duplicate the effect of other statutory controls (eg the legislation on pollution control). The circular is supplemented with a list of model conditions.[1] Although the above advice on the use of conditions extends well beyond consideration of what is strictly legal, it should be remembered that the Scottish Ministers on appeal have the power to amend or revoke conditions, not just on legal grounds, but also for reasons of planning policy or practice (eg if their advice has not been followed!).

1 SODD Circular 4/1998 Addendum 'Model Planning Conditions' (1998).

Planning obligations

6.129 These are either a unilateral obligation or contract entered into with a planning authority, the terms of which can achieve a similar purpose to the imposition of planning conditions. It is the government's policy that a planning authority should seek to regulate a development by planning conditions rather than by means of a planning agreement, though this advice is not always followed in practice. Planning obligations are considered in some depth in Chapter 8.

Grampian conditions

6.130 A 'Grampian condition' is a planning condition which takes the form of a suspensive condition and is so named from the case of *Grampian Regional Council v Aberdeen District Council.*[1] Grampian conditions are dealt with more fully in Chapter 8.

1 1984 SLT 197, HL.

Chapter 7

Reviews, appeals and other forms of challenge

1. INTRODUCTION

7.1 Typically less than ten per cent of applications for planning permission are refused.[1] Therefore; most applicants for planning permission will be content with the outcome of their experience of the development management system in Scotland. However, an applicant whose application for planning permission is refused may naturally be disappointed, and even where planning permission has been granted, an applicant may be dissatisfied with conditions that have been imposed on the grant of planning permission. Further, there will also be applicants who are dissatisfied because the planning authority has failed to reach a decision within the relevant period prescribed by legislation. In all of these instances the applicant may either require the relevant planning authority's Local Review Body ('LRB') to review the case (of the failure of a planning authority's appointed officer within the prescribed period to take a decision capable of being made on an application for planning permission under a scheme of delegation under s 43A(1) of the Town and Country Planning (Scotland) Act 1997 or a decision under such a scheme of delegation) or may appeal to the Scottish Ministers. Any appeal[2] or review[3] may be based on the planning merits of the case, on legal grounds or be based on both planning merits and legal grounds.

1 In 2011/12 92.2 per cent of applications for planning permission were granted.
2 The Town and Country Planning (Scotland) Act 1997, s 47. See also The Town and Country Planning (Appeals) Regulations 2013 (SSI 2013 No 156) and SG Circular 4/2013 'Planning Appeals'.
3 Ibid, s 43A. See also The Town and Country Planning (Schemes of Delegation and Local Review Procedure) (Scotland) Regulations 2013 (SSI 2013 No 157) and SG Circular 5/2013 'Schemes of Delegation and Local Reviews'.

7.2 Of course, applicants for planning permission are not the only ones who may be dissatisfied with a planning authority's decision. As we saw in Chapter 6, other people have the right to comment on planning applications, and if they have objected to a proposed development they may be unhappy if planning permission is granted. However, while an applicant for planning permission has statutory right to challenge both a failure to take a decision or the decision taken by the planning authority, third parties have no such rights. The only possible avenue third parties have is the limited possibility of an application to the Court of Session for a judicial review of the grant of planning permission.[1]

1 See paras 7.116ff below.

7.3 The introduction of 'Third party rights of appeal' (sometimes referred to as a 'Community right of appeal') against the grant of planning permission has been called for, and considered, on a number of occasions. For instance, the 1988 Report of the Committee of the JUSTICE – All Souls Review of Administrative Law in the United Kingdom concluded that the disadvantages of introducing rights of appeal or a call-in for third parties against the grant of planning permission outweighed any possible advantages and the practical difficulties of doing so are formidable.[1] In 2005 and 2006 the Scottish Parliament considered the issue of third party rights of appeal during the scrutiny of the package of proposed reforms that were eventually enacted in the Planning etc (Scotland) Act 2006. We consider that the option of introducing a third party right of appeal against the grant of planning permission will continue to be a subject of debate when issues such as the effectiveness of, and trust in, the planning system is Scotland is being considered. It appears that the Scottish Government will be reviewing the reformed planning system in the not too distant future as typically the operation and impact of new legislation is considered about five years after it came into operation.

1 *Administrative Justice Some Necessary Reforms* (Clarendon Press) 1988, Chapter 10 at paras 10.62 and 10.63.

7.4 The decision of a planning authority's LRB or the Scottish Ministers is final on the planning merits of the case. However, an applicant who is dissatisfied with the decision of the LRB or the Scottish Ministers (as the case may be); can challenge it, on legal grounds only, in the Court of Session. Alternatively, the planning authority itself may apply, on legal grounds only, to that court if is not content with a Scottish Ministers' decision. Third parties may also have a right to make an application to the court, based on legal grounds only, at this stage.

7.5 In the early parts of the chapter, we will consider first possible informal resolutions (through negotiation and mediation) and then requiring a review by the planning authority's LRB and appeals to the Scottish Ministers, mainly in the context of appeals against refusal of planning permission. Other planning related appeals will be discussed in the chapters relevant to those aspects (eg enforcement (Chapter 9) or listed building control (Chapter 12)). However, in the later parts of the chapter it will be convenient to deal in more general terms with legal challenges in the Court of Session. These can relate not only to planning applications, but also to other planning decisions and orders, as well as to the validity of development plans. Court of Session challenges may take the form of statutory applications under planning legislation or, in limited cases, an application by petition for judicial review. There are also certain other methods of challenge (eg a complaint to the Scottish Public Services Ombudsman) that we will deal with briefly at the end of the chapter.

2. INFORMAL DISPUTE RESOLUTION

7.6 A planning application decision must enable the reader to understand why the decision was reached and should enable a disappointed applicant to assess the prospects of obtaining planning permission for a different development proposal.[1] When planning permission is refused it may be desirable that there should be discussions between the applicant and the planning authority to establish whether the reason(s) for refusal might be overcome by alterations to the proposed development which could then be the subject of a new application for planning permission. It may be that in terms of the relevant planning fees regulations that any further application for planning permission made for a development of the same character or description on the same site within 12 months of the date of the refusal of planning permission would not be liable for payment of a planning application fee. Such discussion and negotiation with a planning authority will assist an applicant in assessing the likely prospect of success of a new application. This can then be balanced against the cost and time taken to prepare for and determine a review or an appeal (as the case may be).

1 *South Bucks District Council and Another v Porter* [2004] UKHL 33.

7.7 Where entering into a formal (review, appeal or court) dispute resolution process appears to be unavoidable or inevitable; opening a dialogue with a planning authority might facilitate producing a statement of matters that are agreed and may clarify and narrow the issues in dispute in any formal dispute resolution process.

7.8 Planning authorities may be willing to enter into mediation. It has been said that mediation cannot replace the statutory planning decision making process, as any planning application will require to be determined by the appropriate decision-maker. However, it has a clear role to play. Mediation has been described as ‘a process involving an independent third party, whose role is to help parties to identify the real issues between them, their concerns and needs, the options for resolving matters and, where possible, a solution which is acceptable to all concerned.' Mediation may, for instance, assist in improving the quality of an application, or may serve to resolve or narrow a dispute – and, as such, it has the potential to help the planning process to flow more smoothly and to arrive at better informed and more cost effective outcomes. Whether mediation will or will not work in a particular matter will depend largely on the willingness, open-mindedness and hard work of those involved to find a resolution. It is difficult to assess the impact that mediation is having in the Scottish planning system as, unless the parties agree otherwise, discussions at mediations are usually a private and confidential process. However, mediation has potential across the spectrum (development planning, development management and enforcement) of the planning system in Scotland. Often its outcome (rather than particular discussions during it) will need to become public as decisions are made about implementing agreements or proposals emanating from the mediation process.[1]

1 See, for instance, *A Guide to the Use of Mediation in the Planning System in Scotland* (Scottish Government 2009).

3. REQUIRING A LOCAL PLANNING AUTHORITY REVIEW

7.9 Section 43A of the 1997 Act empowers a planning authority, specifically its LRB, to review prescribed types of planning applications.[1] The LRB is a committee of the planning authority comprising at least three members of the authority. Decisions about the procedure to be followed by the LRB in conducting the review and its decision about how the case under review is to be determined must be held in public.[2] Otherwise, a council LRB is subject to the rules on the operations of local authority committees.[3] The Councillors' Code of Conduct[4] and the national park authority Codes of Conduct for Members are applicable. Every LRB must act lawfully (eg observe the rules of natural justice).

1 1997 Act, s 43A(8) and The Town and Country Planning (Schemes of Delegation and Local Review Procedure) (Scotland) Regulations 2013 (SSI 2013 No 157, reg 7).

2 The Town and Country Planning (Schemes of Delegation and Local Review Procedure) (Scotland) Regulations 2013 (SSI 2013 No 157), reg 7.

3 Local Government (Scotland) Act 1973, including Part IIIA Access to Meetings and Documents of Local Authorities, Committees and Sub-Committees and s 62 Standing Orders etc.

4 Standards Commission for Scotland, *The Councillors' Code of Conduct* (Standards Commission for Scotland, 2010) available at http://www.scotland.gov.uk/Resource/Doc/334603/0109379.pdf

7.10 The 2005 White Paper 'Modernising the Planning System' envisaged that a LRB would undertake an independent review of the officer's decision, rather than considering the proposal afresh. However the Scottish Government's Chief Planner subsequently issued a letter issued a letter to Heads of Planning indicating that a LRB should consider an application for planning permission being reviewed by it as if that application had been made to the LRB in the first instance (as opposed to being a review of the appointed officer's decision).[1]

1 Letter dated 29 July 2011 available at http://www.scotland.gov.uk/Resource/Doc/1070/0119911.pdf

7.11 The lack of clarity about and the lack of a consistent approach in the LRB process are not the only matters that have attracted comment. Adverse comments have been made about the LRB process both before and after its introduction in 2009. The LRB process has been criticised from a policy perspective (it involved the withdrawal of the right of appeal to the Scottish Ministers, a cornerstone of the post 1947 planning landscape). Further, questions have been raised about whether the LRB process is lawful because it does not offer the guarantees set out in Article 6 of the European Convention of Human Rights.[1] Proposals south of the border for a similar but more modest 'Local Member Review Body' process were abandoned in 2008 by the Whitehall government.[2]

1 Eg *Right to Appeal and Modernising Planning – Local Review Bodies* Administrative Justice & Tribunals Council Scottish Committee (2012) available at http://ajtc.justice.gov.uk/scottish/publications-scottish.htm
2 See (2008) 128 SPEL 76.

7.12 Planning authorities will want to ensure that the LRB is supported by appropriate administrative and legal advice to ensure that LRB members are guided on the review process and that all administrative arrangements required to support the review process locally should respect the principles of fairness and transparency that must underpin operation of the LRB process.[1] The Local Review Body Forum has published a number of guidance notes.[2]

1 SG Circular 5/2013 'Schemes of Delegation and Local Reviews'.
2 Available at http://www.scotland.gov.uk/Topics/Built-Environment/planning/about appeals

Right to require a review

7.13 The applicant for planning permission can require a planning authority's LRB to review an application if the officer appointed by virtue of a scheme of delegation under s 43A(1) of the 1997 Act by the planning authority to determine a relevant application:

(a) refuses an application for planning permission or for consent, agreement or approval;
(b) grants it subject to condition; or
(c) is deemed to have decided to refuse the application (see para 7.15(b),

and where a review is required the decision of the officer to either refuse an application or conditionally grant it is not to be treated as a decision of the planning authority.[1]

1 1997 Act, ss 43A(2), 43A(8), and 43A(9).

7.14 Officer decisions for other types of applications such as applications for planning permission for major developments or national developments; applications for listed building consent, conservation area consent, hazardous substances consent and advertisement consent and applications for certificates of lawfulness and for modification or discharge of planning obligations; remain subject to rights of appeal to the Scottish Ministers.

Notice of Review

7.15 A notice of review must be served on the LRB within the period of three months beginning with:

(a) the date of the notice of the decision on the application for planning permission; or
(b) the date of expiry of the period prescribed for the determination of the application for planning permission (four months after the validation date of the application if that application for planning permission requires environmental impact assessment or in any other case two months after the validation date of the application);[1] or the date of expiry of any period agreed in writing by the applicant and the appointed officer to extend the relevant prescribed period for the determination of the application.[2]

1 The Town and Country Planning (Schemes of Delegation and Local Review Procedure) (Scotland) Regulations 2013 (SSI 2013 No 157), regs 8 and 9.
2 1997 Act, s 43A(8)(c) as amended by the Public Services Reform (Planning) (Local Review Procedure) (Scotland) Order 2013 (SSI 2013 No 24) and the Town and Country Planning (Schemes of Delegation and Local Review Procedure) (Scotland) Regulations 2013 (SSI 2013 No 157), reg 9.

LRB review statement

7.16 The notice of review must include a statement setting out the applicant's reasons for requiring the LRB to review the case and by what, if any, procedure (or combination of procedures) the applicant considers the review should be conducted. The applicant should include in that notice or in the documents accompanying that review all matters which the applicant intends to raise in the review.[1] Those reasons, based on provisions of the development plan and other material considerations and setting out both the planning merits of the proposed development and relevant legal considerations; will seek to persuade the LRB to reverse or vary the appointed officer's decision.[2]

1 The Town and Country Planning (Schemes of Delegation and Local Review Procedure) (Scotland) Regulations 2013 (SSI 2013 No 157), regs 9(3) and 9(4).
2 1997 Act, s 43A(15).

7.17 There is a statutory prohibition against raising any matter which was not before the appointed officer at the time the determination was reviewed was made unless the applicant can demonstrate:

(a) that the matter could not have been raised before that time; or
(b) that it not being raised before that time was a consequence of exceptional circumstances.[1]

However, that prohibition is without prejudice to the requirement to consider development plan provisions and other material considerations.[2]

1 1997 Act, s 43B(1).
2 Ibid, s 43B(2).

LRB procedure

7.18 There are similarities in the review procedures and appeal procedures. Therefore those procedures are considered together below (see section 5 below).

LRB appeals

7.19 Where the requirement to review is made on the basis that there is a deemed refusal and the LRB has not conducted the review within three months the planning authority is deemed to have refused the application and the applicant has three months beginning on the date when the requirement to review was made on the basis of the officer's deemed refusal of the application to submit an appeal to the Scottish Ministers.[1] If the applicant does not appeal to the Scottish Ministers the LRB is required to reach its decision within a reasonable time.[2]

1 1997 Act, s 43A(17) and The Town and Country Planning (Scheme of Delegation and Local Review Procedure) (Scotland) Regulations 2013, reg 8(3).
2 *Lafarge Redland Aggregates Ltd v The Scottish Ministers* 2000 SLT 1361.

7.20 Where a development proposal requires both planning permission and other types of related approval (eg listed building consent), then the appellant needs to submit a requirement for a review by the planning authority's LRB and a listed building consent appeal (in the case of listed building consent this is form P/LBA) or two separate appeals using the appropriate appeal forms (as the case may be).

LRB statutory applications

7.21 An LRB decision is final, subject to a statutory challenge on legal grounds to the Court of Session.[1]

1 1997 Act, ss 47(1A), 237(3A) and 239(4).

4. APPEALS TO THE SCOTTISH MINISTERS

7.22 An applicant whose application for planning permission is not capable of being determined by a planning authority's officer appointed by virtue of a scheme of delegation make under s 43A(1) of the 1997 Act, has a right to appeal to the Scottish Ministers where:

(a) the planning authority refuses the application for planning permission or grants it subject to conditions;[1]

(b) the planning authority refuses the application for any consent, agreement or approval of that authority required by a condition imposed on a grant of planning permission or grants it subject to conditions;[2]

(c) the planning authority refuses the application for any approval of that authority required under a development order (eg the Permitted Development Order) or grants it subject to conditions;[3]

(d) the planning authority has not given notice to the applicant within any period prescribed by regulation or a development order or within such extended period as may be agreed in writing between the applicant and the planning authority of (i) its decision on the application for planning permission within the relevant statutory period (see para 7.24); (ii) its decision (under s 39 of the 1997 Act) to decline to determine the application for planning permission; or (iii) that the application for planning permission has been referred to the Scottish Ministers in accordance with directions given under s 46 of the 1997 Act;[4] or

(e) a deemed refusal by the LRB on a review – where the planning authority has not conducted the review within three months beginning on the date when the requirement to review is made on the basis that the appointed officer is also deemed to have refused the application for planning permission (see para 7.15 above).[5]

1 1997 Act, s 47(1)(a).
2 Ibid, s 47(1)(b).
3 Ibid, s 47(1)(c).
4 Ibid, s 47(2).
5 Ibid, s 43A(17) and The Town and Country Planning (Schemes of Delegation and Local Review Procedure) (Scotland) Regulations 2013 (SSI 2013 No 157), reg 8(3).

7.23 There is no right to appeal to the Scottish Ministers for decisions made or deemed to be refused by an appointed officer appointed by the planning authority under a scheme of delegation under s 43A(1) of the 1997 Act (see para 7.13) or LRB decisions made under s 43A(15) of the 1997 Act (such decisions should be challenged by a statutory application to the Court of Session).[1]

1 1997 Act, ss 47(1A), 237(3A) and 239(4).

Notice of appeal

7.24 A notice of appeal must be lodged with the Scottish Ministers within three months of:

(a) the date of the notice of the planning authority decision on the application for planning permission;[1] or
(b) the date of the expiry of the period prescribed for the determination of the application for planning permission (four months from the validation date of the application if that application for planning permission requires an environmental impact assessment or is for a national development or a major development; in other cases the expiry of two months from the validation date; or the expiry of any period agreed in writing by the applicant and the planning authority for the determination of the application for planning permission).[2]

1 The Town and Country Planning (Appeals) (Scotland) Regulations 2013 (SSI 2013 No 156), reg 3(3).
2 The Town and Country Planning (Development Management Procedure) (Scotland) Regulations 2013 (SSI 2013 No 155), reg 26 and The Town and Country Planning (Appeals) (Scotland) Regulations 2013 (SSI 2013 No 156), reg 3(2) and 3(3). See also *Vattenfall Wind Power Ltd v The Scottish Ministers* 2009 SLT 516.

Appeal statement

7.25 The notice of appeal must include a statement setting out full particulars of the appeal including a note of the matters which the appellant considers require to be taken into account in determining the appeal and by what, if any, procedure (or combination of procedures) the appellant considers the appeal should be conducted. The appellant should include in that notice or in the documents which accompany the notice of appeal all matters which the appellant intends to raise in the appeal.[1] That statement, based on the provisions of the development plan and other material considerations and setting out both the planning merits of the proposed development and relevant legal considerations; will seek to persuade the Scottish Ministers to allow the appeal or reverse of vary the planning authority's decision.[2]

1 The Town and Country Planning (Appeals) (Scotland) Regulations 2013 (SSI 2013 No 156), regs 3 and 14(3).
2 1997 Act, s 48(1).

7.26 There is a statutory prohibition against raising any matter which was not before the planning authority at the time the decision appealed against was made unless the appellant can demonstrate:

(a) that the matter could not have been raised before that time; or
(b) that it not being raised before that time was a consequence of exceptional circumstances.[1]

However, that prohibition is without prejudice to the requirement to consider development plan provisions and other material considerations.[2]

1 1997 Act, s 47A(1).
2 Ibid, s 47A(2).

Appeals and DPEA guidance

7.27 The Scottish Ministers will deal with the application as if it had been made to them in the first instance.[1] Most appeals are delegated to one of more of the Scottish Ministers' reporters for determination and the 1997 Act sets out provisions regarding the determination of appeals by a person appointed by the Scottish Ministers.[2] The Scottish Government's Directorate for Planning and Environmental Appeals has published a suite of guidance notes for reporters.[3]

1 1997 Act, s 48(1).
2 1997 Act, Sched 4.
3 Available at http://www.scotland.gov.uk/Topics/Built-Environment/planning/Appeals/howwework/guidanceforreporters

5. APPEAL/REVIEW PROCEDURES

7.28 The procedures for appeals[1] and reviews[2] are very similar. In the remainder of this section reference is made to the 'appellant' for appeal procedures and the 'applicant' for review procedures. The procedures are very detailed. We have summarised what we consider to be the key features of the procedures.

1 The Town and Country Planning (Appeals) (Scotland) Regulations 2013 (SSI 2013 No 156).

2 The Town and Country Planning (Schemes of Delegation and Local Review Procedure) (Scotland) Regulations 2013 (SSI 2013 No 157).

7.29 Both the Scottish Ministers and LRBs will seek to use the most informal process suitable for the consideration of the application for planning permission of the proposed development. However, there are potential pitfalls in using informal procedures.[1] Whatever process is selected those involved must be aware of the requirements placed upon them. For instance, the RTPI's Code of Professional Conduct[2] requires that in all their professional activities members of the Royal Town Planning Institute shall act with competence, honesty and integrity and they shall not make or subscribe to any statements or reports which are contrary to their own bona fide professional opinions. Further, an expert witness has a number of legal duties and responsibilities.[3]

1 See, eg, Watchman, J 'Informal Dispute Resolution Processes and Potential Pitfalls for Decision-makers' (2013) 156 SPEL 31.

2 Available at http://www.rtpi.org.uk/media/8590/Code-of-Professional-Conduct-Final-_2_Jan-2012.pdf

3 See, eg, Watchman, J 'An Expert's Obligations' (1996) 54 SPEL 25.

7.30 As we noted, most planning application appeals are delegated to one or more of the Scottish Ministers' reporters for determination although the Scottish Ministers could appoint an 'appointed person' who is not one of their reporters to determine an appeal. While most decision are taken by a reporter nowadays, the Scottish Ministers have the power to recall any delegated case for their decision.[1]

1 1997 Act, Sch 4, para 3(1).

7.31 The same procedures apply whether the planning application appeal is decided by the Scottish Ministers after considering a report on the planning application appeal prepared by an appointed person.[1] Similar procedures also apply to applications for planning permission which have been called-in by the Scottish Ministers for their determination.[2]

1 The Town and Country Planning (Appeals) (Scotland) Regulations 2013 (SSI 2013 No 156), reg 26.

2 The Town and Country Planning (Appeals) (Scotland) Regulations 2013 (SSI 2013 No 156), reg 24.

7.32 Electronic communications can be used for any notice, consent, agreement, decision, representation, statement report or other information or communication provided the recipient consents to receiving it electronically. Where a person uses electronic communication, that person is taken to have agreed to the use of electronic communications, unless and until the person gives notice to revoke that agreement.[1]

1 The Town and Country Planning (Appeals) (Scotland) Regulations 2013 (SSI 2013 No 156), reg 32 and The Town and Country Planning (Schemes of Delegation and Local Review Procedure) (Scotland) Regulations 2013 (SSI 2013 No 157), reg 23.

7.33 Until the appeal/review is determined, the planning authority must make available for inspection in its offices the appeal/review papers and afford any person who request the opportunity to inspect and, where practicable, takes copies of those papers.[1]

1 The Town and Country Planning (Appeals) (Scotland) Regulations 2013 (SSI 2013 No 156), reg 6 and The Town and Country Planning (Schemes of Delegation and Local Review Procedure) (Scotland) Regulations 2013 (SSI 2013 No 157), reg 11.

Notice of Appeal/Notice of Review

7.34 An appeal to the Scottish Ministers (under s 47 of the 1997 Act) and the requirement for the review of a case by a planning authority's LRB (under s 43A of the 1997 Act) is made by giving written notice to the Scottish Ministers (per Scottish Government's Directorate for Planning and Environmental Appeals) or the relevant LRB (as the case may be) within the prescribed (three-month) period.[1] A form of the notice of appeal is available from that Directorate.[2] A form of notice of review is available from the relevant planning authority. Those forms set out the particulars etc that are required to be given (including those referred to at paras 7.16 and 7.25) in the notice. It is important to remember that the Scottish Ministers or the LRB might decide to determine the appeal/review without further procedure and therefore the relevant notice and the accompany statement should fully set out the case for the appellant/applicant. An appellant is required at the same time as giving the notice of appeal to the Scottish Ministers to send to the planning authority a copy of the notice of appeal; a list of all documents, materials and evidence which the appellant intends to rely on in the appeal and a copy of all documents, materials and evidence specified on such list which the appellant has not already provided to the planning authority in connection with the application to which the appeal relates.[3] There is no equivalent requirement in the review process. Notice is given to the LRB which is a committee of the planning authority.

1 The Town and Country Planning (Appeals) (Scotland) Regulations 2013 (SSI 2013 No 156), reg 3 and The Town and Country Planning (Schemes of Delegation and Local Review Procedure) (Scotland) Regulations 2013 (SSI 2013 No 157), reg 9.

2 http://www.scotland.gov.uk/Topics/Built-Environment/planning/Appeals/appealformsguidancenotes/ppaform

3 The Town and Country Planning (Appeals) (Scotland) Regulations 2013 (SSI 2013/156), reg 4(1).

Notice to interested parties by Planning Authority/LRB

7.35 The LRB must not later than 14 days following notification of the review send an acknowledgement of the notice to the applicant and inform the applicant how the documents related to the review may be inspected.[1]

1 The Town and Country Planning (Schemes of Delegation and Local Review Procedures) (Scotland) Regulations 2013 (SSI 2013 No 157), reg 10(1)(a).

7.36 If any neighbour notification or consultation procedures on the application for planning permission have not been undertaken or completed, the Scottish Ministers or the LRB (as the case may be) must undertake or complete those procedures.[1]

1 The Town and Country Planning (Appeals) (Scotland) Regulations 2013 (SSI 2013 No 156), reg 29 and The Town and Country Planning (Schemes of Delegation and Local Review Procedures) (Scotland) Regulations 2013 (SSI 2013 No 157), reg 20.

7.37 The Scottish Ministers or the LRB (as the case may be) must not later than 14 days following notification of the appeal/review give notice to every 'interested party' (any statutory consultee from whom the planning authority received representations (which were not subsequently withdrawn) in connection with the application for planning permission and any other person from whom the planning authority received representations (which were not subsequently withdrawn) in connection with the application for planning permission, before the end of the prescribed period).[1]

1 The Town and Country Planning (Appeals) (Scotland) Regulations 2013 (SSI 2013 No 156), reg 5(1) and The Town and Country Planning (Schemes of Delegation and Local Review Procedure) (Scotland) Regulations 2013 (SSI 2013 No 157), reg 10(1)(b).

7.38 Such notice may be given by post or newspapers advertisement depending on the circumstances. The notice includes information about how further representations can be made. An interested party has 14 days from the date on which the notice is given to make representations. The Scottish Ministers/LRB must send the appellant/applicant a copy of such further representations received from interested parties and allow the appellant/applicant at least 14 days after the date on which the copy was sent to make comments on the further representations. In an appeal the Scottish Ministers also send the planning authority a copy of the further representations and give it at least 14 days to make comments on those further representations.[1]

1 The Town and Country Planning (Appeals) (Scotland) Regulations 2013 (SSI 2013 No 156), reg 5 and The Town and Country Planning (Schemes of Delegation and Local Review Procedure) (Scotland) Regulations 2013 (SSI 2013 No 157), reg 10.

7.39 In a review there is no requirement for the LRB to send a copy of the further representations to the appointed officer whose decision is the subject of a review.

Response to Appeal/Review

7.40 The planning authority must not later than 21 days beginning with the date of receipt of notification of an appeal send its response to the Scottish Ministers and the appellant. The planning authority's response must set out the matters which it considers require to be taken into account in determining the appeal and by what, if any, procedure (or combination of procedures) the planning authority wishes the appeal to be conducted. The planning authority must also provide copies of the documents not specified on the appellant's list (other than those specified on the list which were before the planning authority and which were taken into account in reaching its decision and of any 'Report of Handling' prepared in respect of the application and the planning conditions (if any) which the planning authority presently considers should be imposed if the Scottish Ministers or the appointed person, as the case may be, decide that planning permission should be granted.[1] The Scottish Ministers, or their appointed person, may take into account the planning authority's response and related documents even if these are received outwith the prescribed 21-day period.[2]

1 The Town and Country Planning (Appeals) (Scotland) Regulations 2013 (SSI 2013 No 156), reg 4(2).
2 *Greenland Developments (UK) Ltd v The Scottish Ministers* [2011] CSIH 05.

7.41 As we have noted, that is no requirement for a notice of review to be sent to the planning authority's appointed officer. The review process does not afford any opportunity to the appointed offer to submit comments about the notice of review and supporting materials to the LRB.

Counter responses from Appellant/Applicant

7.42 The appellant may, within 14 days beginning with the date of receipt of the planning authority's response, send to the Scottish

Ministers and the planning authority comments on any matters raised in the planning authority's response which had not been raised in the decision notice (if any); and any documents, materials or evidence on which the appellant intends to rely in relation to such comments.[1]

1 The Town and Country Planning (Appeals) (Scotland) Regulations 2013 (SSI 2013 No 156), reg 4(3).

7.43 As we have noted,

(a) there is no requirement to send a notice of review to the appointed officer whose decision is the subject of the review, the review process does not afford the appointed officer an opportunity to make comments on the applicant's notice for review; and

(b) the appellant/applicant must be given not less than 14 days after the date on which copy comments made by interested parties is sent by the Scottish Ministers/LRB to make comments to the Scottish Ministers/LRB about representations made by interested persons.

Determination without further procedure

7.44 In an appeal, the Scottish Ministers will appoint a person (usually one of their reporters) to determine the appeal or to provide them with a report to facilitate them determining the appeal. When the appointed person considers that no further representations are or information is required to enable the appeal to be determined, the appointed person may determine the appeal without further procedure.[1] The Scottish Executive's Directorate for Planning and Environmental Appeals has published guidance which set out examples of appeals where a reporter may consider that no further procedure is necessary.[2]

1 The Town and Country Planning (Appeals) (Scotland) Regulations 2013 (SSI 2013 No 156) reg 7.

2 Available at http://www.scotland.gov.uk/Resource/0038/00387399.pdf

7.45 If the LRB considers that the review documents provide sufficient information to enable it to determine the review, it may determine the review without further procedure.[1]

1 The Town and Country Planning (Schemes of Delegation and Local Review Procedure) (Scotland) Regulations 2013 (SSI 2013 No 157, reg 12.

Determination after further procedure

7.46 Where the appointed person decides that the appeal should be determined after further procedure that person may seek confirmation from interested parties as to whether they wish to be involved in any further procedure. If the interested party wishes to participate in any further procedure conducted in relation to the appeal that person must send a notice ('an opt-in notice') to the appointed person informing the appointed person of a wish to participate in any further procedure.[1] There is no equivalent provision in the LRB process.

1 The Town and Country Planning (Appeals) (Scotland) Regulations 2013 (SSI 2013 No 156), reg 8.

7.47 The appointed person/LRB can decide at any stage of the appeal/review that further representations should be made or further information should be made available or provided to enable the appeal/review to be determined. The appeal/review can be conducted by one or a combination of: written submissions; the holding of one or more hearing sessions; the holding of one or more inquiry sessions (in planning appeals only); and a site inspection.[1] The Scottish Government's Directorate for Planning and Environmental Appeals has published guidance which sets out relevant factors to be considered in deciding what form of further procedure is appropriate.[2]

1 The Town and Country Planning (Appeals) (Scotland) Regulations 2013 (SSI 2013 (SSI 2013 No 2013 No 156), reg 9 and The Town and Country Planning (Schemes of Delegation and Local Review Procedure) (Scotland) Regulations 2013 (SSI 2009 2013 No 157), reg 13.

2 Available at http://www.scotland.gov.uk/Topics/Built-Environment/planning/Appeals/howwework/guidanceforreporters/reportersguidancenote8

7.48 A pre-examination meeting can be held to consider the manner in which the appeal/review (or any stage of it) is to be considered.[1]

1 The Town and Country Planning (Appeals) (Scotland) Regulations 2013 (SSI 2013 No 156), reg 10 and The Town and Country Planning (Scheme of Delegations and Local Review Procedure) (Scotland) Regulations 2013 (SSI 2013 No 157), reg 14.

7.49 The appointed person/LRB initiates further procedures by giving a 'procedure notice'[1] to:

(a) in the case of an appeal both the appellant and the planning authority and any other person from whom the appointed person wishes to receive further representations or information; or
(b) in the case of a review the applicant and any other body or person from whom the LRB wishes to receive further representations or information.

Only matters set out in a procedure notice can be considered in the written submissions, hearing sessions or inquiry sessions (as the case may be).

1 'Procedure notice' is defined in the Town and Country Planning (Appeals) (Scotland) Regulations 2013 (SSI 2013 No 156), reg 2 and the Town and Country Planning (Schemes of Delegation and Local Review Procedure) (Scotland) Regulations 2013 (SSI 2013 No 157), reg 2.

Written submissions

7.50 The written submissions procedure is initiated by a procedure notice served by the appointed person/LRB. Such notices specify the matters on which further representations or information is requested and the date by which such further representations or information are to be sent to the appointed person and state the name and address of any person to whom the procedure notice is given. Any further representations made or information provided in response to the procedure notice ('the procedure notice response') are to be sent to the appointed person/LRB on or before the date specified for that purpose in the procedure notice and a copy of any procedure notice response is to be sent on or before that date to the appellant/applicant, the planning authority (in an appeal only) any other person specified in the procedure notice. They have 14 days from receipt of a copy of the procedure notice response to send comments to the appointed person/LRB in reply to the procedure notice response and must, when doing so, send a copy of such comments to any other person to whom the procedure notice was given.[1]

1 The Town and Country Planning (Appeals) (Scotland) Regulations 2013 (SSI 2013 No 156), reg 12 and The Town and Country Planning (Schemes of Delegation and Local Review Procedure) (Scotland) Regulations 2013 (SSI 2013 No 157), reg 15.

7.51 If the appointed person/LRB proposes to take into consideration any new evidence which is material to the determination of the appeal/review, the appointed person/LRB must not reach a decision on the appeal/review without affording the recipients of the procedure notice with an opportunity of making representations on such new evidence.[1]

1 The Town and Country Planning (Appeals) (Scotland) Regulations 2013 (SSI 2013 No 157), reg 13 and The Town and Country Planning (Schemes of Delegation and Local Review Procedure) (Scotland) Regulations 2013 (SSI 2013 No 157), reg 17.

7.52 A site inspection may be made in conjunction with the written submissions procedure (see below).

Hearings and the Hearing Session Rules

7.53 Of the three further procedure processes (written submissions, hearings and inquiry) it is the hearing process, which requires the appointed person/LRB to lead a discussion at the hearing and to adopt an inquisitorial approach; that is the greatest challenge. The courts have considered the role of an inspector in a hearing and have summarised the role of the inspector at a hearing as:

(a) having the responsibility to bring out such evidence as is required in order to decide the main issues that the inspector has identified;
(b) providing, if necessary, the parties with an opportunity to introduce evidence or documents or other information into the hearing which had not previously been referred to;
(c) obtaining and adducing any relevant or significant evidence;
(d) permitting, where appropriate, cross-examination of all those present or of a particular witness or witnesses or, in an extreme case, to abandon the hearing so as to allow the appeal to be determined as an inquiry; and
(e) having the overriding objective is to conduct the hearing fairly,[1] expeditiously and economically so as to determine the appeal in a single hearing lasting no more than about one day having addressed the main issues and having given the applicant and the planning authority a reasonable opportunity of explaining their respective points of view in a non-technical environment.[2]

1 See, eg *Dyason v Secretary of State for the Environment Transport and the Regions* [1998] JPL 778.

2 AZ v Secretary of State for Communities and Local Government and Another [2012] EWHC 3660 (Admin) [105] – [107].

7.54 Hearings, which may be used in both planning application appeals and reviews, are regulated by the Hearing Session Rules.[1] A summary of the key provisions of these rules is set out below.

1 The Town and Country Planning (Appeals) (Scotland) Regulations 2013 (SSI 2013 No 156), regs 2, 9(5)(b) and Sch 1 and The Town and Country Planning (Schemes of Delegation and Local Review Procedure) (Scotland) Regulations 2013 (SSI 2013 No 157), regs 2, 13(5)(b) and Sch 1.

Notice of hearing session and specified matters

7.55 Where the appointed person/LRB has determined that a hearing session should be held the appointed person/LRB is to give written notice to that effect to the appellant/applicant; the planning authority (in a planning appeal only); any interested party who made representations in relation to specified matters set out in the procedure notice; and any person who the appointed person/LRB wishes to make further representations or to provide further information on specified matters at the hearing session. The notice given by the appointed person/LRB must specify the matters to be considered at the hearing session and only specified matters are to be considered at the hearing session. A person given notice by the appointed person/LRB and who intends to appear at the hearing session must within 14 days of the date of such notice inform the appointed person/LRB in writing of that intention.

Appointment of assessor

7.56 Some hearings may involve highly technical matters and so it can be helpful for the reporter to have access to the advice of an expert on such matters, rather than rely on the (possibly conflicting) technical evidence submitted by experts acting for the parties to the appeal.

7.57 The Scottish Ministers/LRB may appoint a person to sit with the appointed person/LRB at a hearing session to advise the appointed person/LRB on such matters arising as the Scottish Ministers/LRB may specify ('an assessor'). If such an appointment is made the Scottish Ministers/LRB must notify every person entitled to appear at the hearing session of the name of the assessor and of the matters on which the assessor is to advise the appointed person/LRB. Where an assessor has been appointed, the assessor may (and if so required by the appointed person/LRB must), after the close of the hearing session make a report in writing to the appointed person/LRB in respect of the matters on which the assessor was appointed to advise.[1]

1 The Town and Country Planning (Appeals) (Scotland) Regulations 2013 (SSI 2013 No 156), reg 30 and The Town and Country Planning (Schemes of Delegation and Local Review Procedure) (Scotland) Regulations 2013 (SSI 2013 No 157), reg 21.

Appearances at hearing session

7.58 The persons entitled to appear at a hearing session are the appellant/applicant; the planning authority (in a planning appeal only) and any other person who, in response to a procedure notice, has informed the appointed person/LRB in writing within 14 days of the date of the procedure notice of their intention to appear at the hearing session. A review hearing must be held in public.[1] There is no requirement for an appeal hearing to be held in public.

1 The Town and Country Planning (Schemes of Delegation and Local Review Procedure) (Scotland) Regulations 2013 (SSI 2013 No 157), reg 7.

Date and notification of hearing session

7.59 The date, time and place at which the hearing session is to be held is to be determined (and may subsequently be varied) by the appointed person/LRB. The appointed person/LRB is to give to those persons entitled to appear at the hearing session such notice of the date, time and place fixed for the holding of a hearing session (and any subsequent variation thereof) as may appear to the appointed person/LRB to be reasonable in the circumstances.

Service of hearing statements and documents

7.60 Where required to do so by notice given by the appointed person/LRB, a person entitled to appear at the hearing session must, by such date as is specified in the notice, send to the appointed person/LRB, the appellant/applicant, the planning authority (in a planning appeal only) and to such other persons entitled to appear at the hearing session as the appointed person may specify in such notice:

(a) 'a hearing statement' (ie a written statement which fully sets out the case relating to the specified matters which a person proposes to put forward to a hearing session; a list of documents (if any) which the person putting forward such case intends to refer to or rely on; and a list of any other persons who are to speak at the hearing session in respect of such case, any matters which such persons are particularly to address and any relevant qualifications of such persons to do so); and

(b) where that person intends to refer to or rely on any documents when presenting their case a copy of every document (or the relevant part of a document) on the list of such documents comprised in that hearing statement to the appointed person/LRB and in the case of all of the others only those documents which not already available for inspection in terms of the relevant legislation.

7.61 The planning authority is, until such time as the appeal/review is determined, to afford to any person who so requests a reasonable opportunity to inspect and, where practicable, take copies of any hearing statement or other document (or any part thereof) which, or a copy of which, has been sent to the planning authority/LRB (as the case may be).

7.62 Any person who has served a hearing statement must when required by notice in writing from the appointed person/LRB provide such further information about the matters contained in the statement as the appointed person/LRB may specify; and at the same time send a copy of such further information to any other person on whom the hearing statement has been served.

Procedure at hearing

7.63 Except as otherwise provided in the Hearing Session Rules, the procedure at a hearing shall be as the appointed person/LRB determines.

7.64 Having considered any submission by the persons entitled to appear at the hearing session:

(a) the appointed person is to state at the commencement of the hearing session the procedure the appointed person proposes to adopt;
(b) the LRB is to state at or before the commencement of the hearing session the procedure which the LRB proposes to adopt and in particular are to state the order in which (i) the specified matters are to be considered at the hearing session; and (ii) the persons entitled to appear at the hearing session are to be heard in relation to a specified matter (a different order may be chosen for different specified matters).

7.65 Any person entitled to appear at the hearing may do so on that person's own behalf or be represented by another person. Where there are two or more persons having a similar interest in the issues being considered at the hearing session, the appointed person/LRB may allow one or more persons to appear on behalf of some or all of any persons so interested. The appointed person/LRB may proceed with a hearing session in the absence of any person entitled to appear at the hearing session and may need to consider an adjournment if one is unable to attend.[1]

1 *West Lancashire District Council v Secretary of State for the Environment* [1998] EGCS 33.

7.66 A hearing shall take the form of a discussion led by the appointed person/LRB. Cross-examination is not permitted except where a LRB considers that cross-examination is required to ensure a thorough examination of the issues.

7.67 A person entitled to appear at a LRB hearing session is entitled to call evidence. However, the LRB may refuse to permit the giving or production of evidence; the cross-examination of persons giving evidence; or the presentation of any other matter which the LRB considers to be irrelevant or repetitious.

7.68 The appointed person/LRB may from time to time adjourn the hearing session. If the date, time and place of the adjourned hearing session are announced before the adjournment, no further notice is required. Otherwise notice must be given of the date, time and place of the adjourned hearing session to the persons entitled to appear at the hearing session as may appear to the appointed person/LRB to be reasonable in the circumstances.

Inquiries and the Inquiry Session Rules

7.69 An inquiry, which cannot be held in a planning application review, is regulated by both the 1997 Act and the Inquiry Session Rules.[1] A summary of the key points of those rules is set out below.

1 The Town and Country Planning (Appeals) (Scotland) Regulations 2013 (SSI 2013 No 156) regs 2 and 9 and Sch 2.

7.70 In general planning inquiries must be held in public.[1] In general the appointed person may require the appearance of witnesses or the production of evidence. Further the appointed person may administer oaths and may examine witnesses on oath. The appointed person may accept in place of evidence on oath a written statement.[2]

1 1997 Act, s 265A.
2 Ibid, s 265.

Notice of inquiry session and specified matters

7.71 Where the appointed person has determined that an inquiry session is to be held the appointed person is to give written notice to that effect to the appellant; the planning authority; any interested party who made representations in relation to specified matters; and any person who the appointed person wishes to make further representations or to provide further information on specified matters at the inquiry session. The notice given by the appointed person must specify the matters to be considered at the inquiry session and only specified matters are to be considered at the inquiry session. A person given such notice by the appointed person and who intends to appear at the inquiry session must within 14 days of date of such notice inform the appointed person in writing of that intention.

Appointment of assessor

7.72 The Scottish Ministers may appoint a person to sit with the appointed person at an inquiry session to advise the appointed person on such matters arising as the Scottish Ministers may specify ('an assessor'). Where they do so they are to notify every person entitled to appear at the inquiry session of the name of the assessor and of the matters on which the assessor is to advise the appointed person. Where an assessor has been appointed, the assessor may (and if so required by the appointed person, must), after the close of the inquiry session, make a report in writing to the appointed person in respect of the matters on which the assessor was appointed to advise.

Appearances at inquiry session

7.73 The persons entitled to appear at the inquiry session are the appellant; the planning authority; and any other person who, in a response to a procedure notice, has informed the appointed person within 14 days of the date of the procedural notice of their intention to appear at the inquiry.

Date and notification of inquiry

7.74 The date, time and place for the holding of the inquiry session is to be fixed (and may subsequently be varied) by the appointed person. The appointed person is to give to those persons entitled to appear at the inquiry session such notice of the date, time and place fixed for the holding of the inquiry session (and of any subsequent variation thereof) as may appear to the appointed person to be reasonable in the circumstances.

7.75 The appointed person may require the planning authority to take one or more of the following steps:

(a) not less than 14 days before the date fixed for the holding of the inquiry session, to publish:
   (i) in one or more local newspapers circulating in the locality in which the land is situated; and
   (ii) on a website, such notices of the inquiry session as the appointed person may direct; or

(b) to serve notice of the inquiry session in such form and on such persons or classes of persons as the appointed person may specify.

Service of inquiry statements, documents and precognitions

7.76 Where required to do so by notice given by the appointed person, a person entitled to appear at the inquiry session must, by such date as is specified in the notice, send to the appointed person, the appellant and the planning authority and to such other persons entitled to appear at the hearing session as the appointed person may specify in such notice:

(a) an inquiry statement (ie a written statement which contains particulars of the case relating to the specified matters which a person proposes to put forward to an inquiry session; a list of documents (if any) which the person putting forward such case intends to refer to, rely on or put in evidence; and a list of witnesses specifying the persons who are to give, or be called to give, evidence at the inquiry session, the matters in respect of which such persons are to give evidence and the relevant qualifications of such persons to do so);
(b) in the case of the appointed person a copy of every document (or the relevant part of a document) on the list of such documents comprised in that inquiry statement and in the case of any person other than the appointed person a copy of every document (or the relevant part of a document) which is not already available for inspection; and
(c) in the case of the appointed person a precognition (ie a written statement of no more than 2,000 words (unless the appointed person agrees otherwise) of the evidence which it is proposed that a witness will give to the inquiry session in respect of any evidence to be given to the inquiry session by a person included on the list of witnesses comprised in that inquiry statement and in the case of any other person a copy of every precognition which is not already available for inspection.

7.77 The planning authority is, until such time as the appeal is determined, to afford to any person who so requests a reasonable opportunity to inspect and, where practicable, take copies of any inquiry statement, precognition or other document (or any part hereof) which, or a copy of which, has been sent to it.

Procedure at inquiry session

7.78 Except as otherwise provided in the Inquiry Session Rules, the procedure at the inquiry session shall be as the appointed person determines.

7.79 Having considered any submission by the persons entitled to appear at the inquiry session the appointed person is, to state at or before the commencement of the inquiry session the procedure which the appointed person proposes to adopt and in particular is to state:

(a) the order in which the specified matters are to be considered at the inquiry session; and
(b) the order in which the persons entitled to appear at the inquiry session are to be heard in relation to a specified matter (a different order may be chosen for different specified matters).

7.80 Any person entitled to appear may do so on that person's own behalf or be represented by another person. Where there are two or more persons having a similar interest in the matter under inquiry, the appointed person may allow one or more persons to appear for the benefit of some or all persons so interested. the appointed person may proceed with the inquiry session at the appointed person's discretion if any person entitled to appear at the inquiry session fails to do so

7.81 A person entitled to appear at the inquiry session is entitled to call evidence and to cross-examine persons giving evidence and to make closing statements. However, the appointed person may refuse to permit the giving or production of evidence; the cross-examination of persons giving evidence; or the presentation of any other matter, which the appointed person considers to be irrelevant or repetitious.

7.82 The appointed person may from time to time adjourn the inquiry session. If the date, time and place of the adjourned inquiry session are announced before the adjournment, no further notice is required. Otherwise notice of the date, time and place fixed for the holding of the inquiry session (and of any subsequent variation thereof) as may appear to the appointed person to be reasonable in the circumstances.

Site inspections

7.83 A site inspection allows the appointed person/LRB to visit and become familiar with the proposed development site and its surrounding area and to facilitate a better informed decision. Where the appointed person/LRB intends to make an unaccompanied inspection, the appointed person/LRB is to inform the appellant/applicant and the planning authority (in a planning appeal only) of such intention. Where the appointed person/LRB intends to make an accompanied inspection, the appointed person is to give such notice of the date and time of the proposed inspection as may appear to the appointed person to be reasonable in the circumstances to the appellant/applicant; the planning authority (in a planning appeal only); and any interested party. The appointed person/LRB is not bound to defer an inspection if any person to whom notice of the site inspections was given is not present at the time appointed.[1]

1 The Town and Country Planning (Appeals) Scotland) Regulations 2013 (SSI 2013 No 156), reg 12 and The Town and Country Planning (Schemes of Delegation and Local Review Procedure) (Scotland) Regulations 2013 (SSI 2013 No 157), reg 16.

7.84 Great care must be taken by the appointed person/LRB at a site inspection so as to avoid any perception of and, in turn, an accusation of bias. In *British Muslims Association v Secretary of State for the Environment* the decision was quashed because the inspector had discussions with local authority planning officials out of earshot of the appellant and in *R (on the application of Tait) v Secretary of State for the Communities and Local Government* the court held it was unlawful in that case for a pre-arranged site inspection of the enforcement notice appeal property to proceed in the absence of the appellant but in the presence of the planning authority representative.[1] An accusation of bias was also made in *Fox v Secretary of State for the Environment and Dover District Council*[2] because the inspector had lunched with local authority staff and travelled to the site with them. However, the claim of bias was rejected in this case because the appellant's approval of the inspector's travelling arrangements had been sought and given in advance. In the court held that it was unlawful for the inspector to carry out in the If the appointed person/LRB propose to take into consideration any new evidence from the site inspection, an opportunity of making representations must be given to the parties.[3]

1 (1987) P&CR 205 and [2012] EWHC 643 Admin respectively.
2 [1993] JPL 448.
3 See the following parag and, eg, *Bancon Developments Ltd v The Scottish Ministers* [2011] CSOH 137.

New Evidence

7.85 If, after the conclusion of any written submissions, hearing or inquiry (in a planning appeal only) procedure conducted the appointed person/LRB propose to take into consideration any new evidence which is material to the determination of the appeal/review, the appointed person/LRB must not reach a decision on the review without first affording the applicant, planning authority (in a planning appeal only) and any person entitled to appear at the hearing/inquiry session an opportunity of making representations on such new evidence or in the case of further written representation procedure any person to whom a procedure notice was sent.

Decision and decision notice

7.86 If it appears to the Scottish Ministers or their appointed person that the appellant is responsible for undue delay in the progress of the appeal, they may give the appellant notice that the appeal will be dismissed unless the appellant takes, within the period specified in the notice, such steps as are specified in the notice for the expedition of the appeal and if the appellant fails to comply with that notice the appeal may be dismissed.[1]

1 1997 Act, s 48(8).

7.87 An appointed person may allow or dismiss an appeal or reverse or vary any part of the decision of the planning authority.[1] Notice of the decision must be given to the applicant and the planning authority and notify every person who has made (and not subsequently withdrawn) representations in respect of the appeal that a decision on the appeal has been made and where a copy of the notice of the decision is available for inspection.[2]

1 1997 Act, s 48(1).
2 The Town and Country Planning (Appeals) (Scotland) Regulations 2013 (SSI 2013 No 156), reg 31.

7.88 A LRB may uphold, reverse or vary a determination reviewed by it.[1] It must give notice of its decision ('a decision notice') to the applicant and notify every person who has made (and not subsequently withdrawn) representations in respect of the review that a decision on the review has been made and where a copy of the decision notice is available for inspection.

1 1997 Act, s 43A(15).

7.89 A LRB decision notice must set out the matters required by s 43A(12)(a) of the 1997 Act and

(a) in the case of an application for planning permission:
  (i) include the reference number of the application;
  (ii) include a description of the location of the proposed development including, where applicable, a postal address;
  (iii) include a description of the proposed development (including identification of the plans and drawings showing the proposed development) for which planning permission has been granted, or as the case may be, refused;
  (iv) include a description of any variation made to the application in accordance with s 32A(a) of the 1997 Act;
  (v) specify any conditions to which the decision is subject;
  (vi) include a statement as to the effect of s 58(2) or s 59(4) of the Act, as the case may be, or where the planning authority have made a direction under s 58(2) or s 59(5) of the Act, give details of that direction;

(vii) if any obligation is to be entered into under s 75 of the 1997 Act in connection with the application, state where the terms of such obligation or a summary of such terms may be inspected; and

(viii) include details of the provisions of the development plan and any other material considerations to which the LRB had regard in determining the application; or

(b) in the case of an application for a consent, agreement or approval required by a condition imposed on a grant of planning permission include:

(i) a description of the matter in respect of which approval, consent or agreement has been granted or, as the case may be, refused;

(ii) the reference number of the application; and

(iii) the reference number of the application for the planning permission in respect of which the condition in question was imposed.

7.90 A LRB decision notice must in the case of refusal or approval subject to conditions be accompanied by a notification in the terms set out in Schedule 2 to the Town and Country Planning (Schemes of Delegation and Local Review Procedures) (Scotland) Regulations 2013.[1]

1 The Town and Country Planning (Schemes of Delegation and Local Review Procedure) 2013 (SSI 2013 No 157), reg 22.

7.91 Where the decision is taken by the Scottish Ministers (as opposed to one of their reporters) the appointed person will submit a report to the Scottish Ministers. That report will include findings-in-fact, reasoned conclusions and will normally include the reporter's recommendation. The Scottish Ministers are not required to adopt the terms of the report.

7.92 The decision should include reasons that are proper, intelligible and adequate. They should deal with the substantial points raised and enable the reader to know what conclusions have been reached on the principal issues and understand the basis for the decision. Decision notices should be read as a whole and not construed as if they were legislation.[1]

1 See, eg, *Hope v Secretary of State for the Environment* (1975) 31 P&CR 120 (approved in *City of Edinburgh Council v Secretary of State for Scotland* 1997 SCLR 1112 at 1127C, per Lord Clyde); *Bolton Metropolitan Borough Council v Secretary of State for the Environment* [1995] EGCS 94; *MJT Securities v Secretary of State for the Environment* (1997) P&CR 188; and *South Bucks District Council and another v Porter* [2004] UKHL 33.

7.93 The decision of the LRB, appointed person or the Scottish Ministers is final subject only to a statutory challenge to the Court of Session which can only be made on a point of law and within six weeks of the decision (see below).

6. APPEALS TO THE SCOTTISH MINISTERS: EXPENSES

7.94 Normally, the parties to an appeal are expected to meet their own expenses. Planning authorities (acting through their LRBs) are not empowered to make an award of expenses. However, the Scottish Ministers (or their appointed person) has the power to make an award of expenses in an appeal, in certain circumstances.[1] This power applies to an appeal made by written submissions as well as those conducted through a public inquiry or a hearing.[2]

1 1997 Act, s 265(9).
2 Ibid, s 266.

7.95 An award of expenses is not determined by the success or otherwise of an appeal. The key issue is whether the person against whom the claim for expenses is made has acted unreasonably. Circular 6/1990 gives detailed advice on how to claim expenses and also about matters that might be deemed unreasonable conduct. Claims should normally be made before the conclusion of the inquiry/hearing or along with the claimants final submission in written submission cases).[1] Further, the unreasonable conduct must have caused the person applying for an award of expenses to incur unnecessary expenses either because it should not have been necessary for the appeal to come before the Scottish Ministers for determination or because of the manner in which the party against whom the claim is made has conducted that party's part of the proceedings. Examples of unreasonable conduct include the planning authority refusing planning permission without having adequate planning grounds for doing so, the appellant withdrawing an appeal at a late stage or where an adjournment has been caused by unreasonable conduct of the person against whom the claim for expenses is made. It may also be deemed to be unreasonable for any party to introduce new material (eg a new ground for refusal or of appeal) at a late stage or to refuse to co-operate with procedural requirements. It is possible that an award of expenses may be made in favour of or against a third party. This would only happen in exceptional circumstances, for example if an inquiry has to be adjourned because of unreasonable conduct by the third party.[2]

1 SDD Circular 6/1990 'Awards of Expenses in Planning Appeals and Other Planning Proceedings and in Compulsory Purchase Order Inquiries', para 5.1.
2 Ibid, paras 7–10.

7.96 An award of expenses may be made in whole or part[1] and can only be challenged through judicial review.[2]

1 SDD Circular 6/1990 'Awards of Expenses in Planning Appeals and Other Planning Proceedings and in Compulsory Purchase Order Inquiries', para 15.

2 *City of Aberdeen District Council v Secretary of State for Scotland* 1993 SLT 1149 and *R v Secretary of State for the Environment ex parte Rochford District Council* [2000] 3 All ER 1018. See also paras 7.116 ff below.

7. COURT OF SESSION CHALLENGES: GENERAL

7.97 There are two main avenues for challenging planning decisions in court:

(a) a statutory application by an 'aggrieved person';[1] and
(b) an application for judicial review.[2]

In each case the application is to the Court of Session. However, statutory applications are made directly to the Inner House (ie the appeal court) although sometimes the application is remitted to the Outer House (the court of first instance). Petitions for judicial review are made initially to the Outer House. A further appeal is possible from the Outer House to the Inner House if either party is dissatisfied. There could be an ultimate appeal to the UK Supreme Court. However appeals to the UK Supreme Court should be reserved for cases raising a point of law of general public importance.[3] A petition for judicial review will normally only be entertained in cases where a statutory application is not competent; as we will see below, this does not generally include cases where a statutory application would have been competent but has been time-barred.

1 See the 1997 Act, ss 237–239; Planning (Listed Buildings and Conservation Areas) (Scotland) Act 1997, s 58; Planning (Hazardous Substances) (Scotland) Act 1997, s 19.

2 See Court of Session Rules Chapter 58 (Applications for Judicial Review) and Chapter 58A (Protective Expenses Orders in Environmental Appeals and Judicial Reviews).

3 Re appeals to the UK Supreme Court see *Uprichard v The Scottish Ministers* [2013] UKSC 21 at paras 58–63.

7.98 As we saw above, LRB reviews or appeals to the Scottish Ministers can be based on the planning merits of the case or on legal issues, or both. However, the jurisdiction of the court is confined to legal issues, a long-held principle affirmed by the House of Lords:

> '[It is] a fundamental principle of British planning law … that the courts are concerned only with the legality of the decision-making process and not with the merits of the decision. If there is one principle of planning law more firmly settled than any other, it is that matters of planning judgement are within the exclusive province of the local planning authority or the Secretary of State.'[1]

1 *Tesco Stores Ltd v Secretary of State for the Environment* [1995] 2 All ER 636 at 657, per Lord Hoffman. This passage was quoted with approval, also in the House of Lords, in the City of Edinburgh Council v Secretary of State for Scotland and Revival Properties Ltd 1997 SCLR 1112 at 1122, per Lord Clyde.

7.99 There is a limit to the usefulness of an appeal to the Court of Session. It may result in a planning decision being quashed, but the planning authority might ultimately make the same decision but on this occasion a legally sustainable decision. However, objectors may aim to gain something other than ultimate legal victory. So, for instance the media coverage generated about a court challenge may embarrass a planning authority; when the application is to be re-determined there might be a different planning (development plan and material considerations) landscape; an objector may be seeking to gain a commercial advantage by maintaining the status quo for as long as possible or the delay and expense may persuade a developer to give up on the particular project and concentrate using available resources elsewhere.

8. STATUTORY APPLICATIONS TO THE COURT OF SESSION

Scope of statutory applications

7.100 The 1997 Act allows five main categories of legal challenge by any person who is aggrieved by a development plan or by a planning decision that falls within certain specified categories. Those who qualify as 'aggrieved persons' may question the validity of:

(a) a strategic development plan or local development plan, or the alteration, repeal or replacement of such a plan;[1]
(b) a simplified planning zone scheme or an alteration of such a scheme;[2]
(c) certain orders by the Scottish Ministers or a local authority relating to the stopping up or diversion of roads or footpaths etc, the extinguishment of rights of way, or the obligations of statutory undertakers;[2]
(d) certain orders by a planning authority or the Scottish Ministers;[3] and
(e) certain actions by the Scottish Ministers (including planning appeal decisions).[4]

1 1997 Act, s 238(1).
2 Ibid, s 238(3).
3 Ibid, s 239(1)(a).
4 Ibid, s 239(1)(b); Planning (Listed Buildings and Conservation Areas) (Scotland) Act 1997, s 58(1); Planning (Hazardous Substances) (Scotland) Act 1997 s 20.

Orders that may be challenged

7.101 Head (d) above comprises the following types of order which are mostly (but not in all cases) made by a planning authority[1]:

(1) Revocation Orders or Discontinuance Orders under ss 65 or 71 respectively;[2]
(2) Tree Preservation Orders;[3]
(3) orders defining areas of special control for advertisements;[4]
(4) orders relating to the discontinuance of mineral workings;[5]
(5) orders revoking or modifying listed building consent.[6]

1 1997 Act, ss 237(2), 239(4).
2 See Chapter 11.
3 See Chapter 13, pt 1.
4 See 1997 Act, s 183(4) and Chapter 14, pt 2.
5 See 1997 Act, Sch 8 paras 1, 3, 5, 6 and Chapter 14, pt 4.
6 Planning (Listed Buildings and Conservation Areas) (Scotland) Act 1997, s 57(1); see also Chapter 12, pt 1.

7.102 Further any decision or determination (other than a deemed decision) in a review conducted by a LRB of a planning authority by virtue of s 42A(8) of the 1997 Act can be challenged in the Court of Session.[1]

1 1997 Act, ss 47(1A), 237(3A) and 239(4).

Actions by the Scottish Ministers

7.103 Head (d) above renders subject to challenge decisions by the Scottish Ministers on the following:[1]

(1) an application for planning permission for the operation of a marine fish farm, for urgent Crown development, or an application for planning permission that the Scottish Ministers called in for their determination;[2]
(2) an appeal against refusal of planning permission or the granting of permission subject to conditions;[3] also included are appeals against refusals or conditional consents, where the consent was required under the terms of a planning condition, or of a development order (eg where the planning authority's approval is required for an agricultural building erected under part 6 of the permitted development order);[4]
(3) confirmation of a completion notice (ie where a notice issued where developer has failed to complete a development);[5]
(4) an appeal against an enforcement notice or a tree enforcement notice;[6]
(5) a decision either to confirm or not to confirm a purchase notice, or other related decisions;[7]

(6) an appeal against a refusal to grant a Certificate of Lawful Use or Development (in respect of either an existing or a proposed use or development);[8]
(7) an appeal against an amenity land notice;[9]
(8) an application for consent under a Tree Preservation Order[10] or the Advertisement Regulations[11] or any direction or certificate relating to one of these;
(9) orders and decisions relating to listed buildings (including decisions by the Scottish Ministers in relation to listed building consent);[12] and
(10) A decision relating to Hazardous Substances Consent.[13]

This list only includes *actions* by the Scottish Ministers and not their *failure* to make a decision on any matter, though that may be a ground of judicial review.[14]

1 1997 Act, ss 237(3), 239(4).
2 Ibid, ss 31A, 242A and 46; see also Chapter 6, pt 7.
3 1997 Act, s 47.
4 See Chapter 5, pt 4.
5 See 1997 Act, s 62 and Chapter 6, pt 9.
6 1997 Act, s 130 and Chapter 9, pt 4 and s 169.
7 See Chapter 10, pt 2.
8 See 1997 Act, ss 150, 151, 154 and Chapter 9, pt 14.
9 See 1997 Act, ss 179, 180 and Chapter 14, pt 5.
10 See Chapter 13, pt 3.
11 See Chapter 14, pt 2.
12 Planning (Listed Buildings and Conservation Areas) (Scotland) Act 1997, s 57(1); see also Chapter 12, pt 1.
13 Planning (Hazardous Substances) (Scotland) Act 1997, ss 18–20; see also Chapter 14, pt 3.
14 1997 Act, s 237(4); Planning (Listed Buildings and Conservation Areas) (Scotland) Act 1997, s 57(3); Planning (Hazardous Substances)(Scotland) Act 1997, s 20(6). See, eg *Lafarge Redland Aggregates Ltd v The Scottish Ministers* 2000 SLT 136.

Time limits

7.104 In every case there is a six-week limit within which a statutory application must be made.[1] The relevant provisions specify in each case the date from which this time limit runs. In the case of challenges to development plans it is the date its publication.[2] In the case of orders, it is the date on which the order is confirmed, and in the case of actions by the Scottish Ministers, the date on which the action is taken.[3] These time limits must be strictly observed.

1 1997 Act, ss 238(4), 239(3); Planning (Listed Buildings and Conservation Areas)(Scotland) Act 1997, s 58(3); Planning (Hazardous Substances) (Scotland) Act 1997, s 20(1).
2 1997 Act, ss 238(5)(a), 238(5)(aa).
3 Ibid, s 239(3).

'Ouster' clause

7.105 It is expressly provided that the validity of those matters that may be the subject of a statutory application shall not otherwise be 'questioned in any legal proceedings whatsoever.'[1] The effect of this 'ouster clause' in conjunction with the six-week time limit is to require an applicant to lodge any statutory application on time; a late application under the statutory provisions will not be allowed, and in situations where it would otherwise have been competent, an alternative remedy, such as judicial review, will normally be precluded (see below).

1 1997 Act, s 237(1); Planning (Listed Buildings and Conservation Areas) (Scotland) Act 1997, s 57(1); Planning (Hazardous Substances) (Scotland) Act 1997, s 20(5).

Aggrieved Persons[1]

7.106 In contrast to the above lists which so thoroughly catalogue the subject matter involved, the legislation gives virtually no help in deciding who may qualify as an 'aggrieved person', and thus have the right to raise a statutory application. An 'aggrieved person' will obviously include the landowner or developer at the receiving end of an order or decision that is being challenged, eg where the Scottish Ministers have refused planning permission, or of a certificate of lawful use or development, or has upheld an enforcement notice. Equally obviously this right to make a statutory application is not open to absolutely any member of the public. As Lord Denning put it in a much quoted judgment:

> '[Aggrieved persons] do not include, of course, a mere busybody who is interfering in things which do not concern him: but they do include a person who has a genuine grievance because an order has been made which prejudicially affects his interests.'[2]

However, this leaves a rather broad range of potentially interested persons whom it has fallen upon the courts to identify. The trend over the years has been to move from a fairly restrictive to a more liberal interpretation of the term 'aggrieved persons'.

1 See Young, E '"Aggrieved Persons" in Planning Law' 1993 SLT (News) 43.
2 *Attorney General (Gambia) v N'Jie* [1961] AC 617 at 634, per Lord Denning.

7.107 With the possible exception of the situation of the planning authority as the aggrieved party(considered below[1]), it now seems that the 'aggrieved person' has the same meaning where a development plan is being challenged as it does in other statutory appeals.[2] It can include not only people whose property or legal rights have been affected, but anyone who has made representations to the planning authority, or has taken part in an inquiry or in an appeal by written submissions.[3] In *Times Investment Ltd v Secretary of State for the Environment*[4] the plaintiffs had purchased the property concerned after planning permission had been granted on appeal. It was held that they qualified as aggrieved persons because they were bound by a planning condition attached to the permission.

1 See para 7.110 below.
2 *MacKenzie's Trustees v Highland Regional Council* 1995 SLT 218.
3 *Strathclyde Regional Council v Secretary of State for Scotland (No 2)* 1990 SLT 149; 1990 SCLR 11; *North East Fife District Council v Secretary of State for Scotland* 1992 SLT 373; 1990 SCLR 647.
4 [1990] 3 PLR 111.

7.108 In *Mackenzie's Trustees v Highland Regional Council*[1] the pursuers, who had objected to a local plan and whose property was expressly referred to in it, qualified as aggrieved persons. In *Cumming v Secretary of State for Scotland*[2] a neighbour and business rival of a successful appellant felt aggrieved because the original planning application and press advert inadequately described the scope of the development, which posed much more of a threat to the pursuer's business than had appeared to be the case.[3] He had not made representations at the planning appeal (partly because at that time he had not known the true nature of the development), but was held to have enough of an interest to qualify as an aggrieved person. On the other hand, in *Lardner v Renfrewshire Council*[4] it was held that the pursuer was not an aggrieved person because (a) the pursuer's property was not sufficiently affected by the relevant local plan proposal and (b) the pursuer had failed to lodge objections at the proper time. The Lord President drew a contrast between the case of *Cumming*, where the failure to lodge objections resulted from misleading publicity, and Mr Lardner's circumstances, where it was not disputed that the council had followed the proper procedures regarding publicity and consultation:

> 'We do not suggest, of course, that someone who has not objected to a draft plan or taken part in an inquiry can never be "a person aggrieved". On the other hand, there is a difference between *feeling* aggrieved and *being* aggrieved: for the latter expression to be appropriate, some external basis for feeling upset is required ... some denial of or affront to his expectations or rights ... The particular circumstances of any case require to be considered and the question must always be whether the appellant can properly be said to be aggrieved by what has happened. In deciding that question it will usually be a relevant factor that, through no fault of the council, the appellant has failed to state his objection at the appropriate stage of

the procedure. … The nature of the grounds on which the appellant claims to be aggrieved may also be relevant.'[5]

1 1995 SLT 218.
2 1993 SLT 228; 1992 SCLR 831.
3 See para 6.20 above.
4 1997 SCLR 454.
5 1997 SCLR 454 at 457, per the Lord President.

7.109 The above cases show that the courts are willing to show a degree of flexibility in determining who is an 'aggrieved person', depending upon the facts of the case. In the particular circumstances of *Cumming*, failure to lodge an objection was not fatal. On the other hand, the last part of the passage quoted above seems to suggest that, even where objections *have* been made, it may not be enough to make an applicant an aggrieved person if that person's rights have not been sufficiently affected.

Planning authority as an 'aggrieved person'

7.110 In the provisions covering the challenge of planning decisions (ie heads (d) and (e) in para 7.100 above) it is made clear that a planning authority, where it is 'the authority directly concerned' with a decision can qualify as an aggrieved person.[1] This means, for example, that in cases where the Scottish Ministers have overturned a planning authority's decision to refuse planning permission, the authority can challenge the Scottish Ministers' decision on legal grounds. However, there is no parallel provision in s 238 of the 1997 Act (which deals *inter alia* with challenges to development plans). There is some doubt as to whether a challenge by a planning authority to a development plan is competent.[2]

1 1997 Act, s 239(2); Planning (Listed Buildings and Conservation Areas) (Scotland) Act 1997, s 58(2); Planning (Hazardous Substances) (Scotland) Act 1997, s 20(2).
2 *Strathclyde Regional Council v Secretary of State for Scotland* 1989 SLT 821; but see also Young, E '"Aggrieved Persons" in Planning Law' 1993 SLT (News) 43 at 47–48.

Statutory grounds of appeal

7.111 The grounds appear in several statutory provisions, depending on the nature of the challenge. There are minor variations in wording but, in essence, any statutory application must be based on one or more of the following grounds, namely that:

(a) the plan, order or decision is not within the powers of the legislation; or

(b) there has been a failure to comply with a relevant statutory requirement.[1]

Any application under head (b) will only succeed where the court is satisfied that failure to comply with the requirement has caused the applicant substantial prejudice.[2] The relevant requirements are any of those in (1) Part II of the 1997 Act and any regulations thereunder (for challenges to development plans and other appeals under s 238); (2) all of the 1997 Act (in relation to other appeals); (3) the acts relating to listed buildings, conservation areas and hazardous substances (in those cases where they apply); (4) the Tribunals and Inquiries Act 1992 (for all appeals other than those under s 238); or (5) any order, regulations or rules made under heads (2)–(4) above.[3]

1 See the 1997 Act, ss 238(1), 239(1); Planning (Listed Buildings and Conservation Areas) (Scotland) Act 1997, s 58(1); Planning (Hazardous Substances)(Scotland) Act 1997, s 20(1).
2 1997 Act, ss 238(2)(b), 239(5)(b); Planning (Listed Buildings and Conservation Areas) (Scotland) Act 1997, s 58(4)(b)(ii); Planning (Hazardous Substances) (Scotland) Act 1997, s 20(3)(b); *McMillan v Inverness-shire County Council* 1949 SC 77; 1949 SLT 77.
3 1997 Act, ss 238(1), 239(9); Planning (Listed Buildings and Conservation Areas) (Scotland) Act 1997, s 58(6); and Planning (Hazardous Substances) (Scotland) Act, s 20(4).

Judicial interpretation

7.112 The statutory grounds (and their English equivalents) have been given a broad interpretation by the courts, most notably by Lord Denning in the *Ashbridge* case[1]:

> 'The Court can only interfere on the ground that the Minister has gone outside the powers of the Act or that any requirement of the Act has not been complied with. Under this section it seems to me that the court can interfere with the Minister's decision if he has acted on no evidence; or if he has come to a conclusion to which on the evidence he could not reasonably come; or if he has given a wrong interpretation to the words of the statute; or if he has taken into consideration matters which he ought not to have taken into account, or vice versa; or has otherwise gone wrong in law.'[2]

It is generally accepted that the 'Ashbridge formula' applies in Scotland.[3]

1 *Ashbridge Investment Ltd v Minister of Housing and Local Government* [1965] 1 WLR 1320.
2 [1965] 1 WLR 1320 at 1326, per Lord Denning.
3 Wordie Property Co Ltd v Secretary of State for Scotland 1984 SLT 345.

7.113 The scope of the statutory grounds (as derived from the *Ashbridge* case and others and usefully summarised by Forbes J in *Seddon Properties v Secretary of State for the Environment*[1]) is as follows:

1. The decision maker must not act perversely, ie arrive at a conclusion that no reasonable person in his position, properly directing himself, could have reached. This is effectively the same as the *Wednesbury* principle, which applies in cases of judicial review.[2]
2. The decision maker must not take into account irrelevant material or fail to take into account that which is relevant. We have already noted this principle in relation to decisions on planning applications, ie that all material considerations must be taken into account and no account taken of considerations that are not material.[3] However, failure by the Secretary of State when giving his reasons to mention every material consideration is not necessarily fatal.[4]
3. The decision maker must abide by the statutory procedures. These include those laid down by the rules governing public inquiries, which *inter alia* require proper and adequate reasons to be given for a decision following a planning inquiry[5] and, where the Secretary of State disagrees with his reporter's recommendations, require the parties to be afforded a further opportunity to make representations.[6] The duty to give reasons probably also applies in cases where the appeal is by way of written submissions.[7]
4. The decision maker must not depart from the principles of natural justice.[8]

The effect of the court decisions has been to broaden the scope of the statutory grounds well beyond the wording of the legislation. As a result, though evolving from a different source, they in fact include all of the common law grounds available in cases of judicial review.[9]

1 (1978) 42 P&CR 26.

2 *Associated Provincial Picture Houses Ltd v Wednesbury Corporation* [1948] 1 KB 223. See also *Edwin H Bradley and Sons Ltd v Secretary of State for the Environment* (1982) 47 P&CR 374; and para 7.128 below.

3 See Chapter 6, pt 5.

4 *Bolton MBC v Secretary of State for the Environment* [1995] EGCS 94, (1995) 51 SPEL 91.

5 See para *Save Britain's Heritage v Secretary of State for the Environment and Number 1 Poultry Ltd* [1991] 1 WLR 153; *London and Midland Developments v Secretary of State for Scotland and Dawn Construction Ltd* (1996) 55 SPEL 52.

6 *Portsmouth Water plc v Secretary of State for the Environment* (1993) 66 P&CR 410.

7 *Castle Rock Housing Association Ltd v Secretary of State for Scotland* 1995 SCLR 850; see also commentary by Eric Young in (1996) 53 SPEL 7.

8 See eg *Dunfermline District Council v Secretary of State for Scotland* 1995 SCLR 813; 1996 SLT 89.

9 See Rowan-Robinson *Scottish Planning Law and Procedure* (2001) para 21.44.

Court orders including Protective Expenses Orders

7.114 If the Court of Session is satisfied that one of the statutory grounds exists, it may quash the development plan, order or action, as the case may be.[1] It may also, pending the final outcome, grant an interim order suspending its operation.[1] It may quash a development plan etc either in whole or in part, or even only insofar as it affects the property of the applicant.[2] Partial quashing is also competent in relation to tree preservation orders or orders creating areas of special control for advertisements.[3] In all other cases, the court must either quash the order or action entirely or leave it standing; it has no power to vary or amend it.[4] However, it many cases it will be merely a matter of remitting the matter back for re-determination having regard to the court's opinion and any relevant change of circumstances in the intervening period.

1 1997 Act, ss 238(2), 239(5); Planning (Listed Buildings and Conservation Areas) (Scotland) Act 1997, s 58(4); Planning (Hazardous Substances) Act 1997, s 20(3).
2 Ibid, s 238(2)(b). See, *Hallam Land Management Ltd v City of Edinburgh Council* [2011] CSOH 75.
3 Ibid, s 239(7).
4 *British Airports Authority v Secretary of State for Scotland* 1979 SC 200, 1979 SLT 197; see Chapter 6, pt 10.

7.115 The court will normally make an award of expenses against the unsuccessful party. However, the court may in its discretion restrict the award of expenses and in some cases it will do so because a Protective Expenses Order has been made. A Protective Expenses Order limits a person's liability to pay expenses.[1]

1 Eg it has been reported that the UK Supreme Court in *Uprichard v The Scottish Ministers* [2013] UKSC 21 made a Protected Costs Order. See also Court of Session Rules Chapter 58A Protective Expenses Orders in Environmental Appeals and Judicial Review.

9. APPLICATION TO THE COURT OF SESSION FOR JUDICIAL REVIEW[1]

Nature of judicial review

7.116 Judicial review is the term generally used for the supervisory jurisdiction possessed by the Court of Session at common law to ensure that inferior courts, tribunals and other bodies with limited jurisdiction act within the terms of that jurisdiction.[2] It is therefore of general application, but is relevant here because planning authorities as well as the Scottish Ministers and their reporters are included among those whose decisions are subject to this supervisory jurisdiction. It can also extend to the decisions of other bodies involved in the planning process, eg Scottish Natural Heritage, Historic Scotland or the Scottish Environment Protection Agency (SEPA).

1 On judicial review generally see Clyde and Edwards *Judicial Review* (2001); in relation to planning matters see Lord Reed 'Judicial Review', *Scottish Planning Encyclopaedia* Chapter 11.
2 *Reed*, para A.5001.

Scope of judicial review

7.117 There is one major qualification that must be made to the above generalisation. The court will not normally entertain a petition for judicial review in cases where there is an alternative (such as a statutory appeal) available.[1] As we saw above this is partly due to the 'ouster' clauses which appear in the relevant statutory provisions, stating that the subject matter of statutory appeals 'shall not be questioned in any legal proceedings whatsoever'.[2] It also derives from a general rule precluding judicial review in cases where a suitable alternative remedy is available. Judicial review is therefore something of a 'fall-back' remedy, but there remain a number of residual situations where it is available.

1 *Bellway v Strathclyde Regional Council* 1980 SLT 66 and *Howard Wallace and Another v East Lothian Council* [2012] CSOH 195. See also Court of Session Rule 58.3(2).
2 See para 7.105 above.

Decisions outwith the statutory list

7.118 Judicial review may be competent where the decision being challenged does not fall within the long list of orders or actions that may be the subject of a statutory application.[1] Since the relevant actions are all by the Scottish Ministers, this leaves actions by a planning authority, eg a decision to grant planning permission. The applicant may appeal to the Scottish Ministers against a refusal or a conditional permission, but third parties, who may have objected to the application, have no right to appeal to the minister against the *granting* of permission. They may, however, petition for judicial review provided that (1) their challenge is on legal grounds and not the planning merits of the case; and (2) they can establish a title and interest to sue.[2]

1 See paras 7.100ff above.
2 See para 7.122 below.

Challenge by another authority

7.119 It may be that one public authority wishes to challenge the decision of another, as in *Kirkcaldy District Council v Fife Regional Council and Muir Construction Ltd*[1] where a district council sought to legally challenge the regional council's decision in an application which the latter had called in. Although the regional councils no longer exist, it remains possible, for example, that one of the unitary councils may want to challenge a planning permission granted by a neighbouring council, if the development is sufficiently significant to affect the former's area.

1 (1987) 22 SPLP 78.

Failure to take action

7.120 We saw above that the Scottish Ministers' refusal or failure to take one of the actions on the statutory list was specifically excepted from the ouster provisions.[1] Judicial review is therefore available in such cases, eg where the Scottish Ministers have decided not to consider a planning application[2] or where they have refused to entertain an appeal.[3] It may also be competent in relation to their failure to take an action that is not on the statutory list, eg their failure to call in a planning application for their determination.[4] Judicial review has also been held to be competent against a planning authority because of their failure to take enforcement proceedings against an unlawful development.[5]

1 See para 7.103 above.
2 *Hunterston Development Co Ltd v Secretary of State for Scotland* 1992 SCLR 68.
3 *Adams v Secretary of State for Scotland* 1988 SLT 300.
4 *Lakin Ltd v Secretary of State for Scotland* 1988 SLT 780.
5 *Hands v Kyle and Carrick District Council* 1988 SCLR 470.

Appeals outwith the statutory time limit.

7.121 One effect of the ouster provisions relating to statutory appeals is that judicial review is not normally available in cases where a statutory appeal would have been competent except that the six-week time limit has expired. In *Pollock v Secretary of State for Scotland*[1] the petitioners sought to challenge conditions attached to a planning permission which had been granted on appeal to the Secretary of State. The planning permission related to the tipping of waste and the petitioners were owners of property adjoining the tip. They had failed to make a statutory appeal within the six-week time limit for the simple reason that they had not, as they should have, received neighbour notification of the planning application and only found out about it 11 months after the appeal decision. However, the petition for judicial review was held to be incompetent. The petitioners found themselves in a Catch 22 situation: the failure to notify them was a procedural irregularity that was only challengeable by a statutory application, but that very irregularity had been the reason for their failure to make a timeous application!

1 1992 SCLR 972, but see also *McDaid v Clydebank District Council* 1984 SLT 162.

Title and interest to sue[1]

7.122 We saw above in relation to statutory applications that only 'aggrieved persons' can properly make an application. In cases of judicial review the petitioner must have both title to sue and interest to sue (sometimes referred to as *locus standi* or standing) Although the case law on each has evolved separately, the criteria required to establish a title and interest to sue are similar to those for identifying aggrieved persons.

1 See *Reed*, paras A.5023–A.5026; Mungo Deans 'Judicial Review in Planning' (1991) SPLP 32:4.

7.123 Broadly speaking, the petitioner must show both some kind of legal right in the matter as well as a sufficient interest (not necessarily pecuniary). Both title and interest are possessed by the applicant and by the planning authority. In *Lakin Ltd v Secretary of State for Scotland*[1] the petitioners had title and interest to challenge the Secretary of State's failure to call in a rival application on the basis that they were the appellants under an ongoing appeal that related to a rival site. In *Simpson v Edinburgh Corporation*[2] a neighbouring proprietor was denied title to sue, but that was before neighbour notification was a statutory duty or neighbouring proprietors had a right to make representations to the planning authority. It now appears to be accepted that neighbours and others with a notifiable interest have both title and interest to sue. Those who have lodged objections, even if they do not have a notifiable interest, may also qualify, but probably only if they can also establish sufficient interest. In *Bondway Properties Ltd v City of Edinburgh Council and Scottish & Newcastle plc*[3] the petitioners sought to challenge the grant of planning permission to a rival developer. It was held that the possibility of the other development affecting them commercially was not enough to give them an interest to sue.

1 1988 SLT 780.
2 1960 SC 313.
3 (1998) 66 SPEL 31

7.124 In more recent times the UK Supreme Court has indicated that the time has come to move away from the test for standing being based on 'title and interest' to sue (now viewed as too restrictive) and towards a test based on interests (a person who is 'directly affected' or who has 'sufficient interest'). However the detail and the extent of this new approach is still unclear.[1]

1 *Axa General Insurance Ltd v Lord Advocate* [2011] UKSC 46.

Time limits

7.125 At the time of writing a consultation about the introduction of a three-month time limit for applications for judicial review of planning decisions and a new requirement to seek leave from the Court of Session before a judicial review can be brought (and, in turn, the introduction of a mechanism to sift out applications with limited prospects of success). However, in the interim there are considerations about when an application for judicial review can be made and whether the right to challenge a decision by judicial review is barred on the basis of a plea of 'mora, taciturnity and acquiescence'. The courts have held that it is competent to launch a challenge when a planning authority has resolved to grant planning permission.[1] However we consider that a better view is that the time limit for seeking judicial review of the grant of planning permission starts when the planning permission is granted (as opposed to the date of the resolution to grant planning permission).[2] A plea of 'mora, taciturnity and acquiescence' is essentially based on the ground that the claimant by reason of delay in raising proceedings has abandoned and is personally barred from insisting on the legal challenge made. It is recognised that, for instance, a grant of planning permission may trigger other actions such as the conclusion of a land purchase, initiating other costly technical works or the letting of a contract and so any challenge must be made promptly. Whether a plea of mora, taciturnity and acquiescence will ultimately be successful will very much depend on the facts of the case, however it has been said that plea 'is frequently doomed to failure and will only succeed in the most exceptional circumstances'.[3]

1 *Simson v Aberdeenshire Council and Others* [2007] CSIH 10.
2 *R v Hammersmith and Fulham London Borough Council ex parte Burkett* [2002] UKHL 23.
3 See, eg O'Carroll, M 'The Plea of Mora, Acquiescence and Taciturnity in Judicial Review Proceedings' (2000) 79 SPEL 56.

Grounds of judicial review[1]

7.126 There are many grounds of judicial review at common law, and we will only consider the main ones, with particular reference to a planning context. We will see that in many cases these are similar, or even identical, to the grounds of a statutory appeal, as the latter have been developed by the courts; as a result, the case law relating to statutory applications may often be relevant to cases of judicial review (and vice-versa). The grounds of judicial review can be divided into three main headings: (1) Illegality; (2) Irrationality (or '*Wednesbury* unreasonableness'); and (3) Procedural impropriety.[2] As observed above, these are not exhaustive, and there can be a degree of overlap between them.

1 *Reed*, paras A.5030ff.
2 These are the main headings adopted by Reed (see note 1 above).

Illegality

7.127 The decision maker must correctly understand and apply the law that governs the decision. The decision maker will be acting unlawfully if the decision maker exceeds powers or makes a fundamental error in law. Examples of illegality include the failure of a planning authority to determine a planning application, an *ultra vires* planning condition,[1] the failure to take into account a material consideration, or the taking into account of an irrelevant or non-material consideration.

1 See Chapter 6, pt 10.

Irrationality (or 'Wednesbury' unreasonableness)

7.128 In the leading English case of *Associated Provincial Picture Houses Ltd v Wednesbury Corporation*[1] Lord Greene coined what has come to be known as the 'Wednesbury principle', namely that bodies exercising a discretionary administrative power conferred by Parliament have an overriding duty to exercise that discretion in a reasonable fashion. A court can therefore quash an administrative decision that is 'so unreasonable that no reasonable authority could ever have come to it.' The case did not relate to planning but the principle, which applies to administrative decisions generally, does apply in planning law and, as we noted above, it is considered to be identical to the '*Ashbridge* formula' used in statutory appeals.[2]

1 [1948] 1 KB 223.
2 See para 7.112 above.

7.129 Although the '*Wednesbury*' principle is recognised in Scotland, the Court of Session has been slow to acknowledge cases where it is applicable.[1] However, in *James Aitken & Sons (Meat Producers) Ltd v City of Edinburgh District Council*[2] a developer appealed against a deemed refusal of planning permission and, before the appeal was determined, submitted an amended application which the planning authority approved. It was held that the planning authority had acted unreasonably in approving the amended application while the appeal was still pending, as the outcome of the latter was material to the amended application.

1 See *Reed*, paras A.5034–A.5038.
2 1990 SLT 241; see also *Trusthouse Forte(UK) Ltd v Perth and Kinross District Council* 1990 SLT 737 and para 6.28 above.

Procedural Impropriety[1]

7.130 This includes not only a decision maker's failure to observe a statutory procedure but also, more generally, any failure to observe the rules of natural justice; the latter includes the duty not to show bias and the duty to act fairly[2], including giving interested parties a fair hearing; as a result, not only must the applicant be fairly dealt with, but objectors must be given a fair opportunity to make representations.[3]

1 See *Reed*, paras A.5042–A.5050.
2 See *Lakin Ltd v Secretary of State for Scotland* 1988 SLT 780; but see also *Asda Stores Ltd v Secretary of State for Scotland* 1997 SCLR 661.
3 *Lochore v Moray District Council* 1992 SLT 16; *Henderson v Cumnock and Doon Valley District Council* 1992 SCLR 489; but see also *Watson v Renfrew District Council* 1995 SCLR 82.

Court orders including Protective Expenses Orders

7.131 The court has within its power the full range of civil remedies normally available to the Court of Session. It may *inter alia* quash any decision that is being challenged and also, where appropriate, grant an interdict, or make a financial award such as damages.[1] When the court finds that eg the planning authority has acted unlawfully it still has discretion whether to quash the decision. So even after establishing that the planning authority has acted unlawfully in granting a planning permission, the court may decline to quash the planning permission.[2]

1 Court of Session Rules, Chapter 58 Applications for Judicial Review.
2 See, eg *R (on the application of Burridge) v Breckland District Council* [2013] EWCA Civ 228.

7.132 The court can also make a Protective Expenses Order limiting the liability of an individual or non-governmental organisation promoting environmental protection for another person's court expenses where the court is satisfied that the proceedings are prohibitively expensive for that individual etc.[1] The courts have also made and refused to make protective expenses orders at common law.[2]

1 Court of Session Rules, Chapter 58A Protective Expenses Orders in Environmental Appeals and Judicial Reviews.
2 See, eg *McGinty, Petitioner* [2010] CSOH 5 and *Newton Mearns Residents Flood Prevention Group for Cheviot Drive, Petitioners* [2013] CSIH 70 and [2013] CSOH 68.

10. OTHER TYPES OF CHALLENGE

7.133 There are a number of other methods of challenge which may be relevant. However, whether a person will resort to using those methods will normally depend on matters such as cost and the potential outcome(s) of the challenge.

Defence to a criminal prosecution

7.134 There are a number of breaches of planning control that can result in a criminal prosecution, eg breach of an enforcement notice or of listed building control. It is sometimes a competent defence to dispute the legality of the proceedings, though in *R v Wicks*[1] it was held that the validity of an enforcement notice could not be challenged at a prosecution for its breach; however, the validity of breach of condition notices or stop notices *can* be challenged in this way, the reason being that in these cases there is no right of appeal to the Secretary of State, as there is with enforcement notices.[2]

1 [1997] 2 All ER 81; see also paras 9.28 and 9.29 below.
2 See para 9.29 below.

Negligence by planning authority

7.135 There has in the past been some doubt as to whether planning authorities can be liable for negligence in the exercise of their statutory functions. The most recent opinion seems to be that they cannot, since it would be against public policy for them to incur such liability when performing duties that were for the benefit of the public as a whole.[1]

1 See *Ryeford Homes v Sevenoaks District Council* [1990] JPL 36, and commentary thereon by Colin Crawford (1989) 27 SPLP 54; see also Mungo Deans *Scots Public Law* (1995) pp 177–181; *Tidman v Reading BC* [1994] EGCS 180, (1994) Times, 10 November, *Chung Tak Lam v Brennan* [1997] PIQR P488 and *Kane v New Forest District Council* [2001] 3 All ER 914.

Standards Commission for Scotland

7.136 A complaint that a councillor has breached the Standards Commission for Scotland's Councillors Code of Conduct or a member of a public body has breached that body's Code of Conduct for Members[1] should be made to the Public Standards Commissioner.[2] The Public Standards Commissioner investigates complaints and refers cases to the Standards Commission for Scotland. The Standards Commission considers whether there has been a breach of the relevant Code of Conduct and what sanction, if any, should be imposed for a breach of the relevant Code of Conduct. The Standards Commission for Scotland has, for instance, disqualified, suspended and censured councillors for their conduct in relation to planning matters.[3]

1 Codes (including those for the national park authorities) available at http://www.standardscommissionscotland.org.uk/content/which-bodies-have-codes
2 See http://www.publicstandardscommissioner.org.uk/
3 See, for instance, McFadden, J 'Standards Commissioner Disqualifies Councillor' (2010) 140 SPEL 85 and (2012) 150 SPEL 37. Standards Commission for Scotland decisions available at http://www.standardscommissionscotland.org.uk/advanced_search

Royal Town Planning Institute

7.137 A complaint may be made against a member of the Royal Town Planning Institute.[1] RTPI members must observe the RTPI Code of Professional Conduct.[2] That code includes requirements about RTPI members acting with competence, honesty and integrity; discharging their duties with due care and diligence and not making or subscribing to any statements or reports which are contrary to their own bona fide professional opinions.

1 Available at http://www.rtpi.org.uk/membership/professional-standards/how-to-make-a-complaint-about-rtpi-members/
2 Available at http://www.rtpi.org.uk/media/8590/Code-of-Professional-Conduct-Final-_2_Jan-2012.pdf.

Scottish Public Services Ombudsman

7.138 If a person is still dissatisfied after exhausting the complaint processes of the Scottish Government, the council or the national park authority (as the case may be) a complaint about maladministration can be made to the Scottish Public Services Ombudsman.[1] This includes, though it is not confined to, complaints relating to the exercise of planning powers. The SPSO will issue a 'Decision Report' or an 'Investigation Report' on the complaint. Any recommendation of the SPSO is not legally enforceable. However, it may be acted upon by the authority concerned.

The SPSO has published a number of information leaflets for the public.[2] These include leaflets about how to complain[3] and specific leaflets for both applicants for planning permission[4] and objectors to applications for planning permission.[5]

1 See generally Logie and Watchman The Local Ombudsman (1990).
2 Available at http://www.spso.org.uk/online-leaflets/leaflets-for-the-public.
3 Available at http://www.spso.org.uk/how-complain.
4 Available at http://www.spso.org.uk/files/webfm/Publications/Leaflets/Planning%20Leaflet%20(applicants)%20Sept%2009.pdf.
5 Available at http://www.spso.org.uk/files/Planning%20leaflet%20(objectors)%20Sept%2009.pdf.

Chapter 8

Planning obligations and good neighbour agreements

1. INTRODUCTION[1]

8.1 We saw in Chapter 6 that planning approval for a proposed development can be sought either by an application for a planning permission, or in two stages, by first applying for a planning permission in principle and then seeking approval of matters specified in conditions imposed in the related planning permission in principle. It is unlikely, however, particularly in the case of larger developments; that these formal steps will be the only matters discussed between the would-be developer and the planning authority and which will be considered by that authority in considering whether to grant the relevant planning application. A developer will want to ascertain from the planning authority, where possible, during pre-application discussion what might be acceptable to it regarding related infrastructure (education, roads etc) provision. There are likely to be preliminary consultations, or even negotiations, about infrastructure provision especially the details of infrastructure contributions (which ought to have been foreshadowed by the development plan and related supplementary guidance). Frequently the outcome of those discussions will lead to an agreement setting out matters including payment for, or contributions to, the cost of development related infrastructure.

1 See Rowan-Robinson & Young *Planning by Agreement in Scotland* (1989); Rowan-Robinson & Durman *Section 50 Agreements* (1992); *The Use and Effectiveness of Planning Agreements* (Scottish Executive, 2001); *Planning Agreements and Positive Planning for Sustainable Communities in Scotland* (Scottish Executive, 2005) and *An Assessment of the Value of Planning Agreements in Scotland* (Scottish Executive, 2008).

8.2 Section 75 of the Town and Country Planning (Scotland) Act 1997 recognises this. It does so by providing that planning obligations (including a unilateral obligation by any person in favour of a planning authority) may restrict or regulate the development or use of land; include provisions about the payment of money; and also include incidental and consequential provisions that the planning authority considers are necessary or expedient for the purposes of the planning obligation.

A planning obligation does not need to be linked with an application for planning permission. However in practice it nearly always is.

8.3 Planning agreements (known as Section 75 agreements, and formerly as Section 50 agreements under the Town and Country Planning (Scotland) Act 1972) are a special type of contract between planning authorities and landowners. Planning authorities can enter into agreements under other legislation (eg councils under the general powers given by the Local Government (Scotland) Act 1973, s 69)[1] but a notable feature of planning (including unilateral) obligations is that they may be recorded in the General Register of Sasines or registered in the Land Register of Scotland, and such recording or registration (as the case may be) makes them binding on successors in title and others (including, possibly, former landowners).[2] In other words, a planning obligation can be made to 'run with the land' and in turn remain enforceable at the instance of the planning authority, and, in general, not only against the owner who gave the obligation, but also against others including subsequent owners of the property. Further the authority can, after giving due notice, enter the planning obligation land, carry out the operations set out in the planning obligation and seek to recover any expense reasonably incurred in carrying out the operations.[3]

1 See SG Circular 3/2012 'Planning Obligations and Good Neighbour Agreements' and, in particular, para 15 for more details.
2 1997 Act, s 75(5) and s 75C.
3 Ibid, s 75(7) and s 75(8). See also para 8.21 below.

8.4 A planning obligation agreement is usually negotiated while the planning application is being considered (especially after a planning authority has resolved to grant planning permission subject to the conclusion of an agreement or agreements addressing specified matters) and frequently will have to be concluded and recorded or registered (as the case may be) before the planning authority grants planning permission. Alternatively a planning agreement may provide that the (recorded or registered) agreement does not come into force until the planning permission is granted or until a specified 'material operation' begins to be carried out. In addition to the planning agreement provisions there will normally also be a conditional planning permission. In some instances, particularly in the past, planning authorities may have taken a 'belt and braces' approach by imposing planning conditions which duplicate planning agreement provisions.[1] This is contrary to government policy, which includes a 'sequential test of necessity', that is that planning authorities should consider where the relevant issue can be resolved by using a planning condition, then if not by a statutory agreement (eg an agreement under the Local Government in

Scotland Act 2003, s 20) and then, as an option of last resort, a planning obligation.[2]

1 Rowan-Robinson and Durman *Section 50 Agreements* (1992).
2 SG Circular 3/2012 'Planning Obligations and Good Neighbour Agreements' para 15; see also paras 8.29–8.31 below. On the lawfulness of planning conditions, see Chapter 6, part 10.

8.5 The use of planning agreements and other agreements has increased over the years, especially because of restrictions on local government finance and, in turn, a desire to transfer infrastructure provision costs from the state to what is perceived to be 'the developer' (which in this context means the landowner, the developer, the occupier of the development or a combination of them). These restrictions give local authorities an incentive to find alternative ways of funding infrastructure, and, as we shall see below, a planning agreement can offer the possibility of securing a financial contribution from a developer.

Advantages to the planning authority

8.6 Planning obligations are attractive to a planning authority because they can be used in place of a condition imposed on a planning permission where the subject matter involved would (or might) make the condition *ultra vires*.[1] They can also be used by the planning authority to achieve *planning gain*, extra features within the development (or elsewhere) which the developer, left to its own commercially-oriented devices, might not have provided.

1 See para 8.7 below and Chapter 6, pt 10 above.

Advantages to the developer

8.7 From the developer's perspective, the use of planning obligations (including planning agreements) can add speed and certainty to achieving the aim of obtaining planning permission. The use of a planning obligation may persuade a planning authority to grant planning permission and, in turn, the applicant is spared from having to go through a time consuming and expensive planning appeal process with no guarantee that the Scottish Ministers will grant the application for planning permission. The provisions of the relevant planning obligation (which may be wider in scope than planning conditions) might persuade a planning authority to grant permission for a development which might otherwise be refused. A planning obligation might provide for desirable, as opposed to essential, infrastructure. Occasionally, developers may also see planning agreements as affording an opportunity to secure planning permission for an otherwise unacceptable development (perhaps because it is in green belt) by offering new community facilities or community trust funds which while desirable do not directly serve a planning purpose. Where the proposed development does not, for instance, create the need for particular facilities or particular requirements, what is being offered goes beyond what is required to mitigate the impacts of the proposed development and such benefits are sometimes referred to as 'planning gain'.

8.8 Many consider that planning obligations are controversial, and some of the reasons for this will be touched upon in the course of the chapter. Their increasing popularity in recent years has not entirely found favour in certain quarters, particularly with central government which (understandably) has reservations about the ways in which some types of planning obligation make onerous requirements of landowners in particular but also possibly developers or the purchasers/occupiers of new developments through 'planning gain'. They have also attracted the interest of the Nolan Committee.[1] We shall examine these concerns later in this chapter.

1 *Third Report of the Committee on Standards in Public Life: Standards of conduct in Local Government in England, Scotland and Wales* (Cm 3702–1) (1997).

2. PROCEDURAL MATTERS

The parties to a planning obligation

8.9 Any person may grant a unilateral planning obligation in favour of a planning authority. Such unilateral planning obligations may be useful where no planning authority obligation is required, for instance where no planning authority obligation is required (eg where the owner wishes to restrict use of the land) or as one of the documents submitted a as part of a planning application and. possibly, a planning appeal document. However, great care should be taken in drafting and considering a unilateral planning obligation.[1]

1 See, for instance, *R (on the application of Millgate Development Ltd) v Wokingham Borough Council* [2011] EWCA Civ 1062 and *Hertfordshire County Council and Another v Secretary of State for Communities and Local Government and Others* [2011] EWHC 1572 (Admin).

8.10 More commonly, the two main parties to a planning obligation are the planning authority and the owner of the relevant land.

8.11 However, other potential parties have to be considered in light of the relevant statutory provisions. A planning obligation to which the 'owner' is a party may be recorded in the General Register of Sasines or registered in the Land Register of Scotland and such recording or registration (as the case may be) makes the obligations enforceable against the owner in all cases. A planning obligation may in certain circumstances be enforceable against others, including a tenant or other person having use of the land in respect of any planning obligation requirement other than an obligation which requires: payment of money; operations or activities to be carried out; or land to be used in a specified way. So where a tenant or a licensee should be a party to a planning obligation should also be considered. Further, consideration should be given to whether others such as any heritable creditor or a key agency such as Scottish Natural Heritage should be a party to the planning obligation.

Planning authority

8.12 Planning authority means the planning authority but in this case not the Scottish Ministers. The Scottish Ministers are not empowered to enter into planning agreements. So while one of the Scottish Ministers' reporters may be prepared to grant planning permission subject to a planning agreement being entered into, that reporter has no power to require this. In order to get round the problem the reporter may issue a 'Notice of Intention' to grant planning permission following the recording or registering (as the case may be) of a planning obligation which addresses specified matters (such as affordable housing and transportation contributions). Provided that terms can be agreed with the local authority, the formal decision letter is issued once the agreement is recorded or registered. Problems can arise if an agreement is not concluded. There may be an informal suggestion by the reporter that planning permission will be granted without an agreement and for instance a conditional planning permission including a 'Grampian' condition will resolve the difficulty of a failure to conclude an agreement.[1] Alternatively the solution to this problem might be for the landowner to enter into an obligation unilaterally, the terms of which are then enforceable at the instance of the local planning authority.

1 Rowan-Robinson & Young *Planning by Agreement in Scotland*. See, for instance, DPEA appeal ref. P/PPA/200/242 where 'Grampian' planning conditions requiring payments of money and conclusion of specified agreements (for a replacement sports centre and the provision of affordable housing) were imposed. See also part 5 below.

The owner and any other person

8.13 Where the owner is party to a planning obligation, it can be recorded in the General Register of Sasines or registered in the Land Register of Scotland and upon such recording or registration (as the case may be) the statutory enforcement provisions apply. 'Owner' is defined as a person who has right to the land to which the planning obligation relates (whether or not that person has completed title) and includes a heritable creditor in lawful possession of that land. It is also possible for other persons or bodies to be parties to the planning obligation, for example, a lessee under an unrecorded lease, the superior, a person having the benefit of a servitude or a body such as Scottish Natural Heritage (where the planning obligation relates to the conservation, management or monitoring of the effects of the development on the natural heritage).[1]

1 See SODD Circular 12/1996 'Town and Country Planning (Scotland) Act 1972 Planning Agreements', Annex 2 para 7.

Procedural issues

Application by non-owner

8.14 The need for the owner to be a party to a planning agreement can present difficulties in the common situation where a developer has submitted a planning application before becoming the heritable proprietor, eg where missives have been concluded conditional upon the obtaining of planning permission. This can be resolved if the existing owner is willing to enter into the agreement. The landowner may be required to enter into a planning agreement in terms of a contract with a developer or the landowner might consider that its interests are best served by entering into the agreement to secure an increase in the value of land arising from the grant of planning permission. In cases where the owner has agreed to become a party to a planning agreement, research has shown that it is common for the prospective developer also to be a party.[1] However, if the current owner is unwilling to be a party to the agreement a stalemate may occur. The developer may be unwilling to complete the purchase without planning permission, but will be unable to enter a planning agreement until he becomes owner. On the other hand, the planning authority may be unwilling to grant permission without such an agreement.

1 *Rowan-Robinson & Durman*, paras 14–9.

8.15 In some cases this difficulty can be resolved if the planning authority can properly grant planning permission subject to a type of planning condition known as a 'Grampian' condition.[1] Where this is not appropriate, the most straightforward solution is for the planning authority to pass the necessary resolution for the granting of planning permission, but to delay issuing its decision until the planning agreement has been recorded. This protects the planning authority's position since planning permission is only effective from the date of its decision letter.

In such a case the developer can take comfort from the minuted planning authority resolution that it is minded to grant planning permission. However, the delay in obtaining planning permission can be risky for the developer since, as we will see below, a planning authority is entitled to change its mind in the interim.

1 See part 5 below.

Other causes of delay

8.16 As well as the difficulties discussed above, there are other ways in which the decision to enter a planning obligation can prolong the process of obtaining planning permission. For example, planning authorities will carry out considerable research into the title of a property before entering into a planning agreement. This is in order to be sure not only of the position regarding ownership, but also to check that other relevant legal interests (eg those of lessees, heritable creditors, or servitude holders) are taken into account. Research has indicated that negotiating a planning agreement is likely to add anything up to six months to the time taken to get a decision, and that delays of over ten months are not uncommon.[1] Some planning authorities have planning policies in place about conclusion of planning agreements within a specified period. Recent government advice has suggested ways of speeding up the process.[2]

1 *Rowan-Robinson & Durman*, p 60.
2 SG Circular 3/2012 'Planning Obligations and Good Neighbour Agreements', paras 28 – 43; see also para 8.24 below.

Dangers to developer

8.17 As we indicated above, such delays in obtaining planning permission can present serious risks for the developer. There is no guarantee that planning permission will eventually be issued, even after the planning obligation has been signed. This is because there is a general legal principle that a planning authority must not fetter its exercise of discretionary powers. In other words; a planning obligation cannot be used to bind a planning authority to grant planning permission. Nor can it prevent a planning authority from exercising any other planning powers, even where such an exercise may be inconsistent with the proposed development. In *Windsor and Maidenhead Royal Borough Council v Brandrose Investments Limited*,[1] a developer and the local planning authority had entered into a planning agreement under which the developer would demolish a number of buildings prior to redevelopment, and this was followed by a grant of planning permission. However, before the developer began demolition, the council also decided to designate the locality within which the site lay as a conservation area. As a result, it became necessary for the developer to obtain conservation area consent for the demolition, and when demolition work began without that consent the planning authority sought an injunction to halt the work. The Court of Appeal held that the planning agreement could not fetter the authority's power to designate a conservation area, even if an effect of this would be to frustrate that agreement.

1 [1983] 1 WLR 509.

8.18 Where delays have occurred, a further danger can arise from the council's obligation, before finally granting planning permission, to take into account any new material considerations that might have arisen. In *John G Russell (Transport) Ltd v Strathkelvin District Council*[1] a considerable period of time elapsed before the terms of a planning agreement were concluded. In the meantime, a number of material circumstances had changed which led the council to take the view that it could not grant permission for the proposed development. Supporting the council's position, Lord Cullen said that this case demonstrated the perils inherent in a situation where planning agreement negotiations extend over a considerable period of time.

1 1992 SLT 1001.

8.19 Another potential stalemate could result where a planning authority refuses to grant planning permission without a planning agreement and the applicant is not prepared to enter into one. Here the remedy is for the applicant to appeal to the Scottish Ministers on the basis of a deemed refusal of the application provided it is competent for the applicant to do so.[1]

1 See *Vattenfall Wind Power Ltd v The Scottish Ministers* [2009] CSIH 27.

Sale to third party

8.20 We saw above[1] that recording (or registration) of a planning obligation has the effect of making its terms binding, upon the owner and others. However, a planning obligation cannot be enforced against a 'third party who has acquired right to the land (whether or not that person has completed title)' prior to the planning obligation being recorded or registered.'[2] Such a situation could arise where missives were concluded for the sale of the land to a third party before the planning obligation was recorded or registered.

1 See para 8.3 above.
2 1997 Act, s 75(6).

Enforcement

8.21 In addition to the statutory rights of enforcement referred to in para 8.3 above, a planning authority may enforce a planning obligation at common law. Planning obligations, like any other undertaking or contract, may be enforced by the usual common law remedies for breach of contract, particularly interdict or specific implement. This has the advantage of providing the planning authority with an alternative enforcement mechanism (although, interdict is now available as part of an authority's normal enforcement powers).[1] Research has shown[2] that many planning agreements build in other remedies, eg the authority having the right to withdraw planning permission without compensation or land ownership being transferred to the council on default. (It is doubtful, however, whether the latter remedy would be enforced in court.) A planning obligation will remain valid and enforceable even if a new planning permission, which is not tied to a planning obligation, is later granted for the same development. If carrying out the development would conflict with the terms of an existing planning obligation, the fact that planning permission has been granted for that development does not overcome the problem.[3] Furthermore, a developer cannot get out of an a planning obligation by allowing a planning permission to lapse, if another part of the development has been implemented.[4]

1 See Chapter 9, pt 7.

2 *Rowan-Robinson & Durman*, para 17–1.

3 *R v Tunbridge Wells BC, ex p Blue Boys Developments Ltd* [1990] 1 PLR 55, *R v Secretary of State for the Environment and Brixton Estates, ex p Ealing Borough Council* [1993] NPC 10.

4 *Hertsmere Borough Council v Brent Walker Group* [1994] 1 PLR 1.

Modification and discharge of planning obligation

8.22 There might be various reasons why modification or termination of an agreement would be desirable. New development in an area may make it redundant, or there may be a change in local plan policy. An appeal to the Lands Tribunal for Scotland, for example, is not possible because planning obligations do not fall within the definition of a 'land obligation' in terms of the Conveyancing and Feudal Reform (Scotland) Act 1970.[1] Also, it was held in *McIntosh v Aberdeen Council*[2] that it was not competent for a developer to petition for judicial review in order to obtain the discharge of a planning agreement to which he was a party. By signing the agreement Mr McIntosh had consented to any element in it that might have been *ultra vires* on the part of the planning authority, and in any case by implementing and acting upon the agreement he had waived any objection he might have had. Third parties might apply for a judicial review of a planning authority decision to enter into an agreement or a decision by a planning authority based on the planning obligation. Grounds of challenge include that a planning authority has exceeded the powers specified in s 75 of the 1997 Act or that the authority has acted unreasonably. For instance in *R v South Holland District Council, ex. p. Lincoln Co-operative Society Ltd*[3] the court quashed the council's decision to grant planning permission because the planning obligation which underpinned the decision to grant planning permission was *Wednesbury* unreasonable.

1 Section 1(2).
2 1998 SCLR 435; see also comment in (1998) 67 SPEL 56.
3 [2000] EWHC Admin 419.

8.23 Applications for modification or discharge of a planning obligation (including pre-1 February 2011 planning agreements) may be made to the planning authority and an appeal may be made within three months to the Scottish Ministers of either the authority failing to give its decision within the two month period allowed or if the authority does not decide that the planning obligation is discharged or is to have effect subject to the modification specified in the application.[1] Relevant Government guidance about the determination of an application for modification or discharge of a planning obligation (including considering any change in circumstances since the obligation was entered into and the five planning obligation policy tests referred to below) and related appeals to the Scottish Ministers has to be taken into account.[2] The planning authority's decision to discharge or modify a planning obligation does not take effect until the relevant determination notice has been recorded in the General Register of Sasines of registered in the Land Register of Scotland (as the case may be).

1 1997 Act, s 75A and s 75B; The Town and Country Planning (Modification and Discharge of Planning Obligations) (Scotland) Regulations 2010 (SSI 2010 No. 432) and The Planning etc. (Scotland) Act 2006 (Saving and Transitional Provisions) Amendment Order 2011 (SSI 2011 No. 348).
2 SG Circular 3/2012 'Planning Obligations and Good Neighbour Agreements' at paras 70 – 75 and 76 – 81 respectively. See also Watchman, J 'Planning Obligations Appeal Decisions' (2013) 156 SPEL 36.

Government advice about planning agreement provisions

8.24 SODD Circular 12/1996: *Town and Country Planning (Scotland) Act 1972 Planning Agreements* gave advice on the negotiation and conclusion of planning agreements, as well as detailed advice to solicitors on their drafting.[1] However, that advice will now have to be considered in light of the different, current, regulatory regime. While that guidance seemed to be primarily aimed at planning authority solicitors, its advice was also useful to those representing an applicant for planning permission. It suggested, for example, that arbitration provisions should be included, as well as a mechanism for the review and variation of the agreement. In terms of enforcement, it recommended that consideration be given to the inclusion of provisions dealing with breach of the agreement by any of the parties, including the possibility of the council taking direct action to implement obligations and recovering its costs.[2] Provision should also be made for entry and inspection of the relevant land by the council. How obligations will be allocated in the event of future subdivision of the property may also need to be addressed. Once the agreement is signed by the applicant (and by any other parties involved) it should be signed as quickly as possible by the planning authority and sent to the General Register of Sasines (or the Land Register of Scotland, as the case may be). The grant of planning permission should normally be dated and issued after receipt of the Keeper's acknowledgement. It is also suggested that in urgent cases planning permission could be issued on receipt of the executed agreement from the applicant's solicitors. However, this involves the risk of the land being sold before the agreement is recorded or registered in which case, as we saw above,[3] the planning authority may not be able to enforce the agreement against the new owner. The circular suggested that it is up to the planning authority to judge the extent of this risk for itself.

1 SODD Circular 12/1996 'Town and Country Planning (Scotland) Act 1972 Planning Agreements', Annex 2.
2 See para 9.66 below.
3 See para 8.20.

3. SCOPE OF AGREEMENTS

8.25 Given that planning agreements derive from planning legislation, it is clear that they must be confined to a planning purpose and not ulterior matters.[1] However, as a planning purpose encompasses any purpose related to the use and development of land, this can be interpreted very widely. The content of agreement is also subject to the test of *Wednesbury* reasonableness.[2] In other words they must not be irrational, imposed for an improper motive or involve bad faith. Beyond this, there has been some debate about just exactly what agreements may, or may not, be used for. This was due, in part, to the previous wording used in s 75 to define what the purpose and scope of agreements may be:

'...for the purpose of restricting or regulating the development or use of the land, either permanently or during such period as may be prescribed by the agreement.'[3]

'Any such agreement may include such incidental and consequential provisions (including financial ones) as appear to the planning authority to be necessary or expedient for the purposes of the agreement.'[4]

Clearly, the words used leave some scope for interpretation.

1 *R v Gillingham Borough Council, ex p F Parham Ltd* [1988] JPL 336.
2 *Associated Provincial Picture Houses Ltd v Wednesbury Corporation* [1948] 1 KB 223; see Chapter 7.
3 1997 Act, s 75(1).
4 Ibid, s 75(2).

8.26 The current s 75 replaced planning agreements with the broader concept of planning obligations which, like before, can derive from a bilateral planning agreement, but can also take the form of a unilateral undertaking in favour of a planning authority. It states that planning obligations may restrict or regulate the development or use of the land, either permanently or during such period as may be specified in the planning obligation and without prejudice to that provision, may:

(a) require specified operations or activities to be carried out;
(b) require the land to be used in any specified way;
(c) require a sum or sums of money to be paid; and
(d) contain such incidental and consequential provisions as appear to be necessary of expedient

8.27 In fact, this much more specific wording still leaves doubts about the scope of obligations, as we will see later in this chapter. Returning to the legislation, the words 'restricting' and 'regulating' which appear in s 75(1) might suggest that agreements should primarily involve negative obligations, aimed at controlling the development and use of land. However, it was widely accepted before the recent change in the relevant legislation that positive obligations can also be entered into, provided that the primary purpose of such obligations is to regulate the use and development of land.[1]

1 See Young & Rowan Robinson *Scottish Planning Law and Procedure* (1985) p 282 and SODD Circular 12/1996 'Town and Country Planning (Scotland) Act 1972 Planning Agreements'.

8.28 There is a significant difference between the government's policy on the use of planning obligations[1] and the extent of their lawful use as defined by the courts. The courts have recognised that as a mater of law planning obligations agreements need not be proportionate to the impacts of the proposed development despite the fact that current government policy statements were issued following (and taking into account) the court decisions. It should also be noted that there is very little Scottish authority on this issue, and that the English cases should as usual be treated with some caution.

1 SG Circular 3/2012 'Planning Obligations and Good Neighbour Agreements', ODPM Circular 05/05: 'Planning Obligations'.

Government policy

8.29 The government's view is that planning obligations have a 'limited but useful role to play in the development management process' and it has indicated that a planning obligation is only necessary where successors in title need to be bound by the planning obligation (eg where phased contributions to infrastructure are required) and that the need for a planning obligation should be foreshadowed in the development plan.[1] The use of planning obligations should be an option of last resort. A planning obligation should only be used where a planning permission cannot be granted without some restriction or regulation, and before deciding to seek a planning obligation, a planning authority should apply what might be called a 'sequential test of necessity'. Planning obligations should only be used when an appropriate restriction or regulation cannot be imposed by planning condition and failing that a statutory agreements (made under legislation including the Countryside (Scotland) Act 1967, the Sewerage (Scotland) Act 1968, the Local Government (Scotland) Act 1973, the Roads (Scotland) Act 1984 and the Local Government in Scotland Act 2003). The government has stated that such statutory agreements should be used where all the policy tests required of planning obligations are not satisfied. Such agreements may be required in circumstances where, for instance, contributions are being sought for community benefits which, while desirable, do not directly serve a planning purpose (eg benefits such as the provision of infrastructure which is desirable but which is not essential) or seek contributions which were not fairly and reasonably related in scale and kind to the proposed development. However if the benefits sought or offered do not serve a planning purpose how can they properly be taken into account in deciding whether to grant planning permission?

1 SG Circular 3/2012 'Planning Obligations and Good Neighbour Agreements', paras 12 and 15 and SG Circular 1/2009 'Development Planning' at paras 96 and 97.

8.30 Government guidance states that a planning obligation should only be used where all of the following five tests are satisfied, namely where the obligation:

- is necessary to make the proposed development acceptable in planning terms (see para 8.26 above);
- serves a planning purpose and, where it is possible to identify infrastructure provision requirements in advance, should relate to development plans;
- relates to the proposed development either as a direct consequence of the development or arising from the cumulative impact of development in the area;
- is fairly and reasonably relate in scale and kind to the proposed development; and
- is reasonable in all other respects.

8.31 A planning obligation should restrict or regulate the use or development of land and requirements for a planning obligation should be foreshadowed in the development plan and related (statutory and non-statutory) planning guidance (which ought to include exact levels of contributions of methodologies for their calculation). There should be a link between the proposed development and the proposed mitigation provisions of the planning obligation. Offers to undertake works; donate monies, contribute to trust funds etc should not be taken into account if this test about connection between the proposed development and the planning obligation provisions is not satisfied. Further planning authorities should not be swayed by the absence of such offers. Any offer of a planning obligation which has nothing to do with a proposed development, other than being offer by the developer, will not be a material consideration and could only be regarded as an attempt to buy planning permission. The scale and kind test is not required by law. It is a policy test that requires that the planning obligation provisions are proportionate to the proposed development and Circular 3/2012 (picking up on other planning policy references to planning authorities understanding the 'underlying economics of development') refers to considering economic viability, understanding what costs a proposed development can reasonably be expected to bear and considering options including phasing of staging payments to address cash flow issues. The reasonableness test poses four questions, namely:

1. is a planning obligation needed to enable a development to go ahead?
2. will financial payments contribute to the cost of providing necessary facilities required as a consequence of, or in connection with the development in the near future?
3. is the planning obligation requirement so directly related to the regulation of the proposed development that it should not be permitted without it?

4. will the planning obligation mitigate the loss of, or impact on, any amenity or resource present on the site prior to development?

and where the answer to any of the above four questions would be no, a planning obligation is generally not appropriate.[1]

1 SG Circular 3/2012 'Planning Obligations and Good Neighbour Agreements', paras 24 and 25.

8.32 Overall, it is clear that the government remains committed to its long-held position that planning permission should not to be bought or sold. Planning obligations should only be sought where these are necessary and there is no othcr lcgal option for achieving what is required to make the proposed development acceptable in planning terms.

Case law

Scope of planning agreements

8.33 In contrast to the government's view that planning agreements should only be used as a last resort, the Court of Appeal in *Good v Epping Forest District Council*[1] held that it is lawful for a planning authority to use a planning agreement in a situation where planning conditions could achieve the same objective, even although in that case the local authority had deliberately used the agreement to circumvent ministerial policy.

1 [1994] 27 EG 135.

8.34 As we have already seen, planning obligations do not have to be linked to a planning application. Where they are not, the only limit on their scope is the need for them to have a planning purpose and not be *Wednesbury* unreasonable. However, planning agreements usually *are* linked with a planning application, and here the situation has in the past been less certain. It is now clearer, mainly resulting from judicial consideration of the role of planning obligations as material considerations.[1]

1 See paras 6.69–6.71 above.

Planning agreements as material considerations

8.35 As we saw in Chapter 6, when reaching a decision on any planning application, the planning authority must take into account all material considerations and must not have regard to anything that is immaterial to the application. This means that where an application is linked to a planning obligation, the authority can be assumed to have considered the terms of that obligation when deciding whether to grant planning permission. As a result, the contents of the obligation must relate to matters that are material (ie relevant) to the application, otherwise the planning permission may be open to legal challenge. While it is unlikely that an applicant would want to challenge a decision to approve the application, a rival developer might well do so, for example when developers are competing for planning permission to build on different sites in the same area. If one gets planning permission by offering planning benefits through a planning obligation, another developer may well try to challenge this on the ground that an inducement of this kind is not relevant to the application and therefore not a material consideration. Any such challenge will create uncertainty and may deter a developer from proceeding to implement a planning permission. Further if an application for judicial review of a grant of planning permission is successful, the court may quash the planning permission thus preventing the development from taking place, and perhaps improving the prospects for the challenger's scheme. Several important cases, including the *Tesco* and *Plymouth* cases[1] have arisen from such situations.

1 See paras 8.33 – 8.40 below and *R (on the application of Sainsbury's Supermarkets Ltd) v Wolverhampton City Council and another* [2010] UKSC 20 which reviews case law including the decisions in the *Tesco* and *Plymouth* cases and other related cases).

The Tesco case[1]

8.36 Two developers, Tesco and Tarmac (who had links with Sainsbury) each applied for planning permission to build a superstore on different sites in the town of Witney, Oxfordshire. Only one superstore development could be justified in planning terms. There had been a long-standing traffic congestion problem in the town and a plan existed for the construction of a new road to relieve this; however, the highways authority did not have the funds to construct it. Tesco offered to give the local authority £6.6m to construct the road in return for planning permission. Tarmac was not prepared to make such an offer and appealed to the Secretary of State on the basis of a deemed refusal of their application. The Tesco application was then called in for determination by the Secretary of State and the two applications were considered together at a conjoined public inquiry (see Chapter 7).

1 *Tesco Stores Ltd v Secretary of State for the Environment* [1995] 1 WLR 759, [1995] 2 All ER 636.

8.37 The inspector considered that the link between the new road and the proposed superstore was tenuous, but nevertheless recommended that Tesco's application should be approved. The Secretary of State, however, disagreed, taking the view that, because the road was not absolutely necessary for the superstore to operate satisfactorily, it would be contrary to government policy to accept such a planning gain. He attached no weight, therefore, to Tesco's offer and, on the balance of the remaining planning arguments, decided to grant permission for the Tarmac development instead.

8.38 Tesco challenged the decision in court, on the basis that its offer to fund the road was a material consideration which the Secretary of State had failed to take into account, and this failure made the decision *ultra vires*. It was held that, provided that there was more than a *de minimis* link between what was offered and the proposed development, the offer would be relevant and thus a material consideration. Here there *was* such a minimal link, and so Tesco's offer was a material consideration that had to be taken account of. However, the Secretary of State *had* taken it into account, though he had attached no weight to it and, as we have already seen in Chapter 6,[1] it is up to the decision maker to determine what weight should be given to a material consideration, or even to attach no weight to it at all.

1 See para 6.50 above.

8.39 It was therefore perfectly legal for the Secretary of State to attach no weight to Tesco's offer. More importantly, however, it would have been equally within the Secretary of State's discretion, and equally legal, to have attached considerable weight to it and to have allowed it to influence the Secretary of State's decision in Tesco's favour. In the words of Lord Hoffman:

> '…the choice between a policy which emphasises the presumption in favour of development and fairness between developers … and a policy of attempting to obtain the maximum legitimate public benefit … lies within the area of discretion which Parliament has entrusted to planning authorities. It is not a choice which should be imposed upon them by the courts.'[1]

1 [1995] 2 All ER 636 at 660.

8.40 It is therefore lawful for a planning authority to accept an inducement in return for granting planning permission, as long as what is offered is sufficiently related to the development to be a material consideration. And to thus qualify the subject of the offer need not be necessary to the development, or related to it in scale; there only has to be a connection that is more than *de minimis*.

8.41 The *Tesco* case concerned a unilateral planning obligation which, as we saw above, can now be used in Scotland instead of a bilateral planning agreement. There is no reason why the same principles should not apply in Scotland to a planning agreement that is linked to a planning application.

8.42 Limiting agreements to matters that are material considerations does not seem to impose much of a restriction, given the House of Lords' definition of material considerations in this case. With some care and skill, a legitimate case could be made that a wide range of benefits are material. To a large extent, this had already been demonstrated by the Court of Appeal in *R v Plymouth City Council, ex p Plymouth and South Devon Co-operative Society Ltd.*[1] Three planning applications were submitted for superstore developments on different out-of-centre sites. The council granted planning permission for those submitted by Sainsbury and Tesco but continued consideration of the third one submitted by the Coop. Not unnaturally, the Co-op was unhappy with this especially since, unlike it, Tesco and Sainsbury had agreed to give the council a number of planning gains in return for planning permission. The complete package of benefits was worth over £3.6m and included a bird watching hide, tourist information centre, art gallery display, and contributions to the city's park-and-ride scheme. The Co-op submitted that these matters were not material considerations because they were not necessary and did not fairly and reasonably relate to the developments. By taking them into account when granting planning permission, the council's decisions were unlawful. However, while one cannot help having some sympathy with the Co-op's position, the Court of Appeal unanimously rejected its case, finding that all of the benefits offered were fairly and reasonable related to the developments. Consequently, they could be regarded as material considerations.

1 (1993) 67 P&CR 78.

8.43 It therefore seems that planning authorities may legitimately seek a wide range of benefits. Equally, developers may now offer a range of 'sweeteners' to try to gain planning permission, confident in the knowledge that these can lawfully be taken into account and so are unlikely to be subject to legal challenge from rival developers. This has led some commentators to suggest that the *Tesco* decision 'will not cure the planning system of the excesses of planning gain seen in recent years'.[1] In view of this, it is tempting to conclude that the Government's policy on the use of planning agreements and obligations is not sustainable. However, this would ignore the fact that the Scottish Ministers often have the final say in whether or not a development gets planning permission, through called-in applications and appeals. Furthermore, the kinds of application that are likely to end up with the Scottish Ministers (eg major retail developments) will often involve some kind of agreement. Obviously, the Scottish Ministers can be expected to implement their own policy on planning agreements when dealing with such applications. As a result, any inducement is unlikely to be accepted unless it is consistent with government policy. In addition, where a local authority and developer negotiate an agreement linked to a development which has to be notified to the Scottish Ministers and thus the relevant planning application may be called in for their determination, this possibility *may* temper the negotiations.

1 See eg Edwards and Martin *Planning Gain – The final word?* Estates Gazette (1995) 9521, p 44–45.

4. TYPES OF AGREEMENT

8.44 There are essentially two types of planning agreement, those which regulate or restrict the use of property and those which impose a positive obligation. Positive obligations can be further sub-divided as we explain later.[1] None of these categories is mutually exclusive and so agreements may include elements from several, or even all of them.

1 Para 8.48.

Restrictive/regulative obligations

8.45 Examples of these agreements include restricting the occupancy of private sheltered housing to the elderly and tying occupancy of houses to people employed in certain areas (eg ensuring that houses for farm workers are so occupied). However, Circular 3/2012: *Planning Obligations and Good Neighbour Agreements* states, at para 51, that *it should not be necessary to use a planning obligation as a formal mechanism to restrict occupancy or use* [of land or buildings].

8.46 The Planning (Listed Buildings and Conservation Areas) Act 1997 specifies situations where the use of regulating agreements would be appropriate, eg control over the timing of the demolition of a listed building and the work required to replace it.[1]

1 Section 15(3)(a).

8.47 These types of obligation can lead to a planning application being approved which might otherwise have been refused. For example, a planning authority may be prepared to allow a shop unit to be used as a doctor's surgery in spite of a policy protecting shop units for retail use. It might be reluctant to grant planning permission for this as it could have no control over a subsequent change to other class 2[1] uses such as a bookmakers. It could use a condition to prevent this. However, a planning authority may view a planning obligation preventing such a change as a more secure way of overcoming this problem, because it could not be appealed against.

1 Town and Country Planning (Use Classes) (Scotland) Order 1997, SI 1997/3061 (as amended).

Positive obligations

8.48 These are obligations which impose a positive obligation, in other words they require the developer to provide or do something. Positive obligations can be divided into three main types: (a) those directly required to enable the development to function properly; (b) others involving a trade-off to compensate for some objection to an adverse impact; and (c) those which involve extraneous planning gain.

Those required for the development to function properly

8.49 A common example is where the obligation is designed to solve a problem regarding infrastructure. Often a major objection to a proposal such as new retail park will be that the existing road network cannot cope with the likely levels of traffic generation. However, as we saw above[1] unless necessary road improvements can be provided on land completely within the control of the applicant, it would not be lawful to impose conditions on a permission forcing the developer to provide or fund them. On the other hand, given the financial restrictions that local authorities continue to operate under, it is increasingly unlikely that local authorities will be able or willing to fund the necessary improvements. In such situations the application might have to be refused on traffic grounds. However, if the developer can agree to meet the infrastructure requirements himself through a planning agreement the problem can be resolved.

1 Chapter 6, part 10.

Trade-off obligations

8.50 In trade-off obligations the planning obligations contains something which is aimed at mitigating an objection to a proposal rather than disposing of it. For example, if the proposal involves the loss of public open space, the agreement might require the developer to provide some other recreational facility to replace it.

8.51 The controversial aspect of such deals stems from a fear that developers may try to buy planning permission for unacceptable development. At times of financial restraint on local authorities it is quite possible that they could be tempted by such offers. While this could lead to some benefits it could also adversely affect residents who have to live next to the new development. In the *Monahan* case, for example, there was considerable local opposition to the decision to grant permission for an undesirable office development in order to fund improvements to the Royal Opera House at Covent Garden.[1]

1 *R v Westminster City Council ex parte Monahan* [1989] 1 PLR 36, CA. See also *Wansdyke District Council v Secretary of State for the Environment and Bath Football (Rugby) Club* [1993] 1 PLR 15.

Extraneous planning gain

8.52 Extraneous planning gain obligations are those which are designed purely to extract something from a developer in return for the grant of planning permission. There is usually no planning objection to the development in such cases. The planning authority hopes that the developer will be prepared to offer some benefit in order to get planning permission without having to go to appeal. This is because an appeal may take up to a year and the outcome is uncertain. The cost of providing some gain may be less than the cost of delay and uncertainty.

8.53 For many years now, there have been concerns about perceived abuses of the planning system caused by this kind of planning obligation. There is a popularly held view that on the one hand, developers of acceptable developments are being held to ransom by local authority demands for planning gain, while on the other, developers of undesirable development are getting planning permission by offering 'sweeteners' of various kinds. This is sometimes summed up by saying that planning permissions are being bought and sold. Cases such as *Tesco* and *Plymouth*[1] seem to have at least partly legitimised such agreements. However, in practice, planning gain will always be limited by economic reality. Even if they are willing to negotiate, developers will only be able to pay for significant planning gains where the development is likely to prove very profitable.

1 See paras 8.36ff and 8.42 above.

Collective infrastructure

8.54 In very large new developments, a problem can arise with infrastructure contributions when more than one developer is involved. For example, there can be a danger that those developers involved in the earlier phases have to bear the bulk of the infrastructure costs while those doing the later stages 'freeload' on the back of that investment. On the other hand, if the authority tries to address this by sharing out the costs, how can this be done fairly and what happens if one or more developers refuse to co-operate? This issue was addressed by the Court of Appeal in *R v South Northamptonshire District Council, ex p Crest Homes.*[1]

The background to this case was a structure plan requirement that the town of Towcester would have to absorb a considerable amount of new residential development. The problem with this requirement was that the town's existing infrastructure would be unable to cope with the new housing and the local authority did not have the funds to increase capacity. In order to tackle this problem equitably, the council promoted the establishment of a development consortium. Crest Homes was originally a member of it but later withdrew. It did not prove possible to conclude a planning obligation with the consortium as a whole and so separate agreements were sought with individual developers for a contribution based on a percentage of the enhanced land value,[2] in line with a draft local plan policy to this effect. Crest Homes submitted a planning application and refused to enter into a planning obligation. Following dismissal of their appeal to the Secretary of State, they sought judicial review of the council's decision. In particular, they tried to argue that the council was in fact unlawfully operating its own local development land tax. In support of this view, they pointed out that the formula used to calculate contributions was based on land values, not the true costs of providing infrastructure. The court rejected these arguments and took the view that the council's actions were lawful. However, Henry LJ, in the leading judgment, concluded with a word of caution about the use of such formula-based approaches:

> 'I would re-emphasise the crucial importance in this case of the facts: the genuineness and lawfulness of the policy of the treatment of Towcester as a unity, the identification of the infrastructure required and the attempts to distribute the costs … equitably among the developers. Those facts are crucial because they legitimise a formula which if used in other factual contexts could be struck down as constituting an unauthorised local development land tax.'

1 [1995] JPL 200.
2 Ie the market value of the land after planning permission less its previous value.

8.55 South Northamptonshire District Council's approach seems only just to have survived legal scrutiny. Commenting on the case, Edwards and Martin[1] consider that the judgment gives clear guidelines to any local planning authority faced with a similar situation. They suggest that, provided there is a local plan policy that is lawful and consistent with government policy, a method of implementation in line with the South Northamptonshire approach should be upheld. However, it has been pointed out elsewhere[2] that the formula approach poses practical difficulties in implementation. Given local authority funding difficulties, necessary infrastructure will only be provided once all of the contributions have been secured and, in some cases the infrastructure may need to be there before development takes place. This suggests high 'front-loaded' construction costs for developers, which may undermine the financial viability of their development. Further, a planning authority might be required to carry out a single consultation process with all relevant landowners if infrastructure costs apportionment is an issue.[3]

1 Edwards & Martin 'Legality of Related Development' Estates Gazette [1994] 9424, p 144.
2 Rowan-Robinson, J 'The Limits of Planning Agreements' (1995) 50 SPEL 60.
3 *R (on the application of Lichfield Securities Ltd) v Litchfield District Council and Another* [2001] EWCA Civ 304.

Nolan committee

8.56 During 1996–97 planning agreements, and in particular planning gain, were investigated by the Committee of Standards in Public Life (initially chaired by Lord Nolan) as part of its general investigation into the standards of local government.[1] The Committee found planning agreements to be 'the most intractable aspect of the planning system' which it had to deal with. It saw little evidence of corruption but did conclude that there was a lack of openness in the negotiation of agreements and that planning permissions *were* being bought and sold. However, the Committee was not prepared to recommend that the system of planning agreements be abolished and in fact recognised its benefits thus:

> 'Most large developments have an effect on traffic flows with implications for roads and public transport. Some, such as out of town shopping centres, mineral sites, or large developments in remote areas, may have effects which impose costs on the community in places quite distant from the actual site of the development. In our view the community is quite entitled to seek a contribution from the developer to offset such costs, and we can readily envisage circumstances in which a development would only be made acceptable if this was forthcoming.'[2]

1 *Third Report of the Committee on Standards in Public Life: Standards of conduct in Local Government in England, Scotland and Wales* (Cm 3702–I) (1997).
2 Ibid, para 30.

8.57 The following were the main problems identified by the Committee and its recommendations for dealing with them:

- in some cases, unsuitable developments were being granted planning permission in return for offers of planning gain, and thus planning permission was clearly 'for sale'. The Committee recommended that the Department of the Environment (and the Scottish and Welsh Offices) should consider whether the present legislation is sufficiently tightly worded to prevent planning permissions from being bought and sold. Unhelpfully, the Committee did not suggest ways in which the legislation might achieve this.
- many developers felt they had no choice but to co-operate with a local planning authority which was demanding a planning gain, largely because the alternative option of an appeal to the Secretary of State takes so long to process. The Committee suggested that the answer was to speed up the appeals process. However, while this would possibly help a little, developers would still have to face expensive appeals of which the outcome was uncertain. Set against this, paying for a planning gain to guarantee planning permission might seem attractive.
- the amount of secrecy in the negotiation of planning agreements undermines public confidence in the planning system. The Committee recommended that local authorities should adopt rules on openness that allow planning agreements to be subject to discussion between councillors and the public. They should also give unrestricted access to supporting documents except where justified by commercial confidentiality (which should be narrowly interpreted).

8.58 In its preliminary response to these recommendations,[1] the government has said that it intends to make it a legal requirement for planning authorities to enter planning agreements in their planning register (see Chapter 6). However, it did not believe that changes to the wording of the primary legislation or to policy guidance were required (although it would be prepared to reconsider this position if any case for change became evident). It was also satisfied with the steps already taken to speed up the appeals process. Section 36(1)(d) of the Town and Country Planning (Scotland) Act 1997 makes provision for the entry of planning obligations in a planning authority's planning register. Further, there is a requirement that a planning application decision notice include a statement as to where the terms of a planning obligation or where summary of the terms of the planning obligation may be inspected.[2]

1 Scottish Office *A New Ethical Framework for Local Government in Scotland* (1998).

2 The Town and Country Planning (Development Management Procedure) (Scotland) Regulations 2013 (SSI 2013 No 155), reg 28(3)(vi) and SG Circular 3/2012 'Planning Obligations and Good Neighbour Agreements' at para 27.

5. 'GRAMPIAN' CONDITIONS

8.59 In many cases, a special type of planning condition know as a 'Grampian condition' offers a perfectly viable and more straightforward alternative for achieving the kinds of planning objectives that planning obligations are commonly used for. This is a type of suspensive condition that involves granting approval of a proposed development conditional upon something else happening first (eg the construction of a roundabout) *but without specifying who has to implement it.* Such conditions are called 'Grampian' conditions after the case which established the legality of this approach, ie *Grampian Regional Council v Aberdeen District Council.*[1] In this case a reporter had to deal with an appeal against deemed refusal of planning permission. While the reporter favoured granting permission for the development involved, he refused it on traffic safety grounds. A road closure some way from the site was necessary to resolve the problem and the reporter took the view that a condition requiring the applicants to close that road would not be lawful as it was a matter outwith their control. The House of Lords held that the reporter could validly have imposed a negatively-worded condition to resolve the problem.

1 1984 SLT 197 (HL).

8.60 It was originally thought that Grampian conditions could only be used if there were good prospects of the condition being implemented.[1] However, following the House of Lords decision in *British Railways Board v Secretary of State for the Environment*[2] it is clear that Grampian conditions do not need to pass such a test. In this case, planning permission had been refused on appeal because of an access difficulty. This could have been solved by the use of adjoining land but the owners (who happened to be the local authority) were not prepared to sell it for this purpose. The inspector had been minded to grant permission subject to a planning agreement but the council was not prepared to co-operate with this either. While a Grampian condition would have offered a solution to this stalemate, the inspector took the view that it would be unlawful for him to impose one because there was no reasonable prospect of what was required being implemented. The inspector therefore refused permission. Their Lordships rejected that reasoning, pointing out that there is no legal obligation for an applicant to own land when applying for planning permission. In the words of Lord Hirst:

> 'A would-be developer may be faced with difficulties of many kinds, in the way of site assembly or securing the discharge of restrictive covenants. If he considers that it is in his interest to secure planning permission notwithstanding the existence of such difficulties, it is not for the planning authority to refuse it simply on their view of how serious the difficulties are.'[3]

1 *Jones v Secretary of State for Wales* (1991) 61 P&CR 238.
2 [1993] 3 PLR 125, [1994] 02 EG 107.
3 [1994] 62 EG 107 at 110.

8.61 This judgment should change long-established planning practice and offer a solution to some problems with planning agreements. Where a positive obligation is needed, for example, it should now be enough to grant permission subject to a suspensive condition and leave the developer to sort the problem out. This could speed up development management because of the time delay involved in negotiating planning obligations and completing the necessary legal procedures. On the other hand, since Grampian conditions can be appealed against, planning authorities may still want the security of a planning obligation, especially if the desired objective of the planning condition is not absolutely necessary in order to allow the development to proceed.

8.62 This could also be a way of getting round the difficulty of using a planning obligation when the applicant does not yet own the site. A suspensive condition could simultaneously protect the position of the planning authority and give the applicant the security of planning permission before concluding the purchase of the site. At appeals, the reporter can now more easily issue permission with a Grampian condition rather than issuing a 'notice of intention' and relying on the local planning authority and developer to conclude a planning obligation. In *Strathclyde Regional Council v Secretary of State for Scotland*[1] following an appeal against refusal of planning permission for a housing development in Neilston, the reporter indicated that he would be prepared to grant permission if the developer and local authority first entered into an agreement. When the local planning authority refused to do so, he granted planning permission subject to a Grampian condition. The council challenged this decision on the ground that there was no reasonable prospect of the condition being met. However, the court followed the *British Railways Board* case and upheld the reporter's decision.

1 1996 SLT 579.

6. GOOD NEIGHBOUR AGREEMENTS

8.63 The value of local people being able to enter into agreements with site operators of 'bad neighbour' developments encompassing community liaison matters such as hours of operation, the pattern and frequency of vehicle movements and general information about performance was recognised by the introduction of legislative provisions about 'good neighbour agreements'.[1] A good neighbour agreement should not be viewed as an alternative to a planning obligation. A planning authority should not seek to make it a requirement for the grant of planning permission that a good neighbour agreement be put in place.[2]

1 See, for instance, *Love Thy Neighbour The Potential for Good Neighbour Agreements in Scotland* (2004) http://www.foe-scotland.org.uk/sites/files/gna_report.pdf and 1997 Act ss 75D – 75G and SG PAN 3/2010: *Community Engagement* at para 62.
2 SG Circular 3/2012 'Planning Obligations and Good Neighbour Agreements', para 60.

8.64 A good neighbour agreement is an agreement between a person (such as a landowner and/or operator) and a 'community body', namely

- the community council for the area in which the land in question (or any part of that land) is situated; or
- a body or trust whose members of trustees have a substantial connection to the land in question and whose object or function is to preserve or enhance the amenity of thc local arca where the land is situated

and in the case of a body or trust, other than a community council, the body or trust (as the case may be) must be recognised (and notified) by the planning authority for the area in which the land is situated as meeting the criteria set out in the second bullet point above.

8.65 A good neighbour agreement may govern operations or activities relating to the development or use of land, wither permanently or during the period specified in the agreement. It may require the provision to the community body about the development and use of land. A good neighbour agreement cannot include any provision about the payment of money.

8.66 Where the owner of the land is a party to a good neighbour agreement it may be registered in the Land Register of Scotland or the General Register of Sasines and if it is it becomes enforceable against future owners and occupiers of the land and unless the agreement otherwise provides it is enforceable against former owners of the land.

8.67 A good neighbour agreement may be modified or discharge by agreement among the parties to the agreement. Alternatively the person against whom a good neighbour obligation is enforceable may make an application to the relevant planning authority for modification or discharge of a good neighbour agreement.[1] An appeal may be made within three months to the Scottish Ministers of either the planning authority failing to determine the application within the two month period allowed or if the authority does not decide to discharge the good neighbour agreement or modify the good neighbour obligation as specified in the application. Relevant government guidance about the determination of an application for modification or discharge of a good neighbour agreement (including any change in circumstances since the agreement was entered into and the five planning obligation tests referred to at para 8.30 above) and related appeals to the Scottish Ministers have to be taken into account.[2] The planning authority's decision to discharge or modify a good neighbour agreement does not take effect until the relevant determination notice has been recorded in the General Register of Sasines or registered in the Land Register of Scotland (as the case may be).

1 1997 Act, s 75E and the Town and Country Planning (Modification and Discharge of Good Neighbour Agreements) (Scotland) Regulations 2010 (SSI 2010 No 433).

2 SG Circular 3/2012; 'Planning Obligations and Good Neighbour Agreements' at paras 70 – 75 and 76 – 81 respectively.

Chapter 9

Enforcement of planning control

1. INTRODUCTION

9.1 Alongside the requirement to seek planning permission for 'development' are discretionary powers available to panning authorities to apply sanctions against those in breach of this requirement. These enforcement powers, first introduced in the 1947 Act, were significantly enhanced through changes made by the 1991 Planning and Compensation Act[1] and then the 2006 Planning etc (Scotland) Act. Enforcement is seen as a key component of an effective planning system. Scottish Government Circular 10/2009 *Planning Enforcement*[2] sets out the policy context for planning enforcement as part of a modernised planning system. This chapter outlines the current range of enforcement powers available to planning authorities in Scotland.

1 The extended enforcement powers introduced in the 1991 Act followed the report by Robert Carnwath *Enforcing Planning Control* (1989).
2 SG Circular 10/2009 'Planning Enforcement'.

9.2 To commence 'development' (except 'permitted development' – see Chapter 5) without planning permission, or to ignore one or more conditions or limitations attached to a permission, or (since the 2006 Act) to commence development without first notifying the planning authority or without displaying the required statutory notice on planning permission land, comprises unauthorised development, ie a breach of planning control. Whilst a breach of planning control is not normally a criminal offence, once enforcement proceedings have been taken non-compliance can lead to criminal prosecution. Also, a breach of certain special controls (eg those on listed buildings - see Chapter 12) can be an offence as such. Impact on Human Rights may be a relevant factor in deciding whether to take enforcement action, since it is unlawful for a planning authority to act or fail to act in a way incompatible with any right under the European Convention on Human Rights and Fundamental Freedoms.[1] The planning authority must take into account any relevant Convention rights[2] for example:

- Right to a fair trial (Art 6);
- Right to respect for private and family life, home and correspondence (Art 8);

- Protection of property (First Protocol, Art 1).

1 Human Rights Act 1998 s 6.
2 For a fuller discussion of the implications of the 1988 Human Rights Act on planning enforcement see Collar,N *Planning and Human Rights*, W Green 2001; see also Scottish Human Rights Commission at www.scottishhumanrights.com.

9.3 Whilst the enforcement powers are primarily available to planning authorities, there are certain circumstances in which Scottish Ministers may take enforcement action themselves (see below). Also, the Planning Acts empower Scottish Ministers to make Regulations to prescribe:

- the level of a Fixed Penalty Notice;
- the information to be submitted in a Notice of Initiation of Development;
- the information to be displayed in a Site Notice;
- activities that may not be prohibited by a Temporary Stop Notice.

9.4 There is no obligation on a planning authority to respond to a breach in its area by taking enforcement proceedings (but see implications of Human Rights Act above). A development undertaken without permission may nevertheless be acceptable to the authority, in which case it may invite a retrospective application for planning permission. As well as the general provisions relating to enforcement in Part VI of the 1997 Act (as amended by the 2006 Act), there are special enforcement provisions relating to listed buildings and other special controls, which are dealt with elsewhere (see Chapters 12 and 13).

9.5 The enforcement powers essentially take two forms: ***Statutory Notices*** and ***court action***. As we discuss below, issuing a statutory notice is not necessarily a pre-requisite for court action. All enforcement offences are subject to a six month time limit for commencing summary court proceedings.[1] The scope and terms of each of these powers are summarised in turn.

1 *Criminal Procedure (Scotland) Act* 1995 s 136.

2. PLANNING CONTRAVENTION NOTICE

9.6 The 1991 Planning and Compensation Act introduced a new section 125 of the 1997 Act providing planning authorities with the power to issue a planning contravention notice, intended as a prelude to the enforcement process. This notice was intended to supplement, for enforcement purposes, the more limited power under s 272 of the 1997 Act which enables planning authorities to require information about interests in land. In cases where a breach of planning control is suspected, a planning contravention notice requires the recipient to furnish the planning authority (in writing) with any information which it needs in order to determine the situation. Compliance is mandatory where the Notice is properly served.[1] Suspicion of a breach (eg following a complaint by a member of the public) may be sufficient, whereas absence of suspicion may invalidate the Notice.[2] Recipients of a notice are required to provide such information as the notice may specify regarding:[3]

- any operations being carried out on the land, any use of the land and any other activities being carried out on the land; and
- any matter relating to the conditions or limitations which apply to any planning permission that has been granted in respect of the land.

1 *R v Teignbridge District Council ex parte Teignmouth Quay Co Ltd* [1995], JPL 828.
2 op cit.
3 SG Circular 10/2009 'Planning Enforcement', Annex D.

9.7 Recipients may be required to provide, to the best of their ability, any or all of the following:[1]

- a statement declaring whether the land is subject to any of the operations, activities or uses specified in the notice;
- a statement declaring when any operation, activity or use began;
- the names and addresses of any other persons who use or have used the land, or who carry out or have carried out any operations or activities on the land;
- information regarding any planning permission for any use or operation, or any reason why such permission is not required; and
- a statement declaring the nature of their interest (if any) in the land and the names and addresses of any other persons with an interest in the land.

1 *R v Teignbridge* Ibid.

9.8 Serving a planning contravention notice does not constitute 'taking enforcement action' for the purposes of s 123 of the 1997 Act. Nor is it a pre-requisite to taking formal enforcement action. However it may act as a formal warning to the recipient that the planning authority has heard of the breach, and so may help to avoid the necessity of further enforcement action. However, a planning authority may not serve such a notice without grounds for believing that a breach of planning control has occurred, otherwise the recipient may refuse to supply the information requested.[1]

1 *R v Teignbridge* ibid.

9.9 A planning contravention notice may be served on the owner or occupier of the land in question, or on any person who has any other interest in it, or who is carrying on operations there or is otherwise using it. The notice must inform the recipient of the likely consequences of failing to respond; in particular the recipient should be informed that enforcement action could follow and also that failure to respond could deprive of any right to compensation for withdrawal of a stop notice (in cases where that would otherwise have been appropriate). Planning authorities may therefore serve several notices on different people in respect of the same suspected breach. There is no need for the planning authority to obtain clear evidence of a breach of control before issuing the notice; it is sufficient for the authority to suspect that a breach may have occurred, eg from a complaint by a member of the public. A notice may suggest a time and place for a meeting between the recipient and the planning authority in order to try and resolve the matter.[1]

1 1997 Act, s 125(4).

9.10 A planning authority may receive responses from recipients of the notice at its discretion. Respondents cannot reasonably be expected to provide information they do not possess or could not reasonably find out. A notice must inform recipients of the possibility of formal enforcement action if they fail to respond and of the effect of the provisions of s 143(5) of the 1997 Act, ie that where a stop notice is served, no financial compensation is payable in respect of any loss or damage which could have been avoided if the information had been furnished in response to a planning contravention notice, or if the recipient had co-operated with the planning authority when asked to do so. It should state that failure to comply with a planning contravention notice within 21 days of service of the notice is an offence.[1] Those found guilty are liable on summary conviction to a fine not exceeding level 3 on the standard scale. An offender may also be convicted of subsequent offences by reference to any period of time (eg each additional day) following a preceding conviction for such an offence (s 126 of the 1997 Act). It is a defence for persons charged with such an offence to prove that they had a reasonable excuse for failing to comply.

1 Ibid, s 126.

9.11 The *Review of Planning Enforcement*[1] found that the planning contravention notice is generally regarded as an effective means of gathering information on alleged breaches of planning control, but that there was significant underuse of it by most planning authorities, as well as wide variation between authorities in the incidence of its use. Authorities continued to prefer other tried and tested methods of enforcement, such as negotiation and persuasion, and the pre-existing power available in s 272 of the 1997 Act, whereby local authorities or Scottish Ministers can require information from owners and occupiers of land.

1 *Review of Planning Enforcement*, School of Planning and Housing, Edinburgh College of Art/Heriot-Watt University and Brodies WS, Scottish Office Development Department, 1997 paras 5.8–5.19.

3. NOTICE REQUIRING APPLICATION FOR RETROSPECTIVE PLANNING PERMISSION

9.12 Section 9 of the 2006 Act introduced into the 1997 Act a new section 33A providing planning authorities with the power to issue a Notice requiring a retrospective planning application to be submitted for development already carried out in breach of planning control. Previously, where the planning authority determined that development had taken place without permission, but were favourably disposed towards it, they could only invite such an application; there was no obligation to submit one. The purpose of this Notice is to encourage the submission of a retrospective application, so that the planning authority can then consider granting permission subject to any conditions or limitations that would make the development acceptable. Such a retrospective application is determined in the same way as any planning application submitted in advance, including the normal consultation and notifications, and payment of the requisite planning fee. Before issuing such a notice, the planning authority should consider whether its action is commensurate with the breach, since there would be no point in requiring the submission of a retrospective application where the development could not be made acceptable with the imposition of conditions. In such circumstances the planning authority should consider the other enforcement powers at its disposal. The notice must:

- describe the development in a way that is sufficient to identify it;
- specify a date by which the application is to be made; and
- set out the terms of s 123(1) stating that carrying out development without the required permission constitutes a breach of planning control.

9.13 When a notice under s 33A is issued it must be recorded in the planning authority's register of notices maintained under s 147 (see below). The information to be recorded is set out in the Town and Country Planning (Enforcement of Control) (No.2) (Scotland) Regulations 1992, as amended by the Town and Country Planning (Miscellaneous Amendments) (Scotland) Regulations 2009. Where a planning application is not submitted by the specified date, the planning authority is able to consider further enforcement action, particularly if it considers that a retrospective application would have been granted only if it were subject to conditions or limitations. In such cases an enforcement notice could be issued, imposing restrictions on the use of the land or on activities carried out on the land.

9.14 Issuing a notice requiring submission of a retrospective planning application constitutes taking enforcement action. Regardless of any subsequent action, issuing the notice is relevant should a person subsequently seek a certificate of lawful use or development in respect of the development (see below), or where a planning authority considers further action necessary beyond the normal time restrictions on enforcement action.

4. ENFORCEMENT NOTICE

Service of Notice

9.15 Sections 127–129 of the 1997 Act empower a planning authority to serve an enforcement notice, where:

- it appears to the planning authority that there has been a breach of planning control in its area, requiring the breach to be remedied, and
- the planning authority considers it expedient to do so having regard to the provisions of the development plan and to any other material considerations.

9.16 In other words, the notice must be served for planning reasons and not (for example) because the planning authority wants to punish the person in breach. If the unauthorised development is one for which an environmental assessment should have been carried out (which will only be in a small minority of cases), the authority will have to serve a *notice of unauthorised development* along with the enforcement notice.

9.17 The notice should be served on the owner and occupier of the land to which it relates, and also on any other person having an interest in the land if that interest is materially affected by the notice. 'Owner' is defined widely by s 277(1) of the 1997 Act to include a tenant whose lease has more than three years to run. The planning authority may later withdraw or vary an enforcement notice, or waive or relax any particular requirement of it (s 129), and the notice will cease to have effect with the later grant of planning permission for an existing development that is inconsistent with it (s 137). This also applies to breach of condition notices.

9.18 The Scottish Ministers (after consultation with the relevant planning authority) are empowered to serve an enforcement notice, and such a notice will have the same effect as if it had been served by the planning authority itself (s 139).

Form of enforcement notice

9.19 An enforcement notice must contain the following information:[1]

(1) The matters which appear to the planning authority to constitute the breach of planning control; the notice should make it clear whether the alleged breach is an unauthorised development or a breach of a planning condition.[2]
(2) The steps that have to be taken (or any activities that have to cease) in order to remedy the breach; this could include discontinuing any use, restoring the land to its previous condition, remedying any injury to amenity caused by the breach, the alteration or removal of any buildings or works, and even the carrying out of building operations, including the provision of a replacement building or buildings.
(3) The date on which the notice is to take effect; this must be not less than 28 days after service of the notice.
(4) The period or periods of compliance within which any steps specified are to be carried out, or any activities have to cease; different periods may be specified for different steps or activities.
(5) The reasons why the planning authority considers it expedient to issue the notice.[3]
(6) The precise boundaries of the land to which the notice relates, either by reference to a plan or otherwise.[4]
(7) An explanatory note, including information regarding appeal rights.[5]

1 1997 Act, s 128, in respect of steps 1–4 only.
2 Op cit; *Kerrier District Council v Secretary of State for the Environment* (1980) 41 P&CR 284.
3 Town and Country Planning (Enforcement of Control) (No 2) (Scotland) Regulations 1992 (as amended), SI 1992/2086, reg 3(a).
4 Op cit, reg 3(b).
5 Ibid, reg 4.

9.20 Just because a development is unlawful, it does not follow that it will be entirely unacceptable to the planning authority. These provisions make it clear, therefore, that the planning authority has the power to *under enforce*, ie the recipient of a notice may be asked to modify a development, rather than remove it altogether, if this would make it satisfactory to the planning authority. However, the planning authority also needs to have regard to the 1988 Human Rights Act, particularly with respect to any impact on the human rights of third parties such as neighbours. While enforcement action should always be proportionate to the nature of the breach, planning authorities are under an obligation to take enforcement action where it is plainly necessary.

9.21 If an enforcement notice is unclear about the steps that need to be taken, it may be invalid.[1] Moreover, the steps prescribed must not go beyond what is reasonably necessary to remedy the breach.[2] Enforcement of the prescribed steps must also be possible; in *Bennett v Secretary of State for the Environment*[3] the court removed part of a notice that required the restoration of the use of premises as a single dwellinghouse, as it would have been impossible to require someone actually to live on the premises.

1 *Metallic Protectives Ltd v Secretary of State for the Environment* [1976] JPL 166.
2 *Cleaver v Secretary of State for the Environment* [1981] JPL 38; *Mansi v Elstree RDC* (1964) 16 P&CR 153.
3 [1993] JPL 134.

9.22 It may be that an enforcement notice could have required buildings or works to be removed or an activity to cease, but it does not do so. In such a case (provided that all requirements that *are* in the notice have been complied with) planning permission will be treated as having been granted for the unauthorised development. The same applies to any replacement buildings erected in accordance with the terms of the enforcement notice. Compliance with an enforcement notice does not discharge the notice.[1] For example, if the recipient of a notice discontinues an unauthorised use, but later resumes it, it will not be necessary for the planning authority to serve a fresh notice; the recipient will be in breach and open to prosecution.

1 1997 Act, s 138.

9.23 Planning authorities must keep a public register of enforcement notices, which must also contain any breach of condition notices and stop notices (see below). The information to be entered on the register is prescribed by regulations.[1]

1 Town and Country Planning (Enforcement of Control) (No 2) (Scotland) Regulations 1992, as amended.

Appeal against Enforcement Notice

9.24 A person on whom an enforcement notice is served, or any other person having an interest in the land, may appeal to Scottish Ministers[1] on any one or more of the following grounds:

- that the matters which, by virtue of s 128(1)(a) have been stated in the notice, have not occurred;
- that those matters (if they occurred) do not constitute a breach of planning control;
- that the alleged breach was immune from enforcement;
- that the enforcement notice was not served in accordance with the statutory requirements;
- that the steps required by the notice to be taken (or any activities that were required to cease) exceed what is necessary to remedy any breach of planning control or any injury to amenity caused by the breach; or
- that the period specified for compliance with the notice falls short of what should reasonably be allowed.

1 Section 130(1) of the 1997 Act. The 2006 Act removed the provision at s 130(1)(a) to appeal on the basis that planning permission ought to be granted for the breach of control contained in the enforcement notice, or that the relevant condition or limitation should be discharged. The related provision at s 133 enabling Scottish Ministers to grant planning permission on determination of an enforcement notice appeal has also been revoked by the 2006 Act.

9.25 An appeal should be in writing and must be made before the date on which the enforcement notice is to take effect. However an appeal will be timeous if the notice was sent by post in a properly addressed and stamped envelope, provided that it was sent in time, by the normal course of post, to arrive before the effective day. The latter provision was added in 1991 to mitigate hardship in cases where posted notices fail to arrive in time by a narrow margin. It has been held that the enforcement appeals process complies with the requirements of Art 6 of the European Convention on Human Rights.[1]

1 *Bryan v UK* [1996] 1 PLR 47.

9.26 The grounds of appeal must also be stated in writing, either along with the notification of the appeal or within 14 days of being asked for them by Scottish Ministers.[1] The planning authority must forward its submissions within 28 days of being asked for them by Scottish Ministers.[2] Where a notice of appeal has been served, the enforcement notice is of no effect pending the final determination of the appeal. However, this is subject to the planning authority's power to serve a stop notice. In making an appeal, the appellant is deemed to have applied for planning permission. An appeal may proceed by written submissions but (as in the case of appeals against adverse decisions) if either the applicant or the planning authority so desire, a hearing will be granted.

1 *Town and Country Planning (Enforcement of Control) (No 2) (Scotland) Regulations* 1992, reg 5.
2 Op cit, reg 6.

9.27 Schedule 4 to the 1997 Act (relating to the determination of appeals by a Reporter) applies to appeals against enforcement notices as well as to those against adverse decisions. Scottish Ministers (or the Reporter appointed to hear the appeal) are empowered as regards enforcement notices to:

(1) Give directions for the enforcement notice to be quashed.
(2) Correct any defect in the enforcement notice, or vary its terms, where this will not cause injustice either to the appellant or to the planning authority.
(3) If satisfied that there is no breach of planning control or that any existing use of the land is lawful, issue a certificate of lawful use or development.

Alternatively Scottish Ministers may uphold the enforcement notice.

Challenge in Court

9.28 The legal validity of an enforcement notice can be challenged by (a) an appeal to the Court of Session against the Scottish Ministers' decision within six weeks of the decision; or (b) even where an appeal may not have first been made to Scottish Ministers, by a petition to the Court of Session for judicial review. The latter avenue would normally be precluded by s 134 of the 1997 Act which prohibits the validity of an enforcement notice from being questioned in any proceedings whatsoever where the ground of appeal is one specified in s 130(1)(b) to (e) and which by virtue of s128(1)(a) have been stated in the notice.[1] However, judicial review is competent for any residual grounds of invalidity not listed in s 130(1), for example bad faith, bias or other procedural impropriety in the planning authority's decision to issue the notice.[2]

1 Section 54 of the *Planning etc (Scotland) Act* 2006 amended s130(1)(b) of the *Town and Country Planning (Scotland) Act* 1997, clarifying that the matters referred to under s130(1)(b) referred specifically to the matters referred to in the Enforcement Notice.
2 *R v Wicks* [1997] 2 All ER 801 at 818, per Lord Hoffman.

9.29 An enforcement notice, whose effect is suspended pending the outcome of an appeal, will normally come into effect if and when the notice is upheld by the Scottish Ministers. However, if the Scottish Ministers' decision is challenged in court, the effect of the notice will continue to be suspended until the court has reached its decision.[1] This potentially gives developers the opportunity to buy time by lodging appeals.

1 *R v Kuxhaus* [1998] 2 WLR 1005, CA.

Non-compliance with an enforcement notice

9.30 Under s 136 of the 1997 Act, if an enforcement notice is not complied with, the owner and anyone else in breach of the notice will be guilty of an offence and may be liable to a fine (currently) of up to £20,000 on summary conviction (or an unlimited one if convicted on indictment). In determining the amount of any fine payable, the court must take into account any financial benefit which might accrue to the offender as a result of the breach. In the case of an owner, it is a defence that the person did everything that could be expected to be done to secure compliance with the notice, and this may include a situation where the non-compliance was due to the owner's personal and financial circumstances.[1] It is also a defence for any persons charged (including the owner) that they were not aware of the existence of the notice; however, this defence will only apply if (a) the person was not served with a copy of the notice and (b) the notice did not appear in the planning authority's register. If the breach is a continuing one, the person concerned may be charged again at a later date.[2] Where an enforcement notice has been rendered ineffective by the retrospective grant of planning permission, this will not affect the criminal liability of anyone who has earlier failed to comply with the notice.[3] (Presumably, though the Act does not say so, this could only be the case if the person concerned had actually been charged with the offence prior to the grant of planning permission; otherwise it is difficult to see in what respect the enforcement notice could have been rendered ineffective). Also, where a prosecution has already commenced, the making of a planning application in respect of the unauthorised development will not normally be a ground for the case to be adjourned pending the outcome of the application.[4]

1 *Kent County Council v Brockman* [1996] 1 PLR 1; but see also *R v Beard* [1996] CLY 4719.
2 1997 Act, s 136(6).
3 1997 Act, s 137(3).
4 *R v Beaconsfield Magistrates, ex p South Buckinghamshire District Council* [1993] COD 357.

9.31 Powers for the courts to confiscate proceeds of crime were extended under the Criminal Justice (Scotland) Act 1995.[1] These allow the courts to confiscate any benefit obtained by a defendant as a result of or in connection with the commission of a criminal offence and to impose a prison term in default. This includes planning enforcement cases. In a 2010 judgement, the Criminal Court of Appeal in England considered the financial gain to two defendants arising from non-compliance with an enforcement notice to cease using land in St Alban's for the operation of an unauthorised car park.[2]

1 Consolidated in the *Proceeds of Crime (Scotland) Act* 1995.
2 *Luigi del Basso and Bradley Goodwin v Regina* [2010] EWCA Crim 1119.

9.32 The defendants operated an airport park and ride business from land at a local football club. This use was in excess of its permitted use for parking restricted to match days. The planning authority brought enforcement proceedings, but in the period during which the enforcement notice was appealed (and dismissed), the parking operation expanded rather than ceased. A successful prosecution under s 179 of the Town and Country Planning Act 1990 still did not cause the business to cease operating and so this was followed by a second prosecution. On conviction, Mr Del Basso was fined a total of £15,000 for five offences and ordered to pay £20,000 costs. It would appear that the operators regarded the fine as a necessary business expense. However this was followed by a confiscation order. The court held that the operation of the park and ride business became 'criminally unlawful' from the moment the enforcement notice became effective and the defendants were to be treated as having a criminal lifestyle from then onwards, within the meaning of the Proceeds of Crime Act. It was adjudged that the benefit obtained from the illegal activity was £1,881,221.19. The amount that Mr Del Basso was able to pay was £760,000, which was the total value of all his assets, and he was ordered to pay that sum with 18 months imprisonment in default. A nominal order was made against Mr Goodwin, since he was by then bankrupt. The benefit figure was calculated by adding up the gross receipts of the defendants' criminal conduct, namely the operation of the car park during the relevant period. The trial judge concluded:

> *'Those who choose to run operations in disregard of planning enforcement requirements are at risk of having the gross receipts of their illegal businesses confiscated. This may greatly exceed their personal profits. In this respect they are in the same position as thieves, fraudsters and drug dealers ...'*

5. STOP NOTICE

9.33 There may be situations where the planning authority considers that stopping a breach of planning control is a matter of urgency and cannot wait until the end of the minimum 28-day period before an enforcement notice takes effect. Moreover, if the recipient of an enforcement notice lodges an appeal (see below), thereby suspending the effect of the notice, there could be a danger of the breach continuing until the appeal has been heard. In such cases the planning authority may take emergency measures by issuing a stop notice under s 140 of the 1997 Act.

9.34 A stop notice may be issued at the same time as the enforcement notice or at any time thereafter before the enforcement notice takes effect, ie before the date stated in the notice or (as the case may be) the date when the enforcement notice has been upheld on appeal. A stop notice must state the date when it comes into effect, which must not be more than 28 days after its issue, or less than three days, unless the planning authority considers that there are special reasons to justify it taking effect immediately.

9.35 A stop notice may be selective in its effect, ie it may relate only to part of the land in question or only to certain of the breaches referred to in the enforcement notice. This makes it possible for the planning authority to restrict the effect of the stop notice to what is essential to safeguard amenity or public safety in the neighbourhood, or to prevent serious or irreversible harm to the environment in the surrounding area.[1] In this way harm or disruption to the recipient's business can be minimised.

1 SG Circular 10/2009 'Planning Enforcement', Annex H.

9.36 If a use of land (as opposed to a building, engineering, mining or other operation) has been carried on for more than four years, it may not be the subject of a stop notice.[1] Most material changes of use do not become immune from enforcement until after ten years. However, if four years have elapsed, the use will at least be protected from the peremptory effect of a stop notice. This exemption does not apply to the deposit of refuse or waste materials.

1 1997 Act, s 140(5).

9.37 A stop notice may not be used to prohibit the use of any building as a dwellinghouse. Here it should be pointed out that a building does not become a 'dwellinghouse' simply because, after four years, it is immune from enforcement action. There is no definition in planning law of what constitutes a dwellinghouse,[1] however '*if no reasonable person would identify a particular structure as a dwellinghouse, it is justifiable to conclude, as a matter of fact, that it is not a* *dwellinghouse, even if it is being used as such'*.[2] This means that a building may be used lawfully as a dwellinghouse without acquiring the 'permitted development' rights associated with a building that is a dwellinghouse. For the purposes of the 1997 Act, a single, self-contained set of premises can properly be regarded as being in use as a single dwellinghouse if:[3]

- it comprises a unit of occupation, which can be regarded as a 'planning unit' separate from any other part of a building containing it;
- it is designed or adapted for residential purposes, containing the facilities for cooking, eating and sleeping normally associated with use as a dwellinghouse;
- it is used as a permanent or temporary dwelling by a single person, or by persons living together as, or like, a single family.

1 Article 2 of the *Town and Country Planning (General Permitted Development) (Scotland) Order* specifically excludes a flat from the definition of a dwellinghouse.
2 SG Circular 10/2009 'Planning Enforcement', Annex H para 7.
3 SG Circular 10/2009 'Planning Enforcement' Annex A para 8.

9.38 A stop notice may be served on any person who appears to the planning authority to have an interest in the land or to be engaged in activities which constitute or involve the breach of planning control alleged in the enforcement notice. After serving a stop notice, the planning authority may publicise it by displaying on the land a site notice, stating the requirements of the stop notice, that it has been served on a particular person or persons, and the consequences of contravening it. This has the effect of bringing people who have not been served with the stop notice within the prohibition.

9.39 There is no right of appeal against a stop notice. However, the legal validity of the notice may be challenged by an application to the Court of Session for judicial review on the ground that the planning authority is acting beyond its powers. Any ground of challenge that would be competent at an enforcement notice appeal (for example there has been no breach of planning control) falls to be decided at such an appeal, and the recipient's remedy would be a possible compensation claim for loss caused by the stop notice should the enforcement notice be quashed (see below).[1] It is also possible to challenge a stop notice by a defence lodged by the offender to any criminal proceedings resulting from a contravention of the notice. For example, in *R v Dhar*[2] a stop notice so widely framed as to include activities that were not actually in breach of planning control was quashed and the defendant's appeal against his conviction was allowed (it was held not to be permissible to look at the enforcement notice in order to ascertain the actual extent of the prohibition). Unless previously withdrawn by the planning authority, a stop notice stands or falls with the enforcement notice to which it relates, ie if the enforcement notice itself is withdrawn or quashed on appeal. It will also be superseded by the enforcement notice if and when the latter comes into effect.

1 *Central Regional Council v Clackmannan District Council* 1983 SLT 666; *Earl Car Sales (Edinburgh) v City of Edinburgh District Council* 1984 SLT 8.
2 [1993] 2 PLR 60, CA.

9.40 Scottish Ministers, after consulting the relevant planning authority, also have power to serve a stop notice, subject to the same provisions that apply to stop notices served by a planning authority.

Penalty for contravention

9.41 Under s 144 of the 1997 Act, contravention of a stop notice is an offence, which can (currently) lead to a fine of up to £20,000 on summary conviction (or an unlimited fine if convicted on indictment). In determining the amount of any fine payable, the court must take into account any financial benefit which might accrue to the offender as a result of the breach. As with enforcement notices, if the breach is a continuing one, the person concerned may be charged again at a later date. It is a valid defence that the stop notice was not served on the accused *and* that the accused had no reasonable cause to believe that the activity was prohibited by a stop notice.

Compensation for loss due to stop notice

9.42 It would obviously be unfair to the recipient of a stop notice if the effect of the notice was to cause that person loss or damage and the notice turned out to be unnecessary or otherwise unjustified. In certain circumstances, therefore, s 143 of the 1997 Act provides that compensation may be payable in respect of any loss or damage suffered as a result of a stop notice to any person who had an interest in the land when the notice was first served.[1] These circumstances are: (a) where the enforcement notice is quashed on appeal; (b) where it is varied in such a way that excludes the activity which is the subject of the stop notice; (c) where the enforcement notice is withdrawn; or (d) where the stop notice itself is withdrawn. However, no compensation will be payable if the enforcement notice's demise results from planning permission being granted for the unauthorised development, either by the planning authority itself or by Scottish Ministers on appeal. The compensation may include a sum payable in respect of a breach of contract, eg if compliance with a stop notice has caused the recipient to be sued for damages. A compensation claim for loss due to a stop notice is not time-barred after five years under the short negative prescription.[2] Despite this, there was evidence suggesting that planning authorities were often deterred from using stop notices because of the possibility of having to pay compensation.[3] Any disputes regarding the amount of compensation should be referred to the Lands Tribunal.

1 See *Sample (Warkworth) Ltd v Alnwick District Council* (1984) 48 P & CR 474; *Robert Barnes & Co Ltd v Malvern Hills District Council* (1985) 274 EG 733; *Graysmark v South Hams District Council* [1989] 03 EG 75.

2 *Holt v Dundee District Council* 1990 SLT (Lands Tr) 30.

3 *Review of Planning Enforcement*, School of Planning and Housing, Edinburgh College of Art/Heriot-Watt University and Brodies WS, HMSO 1998, paras 7.15–7.20.

9.43 No compensation will be payable where the activity prohibited constitutes or contributes to a breach of planning control, or where the loss could have been avoided by proper compliance with a planning contravention notice.

Temporary Stop Notice

9.44 In order to address planning authorities' perceived shortcomings of the stop notice, the 2006 Act introduced ss 144A to 144D into the 1997 Act enabling a planning authority to issue a temporary stop notice, to take effect immediately (as opposed to the three-day notice period for a Stop Notice) and without the requirement for an Enforcement Notice (a pre-requisite for a Stop Notice). A temporary stop notice requires the immediate cessation of an activity from the moment it is displayed on site. Displaying the notice on site (along with a notice stating under s 144B that it is an offence to contravene the temporary stop notice) is sufficient for it to be regarded as having been served, even if it is later removed. The planning authority therefore needs to take steps to ensure that there is evidence that the notice has been correctly displayed (eg by using time/date photography).

9.45 Copies of the notice may also be served on any person who, in the view of the planning authority, has an interest in the land or is engaged in the activity. This is also desirable to ensure that such persons are aware that a temporary stop notice has been displayed.[1] Such a notice would be used to stop an activity that would, in the view of the planning authority, cause damage to the environment and/or local amenity. The Notice could restrict the activity to certain times or parts of the site, rather than the whole site, and at all times, as appropriate. Since it can be served independently of an enforcement notice, there is no provision for appeal and consequent suspension of the notice.

1 SG Circular 10/2009 'Planning Enforcement,, Annex I.

9.46 A planning authority may issue a temporary stop notice where it considers that:

- there has been a breach of planning control in relation to any land in its area; and,
- the breach consists of engagement in an activity; and
- it is expedient that the activity is stopped immediately.

The notice must be in writing and must:

- specify the activity in question;
- prohibit engagement in the activity (or in so much of the activity as is specified in the notice); and
- set out the authority's reason for issuing the notice.

9.47 A temporary stop notice applies for 28 days, though the planning authority can specify a shorter period. In addition, the authority can withdraw the notice at any time before it is due to expire. Such a notice can be issued only once, ie there is no scope to issue a second or subsequent notice on expiry of the first unless between the issue of the notices the planning authority has taken some other form of enforcement action. This action must relate to the same activity as the temporary stop notice. This would usually be through the issue of an enforcement notice and associated stop notice, or the granting of an interdict (see below).

9.48 There are a number of restrictions to the use of a temporary stop notice:

- as for a stop notice, it may not be used to prohibit the use of a building as a dwellinghouse (but may be used to stop additional development of the dwellinghouse); and
- it may not stop an activity which has been ongoing (whether continuously or not) for at least four years, ending with the day on which a copy of the notice is first displayed; however, this restriction does not apply in the case of building, engineering, mining or other operations, or the deposit of waste materials.

9.49 Scottish Ministers have the power to prescribe other activities which may not be the subject of a temporary stop notice. In the interests of equality and fairness, and in particular the special needs of gypsies and travelers, the Town and Country Planning (Temporary Stop Notice)

(Scotland) Regulations 2009 state that a temporary stop notice may not prohibit the siting of a caravan on land[1] provided that:

- the caravan is stationed on the land immediately prior to the issue of the temporary stop notice; and
- the caravan is at that time occupied by a person as his/her main residence.

1 However, a temporary stop notice could be used to prohibit additional caravans appearing on a site. In England the position was similar (but not the same as in Scotland) until 4 May 2013 when the Town and Country Planning (Temporary Stop Notice) (England) (Revocation) Regulations 2013 (SI 2013/830) came into force and revoked the Town and Country Planning (Temporary Stop Notice) (England) Regulations 2005 (SI 2005/206). The position now in England is that there are no restrictions on the use of temporary stop notices.

9.50 It is an offence for a person to contravene a temporary stop notice which has been served on them, or which has been correctly displayed on the land. It is also an offence to permit or cause a contravention of the notice (eg by a landowner allowing another person to carry out a prohibited activity on the land in question). If a person repeatedly breaches the terms of a temporary stop notice over a period of days, they may be convicted of more than one offence. It is a defence to prove that the temporary stop notice was not served on the person accused of contravening it and that the accused did not, and could not reasonably be expected to, know of its existence. So it is important that the notice is prominently displayed (eg at the entrance to the site in question) and to record proof that it was correctly displayed. On larger sites it may be appropriate to display several copies of the notice. It is also good practice to serve copies of the notice on individuals, for the avoidance of doubt.

9.51 A person convicted of contravening a temporary stop notice is liable on summary conviction, to a fine (currently) not exceeding £20,000, and on conviction on indictment, to an indeterminate fine. In determining the amount of the fine, the court will take into account any financial benefit which the convicted person has made from the activity which constituted the offence.

9.52 The scope for compensation arising from the serving of a temporary stop notice is much more restricted than for a Stop Notice served with an Enforcement Notice (a main reason for its introduction was to address the perceived underuse of the Stop Notice by planning authorities, as revealed by previous research[1]). A person who at the time the temporary stop notice is issued has an interest in the land to which the notice relates, whether as owner or occupier or otherwise, may be entitled to compensation for any loss or damage directly attributable to the prohibition effected by the notice. However this only applies if either:

- the activity specified in the notice had already been granted planning permission by the planning authority; or
- a certificate of lawful use or development applied to the activity; or
- the planning authority withdraws the notice (unless the notice is withdrawn as a result of planning permission being granted after the notice had been served).

The likelihood of the planning authority being liable for compensation is therefore low. This can be minimised further by the planning authority checking its records to establish whether there is any current planning permission for the site, and if so what activities the permission allows.

1 *Review of Planning Enforcement*, School of Planning and Housing, Edinburgh College of Art/Heriot-Watt University and Brodies WS, HMSO 1998.

9.53 The provisions of s 143(3)–(7) which apply to compensation in respect of a stop notice apply also to a temporary stop notice ie:

- if, at any time when the notice is in force, the prohibited activity was a breach of planning control, the planning authority are not liable to pay compensation for any consequent loss or damages (s 143(5)(a));
- anyone who failed to respond to a planning contravention notice, or other statutory notice requiring information, cannot obtain compensation from the planning authority in respect of any loss or damage which could have been avoided if they had provided the information requested, or had otherwise co-operated with the planning authority when responding to the notice (s 143(5)(b)).

6. BREACH OF CONDITION NOTICE

9.54 The breach of condition notice was first introduced through the Planning and Compensation Act 1991, specifically for breaches of planning conditions. The intention was to provide a simpler and quicker remedy in such cases, thereby cutting down the number of enforcement notices and enforcement notice appeals. Under s 145 of the 1997 Act, a planning authority may serve a breach of condition notice on any person who is carrying out or has carried out the development, or any person having control of the land. However, the latter will only apply if the breach consists of a continuing use of the land rather than a one-off operation; for example, if the developer of a residential estate is in breach of a condition requiring landscaping to be carried out, it is only reasonable that this should be enforced against the developer rather than the future residents.

9.55 A breach of condition notice must not only specify the activities which must cease, but also the steps to be taken, otherwise it could be invalid.[1] It must also allow a period of time (not less than 28 days) for compliance. Non-compliance with a breach of condition notice is an offence which is subject to a summary prosecution in the sheriff court and, as with enforcement notices, in the case of a continuing offence the person concerned may be charged again at a later date. It is a defence for the person charged that the accused took all reasonable measures to secure compliance with the conditions specified in the notice or (where that was the ground for serving the notice) that accused no longer had control of the land.[2] As with enforcement notices, a breach of condition notice will cease to have effect with the retrospective grant of planning permission for a development that is inconsistent with it, and will also be rendered ineffective in relation to any condition that is discharged after the service of the notice.

1 *Scottish Coal Ltd v East Lothian Council*, 2001 SLT 495; [2001] 1 PLR 1.
2 See *Quinton v North Cornwall District Council* 1994 CLY 4315.

9.56 There is no right of appeal against the issue of a breach of condition notice, since applicants for planning permission had the right of appeal to the Scottish Ministers against any conditions or limitations attached to the permission. As a planning condition should only have been imposed out of necessity, it is likely that a failure to comply with it will be damaging and justify enforcement action. However the legal validity of the notice may be challenged by judicial review[1] or in a defence to a prosecution in the sheriff court for non-compliance with the notice.[2] The planning authority also has the discretionary power to withdraw a notice, by serving a withdrawal notice on recipients of the original notice, at anytime (including after the expiry of the compliance period). The withdrawal of a notice does not affect the planning authority's power to serve a further notice.

1 See eg *R v Kensington & Chelsea RLBC*, ex p Lawrie Plantation Services [1997] NPC 30.
2 See *Dilieto v Ealing London Borough Council* (1998) Times April 10.

9.57 A breach of condition notice may normally only be served within 10 years of the breach of planning control to which it relates having occurred. However, these immunity provisions are qualified by s 124(4) of the 1997 Act which provides that, even when the standard time limits have expired, a notice may still be served if an enforcement notice relating to the same breach is in effect or, in the preceding four years, the planning authority have taken or purported to take enforcement action in respect of that breach.[1]

1 SG Circular 10/2009 'Planning Enforcement', Annex A para 12.

9.58 A breach of condition notice must specify the steps which the authority requires to be taken, or the activities which they require to cease, in order to ensure compliance with the condition(s) specified in the notice. These may include:

- *specific actions* (such as requiring submission for approval of a landscaping scheme as a condition of the permission) and/or
- *prohibitions* (such as requiring a restaurant or hot food takeaway to comply with the specified opening hours in a planning permission).

9.59 Section 145(9) of the 1997 Act states that it is an offence for a recipient of a notice to be in breach of a breach of condition notice. A notice is breached if, after the expiry of the compliance period (a) any condition specified in the notice has not been complied with and (b) the specified steps have not been taken, or the specified activities have not ceased. Depending on the planning authority's assessment of the nature of the breach, it may issue a fixed penalty notice (see below). The person would then have the option to pay the fixed penalty within 30 days, which would indemnify them from prosecution. Alternatively, a summary prosecution in the Sheriff or District Court may be sought, under s 145(9), for the offence of contravening a Breach of Condition Notice. The maximum penalty on conviction is a fine not exceeding level 3 on the standard scale (currently £1,000). It is a defence for those charged to prove that they took all reasonable measures to secure compliance with the conditions specified in the notice, or that they did not have control of the land at the date when the offence is alleged to have taken place.

9.60 The planning authority still has the option of using an enforcement notice for breach of planning conditions, though one would have expected the more summary form of the breach of condition notice (particularly considering the curtailing of appeal rights) to have become the normal method of enforcing this type of breach. However, research[1] found that, while there has been widespread use of breach of condition notices, planning authorities still prefer in many cases to use an enforcement notice for breach of a planning condition. The main reason appears to be that the enforcement notice is a more flexible tool for enforcing planning conditions that have been imperfectly worded, presumably because of the Scottish Ministers' power on appeal to amend the wording of conditions. It may also be preferred in cases where remedies are needed that can only flow from an enforcement notice, for example where stopping the breach is a matter of urgency requiring the use of a stop notice, or where the planning authority needs to take direct action to remedy the breach by stepping in and doing the work itself.

1 *Review of Planning Enforcement*, School of Planning and Housing, Edinburgh College of Art/Heriot-Watt University and Brodies WS, HMSO 1998, paras 7.21–7.26.

7. INTERDICT

9.61 Section 146 of the 1997 Act enables planning authorities to apply for an interdict to restrain actual or anticipated breaches of planning control. The planning authority may apply either to the sheriff court or the Court of Session for this civil remedy. Application for interdict can be made independently of any other enforcement power. It is entirely at the discretion of the court whether or not to grant such an interdict. A planning authority may also apply for an *interim* interdict, which is an interim measure designed to preserve the status quo or prevent temporary and imminent wrong. The planning authority must be able to establish a *prima facie* case whereupon the court consider whether the planning authority has presented sufficient facts to establish a compelling need for immediate protection by the grant of an interim interdict.

9.62 In the case of a breach that has already occurred, an interdict will not necessarily achieve anything that could not be done by an enforcement notice followed, if necessary, by a stop notice. Indeed, in view of the court's discretion, the latter would provide in the first instance more certainty of the outcome, though the enforcement notice could of course be subject to appeal. On the other hand, an enforcement notice can only be used in relation to the breaches of planning control specified in s 123 of the 1997 Act, ie carrying out a development without planning permission or failing to comply with a planning condition. In *Perth and Kinross Council v Alexander Lowther* [1] council officers had been stopped by the defenders from taking direct action to remove caravans, in implementation of an enforcement notice. It was held that interdict could be employed more widely than an enforcement notice in order to enforce other controls conferred by the legislation, in this case to prevent the defenders from wilfully obstructing council officers in the exercise of their powers. In relation to a future breach, interdict provides a useful alternative to a planning contravention notice. Moreover, unlike the latter, which can only be enforced if followed by an enforcement or breach of condition notice, interdict has the court's backing from the outset. Earlier research [2] found that interdict, when used, has proved to be very effective, but that it has been employed very rarely. This is because the planning authority runs the danger of becoming liable in damages if an interim interdict is used excessively, or if an interdict is used in conjunction with an enforcement notice against which there is a successful appeal.

1 (1996) 58 SPEL 119.
2 *Review of Planning Enforcement*, op cit paras 7.33–7.37.

9.63 As a consequence of the Human Rights Act 1988, the use of the equivalent to interdict in England and Wales (injunction) under the Town and Country Planning Act 1990 to control breaches of planning law has been considered and clarified by the House of Lords,[1] which sets out the basis of the court's powers to grant an injunction under the equivalent section of the 1990 Act.[2] The court considered a number of cases relating to the stationing of gypsy caravans in the green belt. The House of Lords set out the principles governing the grant of an injunction. In summary these are:

(i) the discretion of the court to decide whether an injunction should be granted should be exercised with due regard to the purpose for which it is conferred (in this case to restrain threatened breaches of planning control). This is an original and discretionary, not a supervisory, jurisdiction. The power exists mainly to permit abuses to be curbed and urgent solutions provided where these are called for;
(ii) the court need not examine matters of planning policy or judgement that are the exclusive preserve of the authorities administering the planning regime;
(iii) nevertheless the court is not obliged to grant relief because a planning authority considered it necessary or expedient to restrain a planning breach;
(iv) having regard to s 6 of the Human Rights Act 1998 and Article 8 of the European Convention on Human Rights and Fundamental Freedoms,[3] the court should only grant an injunction where it is just and proportionate to do so.

1 *South Bucks District Council v Porter* [2003], JPL 1412.
2 Section 187B.
3 Right to respect for private and family life, home and correspondence.

8. RIGHT OF ENTRY

9.64 Section 156 of the 1997 Act provides that a person with written authorisation from a planning authority may enter any land to find out if there has been a breach of control requiring use of the authority's enforcement powers, or to determine how these powers should be exercised. There is also a right of entry in order to check whether enforcement action already carried out has been complied with. The right of entry should be exercised at a reasonable hour and only if there are reasonable grounds for entering, with 24 hour notice required before entry to a dwellinghouse. Similar rights may be exercised by Scottish Ministers, after consultation with the appropriate planning authority. If admission is refused, or a request for admission is not replied to within a reasonable time, entry can only be obtained with a warrant from the sheriff. A warrant may also be obtained if refusal is reasonably apprehended or the case is one of urgency.

9.65 A person who has taken entry should leave the property secured to the same standard against trespass as it was secured immediately before taking entry. If exercising the right of entry causes damage to any moveable property, the planning authority (or Scottish Ministers, as the case may be) may be liable to pay compensation. The powers also allow that if necessary, neighbouring land can be entered, whether or not it is in the same ownership, or is occupied by the person whose land is being investigated.

9.66 In addition to the above provisions, rights of entry for a number of purposes are conferred by ss 269 and 270 of the 1997 Act, including for the purpose of ascertaining whether a stop notice or an enforcement notice is being complied with.

9. DIRECT ACTION

9.67 If compliance with an enforcement notice requires steps to be taken (ie works to be carried out as opposed to mere cessation of an unlawful use) and this has not been done within the specified period, under s 135 of the 1997 Act the planning authority may enter the land and do the work itself. Any expense so incurred is recoverable from the owner or lessee of the land and, if someone else is responsible for the breach, the owner or lessee may in turn recover the expense from that person. A warrant may be obtained from the sheriff if necessary. The planning authority may sell any materials recovered by it from the land, unless the owner claims them within three days, but the proceeds must be paid to the owner, after deducting any expenses due to the planning authority. In one English case, a landowner responded to enforcement proceedings by submitting a retrospective planning application which was refused. It was held that the planning authority was entitled to go ahead with the demolition of an unauthorised building, even though the owner's appeal against the refusal of permission, which had little chance of success, had still not been finally concluded.[1] The *Review of Planning Enforcement* [2] found that direct action is in fact hardly ever used because the costs, although legally due to the planning authority, often prove to be irrecoverable in practice.

1 *R v Chiltern District Council, ex p Dyason* [1997] EGCS 147.
2 *Review of Planning Enforcement,* ibid, paras 7.27–7.32.

10. IMMUNITY FROM ENFORCEMENT ACTION

Four-year rule

9.68 Certain types of breach become immune from enforcement after four years namely (a) the carrying out of an unauthorised building, engineering, mining or other operation or (b) an unauthorised change of the use of any building to that of a single dwellinghouse.[1] In the case of (a) the four-year period runs from the date on which the operations were substantially completed. In the case of (b) the period runs from the date of the breach. A breach that falls under (b) above can come about in either of two ways: (i) as a development that should have required planning permission, ie an unauthorised material change of use; or (ii) as a breach of a planning condition which prohibited change to a single dwellinghouse.

1 See *Beesley* case below.

9.69 In relation to the equivalent English provision, the Court of Appeal has held that changing the use of a building to that of a single dwellinghouse includes not only obvious examples such as the amalgamation of dwellings or the change from a commercial to a residential use, but also the common situation where a house is subdivided into flats;[1] the latter is specifically declared to be a material change of use under s 26(3)(a) of the 1997 Act. The reasoning behind this interpretation is that the word 'building' is defined (in both the English and Scottish legislation) to include 'any part of a building' (s 277(1)). If part of a building, therefore, becomes a separate flat this means that, in terms of the statutory definition, a 'building' will have become a single dwellinghouse, and the same will be individually true of all the other flats created by the subdivision. On the other hand, if a material change of use results from multiple occupation of a dwellinghouse where facilities are shared (that is from an intensification of the use rather than subdivision of the building), it will not be included within the above exception and, like all other material changes of use, will be subject to the ten-year rule.

1 *Van Dyck v Secretary of State for the Environment and Southend on Sea Borough Council; Doncaster Borough Council v Secretary of State for the Environment and Dunhill* [1993] JPL 565, [1993] 29 EG 112.

Ten-year rule

9.70 All other breaches become immune ten years after the date of the breach, ie all material changes of use and all breaches of planning conditions apart from those involving a change to a single dwelling-house (in the wider sense of the term explained above). An unauthorised development which is more than four years old may nevertheless still be subject to enforcement proceedings if an unlawful material change of use is also involved, eg where the termination of an illegal use involving the parking of commercial vehicles also required the removal of hard-core which had been laid more than four years before.[1]

1 *Murfitt v Secretary of State for the Environment* (1980) 40 P&CR 254.

9.71 Provided that enforcement action has taken place within the appropriate time limit, further enforcement action may follow outwith the limit, as long as less than four years has passed since the first enforcement action. This means that where a planning authority has served an enforcement notice in time but the notice turns out to be legally invalid, it may take a 'second bite at the cherry' by serving a fresh notice after the time limit has expired. However, the new notice must itself be served within four years of the original notice, and this further limit applies irrespective of whether the breach was subject to the four-year or to the ten-year rule; for example, if a defective enforcement notice for an unauthorised material change of use to which the ten-year rule applies is served within the ten year limit, any new notice outwith that limit will have to be served within four years of the defective notice.[1]

1 See *Barn Properties Ltd v Secretary of State for Scotland* 1995 SCLR 113; (1995) SPEL 49:52.

9.72 Although the apparent purpose of the above provision was to provide for situations where the original notice, served within the appropriate time limit, was defective, the actual requirement laid down by the 1997 Act is that the planning authority, in its first attempt, should 'have taken or purported to take enforcement action.' This suggests that the provision may be wider in scope and may cover situations where the first notice was not actually invalid; eg if a valid notice served within the time limit was later withdrawn, the planning authority could serve a new notice outwith the limit.

9.73 It should also be noted that enforcement action is defined as the issue of either an enforcement or a breach of condition notice, and so it follows that it is not enough, in order to preserve its enforcement rights, for a planning authority merely to serve a planning contravention notice within the time limit unless it is followed by one of the other types of notice before the limit expires. If an enforcement notice has been served within the appropriate time limit, it may be followed by a breach of condition notice outwith the limit. The above provisions do not provide immunity against breaches of listed building control. Breaches of listed building control *never* become immune (see Chapter 12).

11. REGISTER OF NOTICES

9.74 Under s 147(1) of the 1997 Act, every planning authority must keep a register of enforcement notices, breach of condition notices and stop notices which have been served in relation to land in their district. Under s 147(2) the register should be available for inspection by the public at all reasonable hours. Applications for certificates of lawful use or development (see below) should be kept in the planning authority's register of planning applications, in accordance with the Town and Country Planning (General Development Procedure) (Scotland) Order 1992 (as amended).

12. NOTICE OF INITIATION AND COMPLETION OF DEVELOPMENT

9.75 Section 6 of the 2006 Act introduced a new requirement (s 27A (1) of the 1997 Act) that the planning authority must be notified of the date work is expected to commence on any development for which planning permission has been granted, and before commencement of that work. It is not a breach of panning control if the work does not actually commence on the date specified in the notice, but some time afterwards, as there may be a number of reasons (not under the control of the developer) why the development does not commence on the specified date. When granting planning permission, the planning authority is required under s 27A(2) to make the applicant aware that they are required to submit such a notice, and that failure to do so may result in a breach of planning control, in response to which enforcement action may be taken. Under s 27B(1) developers are further required to notify the planning authority when the work is completed. If the development is to be carried out in phases, then each phase is subject to the requirement for a notice of completion.

9.76 Under s 27C of the 1997 Act, information regarding the development must be displayed in a notice on site for any category of development specified by Scottish Ministers.[1] The information must be displayed in such a way that it is accessible to the public. Failure to display such a Notice would be a breach of planning control. These notices are intended to alert the planning authority and, in the case of any notice under s 27C the general public, to active development in their area, and to assist the planning authority in monitoring the implementation of planning permissions in their area.[2]

1 The *Town and Country Planning (Development Management Procedure) (Scotland) Regulations* 2013 (SSI 2013 No 155) reg 41 and SG Circular 3/2013 'Development Management Procedures'.

2 SG Circular 9/2009 'Planning Enforcement, Annex B.

13. FIXED PENALTY NOTICE

9.77 Section 136A gives planning authorities the power to issue a fixed penalty notice as an alternative to prosecution for failure to comply with the terms of an Enforcement Notice (remember that the offence is failure to comply with the terms of a statutory notice, not a breach of planning control in itself). Section 145A provides similar powers for breaching the terms of a Breach of Condition Notice. A fixed penalty notice must be issued within six months of the end of the compliance period specified in the Enforcement Notice and provided that the breach is not already subject to prosecution proceedings.

9.78 For planning purposes, a fixed penalty notice is a notice offering a person the opportunity of discharging any liability for prosecution for failing to comply with an enforcement notice or breach of condition notice, by paying the planning authority a penalty of an amount specified in the notice within 30 days. The 30 day period starts the day the notice is served, but if payment is made within the first 15 days then the amount payable is reduced by 25%. The planning authority retains any sums paid. During the 30-day period no court proceedings can be initiated. If the penalty is not paid within this period, then it is open to the planning authority to consider prosecution.

9.79 Only one fixed penalty notice may be issued in relation to a particular step or activity. Since an enforcement notice may list several steps to be taken (or activities to be ceased) in order to comply with the notice, and since failure to comply with any step or activity is a breach of the notice, it follows that there could be several fixed penalty notices issued, each relating to a *different* step or activity. By paying the fixed penalty, the person discharges any liability for prosecution. However, payment does not discharge the requirement to comply with the terms of the original enforcement notice or breach of condition notice (since the payment may be made but the breach remains) and the planning authority retains the power to take direct action to remedy the breach and recover any costs associated with such work.

9.80 There is no right of appeal against the serving of a fixed penalty notice. It is open to the person in receipt of the notice to make representations to the planning authority that they have in fact remedied the breach and should not therefore be required to pay the fixed penalty. Whilst there is no formal process for withdrawing a fixed penalty notice once served, it is open to the planning authority to take no further action if payment is not made.

9.81 It is at the discretion of the planning authority whether to issue a fixed penalty notice, and indeed it is open to the authority not to take further action in respect of the failure to comply with the Enforcement Notice. It is also at the discretion of the authority whether to take direct action to remedy the breach at the expiry of the Enforcement Notice period, regardless of whether any other action is considered appropriate. In reaching a decision as to whether or not to issue a fixed penalty notice or to take alternative action, planning authorities should apply the principles of planning enforcement that any action should be commensurate to the nature and scale of the breach.

9.82 The level of penalty in a fixed penalty notice is set by Scottish Ministers under the Town and Country Planning (Amount of Fixed Penalty) (Scotland) Regulations 2009. At the time of writing the penalty for breach of the terms of an Enforcement Notice is £2,000, and for breaching the terms of a Brach of Condition Notice it is £300.

14. CERTIFICATE OF LAWFUL USE OR DEVELOPMENT

9.83 In cases where a completed operational project or an existing use does not have the benefit of planning permission, there may nevertheless be no breach of planning control because the project or use falls outside the definition of development, or because it has become immune from enforcement by the passage of time. Nevertheless, the owner may suffer a disadvantage, eg if prospective purchasers are deterred by the lack of planning permission, fearing the possibility of enforcement proceedings. In such cases any person may acquire the evidence needed by obtaining from the planning authority a certificate of lawful use or development. This has replaced the former certificate of established use, which only applied to uses of land and not to completed building or other operations. A would-be developer may also be unsure whether a proposed activity will require planning permission. The formal method of checking the position is to apply for a certificate of lawful use or development in respect of a proposed or future development. The procedure provides a means for establishing the planning status of land, ie whether an existing or proposed use or development is lawful for planning purposes.

9.84 Section 150(2) of the 1997 Act provides that, for the purposes of the Act, uses of land and operations are lawful at any time:

- if no enforcement action may then be taken in respect of them, whether because they did not involve development or require planning permission, or
- because the time for enforcement action against them has expired, or
- for any other reason; and
- that they do not contravene any of the requirements of any enforcement notice then in force.

Existing use or development

9.85 Under s 150, any person (not just one with a legal interest in the land) may apply for a certificate in order to ascertain whether any existing use, any operations that have already been carried out, or any breach of a condition or limitation, are lawful. Breaches which have become immune from enforcement are specifically declared to be lawful. The onus is on the applicant to prove the lawfulness of their development or use and to provide the information and evidence necessary to satisfy the planning authority. However, if that is done, the planning authority is bound to grant the certificate. A fee is payable to the planning authority in respect of an application.

9.86 The existence of a lawful use is something which, because of the lapse of time, could be difficult to prove. Although the onus of proof rests with the applicant, the evidence provided does not need to prove the case beyond reasonable doubt, but only need show that on the balance of probability the use is lawful.[1] There appears to be no guidance on what would constitute evidence, but business records (for example correspondence on the headed notepaper of reputable firms), or signed statements by third parties would probably be acceptable. The evidence produced by the applicant does not need to be corroborated by an independent source, which means that the planning authority, in the absence of any contradictory evidence of its own, may find it difficult to refuse a certificate. If a certificate is refused on the grounds of insufficient evidence, but better evidence comes to light at a later date, the applicant may apply again.

1 See SG Circular 10/2009 'Planning Enforcement', Annex F para 21.

Proposed use or development

9.87 Basically the procedure and nature of the certificate are the same, although the use or operational project referred to has not yet begun. If a certificate is granted, there is no need for the applicant to obtain planning permission before going ahead; if the certificate is refused, planning permission *is* required. This device has been used by major retailers in recent years to enable the installation of extra floor space through mezzanines.[1] In this case the High Court struck down a Planning Inspector's decision to grant a lawful development certificate on appeal for the use of a mezzanine at a retail park. The planning authority had served an enforcement notice alleging the installation of the mezzanine floor breached a 1987 planning permission restricting the amount of retail floorspace. The Court determined that although the construction of the mezzanine was lawful because it did not materially affect the external appearance of the building, its use for trading breached the terms of the 1987 permission. In an earlier case,[2] the Court granted a lawful development certificate because it determined that the construction of a mezzanine floor did not comprise a material change in the character of the land because the 1972 planning permission for the construction of the retail unit did not include a condition restricting the total floor area.

1 *Northampton BC v First Secretary of State* [7 February 2005]; CO/5625/2004.
2 *Eastleigh BC v First Secretary of State* [28 May 2004]; CO/1700/2004.

9.88 Sometimes a developer, on making a more informal approach to the planning authority, may be given an assurance by a planning officer that planning permission is not necessary for a project, and there have been cases where this has happened but the planning authority has later taken a different view. In such a case, the planning authority may be bound by its officer's statement and barred from taking enforcement action, but only in the following circumstances: (a) where the power to make such a decision has been formally delegated to the officer; or (b) where the officer not only has ostensible (that is apparent) authority to make the decision, but this apparent authority is backed up by other evidence, such as a widespread practice within that authority of officers making similar decisions. In the latter case the developer must also have acted upon the officer's assurance to his detriment (for example by going ahead with the development).[1] The decided cases are mainly English and are an application of the English doctrine of estoppel; however, similar principles would probably apply in Scotland under the doctrine of personal bar.

1 See Young & Rowan Robinson *Scottish Planning Law and Procedure* (1985) pp 34–39 and cases cited there, in particular *Lever Finance Ltd v City of Westminster London Borough Council* [1971] 1 QB 222 and *Western Fish Products Ltd v Penwith District Council* [1981] 2 All ER 204; see also *London Borough of Camden v Secretary of State for the Environment* (1993) 67 P&CR 59, *East Lindsey District Council v Secretary of State for the Environment* [1994] EGCS 119 and *Garner v Secretary of State for the Environment* [1997] CLY 4063.

Contents of certificate

9.89 Section 150(5) provides for certain matters a certificate must contain. A certificate should: (a) specify the land to which it relates; (b) describe the use or operations to which it relates; (c) give the reason why the use or operation are lawful; and (d) specify the date of application. In the case of (b), if a use falls within one of the classes of the Use Classes Order,[1] it should be identified by reference to that class. In the case of a certificate in respect of an existing (rather than a proposed) use or development, (b) or (c) may relate instead to breach of a planning condition or limitation.

1 Town and Country Planning (Use Classes) (Scotland) Order 1997 (as amended).

9.90 A certificate may relate to the whole or only part of the land specified in the application. Where an application specifies two or more uses, operations or planning conditions, the certificate may relate to one or more of these rather than all of them. This gives a planning authority some flexibility in situations where it is unhappy with parts of the application; the applicant can be given some (as opposed to all) of what has been sought rather than be refused outright. Certificates of lawful use or development should be placed on the planning authority's register of planning applications and decisions.

False or misleading applications

9.91 If, after a certificate is granted, it is found that a statement or document used in the application was materially false or that any material information was withheld, the planning authority may revoke the certificate. If this was done knowingly or recklessly or with intent to deceive, the person responsible is guilty of a criminal offence.

Right of appeal

9.92 An applicant may appeal to the Scottish Ministers against either an outright or partial refusal to grant a certificate, and also against a deemed refusal where the planning authority fail to respond in time. The appeal must be lodged within a prescribed period, which should not be less than 28 days. As with other planning appeals,[1] the appointed Reporter decides whether there is sufficient information to make a decision or whether further processing is required and, taking due account of the views of the applicant or appellant and the planning authority, what form it should take.

1 The Planning etc (Scotland) Act 2006 removed the right to be heard for appellants and planning authorities in a number of areas of planning.

9.93 In *Whitley and Sons v Secretary of State for Wales* [1] it was established that, where works have begun without a condition precedent (pre-commencement condition) being fully discharged, those works would not constitute a lawful implementation of the consent to prevent it from lapsing, and would result in an unauthorised development. This has become known as the 'Whitley Principle'. However, where a developer commences operations in breach of such a condition precedent, provided details are submitted for approval (a) before the consent expires and (b) those details are approved, this can prevent the permission from lapsing. In *Greyfort Properties v Secretary of State for Communities and Local Government*,[2] the Court of Appeal rejected an attempt by Greyfort Properties to apply the Whitley principle to a planning permission granted in 1974 to build 19 flats in Torquay. Greyfort had submitted an application for a Certificate of Lawful Use or Development that would allow it to carry out the development without submitting a fresh planning application. However, the 1974 permission included a condition that *'before any work is commenced on the site, the ground floor levels of the building hereby permitted shall be agreed with the Local Planning Authority in writing.'* The permission stipulated that work had to begin within five years. In 1978 Greyfort carried out some access work, and argued that this work amounted to commencement of the development, meaning that the planning permission remained in force (and therefore a fresh application would not be needed). However, the planning inspector said that the access works had been carried out in breach of the planning condition, and that the works did not amount to commencement of the development. The planning inspector's decision was upheld by the High Court. Greyfort appealed this ruling at the Court of Appeal, which held that, although preparatory works relating to access for the development were carried out on the site in 1978 within the five-year time limit, these works did not implement the planning permission because the ground levels condition had not been satisfied. So it may not be sufficient to seek to protect an extant permission by physically commencing development before the end of the three-year period; any pre-commencement conditions must also be dealt with before commencement of building works.

1 (1992) 64 P&CR 296.
2 [2011] EWCA Civ 908, appealing [2010] EWHC 3455 (Admin).

Deception

9.94 The *Beesley* decision in England[1] has significance for the interpretation of time limits and the application for a certificate of lawful use or development. In 2001 Mr Beesley applied for and was granted planning permission for the construction of a hay barn on land which he owned in the Green Belt. In 2002 he constructed what appeared externally to be a barn but which internally was a dwellinghouse with garage and gym. In August 2002 he moved in with his family and lived there continuously for four years. The planning authority, Welwyn Hatfield Borough Council, was unaware of this. In August 2006 Mr Beesley applied for a certificate of lawfulness for use of the building as a dwellinghouse, contending that the four-year time limit for taking enforcement action had elapsed.[2] The certificate was granted and subsequently upheld by the Court of Appeal, which decided that there had been a change of use such that immunity from enforcement action was established. Welwyn Hatfield Borough Council appealed to the Supreme Court, challenging the Court of Appeal's decision on two grounds: (1) that there had not been a change of use; (2) that even if there had been, the principle of public policy that no one should be allowed to profit from his own wrong should apply, thus precluding Mr Beesley from relying on the relevant planning law (s 171B(2) of the 1990 Town and Country Planning Act). The Supreme Court unanimously allowed the Council's appeal. It concluded that the building Mr Beesley constructed was not the permitted barn, but was a dwellinghouse. Therefore there had been no change of use. It also concluded that deliberately misleading statements by an applicant take the development outside the rationale for the time limits specified in the planning acts.

1 *Secretary of State for Communities and Local Government and another v Welwyn Hatfield Borough Council* [2011] UKSC 15 (on appeal from the Court of Appeal [2010] EWCA Civ 26.)
2 Unauthorised change of the use of any building to that of a single dwellinghouse.

9.95 The Supreme Court appears to have established that: the four year time limit only applies where there has been a change in the use of a building to use as a single dwelling; s171B(2) can only apply where the building is already in existence and has already been used for some other purpose; the time limits for operational development and change of use, even when they occur together, can be enforced against separately, subject to their own limits. The statutory provisions governing the time limits for enforcement action make no reference to the date on which the breach became known to the planning authority; time begins to run from either the date of substantial completion of operational development, or from the date of the breach. Deliberate concealment or fraud by the landowner or developer has previously been regarded as irrelevant. The Supreme Court accepted the Council's argument that Mr Beesley's conduct precluded him from relying on the normal time limits for enforcement.

9.96 This aspect of the *Beesley* case has been subsequently applied by the Court of Appeal in the case of *Fidler*,[1] who concealed the construction of a mock-Tudor mansion behind straw bales. In this case, the deception was not the making of a false planning application, but the deliberate hiding of building operations behind a shield of straw bales. Four years after completion of construction, Mr Fidler applied for a certificate of lawfulness. The planning authority refused the application on the grounds that the removal of the straw bales was a necessary part of the building operations, and so the time for enforcement did not begin to run until the straw bales had been removed. This argument was accepted by the planning inspector on appeal, and upheld by the High Court. Mr Fidler was initially given permission to appeal to the Court of Appeal. However, when the Supreme Court overruled the Court of Appeal on the Beesley case, the Secretary of State applied to have Mr Fidler's permission to appeal set aside. In a judgement given on 1 September 2011, the Court of Appeal allowed that application on the basis that Mr Fidler's deliberate concealment brought his case squarely within the principles set out in the Beesley case.[2]

1 *R (Fidler) v. Secretary of State for Communities and Local Govenment* [2011] EWCA Civ 1159.

2 As a consequence of these cases, Part 5 of the *Localism Act* 2011 for England introduces new ss 171BA, 171BB and 171BC into the 1990 *Town and Country Planning Act*, providing for an extended time limit for 'cases involving concealment'. This provides a new procedure whereby a planning authority in England may obtain a 'planning enforcement order' from a magistrate's court within six months of the date on which evidence of the apparent breach of planning control came to the authority's knowledge. If granted, a planning efocement order enables the planning authority to take enforcement action at any time within the 'enforcement year', commencing 22 days from the date of the planning enforcement order.

15. ENFORCEMENT CHARTERS

9.97 The 2006 Act introduced a new section 158A into the 1997 Act requiring a planning authority to prepare an enforcement charter, requiring the planning authority to set out enforcement priorities and procedures in its area, together with the service standards it sets itself. The charter consists of a document setting out:

- the planning authority's policies for taking enforcement action;
- how members of the public can report alleged breaches to the planning authority;
- the procedure by which the public can complain to the authority about its performance in taking enforcement action.

9.98 Scottish Ministers may issue guidance on the form and content of enforcement charters (which planning authorities must have regard to), and currently they do this through a model charter displayed on the Scottish government planning website.[1] Charters must be kept up to date and re-published at least every two years. Notwithstanding this requirement, Scottish Ministers may require an individual authority to review its charter or require all authorities to review their charters (eg following changes to the enforcement system).

1 www.scotland.gov.uk/Topics/Built-Environment/planning

9.99 When publishing (or re-publishing) their charter, the planning authority must send two copies to Scottish Ministers, place a copy in each public library in their district, and publish the charter electronically, for example on their website. Scottish Ministers will then consider whether the charter meets the requirements as to form and content, and determine whether further review is required.

16. ENFORCEMENT PERFORMANCE

9.100 As previously stated, the enforcement powers introduced in the 1947 Act were extended by the Planning and Compensation Act 1991 and consolidated in the 1997 Town and Country Planning (Scotland) Act. Enforcement powers were further extended in the Planning etc (Scotland) Act 2006, principally by introducing a Temporary Stop Notice, Notices of initiation and Completion of development, and Fixed Penalty Notices as an alternative to prosecution. The changes in 1991 and 2006 were intended to strengthen the enforcement powers of planning authorities, discourage unauthorised development, and address the issues identified in research on the performance of planning authorities in implementing the enforcement powers then available, particularly their underuse.[1] Scottish Government statistical data for 2011/12 (the most recent available at the time of writing) indicates continued wide variation among planning authorities in the deployment of their enforcement powers, with: more than half of all Councils serving no Breach of Condition Notices; a similar proportion issuing 0–2 Enforcement Notices (although four of the larger authorities served 20 or more such notices); only four serving the new Temporary Stop Notice, with a similar number making use of the new Fixed Penalty Notice (between 1–4 Notices).[2] Whilst it may be too early to judge the impact of the new powers, use of the well-established powers continues at a low level, perhaps indicating issues relating to the resources for and organisation of enforcement, rather than the powers themselves.

1 *Review of Planning Enforcement*, ibid; for a summary, and comparison with equivalent research for England and Wales, see Prior A (2000) *Problems in the Theory and Practice of Planning Enforcement*, Planning Theory and Practice 1 (1), September, 53–69.
2 Scottish Government, Planning Performance Statistics 2011/12, at www.scotland.gov.uk/Topics/Statistics/Browse/Planning.

17. SUMMARY

9.101 Planning authorities have statutory powers to investigate alleged breaches of planning control and the conditions attached to planning permissions, and to take formal action where a satisfactory outcome cannot be achieved by negotiation. These powers have been recently modernised, to ensure compliance with the requirements of the development management system, a means of implementing planning policy, and to ensure justice and fairness for all.

9.102 The enforcement powers available to planning authorities are wide-ranging and discretionary. A planning authority is not required to take any particular action on a specific breach of planning control, and can decide that no action is necessary; enforcement is a means to implementing planning policy, and not an end in itself. However, planning authorities could be exposed to a potential finding of *maladministration* (and compensation) by the Scottish Public Services Ombudsman where they fail to take enforcement action where it is 'plainly necessary' (especially where it leads to injustice).

9.103 Managing 'development' effectively includes the planning authority's readiness to take enforcement action where necessary. When considering any enforcement action, the planning authority should take into account its Development Plan, and 'whether the breach of control would affect unacceptably either public amenity or the use of land and buildings meriting protection in the public interest.'[1]

1 SG Circular 10/2009: 'Planning Enforcement', para 7.

9.104 While the 2006 Act further extended the powers of planning enforcement, there appear to be continued issues within planning authorities of organisation and resourcing of enforcement, perhaps indicating that enforcement remains a Cinderella activity.

Chapter 10

Acquisition of land by planning authorities

1. INTRODUCTION

10.1 The Scottish Ministers, local authorities and other public bodies have wide powers to acquire land either by compulsory purchase or by agreement. These are often needed for new infrastructure projects such as roads, railways, and electricity lines. The power to acquire land for such projects comes from the relevant legislation (eg the Electricity Act 1989 in the case of power lines) and Scottish Government Circular 6/2011[1] lists 24 different Acts of Parliament giving such compulsory purchase powers. It is outwith the scope of this book to consider in any detail the subject of compulsory purchase law, which is comprehensively dealt with in other texts.[2] However, certain aspects of the topic are of particular relevance to planning law and will be considered briefly in part 4 below.

1 SG Circular 6/2011 'Compulsory Purchase Orders', Appendix B.
2 See particularly Rowan Robinson and Farquarson-Black *Compulsory Purchase and Compensation – The Law in Scotland* (2009).

10.2 We will deal first with two situations where the sale to the relevant public authority is at the initiative of the seller rather than the authority, which may even be compelled to purchase against its will. Nevertheless, in each of these situations (where the would-be seller serves a purchase notice or a blight notice on the authority) the sale, if confirmed, will otherwise proceed like a compulsory purchase, with compensation being paid on the usual statutory basis.

2. PURCHASE NOTICES

10.3 We have already seen that where an owner or lessee of property has received an adverse decision from a planning authority (ie planning permission for a development has been refused or has been granted subject to conditions) they may lodge an appeal with a Local Review Body or, in some cases, the Scottish Ministers.[1] If the appeal should prove unsuccessful, the applicant may feel that the effect of the refusal of permission (or of the conditions attached to the permission) is to make the property unviable or (to use the term employed in the 1997 Act) that the land 'has become incapable of reasonably beneficial use in its existing state'. In such a case the disappointed applicant has another option: they may be able to force the planning authority to buy the relevant property. They can start the relevant procedure by serving a purchase notice on the planning authority (assuming, of course, that they have been unable to negotiate a voluntary sale to the authority).

1 See Chapter 7 above.

Service of notice[1]

10.4 A purchase notice may be served where planning permission has been refused or granted subject to conditions and:

(a) the land has become incapable of reasonably beneficial use in its existing state or (in the case of a conditional permission) the conditions prevent it being put to a reasonably beneficial use; and
(b) it cannot be put to a reasonably beneficial use by carrying out an alternative development, for which planning permission has been or would be granted.[2]

It may also be served where existing planning rights are removed by the planning authority eg through the revocation of an existing planning permission[3] or the discontinuance of an established use.[4]

1 Town and Country Planning (Scotland) Act 1997, s 88.
2 Ibid, s 88(3).
3 Through an order under the Town and Country Planning (Scotland) Act 1997, s 65.
4 Through an order under the Town and Country Planning (Scotland) Act 1997, s 71.

10.5 The existence of a possible purchaser for the land is not necessarily evidence that it is capable of reasonably beneficial use.[1]

1 *Gavaghan v Secretary of State for the Environment & South Hampshire District Council* (1990) 60 P&CR 515, CA.

10.6 A purchase notice must be in writing and served either by hand or by prepaid post.[1] It must relate to *all* and not merely part of the land that was the subject of the adverse decision.[2] Also, for a notice to be successful, all of the relevant land must be incapable of reasonably beneficial use and not only part of it.[3]

1 Town and Country Planning (General) (Scotland) Regulations 1976, SI 1976/2022, reg 4(1).
2 *Smart & Courtenay Dale Ltd v Dover District Council* (1972) 23 P&CR 408; *Cook and Woodham v Winchester City Council* (1994) 69 P&CR 99.
3 *Wain v Secretary of State for the Environment* (1982) 44 P&CR 289.

10.7 The purchase notice should be served on the planning authority in whose area the land is situated and must be served within 12 months of the adverse decision.[1] In cases where the decision complained of was made by the Scottish Ministers on appeal, the 12 month period runs from the date of the appeal decision.[2] Once a purchase notice has been served on the planning authority, it is not possible for the applicant to alter it. However, it is possible to submit a new notice which replaces the original version. In those circumstances the three month period which the planning authority has to respond starts again from the date when the replacement notice is served.[3]

1 1997 Act, s 88(2); Town and Country Planning (General) (Scotland) Regulations 1976, SI 1976/2022, reg 4(2)(b).
2 *Reside v North Ayrshire Council* 2001 SLT 6; [2000] 3 PLR 86; 2000 GWD 19-767.
3 *White v Herefordshire Council* [2008] 2 All ER 852; [2008] 1 P&CR 14.

10.8 A purchase notice cannot be served in response to a deemed refusal of planning permission (ie where the planning authority has failed to reach its decision within the prescribed period). The owner must either wait until the planning authority makes its decision or lodge an appeal. If they do the latter then the purchase notice cannot be served until an appeal has been made to the Local Review Body or the Scottish Ministers and has proved unsuccessful. In the case of other refusals, there is apparently no need for the applicant to have the refusal confirmed on appeal before serving a purchase notice; however, since their main interest will normally be in obtaining permission for the development (or of ridding themself of conditions attached to a permission), it may be better for them to postpone serving a purchase notice until after the appeal; otherwise, if the planning authority was to accept the notice, they could find themselves parted with the land without knowing whether the Local Review Body or Scottish Ministers might have looked upon their proposals sympathetically.

Meaning of 'reasonably beneficial use'[1]

10.9 In determining whether the land can or cannot be put to any reasonably beneficial use, no account should be taken of any prospective development that would count as new development, ie development other than that defined in the 1997 Act as existing use development (mainly rebuilding work or subdivision of a dwelling-house).[2] The fact that the land in question would have been more valuable if the application had been approved is not by itself enough to make it incapable of reasonably beneficial use in its existing state.[3] In determining whether a site is capable of reasonably beneficial use, it is legitimate to take into account the costs involved in bringing the site into use. For example, in *Stafford BC v Secretary of State for Communities and Local Government*[4] the land in question would have been suitable for grazing but only after the removal of a derelict building and other debris. The costs of doing so were greatly in excess of the annual rent for grazing purposes. As a result, it was held that an Inspector had been entitled to confirm a purchase notice on the basis that the site was not capable of reasonably beneficial use in its existing state.

1 1997 Act, s 89.
2 Ibid, sch 11, paras 1, 2.
3 *R v Minister of Housing and Local Government ex parte Chichester District Council* [1960] 1 WLR 587.
4 [2011] EWHC 936 (Admin).

Planning authority's response[1]

10.10 On receiving a purchase notice, a planning authority has three options. It may either: (a) agree to the notice; (b) get another local authority or statutory undertaker to buy the land instead; or (c) contest the notice by referring the matter to the Scottish Ministers. If it fails to respond in one of these three ways by serving a response notice on the applicant within three months, the purchase notice will be deemed to be confirmed.[2]

1 1997 Act, s 90.
2 Ibid, s 90(5).

Scottish Ministers' options[1]

10.11 Where the matter has been referred to the Scottish Ministers they have several options: (a) they may confirm the notice; (b) they may confirm it but require another authority or statutory undertaker to purchase it instead of the planning authority; (c) where the notice has been served on the refusal of planning permission, they may grant the permission; (d) where the notice was in response to a conditional permission, they may revoke or amend the condition or conditions that caused the problem; (e) they may direct that planning permission, if applied for, should be granted for a suitable alternative development; (f) where the notice has been served in respect of a revocation of planning permission order they may cancel that order; (g) where the notice relates to an order discontinuing an existing use they may cancel or modify the relevant order; or (h) if they think that the conditions for service of a purchase notice have not been met (ie that the land can still be put to a reasonably beneficial use) they may refuse to confirm the notice. If the Scottish

Ministers do not respond within six months, the notice will be deemed to be confirmed.[2]

1 1997 Act, s 92.
2 Ibid, s 94(2), (3).

10.12 If the Scottish Ministers exercise option (e) above, it may be that the suitable alternative development, if carried out, would result in the land being worth less than its existing use value. In such a case, the planning authority must pay the owner or tenant compensation based on the difference between the two values.[1]

1 1997 Act, s 95(2)–(6).

10.13 Before making their decision, the Scottish Ministers must give notification of their intention to the applicant, the planning authority and (if appropriate) any other authority or statutory undertaker whom they intend to substitute for the planning authority as purchaser. Any of these parties may within 28 days (or any longer period specified in the notification) require to be heard by the Ministers.[1] If the Scottish Ministers fail to take any action within six months, they are deemed to have confirmed the purchase notice.[2] In certain circumstances, the validity of the Scottish Ministers' decision may be challenged in court.[3]

1 1997 Act, s 91(2), (3).
2 Ibid, s 94.
3 Ibid, ss 239, 237(3)(e).

Amenity land

10.14 Sometimes planning permission may be granted subject to a condition that part of the land (possibly a relatively small part) should be restricted in the use to which it is put, eg that it should be left unbuilt upon and used as amenity land. For example, permission may be granted for a housing development on condition that part of the land be reserved as landscaped open space. In the context of the development as a whole this may be perfectly reasonable. However, the developer may seek to get round the condition by submitting a further planning application in respect of the amenity land on its own. If permission is refused, they may then claim that the amenity land, regarded in isolation from the rest of the development, is incapable of reasonably beneficial use, and serve a purchase notice. This approach was successful in *Adams & Wade v Minister of Housing and Local Government*.[1] However, the Scottish Ministers are entitled to decide not to confirm a purchase notice in such circumstances.[2]

1 (1967) 18 P&CR 60. See however *Strathclyde Regional Council v Secretary of State for Scotland* 1987 SLT 724, and discussion in (1987) 22 SPLP 82.
2 1997 Act, s 93(3).

Effect of confirmation

10.15 If a purchase notice is accepted by the planning authority, confirmed by the Scottish Ministers or is deemed to have been confirmed, the planning authority is deemed to have served a notice to treat upon the applicant.[1] The transaction will then proceed in the same way as a compulsory purchase and the seller will be entitled to full compulsory purchase compensation, even though they initiated the proceedings by serving the purchase notice.

1 1997 Act, ss 90(3), 94(1).

3. PLANNING BLIGHT

10.16 If it is known in advance (eg by an indication in a development plan) that at some time in the future a property may be compulsorily acquired for public works, this is likely to have a depressing effect on that property's market value. Prospective purchasers will tend to be deterred by the proposals with the result that the owner, should they wish to sell, may find that they cannot obtain the sort of price they would normally expect, or even find a purchaser at all. This effect is known as planning blight. If the owner has no immediate intention to sell there should not be a problem, since the rules of compulsory purchase compensation require any such depressing effect caused by the prospect of compulsory purchase to be ignored when calculating the land's market value for the purpose of compensation.[1] But what if the acquiring authority will not be ready to purchase the property until some unspecified time (perhaps a matter of years) in the future, and the owner wants or needs to sell now? It seems unfair that, through no fault of their own, they should be forced to sell at a lower price than they would normally expect, or even be unable to sell at all.

1 Land Compensation (Scotland) Act 1963, ss 13 and 16.

10.17 In recognition of the hardship that planning blight may cause, some project promoters have introduced measures to try to alleviate the problem. Examples include the voluntary advance purchase scheme for the Scottish Borders Railway and the exceptional hardship scheme in connection with the HS2 high speed rail project in England.[1] However, while such schemes are discretionary; the 1997 Act also offers a limited statutory remedy. This provides that in some cases affected owners are entitled to serve a *blight notice* on the acquiring authority. If such a notice is accepted or confirmed, the authority will be required to purchase the land ahead of its requirements. The transaction will thereafter proceed like a compulsory purchase and the owner will receive, in compensation, the full market value of their land, unaffected by planning blight; in other words, what they might have realised on the open market if the proposals to compulsorily acquire the land had never been made, or at least never been known of.

1 In *R (on the application of Buckinghamshire CC) v Secretary of State for Transport* [2013] EWHC 481 (Admin) the Court held that the UK Government's consultation on a blight scheme connected with the high speed rail project was unfair as it had not provided enough information and failed to conscientiously consider representations made by a key stakeholder.

10.18 The right to serve a blight notice is not enjoyed by all persons affected by planning blight, but only by owner-occupiers of dwelling-houses, of certain small businesses and of agricultural units. This is designed to limit the extent of public liability and rests on the (controversial) assumption that large businesses and investment owners are better able to absorb the hardship caused by blight.

10.19 The body on which a blight notice is served may happen to be a local planning authority, but not necessarily so. It may be any government department or other body with compulsory purchase powers that intends to acquire the land in question and has caused planning blight by its intentions becoming known.[1]

1 1997 Act, s 120.

Power to serve blight notice[1]

10.20 Before a blight notice can be served, three conditions must be satisfied: (1) there must (in accordance with the criteria laid down in Schedule 14 of the 1997 Act) be a prospect of the land being compulsorily acquired, that is, it must qualify as 'blighted land';[2] (2) the person serving the blight notice must have the type of legal interest in the land that qualifies for the benefit of the provisions;[3] and (3) because of the planning blight they cannot sell their land except at a price substantially below what would normally be expected.[4]

1 1997 Act, s 101.
2 Ibid, s 100(1).
3 Ibid, s 101(1)(a).
4 Ibid, s 101(1)(c).

Land affected

10.21 The 1997 Act attempts to identify blighted land by listing a number of situations where the prospect of compulsory purchase can be assumed to be a matter of public knowledge.[1] Only land falling within one of these categories can be the subject of a blight notice. The list is long and somewhat complex but, in very broad terms, it comprises cases where the proposals are known because: (a) the land is earmarked (eg in a development plan) for some public purpose (eg for road proposals or for some other function of a public authority); (b) a draft compulsory purchase order has been advertised, or such an order has been confirmed by the Scottish Ministers but the authority has still to proceed with the purchase (eg by serving a notice to treat or of a general vesting declaration on the seller); (c) land is authorised to be compulsorily acquired through a special act of Parliament or under the Transport and Works (Scotland) Act 2007; or the land is identified in a national policy statement relating to certain pipelines. The 1997 Act also still refers to land in New Towns and Housing Action Areas although these designations no longer exist. The Courts have held that land affected by a development brief may qualify as blighted even if it could not be said for certain that the Council would need to use its compulsory purchase powers to implement the brief.[2] In *Halliday v Secretary of State for Transport, Local Government and the Regions*[3] the Lands Tribunal held that a site was not blighted just because it might be affected by plans for the expansion of Stansted Airport outlined in a government consultation paper.

1 1997 Act, s 100(1), Sch 14.
2 *Head v Eastbourne BC* [2010] RVR 83; [2010] JPL 631.
3 [2003] RVR 12.

Entitled persons[1]

10.22 As indicated above, there are three classes of qualifying legal interests: the owner-occupier of the whole or part of (a) a dwellinghouse; (b) non-residential premises (eg a shop or office) with a rateable value not exceeding £30,000;[2] and (c) an agricultural unit. In the case of a dwellinghouse and an agricultural unit, there is a requirement that the owner should be in occupation of the property and using it for that purpose.[3] The Scottish Ministers may make an order from time to time raising the rateable value limit for category (b).[4]

1 1997 Act, s 100(2), (3).
2 Town and Country Planning (Limit of Annual Value) (Scotland) Order, SSI 2010 No 49.
3 *Aardvark SRE Ltd v Sedgefield BC* [2008] EWCA Civ 1109; [2009] RVR 93.
4 1997 Act, s 100(4).

10.23 A blight notice may also be served by a heritable creditor who has become entitled to exercise their power of sale[1] or by the personal representative of a deceased owner.[2]

1 1997 Act, s 113.
2 Ibid, s 112.

10.24 The term 'owner' is somewhat misleading in this context, since an owner's interest is very widely defined to include that of a tenant under a lease with an unexpired term of three years or more as well as a crofter or cottar.[1] To qualify as an owner-occupier the claimant must have occupied the whole of the property (or, in the case of dwelling-houses and non-residential units, at least a substantial part of it) for at least six months.[2] Furthermore, the period of occupation must have ended either immediately prior to the date the blight notice was served or within a year of that date.[2]

1 1997 Act, s 119(4).
2 Ibid, ss 119(1), (2).

10.25 In the case of dwellinghouses and non-residential premises, where the owner-occupier is no longer in occupation when they serve the notice, the property must have remained unoccupied since they moved out. The latter provision does not apply to agricultural units.[1]

1 1997 Act, s 119(1), (2).

10.26 The claimant may be a company or other corporate body, or a partnership.[1]

1 1997 Act, s 115.

Existence of blight[1]

10.27 It has to be established that blight has resulted, ie that the property can only be sold at a price substantially below what could normally be expected and that this situation has been caused by the prospect of a future compulsory purchase.[2] The server of the notice has to establish that they made reasonable endeavours to sell, except in cases where the compulsory purchase procedure has already begun.[3] What will qualify as reasonable endeavours to sell can very according to the circumstances of individual cases, but at the very least the property must have been put on the market.[4] In *Rhodia International Holdings Ltd v Huntsman International LLC*[5] it was held that to meet the test of 'reasonable endeavours' it was only necessary to take one reasonable course of action not all reasonable courses of action available. In extreme situations, for example where compulsory acquisition is close and there is already a great deal of land that has been acquired and cleared in an area, it may be fairly self evident that a site is blighted and in such cases, the test required to show reasonable endeavours will not be high.[6]

1 1997 Act, s 101(1).
2 See *Malcolm Campbell Ltd v Glasgow Corporation* 1972 SLT (Lands Tr) 8.
3 1997 Act, s 101(1)(b).

4 *McGinigle v Renfrew District Council* 1992 SLT (Lands Tr) 97; see also *Perkins v West Wiltshire District Council* (1975) 31 P&CR 427.
5 (2007) EWHC 292.
6 See *O'Neill v Department for Regional Development* 2013 WL 128681.

Service of notice[1]

10.28 If the above conditions have been satisfied, the claimant may serve a blight notice on the appropriate authority requiring it to purchase their interest. The form of notice (and of the counter-notice referred to below) is prescribed in the Town and Country Planning (General) (Scotland) Regulations 1976.[2] The 'appropriate authority' is 'the government department, local authority or other body or person by whom … the land is liable to be acquired or is indicated as being proposed to be acquired'.[3] If there is any dispute regarding which is the appropriate authority, this will be decided by the Scottish Ministers, whose decision is final.[4] If a claimant serves a blight notice and subsequently sells the property which was the subject of the notice, they will be deemed to have withdrawn the notice.[5]

1 1997 Act, s 101(1).
2 SI 1976/2022, reg 3 and Sch 1.
3 1997 Act, s 120(1).
4 Ibid, s 120(2); see also *R v Secretary of State for the Environment ex parte Bournemouth Borough Council* (1987) 281 EG 539.
5 *Carrel v London Underground Ltd* [1995] RVR 234; *Bennett v Wakefield MDC* [1997] 37 RVR 32.

Challenge of notice[1]

10.29 Within two months of the service of a blight notice, the authority on whom it was served may object to it by serving a counter-notice on the claimant. The claimant then has a further two months dating from the service of the counter-notice during which they may refer the matter to the Lands Tribunal for Scotland. The authority has seven grounds of objection, which include that the property is not earmarked for compulsory purchase (ie that no part of it is blighted land)[2] or that the claimant does not have a qualifying interest. The authority may not amend the notice by introducing a new ground of objection during the Lands Tribunal hearing.[3] Generally the onus is on the claimant to establish that the objections are not valid rather than upon the authority to show that they are.[4] There is an exception to this where the ground of objection is that the authority does not propose to acquire the property or only proposes to acquire a part of it (or, in certain cases, that it has no such proposal within the next 15 years). In such a case it is up to the authority to show that the objection is well-founded.[5] Obviously it would be unfair (not to mention impractical) to expect the claimant to demonstrate that the authority is telling the truth with regard to its intentions.[6] The fact that a successful objection might cause the applicant hardship is irrelevant.[7]

1 1997 Act, ss 102–104.
2 See *Sinclair v Secretary of State for Transport* [1997] 34 EG 92.
3 *McGinigle v Renfrew District Council* 1992 SLT (Lands Tr) 97.
4 *Malcolm Campbell Ltd v Glasgow Corporation* 1972 SLT (Lands Tr.) 8.
5 1997 Act, s 104(4); *Kayworth v Highways Agency* (1996) 72 P&CR 433.
6 See *Sabey and Sabey v Hartlepool County Borough Council* (1970) 21 P&CR 448.
7 *Mancini v Coventry City Council* (1985) 49 P&CR 127, CA.

Material detriment

10.30 In situations where only part of a person's property is being compulsorily acquired, the seller can sometimes compel the acquiring authority to purchase the whole of their interest. To do so they have to establish that losing part of the property will cause material detriment to the remainder, ie that it will become unviable on its own. Under the same principle, an owner can serve a blight notice relating to the whole of their property, in situations where only part of it would be required by the acquiring authority.[1] If the authority objects, the Lands Tribunal will determine the matter, applying different tests according to the nature of the blighted land:

(a) In the case of a house, building or factory, whether the part proposed to be acquired can be taken without material detriment to the property.[2]
(b) In the case of a park or garden belonging to a house, whether the part proposed to be acquired can be taken without seriously affecting the amenity or convenience of the house.[3]
(c) In the case of an agricultural unit, whether the unaffected area is reasonably capable of being farmed as a separate agricultural unit, either by itself or in conjunction with other land owned by the claimant.[4]

If the appropriate test cannot be satisfied, the Lands Tribunal will uphold the blight notice.

1 1997 Act, s 117; see also *Norman v Department of Transport* (1996) 72 P&CR 210 and HC Abrahams 'Blight: Loss of Part of Property due to Proposed Public Works Seriously Affecting the Amenity or Convenience' [1996] JPL 8.
2 1997 Act, s 117(2)(a).
3 Ibid, s 117(2)(b); see also *Smith and Smith v Kent County Council* (1995) 70 P&CR 669 and *Blyth v Humberside County Council* (1997) 73 P&CR 213.
4 1997 Act, s 109(2), (3).

Confirmation of notice

10.31 If a blight notice is confirmed (ie if the authority does not serve a counter-notice or it does and later withdraws it, or if the Lands Tribunal finds in favour of the claimant), the authority is deemed to be authorised to acquire the interest compulsorily and to have served a notice to treat.[1] Thereafter the transaction will proceed like a compulsory purchase and (as mentioned earlier) any depressing effect of the blight on the value of the property will be ignored in calculating the compensation due to the owner.

1 1997 Act, s 105(1), (2).

Policy on blight

10.32 Scottish Government policy and advice on good practice in the use of compulsory purchase powers is set out in Circular 6/2011.[1] This states that where an affected property owner asks an authority to purchase land in advance on compulsory purchase terms, then this should, if possible, be considered, especially with residential property. It is also policy that authorities should not normally promote a compulsory purchase order unless they are confident of having the financial resources to meet the costs of purchase within three years and complete the project for which it is required within a reasonable period.[2]

1 SG Circular 6/2011 'Compulsory Purchase Orders' (see especially paras 55 and 85).
2 Ibid, para 32.

4. COMPULSORY PURCHASE

10.33 The function of planning authorities is often seen as a reactive one, particularly in the area of development management, where their role is often to respond, perhaps in a restrictive way, to the initiatives of private developers. However, it is also their duty to encourage development and redevelopment, and the purpose of strategic and local development plans is to provide a framework for the promotion as well as for the regulation of such enterprises. To assist them in this role of 'positive planning' planning authorities are given general powers to compulsorily acquire land for planning purposes. These powers can prove useful, not just for public sector developments, but also to help private sector developments or joint ventures. In this context, compulsory purchase powers can be invaluable, if not essential, in assembling sites where a large number of owners are involved.

10.34 We should also note in passing the power of a planning authority to compulsorily acquire a listed building that is in need of repair.[1]

1 See Chapter 12.

Acquisition of land

10.35 Planning authorities have the legal power to compulsorily acquire any land in their area which is:

(a) suitable for and required in order to secure the carrying out of development, redevelopment or improvement;
(b) required for a purpose which is necessary for the proper planning of an area in which the land is situated.[1]

1 1997 Act, s 189(1).

10.36 The types of situation in which a planning authority might use these powers includes assembling land for a regeneration project, such as a town centre improvement scheme, where the range of activities involved means that no other single compulsory purchase power (eg under roads legislation) would be appropriate. Acquiring sites or derelict and abandoned buildings to enable a private investor to redevelop these or bring them back into productive use are other examples. In deciding whether land is suitable for development, redevelopment or improvement the authority must have regard to planning considerations, eg the provisions of the development plan or the current planning status of the land.[1]

1 1997 Act, s 189(2).

10.37 Legally, compulsory acquisition ought to be resorted to only when this is shown to be necessary and an acquiring authority should not seek to acquire any more land or rights in land than absolutely necessary for the scheme. However, representations that the acquiring authority ought to consider acquisition of a lease rather than outright purchase may be unsuccessful.[1] The authority may also acquire adjoining land if that is required to execute works needed to facilitate the development or use of the land being acquired.[2] Where the land required forms part of a common or open space, it may acquire other land to give in exchange for the land it needs .[3]

1 *Stirling Plant (Hire and Sales) Ltd v Central Regional Council Times*, February 9, 1995. See also (1995) 48 SPEL 35.
2 1997 Act, s 189(3)(a).
3 Ibid, s 189(3)(b).

10.38 The acquisition procedure will be the same as in any other compulsory purchase. The compulsory purchase order will have to be confirmed by the Scottish Ministers and the usual requirements for publicity and notification of interested parties will have to be observed. Compensation will be on the usual statutory basis.[1]

1 Land Compensation (Scotland) Act 1963, s 12ff (as amended); .For a basic outline of compensation rights see McMaster, R 'Compensation' (2006) 114 SPEL 40.

10.39 Authorities also have the power to acquire land by agreement[1]and it is Scottish Government policy[2] that wherever practical, land acquisition should be through negotiation rather than achieved compulsorily. However, the Government recognises that compulsory purchase powers are likely to be needed in cases where the owners are not prepared to sell at a realistic price, it is not practical to reach agreement within the project timescale or because there are so many property interests affected that it is neither feasible nor economic to negotiate with them all. In cases where land ownership is unknown or the owners cannot be found, compulsory purchase may be the only way of creating a clean title to land to enable a development to take place.

1 1997 Act, s 188.
2 SG Circular 6/2011 'Compulsory Purchase Orders'.

10.40 Planning authorities have the power to appropriate land, ie where land acquired for some other local authority function is no longer required for that purpose, it may be used for a planning purpose instead.[1] However, if the land concerned is held for use as garden allotments, the Scottish Ministers' approval is needed for such appropriation.

1 Local Government (Scotland) Act 1973, s 73(1).

Development or disposal of land acquired

Development[1]

10.41 Where a planning authority holds land that has been acquired or appropriated by it for planning purposes, it has a wide power to carry out building or other work on such land. This provision does not apply if such development (by the planning authority or anyone else) could be authorised under another statutory enactment. Where it does exercise this power, the authority is also authorised to repair, maintain, insure, and generally carry out any necessary management of, buildings and works on the land. It may also be required to rehouse any persons displaced from the land because of redevelopment.[2] These provisions are also relevant in cases where the local authority is involved in a joint venture development with a partner from the private sector.

1 1997 Act, s 193.
2 Ibid, s 199.

Disposal[1]

10.42 Where land has been acquired or appropriated for planning purposes, a planning authority also has very wide powers to dispose of such land, in any way and to any person, in order to secure the best use of the land. The only proviso is that it is bound to sell at the best price or on the best terms that can reasonably be obtained. In other words, the authority need not take the highest price but may agree to a deal offering the best planning benefits.[2] This allows a planning authority, for example, to sell the land to a private developer, or even enter into a partnership or joint venture with such a developer. This is often achieved through what is known as a back-to-back agreement. Under this the authority agrees to exercise its compulsory powers, In return, the developer gives an undertaking that they will develop the site in a particular way and indemnify the authority for the money it has expended in assembling the site and making it available.

1 1997 Act, s 191.
2 *Standard Commercial Property Securities Ltd v Glasgow City Council* 2007 SC (HL) 33 2006 SLT 1152.

10.43 If land that has been acquired through (or under the threat of) compulsory purchase becomes redundant or surplus to the requirements of the planning authority, it is expected that under non-statutory guidelines (known as the *Crichel Down Rules*), it will first be offered to the former owner or tenant before being disposed of it elsewhere.[1] This applies not only to planning authorities but to all public bodies who acquired (or could have acquired) the land under compulsory purchase powers. There a number of exceptions, for example where the nature of the land has changed materially since its acquisition. For full details see Circular 5/2011.

1 SG Circular 5/2011 'Disposal of Surplus Government Land – The Crichel Down Rules'.

Certificate of Appropriate Alternative Development (CAAD)

10.44 Where a property owner loses their land as a result of compulsory purchase, they are entitled to an amount of compensation which leaves them no better or worse off than would have been the case if the scheme for which their land has been acquired had never existed. This is sometimes described as being compensation based on the open market value of their site 'in the no scheme world'. As we explained in Chapter 6, one of the ways in which the value of land can be established is by obtaining planning permission for new development. While there is nothing to prevent the owner of land subject to compulsory purchase applying for planning permission in an attempt to establish such development value, if they do so, their application is extremely unlikely to be granted because the land is needed for a public project. Fortunately, compulsory purchase legislation[1] provides an alternative means by which landowners can establish which developments they would have been able to obtain planning permission for 'in the no scheme world'. Affected landowners have the right to apply to the local planning authority for a Certificate of Appropriate Alternative Development (CAAD) which, if granted, is a kind of hypothetical planning permission. A CAAD does not give permission to implement development; it simply establishes a basis on which the development value of the site can be assessed for compensation purposes. The acquiring authority also has the right to apply for a CAAD and may do so, for example, to try to establish that a site does not have development value or, if it does, that this is less than that the value claimed by the owner.

1 Land Compensation (Scotland) Act 1963, Part IV. See also Watchman, J 'Certificates of Appropriate Alternative Development' (2010) 137 SPEL 12.

10.45 An application for a CAAD has to be made to the local planning authority in writing and include a map identifying the application site.[1] Not surprisingly, as the application is about hypothetical development, there is no need for the applicant to provide any detailed plans. The applicant just has to identify, giving reasons, the classes of use which they consider would be appropriate for the site were it not the subject of compulsory purchase.[2] If the applicant is the landowner then they must notify the acquiring authority of their application and advise the planning authority of the date when this was done.[3] Equally, where the acquiring authority is the applicant, it must notify the landowner.

1 The Land Compensation (Scotland) Development Order 1975, art 3.
2 Land Compensation (Scotland) Act 1963, s 25(3).
3 Ibid, s 25(3)(c).

10.46 Having received a CAAD application the planning authority has no less than 21 days and no more than two months to respond.[1] The 1963 Act specifies two possible outcomes.[2] Either the planning authority issues a certificate stating that permission would have been granted for one or more of the uses sought or it certifies that the only use which would obtain planning permission is the one for which the land is being acquired. The authority may also indicate the conditions which it would have attached to any planning permission.

1 Land Compensation Scotland Act 1963, s25(4) and Land Compensation (Scotland) Development Order 1975, art 3(2).
2 Land Compensation (Scotland) Act 1963 s25(4).

10.47 Regardless of who made the CAAD application, the landowner and the acquiring authority both have the right to appeal to the Scottish Ministers if they are dissatisfied with the planning authority's decision.[1] Written notice of this has to be given within one month of the date of receipt of the certificate.[2] They can also appeal if the planning authority fails to issue a certificate within two months. In such cases it is deemed that the authority has issued a certificate stating that the only use for which it would grant planning permission is the one for which the land is being acquired.[3]

1 Land Compensation (Scotland) Act 1963, s 26(1).
2 Land Compensation (Scotland) Development Order 1975, art 4.
3 Land Compensation (Scotland) Act 1963, s 26(4).

10.48 The possible appeal outcomes are confirmation of the certificate as originally issued, variation, or its cancelation and replacement with a new certificate.[1] The Scottish Ministers' decision may only be challenged legally within six weeks and on the grounds specified in s29 of the 1963 Act. In a recent case, the court held that a reporter's decision that an appeal had been withdrawn could be challenged under s29 and subsequently rejected the challenge that the Scottish Ministers' reporter had acted beyond her powers under the 1963 Act by treating the appeal as withdrawn.[2]

1 Land Compensation (Scotland) Act 1963, s 26(2).
2 *Scottish Borders Council v The Scottish Ministers* 2013 SLT 41; (2013) 155 SPEL 19 and *Network Rail Infrastructure Ltd v The Scottish Ministers* [2013] CSIH 64.

Chapter 11

Revocation and discontinuance of planning rights

1. INTRODUCTION

11.1 A planning authority may in certain circumstances consider it expedient to revoke or modify a planning permission or consider that it is expedient in the interests of planning that it should require discontinuance of a use of land, impose a planning condition on the continued use of land, or require that any building should be altered or removed. A planning authority may, for one reason or another, change its mind about a recently granted permission and revoke it before the development has been completed, or even started. A planning authority's discontinuance powers relate to a completed development, perhaps one that has been in existence for many years. It might be considered, for instance, that the right of an owner (or other occupier) to use land in a particular way is no longer appropriate because of a change in the character of the area in question (for example, if a factory is situated in an area that has become predominantly residential). Alternatively, a lawful use which has subsisted for many years may now be contrary to development plan policy.

11.2 When a planning authority exercises its powers of revocation etc of a planning permission or requires a discontinuance of use etc the owner or occupier of the land may suffer loss without being at fault. It is therefore normal for compensation to be payable whenever those powers are invoked. This in turn means that planning authorities do not use these powers very often, as the desirability of using them to carry out improvements to the environment or to amenity has to be balanced against the need to pay for such improvements out of the public purse.

2. ORDERS UNDER SECTIONS 65 AND 71

Revocation or modification of unimplemented planning permission (section 65)[1]

11.3 The power to make an order revoking or modifying a planning permission does not extend to a permission granted by a development order (such as the Permitted Development Order). Making such an order is appropriate where a planning authority has granted planning permission and then changed its mind before the relevant planning permission has been fully implemented. More specifically, s 65 empowers a planning authority, if it appears to it to be expedient having regard to the development plan and to any other material considerations (including the cost to the public of making the order);[2] to revoke or modify a planning permission where:

(a) the planning permission relates to the carrying out of building or other operations, at any time before those operations have been completed; or
(b) the planning permission relates to a change of the use of any land, at any time before the change has taken place.[3]

1 Town and Country Planning (Scotland) Act 1997, s 65.
2 Ibid, ss 24, 25 and 277(1) and *R (on the application of the Health and Safety Executive) v Wolverhampton City Council* [2012] UKSC 34.
3 See *Caledonian Terminal Investments Ltd v Edinburgh Corporation* 1970 SC 271; 1970 SLT 362.

11.4 The revocation or modification of planning permission for the carrying out of building or other operations shall not affect so much of those operations as has been carried out before that date on which the order is confirmed or otherwise takes effect.[1] Where building or other operations permitted by a planning permission *have* been completed; or where a lawful change of use permitted by a planning permission *has* taken place; the appropriate course would be for the planning authority to consider making a discontinuance order under s 71.[2]

1 1997 Act, s 65(4).
2 See para 11.12 below.

Procedure

11.5 In general, an order revoking or modifying planning permission only takes effect when it is confirmed by the Scottish Ministers, who are empowered to modify a planning authority's order.[1] Notice of the order must be served on any owner, lessee and occupier of the land affected and any other person who will be affected by it.[2] Prior to confirmation by the Scottish Ministers of the planning authority's order, anyone receiving such notification is entitled to be heard.[3] After an order is confirmed, it may still be challenged in the court;[4] apart from that it is final. Where there is no opposition to the order, the need for confirmation by the Scottish Ministers may sometimes be avoided, though a press advert will be required.[5]

1 1997 Act, s 66(1), (6).
2 Ibid, s 66(2).
3 Ibid, s 66(3), (4).
4 Ibid, ss 237, 239.
5 Ibid, s 67; see also the Town and Country Planning (General) (Scotland) Regulations 1976, SI 1976/2022, reg 7 and Sch 2.

11.6 The Scottish Ministers also have the power to make an order revoking or modifying a planning permission. They cannot make such an order without consulting with, and giving notice to, the relevant planning authority.[1]

1 1997 Act, s 68.

Compensation[1]

11.7 A person 'interested in' the relevant land must be paid compensation where that person:

(a) has incurred expenditure in carrying out work which is rendered abortive by the revocation or modification of planning permission; or
(b) has otherwise sustained loss or damage which is directly attributable to that revocation or modification.[2]

1 1997 Act, s 76; see also *Colley v Canterbury City Council* [1996] 36 RVR 262.
2 Ibid, s 76(1).

11.8 The compensation payable would include professional costs, for example, architects' fees for the preparation of plans etc, provided these were incurred before the order was made. It may also include the loss of future business profits.[1] A claim for compensation must be made within six months.[2]

1 *Hobbs (Quarries) v Somerset County Council* (1975) 30 P&CR 286.
2 Town and Country Planning (General) (Scotland) Regulations 1976, SI 1976/2022, reg 4.

11.9 To be 'interested in' the land and therefore entitled to compensation, it is not necessary for the person concerned to have a proprietory interest as owner or tenant; a right, for example, to use the land under a licence can also given rise to eligibility for compensation.[1]

1 *Pennine Raceway Ltd v Kirklees Metropolitan Borough Council* [1983] QB 382.

11.10 If compensation is paid in respect of a depreciation in the value of the claimant's legal interest in the land, it is to be assumed that planning permission would be granted for an existing use development (rebuilding work or subdivision of a dwellinghouse).[1] In *Canterbury City Council v Colley*[2] the House of Lords held that this assumption should be applied strictly, even though such existing use development (rebuilding of a dwellinghouse) was in fact prohibited by the revocation order itself. As a result, the claimant's compensation was greatly reduced.

1 1997 Act, s 76(4), and Sch 11, paras 1, 2.
2 [1993] 2 WLR 254, HL.

11.11 When the compensation payable includes an amount in excess of £20 in respect of depreciation in value of the claimant's legal interest, the planning authority is required to record a compensation notice in the Register of Sasines or, where appropriate, register it in the Land Register of Scotland.[1] If the land is subsequently developed, the compensation may have to be repaid to the Scottish Ministers (and paid by them to the relevant planning authority).[2]

1 1997 Act, s 79(1).
2 Ibid, ss 80, 81.

Discontinuance of existing use rights (section 71)[1]

11.12 A discontinuance order empowers a planning authority to alter or extinguish the existing use rights of a piece of land or property, even though the existing use is lawful. It may be lawful for different reasons: (a) because planning permission has been granted at some time in the past; (b) because, even though the use was originally in breach of planning control, it has become immune from enforcement by the passage of time; or (c) because it is a long-subsisting use, predating the modern planning legislation (that is, prior to 1 July 1948).

1 1997 Act, s 71.

Planning authority's powers

11.13 Under s 71 of the 1997 Act a planning authority may make an order requiring that:

(a) any use of land should be discontinued, or that any conditions should be imposed on the continuance of a use of land; or
(b) any buildings or works should be altered or removed.

11.14 Such an order can be made in any case where it appears to the planning authority, having regard to the development plan and any other material considerations;[1] to be expedient in the interests of the proper planning of its area (including the interests of amenity). There are special provisions where the discontinued use involves the working of minerals or the deposit of refuse or waste, including the power to impose conditions regarding restoration and aftercare of the land.[2] Any such order may grant permission for some other development in lieu of that removed by it and only takes effect when confirmed by the Scottish Ministers.[3]

1 1997 Act, s 25.
2 1997 Act, s 71(8), Sch 8; see also Chapter 14, pt 3 below.
3 1997 Act, s 71(2).

11.15 As with revocation orders, the Scottish Ministers have the power to make discontinuance orders.[1]

1 1997 Act, s 73.

Procedure

11.16 The procedure is similar to that under revocation orders,[1] including the need to have the order confirmed by the Scottish Ministers (who again may make modifications to it) and to have notice served on interested parties.[2] In the case of discontinuance orders there is an additional requirement to notify the interested parties after as well as before the confirmation of the order.[3] Once again, a discontinuance order can be challenged on limited legal grounds only.[4] However, unlike the situation with revocation orders, there is no procedure for bypassing confirmation by the Scottish Ministers when the order is unopposed.

1 See para 11.5 above.
2 1997 Act, s 72.
3 Ibid, s 72(5).
4 Ibid, ss 237, 239.

11.17 If residents in premises affected by a discontinuance order are displaced then, provided that no other residential accommodation is available on reasonable terms, it is the duty of the planning authority to provide for such alternative accommodation in advance of the displacement.[1] This may include temporary bed and breakfast accommodation pending discussion of permanent accommodation.[2]

1 1997 Act, s 71(6).
2 *R v East Hertfordshire District Council, ex p Smith* (1990) Times, 25 January.

Compensation

11.18 A person affected by a discontinuance order may claim compensation for the depreciation in value of his interest in the land, or because he has been disturbed in his enjoyment of the land.[1] If the works required by the order (for instance, the removal or modification of buildings) are carried out carried out the person who carries out those works is entitled to the repayment of any expenses reasonably incurred, less the scrap value of materials from buildings etc.[2] As with revocation orders, a claim for compensation must be made within six months.[3]

1 1997 Act, s 83.
2 Ibid, s 83(3), (4).
3 Town and Country Planning (General) (Scotland) Regulations 1976, SI 1976/2022, reg 4.

Enforcement[1]

11.19 If land continues to be used in contravention of a discontinuance order, or the order is contravened in any other way, the person responsible is liable, on conviction, to a fine. If the order requires the removal of a building or buildings or other works and these are not done, the planning authority can take the necessary steps itself and charge the owner or tenant.

1 1997 Act, ss 148, 149.

Purchase notices[1]

11.20 The effect of a revocation order or a discontinuance order being implemented may be to render the land incapable of reasonably beneficial use. In such a case, the owner or tenant may serve a purchase notice on the planning authority.[2] However, in these circumstances the person serving the purchase notice will not be entitled to the usual compensation arising from a revocation order or a discontinuance order, as that person will be receiving full compulsory purchase compensation.[3] In other words, an affected person may respond to the order in one of two ways: (1) keep the land and claim compensation for its loss in value and/or any abortive expenditure or loss; or (2) sell the land to the planning authority for its full value. Accordingly, if a purchase notice is eventually confirmed, any compensation already paid under heading (1) above will be deducted from the sale compensation paid under heading (2). Without this provision, the claimant would be receiving a double payment.

1 See Chapter 10, part 2 above.
2 1997 Act, s 88(1).
3 Ibid, s 95(1), (7).

III Special Planning Controls

Chapter 12

The historic environment[1]

12.1 The historic environment includes archaeological sites, historic buildings and townscapes. It also encompasses historic parks and gardens, designed landscapes and other features such as battlefields and shipwrecks. It is widely accepted that these assets have important cultural and economic benefits, not least for the tourism and leisure industries. Many are covered by statutory designations such as scheduled monuments, listed buildings and conservation areas. The protection and enhancement of this historic legacy is an important function of the planning system and Scottish Government policy and guidance for this are contained in SPP[1] and the Scottish Historic Environment Policy (SHEP).[2] In this chapter we will look in turn at each of the main elements of the historic environment and how these are affected by the planning system.

1 Scottish Government 'Scottish Planning Policy' (2010) especially paras 110–124. See also Scottish Government, 'Scottish Planning Policy Consultative Draft' (April 2013), especially paras 114–124.

2 Historic Scotland 'Scottish Historic Environment Policy' (2011); See also Historic Scotland's Managing Change in the Historic Environment Guidance Notes available at www.historic-scotland.gov.uk; and Historic Scotland 'Scotland's Historic Environment Audit' (2010).

1. LISTED BUILDINGS

Introduction

12.2 The Scottish Ministers have a duty to prepare or approve lists of buildings which are of 'special architectural or historic interest'.[1] About 47,500 buildings in Scotland have been listed.

1 Planning (Listed Buildings and Conservation Areas) (Scotland) Act 1997, s 1(1).

12.3 The character of historic buildings can easily be damaged, even by very minor changes such as replacement windows and small extensions. As these kinds of changes do not normally need planning permission, extra controls become available once a building is listed.[1] For a brief but very useful introduction to this topic see Historic Scotland's 'Guide to the Protection of Scotland's Listed Buildings: What Listing Means to Owners and Occupiers' (2011).

1 Planning (Listed Buildings and Conservation Areas) (Scotland) Act 1997, Ch II.

What can be listed?

12.4 As well as buildings in the usual sense of the word, many objects and structures which the public might not normally regard as 'buildings' can be listed. For example, red telephone boxes and statues have become listed 'buildings'. This is because of the wide definition of 'building' in the 1997 Act.[1] In *Leominster District Council v British Historic Buildings and SPS Shipping*[2] a pile of timbers from a listed barn which had blown down in a storm was still regarded as a listed building and subject to control. In April 2013 a scale model of a village in the Cotswolds was given listed status.[3]

1 Town and Country Planning (Scotland) Act 1997 Act, s 277(1).
2 [1987] JPL 350.
3 'Bourton-on-the-Water model village gets Grade II listed status' *The Guardian*, 19 April 2013.

12.5 Objects and structures (including other buildings) attached to a listed building, or which have been within its curtilage since before 1 July 1948, may be treated as part of the listed building.[1] These can include, for example, garden items such as an old sundial, statue or even a ditch. Internal fixtures, such as interior panelling, ceiling paintings, plasterwork and fireplaces can also be affected. The legal tests for determining whether an item can be viewed as a fixture include: (a) the degree to which it is annexed to the building; and, (b) the purpose for which it was put there.[2] Accordingly a freestanding object (such as a carillon clock) may be capable of being viewed as a fixture.[3] Plant or machinery can be included as an 'object' or 'structure' in this context.

1 Planning (Listed Buildings and Conservation Areas) (Scotland) Act 1997, s 1(4). See Watchman, P and Young, E 'The Meaning of 'Curtilage' 1990 SLT 77.
2 See *Berkley v Poulett* [1977] 1 EGLR 86.
3 *Kennedy v Secretary of State for Wales* [1996] EGCS 17.

12.6 There are no statutory definitions of the terms 'attached' and 'curtilage' and this can cause problems. For instance, are structures within a 100-acre park surrounding a listed mansion within the curtilage of that building? Unfortunately, the courts have only partially clarified the position. Ideally, the statutory list should make clear for each property what is (and by omission what is not) covered by the listing. In the past, Historic Scotland has acknowledged that information provided in the list is not always as specific as it should be.[1] However, the Scottish Government did not take the opportunity to clarify the position in its recent legislation aimed at streamlining and clarifying the rules for managing and protecting the historic environment.[2] The list includes two main columns of information for each listed building, one giving the 'name' of the building and the other a description of it. The 'name' column is the one with statutory force but the House of Lords held that the description column can be used to resolve ambiguities in the statutory column.[3] An inaccuracy in the naming of a building in the list will not invalidate a building's listed status provided it is clear from the description and any other relevant material that the building concerned has been listed.[4]

1 Historic Scotland 'Memorandum of Guidance on Listed Buildings and Conservation Areas' (1998), p 182 (now withdrawn).
2 The Historic Environment (Amendment) (Scotland) Act 2011.
3 *Edinburgh City Council v Secretary of State for Scotland and Revival Properties Ltd* 1998 SLT 120.
4 *Barratt v Ashford BC* [2011] 1 P&CR 21; [2011] JPL 931.

12.7 The tests which can help decide whether an object is within the curtilage of a listed building relate to the physical layout, the structure and its past and present ownership and functions.[1] Generally, the curtilage will be confined to a small area about the building, it will have an intimate relationship with the building but it need not be enclosed.[2] However, there can be cases where the curtilage is not a small area. In *Skerritts of Nottingham Ltd v Secretary of State for the Environment, Transport and the Regions (No.1)*[3] a stable block 200m away from a listed hotel building was held to be within that hotel's curtilage.

1 See for example *Watson-Smyth v Secretary of State for the Environment and Cherwell District Council* (1991) 64 P&CR 156.
2 See *Methuen-Campbell v Walkers* [1979] QB 525; *Dyer v Dorset County Council* [1989] 1 QB 346; *McAlpine v Secretary of State for the Environment* [1995] 1 PLR 16.
3 [2001] QB 59.

12.8 It is possible for other buildings near a listed building to be treated as structures attached to it if some ancillary relationship can be shown. In *Attorney-General v Calderdale Borough Council ex rel Sutcliffe*,[1] a terrace of unlisted mill workers' cottages, linked to a listed mill only by a bridge, was treated as a structure attached to a listed building. This was despite the fact that the cottages were in separate ownership from the mill at the time it was listed. The case, *Debenhams plc v Westminster City Council*,[2] concerned a building on the opposite side of the street from, but linked to a listed building by, a footbridge and tunnel. Both buildings were owned and operated by the same firm. The House of Lords took the view that the physical link, and commercial subordination of the unlisted building to the listed one, was not enough to make it a structure fixed to the listed building. For it to be such a structure, there had to be a relationship which was ancillary and subordinate, such as a stable block in the curtilage of a mansion house.

The circumstances at the date the property was listed are also relevant. Unless structures are specifically named in the list, they will not always be afforded protection if they were in a different ownership from the main listed building at the time of listing. This can be the case even if the structure is physically attached to the listed building and has historical associations with it.[3]

1 [1983] JPL 310, (1983) 46 P&CR 399 CA.
2 [1987] AC 396.
3 *Watts v Secretary of State for the Environment* [1991] 1 PLR 61.

12.9 In some cases a listed building may itself lie within the curtilage of a building that is not listed. For instance, ancillary buildings or structures may have been listed in their own right but the house which they originally served may have been replaced by a modern one. If a listed summer house lies within the garden of a modern unlisted house, for example, the modern house cannot be viewed as being within the curtilage of the summer house. In such situations, the area around the summer house would be treated as its 'setting'. As a result, while any development proposals relating to the garden area would not require listed building consent, they would be subject to extra publicity requirements.[1] 'Setting' is another term which lacks a statutory definition, however, and can only be interpreted according to the circumstances of each case.

1 Planning (Listed Buildings and Conservation Areas) (Scotland) Act 1997, s 60.

Criteria for listing

12.10 The Scottish Historic Environment Policy (SHEP)[1] defines three categories of listing:

Category A:	Buildings of national or international importance, either architectural or historic, or fine little-altered examples of some particular period or style, or building type.
Category B:	Buildings of regional or more than local importance, or major examples of some particular period, style, or building type.
Category C(S):	Buildings of local importance; lesser examples of any period, style or building type, as originally constructed or altered; and simple traditional buildings which group well with others.[2]

The 'S' in brackets stands for 'statutory' to indicate that these buildings are afforded statutory protection. This is to distinguish them from buildings listed as 'C' in an earlier non-statutory list. In addition to the individual categories allocated to buildings, Historic Scotland also operates a group system. There are two groups, A and B, which exist to flag considerations such as 'function, setting, design, planning and historic combinations where the individual value is enhanced by its association with others.'[3]

1 Historic Scotland 'Scottish Historic Environment Policy (2011).
2 Ibid, Note 2.19, p65.
3 Ibid.

12.11 The individual and group categories have little legal significance since all listed buildings are subject to the same controls. They do, however, have some procedural significance[1] and can influence grant award decisions. In addition, the higher the category accorded to a building, the more difficult it will be to obtain listed building consent for any significant alterations or demolition.

1 See para 12.34 below.

12.12 The SHEP gives further clarification on the factors which could lead to a building being listed and in which category.[1] There are three main areas for consideration which are: age and rarity; architectural or historic interest; and, close historical association. The older a building is and the fewer of its type that survive, the more likely it is to be listed. Buildings erected before 1840 have a strong chance of being listed if they are of notable quality and survive in predominantly their original form. Buildings erected between 1840 and 1945 may be listed if they are of definite character either individually or as part of a group. Of these, buildings constructed after 1914 will be treated more selectively. Buildings constructed since 1945 may be listed if their special architectural or historic interest is of definite architectural quality.[2] Buildings less than 30 years old will only be listed if they are of exceptional merit and/or face immediate threat. For example, the replica Georgian-style building at 114–116 George Street, Edinburgh, was listed just four years after it had been built. The original houses on this site had been demolished in 1962, and replaced by Morris and Steedman's Carron House, a 1960s style office block which had itself been listed. However, this was demolished to make way for the current building which copies the facades of the original Georgian building but on a slightly different building line.

1 Annex 2.
2 Examples of post 1945 buildings that have been listed include Adam House, Chamber Street, Edinburgh which was built in 1954, the Royal Commonwealth Pool built for the Commonwealth Games held in Edinburgh in 1970 and the former Cummins Engine Factory in Shotts, North Lanarkshire, part of which was completed in 1983.

12.13 With regard to architectural or historic interest, factors which are of particular importance include the survival of important interior features such as ornate plasterwork, staircases and traditional shop fittings, Also of interest are surviving examples of technological innovations, such as the early use of steel frames. Plan form, the setting of a building and regional variations in design are also important. Buildings may be considered for listing where they are associated with a famous historical figure or event. However, such associations will need to be well documented. In addition, the design of the building will normally need to be of interest in itself and the fabric and character well preserved in a way that links directly with the person or event concerned. 'The transient association of short term guests, lodgers and tenants, however eminent, will not usually justify listing'.[1]

1 SHEP Annex 2.

12.14 The policy on listing is kept constantly under review,[1] and so any building could potentially become listed one day. In 2011, the Secretary of State in England listed the Lloyds Building in the City of London which was designed by Richard Rogers and completed as recently as 1986.[2]

1 SHEP para 2.36f.
2 Richard Waite 'Rogers' Lloyd's becomes youngest Grade-1 listed building' The Architects Journal, 19 December 2011.

12.15 It is possible to come across buildings which meet the present criteria for listing but have not yet been included in the list. This will usually be for one of two reasons. They may not have been identified yet in any survey, either by Historic Scotland or the local planning authority. Alternatively, the authorities may be aware of the existence of the building but have not yet got round to carrying out the assessment required to list it. In either case, if the building suddenly becomes at risk of demolition or any major alteration, there is action which the planning authority can take to protect it.[1]

1 See para 12.55 below.

12.16 Property owners or developers who are planning to carry out work to an existing building may be concerned that their plans could be frustrated if these trigger the listing of their property. This can be the case even where they have had an informal indication that this will not happen. For example, in *Western Power Distribution Investments Ltd v Welsh Ministers*[1] the court found that it was lawful for the Ministers to list a building which they had previously considered for listing and rejected. There had been no change in circumstances; the Welsh Ministers discovered that they had overlooked the building's special interest. So if in doubt, the only way a developer can get certainty that a building will not be listed is by obtaining a Certificate of Immunity which, if granted, prevents their building from being listed for five years.[2]

1 [2010] EWHC 800 (Admin).
2 See para 12.56 below.

Listing procedure

12.17 Only the Scottish Ministers have the power to list a building, change its category or remove it from the list altogether.[1] It is open to anybody, however, to propose additions or changes to the list using an application form available from Historic Scotland.[2] The form requests information relevant to the listing criteria set out in Annex 2 to the SHEP. It should be accompanied by up to date photographs of the building and supporting information including date of construction, historical associations, interesting interior features, townscape/group value, level of risk to the structure and planning history (including any live applications for planning permission). Historic Scotland receives around 350 such applications each year.[3] The Scottish Minsters may reject or approve the proposals with or without modifications.[4] Historic Scotland also continues to identify new listed buildings itself through ongoing list maintenance work and thematic surveys. An example of how list maintenance work can result in a new listed building would be where a large country estate is covered by a single listing. In reviewing this, Historic Scotland might decide that individual buildings or structures within the estate deserve a separate listing in their own right. Thematic surveys look nationally at certain types of building[5] or the work of a particular architect.

1 Planning (Listed Buildings and Conservation Areas) (Scotland) Act 1997, s 1(1).
2 Historic Scotland Listing and Designated Landscapes Application Form available at www.historic-scotland.gov.uk/listingapplicationform.pdf
3 www.historic-scotland.gov.uk/index/heritage/historicandlistedbuildings/listing proposal.htm
4 Planning (Listed Buildings and Conservation Areas) (Scotland) Act 1997, s 1(1).
5 Such as the survey of theatre buildings undertaken in 2008–09.

12.18 In carrying out their duties, the Scottish Ministers are assisted and advised by Historic Scotland. In practice it is the staff of the latter that carries out the bulk of the work and with whom local planning authorities and other interested parties need to consult on historic buildings matters.

12.19 Before a building is listed, or a change is made in the status of an existing listed building, it will be surveyed by Historic Scotland in order to assess it against the selection criteria in Annex 2 of the SHEP. Historic Scotland will then consult with the local planning authority and, although not legally required to do so, the owner and occupier if possible.

12.20 Once the decision to list a building (or remove it from the list) is finalised, Historic Scotland notifies the local planning authority. It is then its responsibility to formally notify the decision to the owners, occupiers and lessees of the building affected as soon as possible.[1] Historic Scotland will normally provide the owner with an informal notification in advance of this along with an information pack.

1 Planning (Listed Buildings and Conservation Areas) (Scotland) Act 1997, s 2(2)(b).

12.21 There is no formal right of appeal against listing but it is open to anyone to make representations to the Scottish Ministers at any time to seek removal from the list. Such requests should use the Historic Scotland Listing and Designated Landscapes Application Form. To be successful they will need to make a strong case on the ground that the building does not merit listing because it is not of sufficient architectural or historic interest.

12.22 The Scottish Ministers have a duty to deposit with local authorities certified copies of those parts of the list relevant to their areas and these must be made available for public inspection.[1] The full list is available for inspection at the headquarters of Historic Scotland in Edinburgh. For ease of identification and administration, it is divided into districts, parishes and burghs. Each listed property is identified by its address. Additional information is also provided in the form of an architectural description, category of listing, and map reference. Any other available useful information is also recorded including, if relevant, any historical associations. List descriptions can also be found on the Historic Scotland Website.[2] A map based search facility is available through 'Pastmap', a resource supported by the Royal Commission on the Ancient and Historic Monuments of Scotland.[3]

1 Planning (Listed Buildings and Conservation Areas) (Scotland) Act 1997, s 2.
2 www.historic-scotland.gov.uk/historicandlistedbuildings
3 www.pastmap.org.uk

Exemptions from listed building control

12.23 While it is possible for any building to be listed, there are some cases where works to, or within the curtilage of, listed buildings are exempt from control. Crown buildings (including government offices, court buildings etc) used to be one of these cases but that exemption was removed in 2006.[1] The exemptions which still apply are set out below.

1 Planning (Listed Buildings and Conservation Areas) (Scotland) Act s73A inserted by Planning and Compulsory Purchase Act 2004, s 90(2).

Religious buildings[1]

12.24 As long as a listed building continues in ecclesiastical use, alterations or extensions are exempt from listed building control. Consent for demolition is still needed, as the ecclesiastical use would obviously have to cease before it could be demolished. Similarly, former church buildings which are now put to another use, or which are vacant, lose exemption. Manses are also subject to control because any building used, or available for use, as a residence by a minister of religion is specifically stated not to be in ecclesiastical use.[2] Notwithstanding this legal position, there is a voluntary agreement between Historic Scotland, the Scottish Churches Committee and the Convention of Scottish Local Authorities (COSLA) which applies listed building controls to works proposed to the exterior of churches used by certain denominations, including the Church of Scotland and the Roman Catholic Church. The Historic Scotland leaflet 'Scheme to Apply Listed Building Control to Exteriors of Churches in Ecclesiastical Use' (2006) gives further information about this arrangement.[3]

1 Planning (Listed Buildings and Conservation Areas) (Scotland) Act 1997, s 54.
2 Ibid, s 54(5).
3 Available online at www.historic-scotland.gov.uk/listed-building-control-churches.pdf

Scheduled ancient monuments

12.25 Sometimes a listed building is also designated as a scheduled ancient monument.[1] Where this is the case, listed building consent is not required,[2] but a special permission known as scheduled monument consent is needed instead.[3]

1 One example is the Victoria Swing Bridge in Leith Docks, Edinburgh.
2 Planning (Listed Buildings and Conservation Areas) (Scotland) Act 1997, s 55.
3 See Part 3 below.

Erection of a new free-standing building within the curtilage of a listed building

12.26 According to Historic Scotland,[1] the erection of a free-standing building within the curtilage of a listed building does not require listed building consent (although it will probably require planning permission). However, it acknowledges that in exceptional cases where the new building would be extremely close to the listed building it might be regarded as an extension to that building and so need listed building consent. This was the case in *Ampliflaire Ltd v Secretary of State for Scotland*[2] where it was held that a free-standing building erected within the curtilage of a listed church so affected the character of that building that it could be regarded as an alteration or extension and as a result needed listed building consent. It seems clear from this that it is a matter of fact and degree in each case whether a free-standing building can be regarded as an alteration or extension and so need listed building consent. In the *Ampliflaire* case the structure was substantial and located very close to the facade of the church.

1 SHEP Annex 8, para 2d.
2 1998 SCLR 565; (1998) 68 SPEL 77.

Works to certain objects or structures within the curtilage of a listed building

12.27 Free-standing structures which lie within the curtilage of a listed building and were erected on or after July 1948 are excluded from the definition of a listed building.[1] Consequently, works to such structures are normally exempt from listed building control.[2] However, in view of the findings in the *Ampliflaire* case discussed above, it is conceivable that in some circumstances, listed building consent may be required for such work. Furthermore, given that some buildings which were erected after 1948 have been listed, it is probable that any associated free-standing structures will be included in the statutory description and thus also be protected anyway.

1 Planning (Listed Buildings and Conservation Areas) (Scotland) Act 1997, s 1(4)(b).
2 See SHEP, Annex 8 para 2a.

Listed building consent

Extent of control

12.28 Once a building is included in the list, unless it is one of the types of property exempt from control, its demolition or any other change which would affect its architectural or historic character needs listed building consent.[1] This can include the effect which a change of use may have on a building's character.[2] We saw when considering the definition of development in Chapter 4 that alterations which affect the interior of a building or do not materially affect its external appearance are not development. Consequently, those types of work do not need planning permission. However, this is not the case with listed building consent. Both the exterior and the interior of the buildings are protected, and in fact many minor, and in some cases seemingly trivial changes, which do not usually require planning permission may need consent; eg removing a fire-place, replacing a bathroom, putting an alarm box on an outside wall, window replacement (including replacing clear glass with tinted) and even changing the thickness of window astragals. External alterations will normally need listed building consent even if they are not visible from normal vantage points, and so roof alterations, for example, may require consent even if only visible from the air.[3] Works of like-for-like repair or other works which do not affect a building's character, will not normally require listed building consent. These could include repointing a wall or altering part of a building which does not contribute to the overall special interest.[4] As the need for listed building consent is essentially a professional judgment,[5] anyone wishing to carry out any work to a listed building would be wise to discuss their intentions with the local planning authority first. If it takes the view that what is proposed would not affect the character of the building, then listed building consent is not needed. In such situations the owner should insist on receiving the authority's judgment in writing. Where the local authority determines that listed building consent is required and the owner disagrees, the only route to challenge the authority's determination is by appealing to the Scottish Ministers. Such an appeal would be on the ground that the works involved do not require listed building consent.[6] An application for listed building consent would first have to be made to the local planning authority. It is also worth noting that some permitted development rights are more restricted within the curtilage of a listed building and so planning permission may need to be sought for minor works that would not normally need this. Examples include erecting domestic outbuildings larger than 4 sq m, and the erection of walls, fences, and gates.[7]

1 Planning (Listed Buildings and Conservation Areas) (Scotland) Act 1997, ss 6, 7.
2 *Heatherington (UK) v Secretary of State for the Environment* (1995) 69 P&CR 374.
3 *Burroughs Day v Bristol City Council* [1996] EGCS 10.
4 SHEP (2011) para 3.33.
5 Guidance is given in Historic Scotland's 'Managing Change in the Historic Environment Guidance Notes' available at www.historic-scotland.gov.uk
6 *Chambers v Guildford BC* [2008] EWHC 826 (QB); [2008] JPL 1459.
7 The Town and Country Planning (General Permitted Development) (Scotland) Order 1992 Sch 1, Part 1 Class 3E and Part 2 Class 7.

12.29 It is also worth pointing out that listed building status can affect other property nearby, even if the latter is not listed. This is because in coming to a decision on any planning applications for sites near to a listed building, the planning authority must take into account any effects on the setting of that listed building.[1] If the planning authority considers that the setting would be affected by the proposed development, it has to advertise the application in a local newspaper and display a notice on the land for seven days. This requirement applies to the setting of all listed buildings, including those which are themselves exempt from listed building control (see para 12.33 below). It should be noted that the requirement here is only that the authority **considers** the impact the proposal would have on the setting; it is not a blanket ban on such development. Even where it can be shown that the setting would be damaged it is open to the authority to decide that other planning considerations in favour of the proposed development outweigh this and so grant planning permission.[2] Further advice on this issue is given in Historic Scotland's Guidance Note 'Setting' (2010)[3] Where new development is proposed which affects a category A listed building or its setting, the Scottish Ministers must be consulted.[4] A planning application for a development categorised as local needs to be accompanied by a design statement if the proposal is within the curtilage of a Category A listed building.[5]

1 Planning (Listed Buildings and Conservation Areas) (Scotland) Act 1997, s 59(1).
2 *Historic Buildings and Monuments Commission for England (English Heritage) v Secretary of State for Communities and Local Government* [2009] EWHC 2287 (Admin); [2010] JPL 451.
3 Part of the Managing Change in the Historic Environment Guidance Note series available at www.historic-scotland.gov.uk
4 Town and Country planning (Development Management Procedure) (Scotland) Regulations 2013, SSI 2013/155 Sch. 5, para. 5(4)(c).
5 Ibid, reg 13.

12.30 Where listed building consent is required, the local planning authority or the Scottish Ministers must make their decision having special regard to the desirability of preserving the building or its setting or any features of special architectural or historic interest which it possesses.[1] In other words, there is a statutory presumption in favour of preserving a listed building and its setting. This statutory presumption is reflected in government policy and practice. However, other material factors may be allowed to outweigh this presumption. For example, in *Glasgow District Council v Secretary of State for Scotland*[2] the fact that a bank's proposed alterations to a listed building would improve operational efficiency, the range of services it offered to the public and the accommodation for staff was accepted by the court as acceptable grounds for departing from the presumption against alterations. *In R. (on the application of Save Britain's Heritage) v Westminster City Council*[3] the Court held that the planning authority was entitled to conclude that the national importance of siting the UK Supreme Court in the Middlesex Guildhall justified the damage caused to that listed building's character by works necessary to accommodate the Court. However, the decision-maker has to attach a significant weight to the desirability of preserving the setting of listed buildings when weighing that factor against other material considerations which do not have that statutory basis.[4]

1 Planning (Listed Buildings and Conservation Areas) (Scotland) Act 1997, s 14(2).
2 1993 SLT 1332; see also *Save Britain's Heritage v Secretary of State for the Environment and Poultry Number 1 Ltd* [1991] 1 W.L.R. 153, *Rolf v North Shropshire Council* [1988] JPL 105 and *R v Westminster City Council ex parte Monahan* [1989] 2 All ER 74.
3 [2007] EWHC 807 (Admin); (2007) 104(15) LSG 22.
4 *East Northamptonshire DC v Secretary of State for Communities and Local Government* [2013] EWHC 473 (Admin); [2013] 12 EG 78 (CS).

Application procedure

12.31 The application procedure for listed building consent is similar to that for making an application for planning permission (see Chapter 6). The relevant regulations are the Town and Country Planning (Listed Buildings and Conservation Areas) (Scotland) Regulations 1987[1] as amended. Listed building consent application forms and guidance notes on how to complete these can be found on the ePlanning Scotland website.[2]

1 SI 1987/1529.
2 https://eplanning.scotland.gov.uk/WAM/staticforms.htm

12.32 The first point to note is that the need for listed building consent is separate from other permissions. Where a change to a listed building constitutes a development which requires planning permission, then *both* planning permission and listed building consent are required and separate applications need to be made for each using the relevant forms. The two systems run in parallel and according to Historic Scotland, such cases are normally dealt with most effectively if both applications are submitted at the same time.[1] This is because the desirability of preserving a listed building and its setting are material considerations in determining applications for planning permission.[2]

1 SHEP, para. 3.34.
2 SPP, para. 113.

12.33 Almost all listed building consent applications must be advertised by the planning authority in a local newspaper and the Edinburgh Gazette[1] and the authority must also display a notice on the site for seven days. The exception are urgent applications relating to Crown properties which must be advertised through the same media but by the Scottish

Ministers rather than the local planning authority.[2] Advertising locally and nationally ensures that both local and national amenity societies can keep themselves aware of all listed building applications. Authorities must give 21 days for representations and cannot make a decision on the application until after this period has expired and they have taken into account representations received during that period.[3] Where the planning authority intends to grant consent for demolition, the Royal Commission on the Ancient and Historical Monuments of Scotland must be notified.[4] This is to allow the Commission time to visit the building to photograph and record it. Consent to demolish will usually be subject to a condition delaying demolition for three months to allow the Commission time to carry out this recording.[5]

1 Town and Country Planning (Listed Buildings and Buildings in Conservation Areas) (Scotland) Regulations 1987, SI 1987/1529, reg 5(1).
2 Ibid, reg 5(1)(A) (added by Town and Country Planning (Listed Buildings and Buildings in Conservation Areas) (Amendment) (Scotland) Regulations 2006 (SSI 2006 No 266), reg 2).
3 Ibid reg 5(2) and 5(3) (added by Town and Country Planning (Application of Subordinate Legislation to the Crown) (Scotland) Order 2006 (2006 No 270), art 7(3)).
4 Planning (Listed Buildings and Conservation Areas) (Scotland) Act 1997, s 7(2)(b).
5 S 7(2)(c)(i).

12.34 All applications have to be submitted in the first instance to the planning authority. While it has the power to refuse any application, many decisions to approve cannot be made until the Scottish Ministers have been given the opportunity to call in the proposal for their determination. The applications which local authorities are able to approve without first notifying the Scottish Ministers are those for the alteration or extension of a Category C(S) building.[1] Following a pilot project in 2008, local authorities also have the option to reach an agreement with Historic Scotland for delegation of certain applications affecting Category B buildings.[2] Historic Scotland had a target that half (16) of all local authorities would opt to do so by March 2011 but only 11 had done so by that date.[3]

1 Direction on Certain Classes of Application for Listed Building Consent (1987) (issued with SDD Circular 17/1987 – Annex III).
2 See The Listed Buildings and Conservation Areas (Removal of Duty to Notify) (Scotland) Direction 2010 and Historic Scotland 'A Joint Working Agreement Between Historic Scotland and Planning Authorities in Relation to Statutory Casework and Consultation' (2009) Appendix 10.
3 See Historic Scotland *Strategic Priorities Key Performance Indicators Outturns 2010/11* at www.historic-scotland.gov.uk/hsb1511kpisannexa.pdf

12.35 In all other cases, including an application to demolish any class of listed building,[1] the Scottish Ministers must be notified if the planning authority intends to grant consent.[2] The Scottish Ministers then have 28 days to decide whether to call in the application, clear it, or request further information. If they ask for more information or time to decide whether to call in the application, the process is frozen indefinitely.[3] No decision can be taken until the Scottish Ministers indicate that the planning authority may grant consent, or they call it in. If the Scottish Ministers do nothing during the 28 days, or state that they do not intend calling in the application, the planning authority may grant consent. If the Scottish Ministers decide to call it in, there is no automatic right to a hearing or public inquiry.[4] While the applicant and the local planning authority have the opportunity to specify what procedure they would like to see used, it is for the Scottish Ministers to select the most suitable means of determining the application. Once an application has been called in, there is no right of appeal against the Scottish Ministers' decision except on a point of law. The courts have held that, despite the lack of a right to appeal on the merits of the case, this arrangement complies with the Human Rights Act 1998 Sch 1 Art 6(1).[5]

1 Planning (Listed Buildings and Conservation Areas) (Scotland) Act 1997, s 13(1).
2 Ibid, s 12(1).
3 Ibid, s 12(3).
4 The right for the applicant or planning authority to have a hearing or inquiry was removed by Historic Environment (Amendment) (Scotland) Act 2011 s.21(a).
5 *County Properties Ltd v Scottish Ministers* 2002 SC 79; 2001 SLT 1125.

12.36 Formal notification to the Scottish Ministers occurs after the planning authority has decided that consent should be granted. In effect, the planning authority resolves to grant consent subject to the views of the Scottish Ministers. However, that decision is not issued to the applicant unless and until authority has been given (or deemed to have been given) to do so. In theory, this could result in considerable delay. It is normal practice, however, particularly with more complex and important applications, for informal consultations to take place with staff of Historic Scotland before or during the initial application process. The views of Historic Scotland are, therefore, often influential in any negotiations between the applicant and planning authority, especially over any amendments to the proposal which make it possible to grant consent. As a result, the Scottish Ministers' power to call in applications is rarely used. This informal process also helps to avoid the need for the applicant to make two sets of alterations to their plans, once for the planning authority and then again for the Scottish Ministers.

Conditions of consent

12.37 Consent may be granted with conditions, some of which are specified in the Listed Buildings Act 1997 itself. Conditions may be imposed with respect to:

(a) the preservation of particular features of the building, either as part of it or after severance from it;
(b) the making good, after the works are completed, of any damage caused to the building by the works;
(c) the reconstruction of the building or any part of it following the execution of any works, with the use of original materials so far as practicable and with such alterations of the interior of the building as may be specified in the conditions.[1]

Other conditions may be granted under the same section to prevent premature demolition.

1 Planning (Listed Buildings and Conservation Areas) (Scotland) Act 1997, s 15.

In principle applications

12.38 It is not possible to make an in principle application for listed building consent. All applications must provide detailed drawings showing the precise nature of the work proposed. They must also show what is to replace the building if demolition is involved. In certain circumstances consent can, however, be granted subject to the approval of further details[1] and this might be appropriate in cases where there are minor, possibly structural, details which it is impossible to determine in advance.

1 Planning (Listed Buildings and Conservation Areas) (Scotland) Act 1997, s 15(2).

Retrospective applications

12.39 Applications for listed building consent can be made retrospectively.[1] In such cases, however, if listed building consent is granted it only applies from the date of approval, not retrospectively.[2] This means that, although a listed building enforcement notice concerning the matter would lapse,[3] the owner could still be liable for prosecution on the grounds of their earlier failure to comply with the notice.[4] Any conviction for the offence of unauthorised works could also still be valid.

1 Planning (Listed Buildings and Conservation Areas) (Scotland) Act 1997, s 7(3).
2 Ibid.
3 Ibid, s 40(1).
4 Ibid, s 40(2).

Applications by planning authorities

12.40 Where a planning authority proposes to carry out work to a listed building, it requires listed building consent from the Scottish

Ministers.[1] In practice, authorities follow the same procedure as for any normal listed building consent application but can only grant it subject to the Scottish Ministers' approval.[2]

1 Planning (Listed Buildings and Conservation Areas) (Scotland) Act 1997, s 73.
2 Town and Country Planning (Listed Buildings and Buildings in Conservation Areas) (Scotland) Regulations 1987, SI 1987/1529, reg 11.

Revocation and modification of listed building consent

12.41 Planning authorities have the power,[1] subject in most cases to confirmation by the Scottish Ministers,[2] to revokc or modify listed building consent. This procedure can only be used before the work has been completed and cannot affect any of the work which has been completed. Unless the order was unopposed, compensation may be payable for any losses caused by it.[3]

1 Planning (Listed Buildings and Conservation Areas) (Scotland) Act 1997, s 21.
2 Ibid, s 22.
3 Ibid, s 25.

Demolition of listed buildings

12.42 Government policy on the demolition of listed buildings is set out in the SHEP.[1] In essence, this is that no listed building should be demolished unless it can bc clearly demonstrated that every effort has been made to retain it. Furthermore, Historic Scotland advises that demolition will only be justified in the following circumstances:

(a) the building is not of special interest; or
(b) the building is incapable of repair; or
(c) the demolition of the building is essential to delivering significant benefits to economic growth or the wider community; or
(d) the repair of the building is not economically viable and has been marketed (unsuccessfully) at a price reflecting its location and condition to potential restoring purchasers for a reasonable period.[2]

The costs of maintenance should be considered but these alone do not override the presumption in favour of preservation of the listed building.[3] Demolition means the destruction or substantial destruction of the whole building.[4] While it will normally be straightforward to identify works that involve demolition, this is not always the case. Historic Scotland's advice is that the question of whether a proposal falls into the category of demolition or alteration is ultimately one of fact and degree, and requires careful consideration by the planning authority.[5] Where only part of a building is listed, the Courts have held that the whole building should be treated as listed and therefore, removal of the listed part will amount to an alteration rather than a demolition.[6]

1 See also Historic Scotland 'Demolition' (2010) part of the Managing Change in the Historic Environment series available at www.historic-scotland.gov.uk/index/heritage/policy/managingchange.htm
2 SHEP, para 3.50.
3 *Cullimore v Secretary of State for the Environment* [1992] EGCS 69.
4 SHEP, Annex 8 para 9.
5 Ibid.
6 *Shimizu (UK) Ltd v Westminster City Council* [1997] 1 WLR 168.

12.43 Demolition is unlikely to be supported by the Scottish Ministers without hard evidence that there is no economic use to which the building can be put. Such evidence might include financial appraisals and proof that the applicants, in spite of conducting a lengthy marketing campaign, have not been able to sell or lease the building. Historic Scotland advises owners to use the services of the local planning authority and the Scottish Civic Trust[1] for advice on the adequacy of any marketing campaign and to help find a purchaser, such as a Building Preservation Trust. The Civic Trust operates a register of Listed Buildings at Risk which helps to raise awareness of such opportunities.[2] In May 2012; the Scottish Ministers refused an application from Perth & Kinross Council for Listed Building Consent to demolish Perth City Hall. The council had made the proposal as part of its plans to create a new civic open space. However, one of the reasons for refusal was that the council had not produced sufficient evidence that, based on marketing to potential restoring purchasers at a price reflecting its location and condition for a reasonable period, there was no alternative to demolition. Historic Scotland guidance note 'Demolition' (2010)[3] gives examples of listed buildings which have been demolished because of a proven lack of economic viability, such as the Ferguslie Mill No 1 in Paisley. It also gives examples of successful conversions of buildings which had previously been threatened with demolition, such as the *Art Deco* 'India of Inchinnan' building in Renfrewshire, now converted to office use.

1 The Scottish Civic Trust is based at The Tobacco Merchants House, 42 Miller Street, Glasgow. Its website is at www.scottishcivictrust.org.uk.
2 www.buildingsatrisk.org.uk.
3 Part of the Managing Change in the Historic Environment series available at www.historic-scotland.gov.uk/index/heritage/policy/managingchange.htm.

12.44 It is unusual, therefore, but not impossible, for the demolition of a listed building to be given consent. It is most likely to be possible when evidence is produced showing no practicable use for a building which is in an advanced state of decay. Having said that, in exceptional circumstances demolition may be allowed of listed buildings which could be capable of economic use. In *Save Britain's Heritage v the Secretary of State for the Environment and Number 1 Poultry Ltd*[1] the House of Lords rejected the interpretation that government policy meant an absolute ban on the demolition of listed buildings which are capable of economic use. In that case, the fact that the replacement building had greater architectural merit was used to justify the decision. However, Lord Bridge said that this factor would not always justify demolition; it was simply to be considered along with other factors in each case. This is an important point because some buildings are listed for their historic rather than architectural merit and would, therefore, be at risk if the greater architectural merit of a replacement could always justify demolition. From *Rolf v North Shropshire District Council*,[2] it seems clear that a planning authority may take into account the financial circumstances of the owner. Other financial considerations can be taken into account, as in *R v Westminster City Council ex parte Monahan*[3] where listed building consent was granted for partial demolition to allow development which would help finance improvements to the Royal Opera House, Covent Garden. The Scottish Ministers have made clear that demolition may be justified in cases where the building's retention would frustrate developments of national or regional significance. For example, Falfield Mill, built in 1818, was demolished to make way for the M74 motorway extension, an infrastructure project of national importance.[4]

1 [1991] 1 WLR 153.
2 [1988] JPL 103.
3 [1989] 2 All ER 74.
4 Historic Scotland 'Demolition' (2010) part of the 'Managing Change in the Historic Environment' series available at www.historic-scotland.gov.uk/index/heritage/policy/managingchange.htm

12.45 Where demolition is to be approved there is great concern that a building may be lost leaving nothing but an ugly gap site for an indefinite period. The Listed Buildings Act[1] makes it possible; therefore, for planning authorities to grant consent for demolition subject to a condition that demolition cannot begin until either or both of the following requirements have been met:

(a) a planning obligation for the regulation of the redevelopment of the site of the listed building has been agreed and recorded under s 75 of the 1997 Act;
(b) the planning authority is satisfied that contracts have been placed either for –
    (i) the acceptable redevelopment of the site; or
    (ii) its conversion to an acceptable open space.

In this way the planning authority can satisfy itself that demolition can only happen once it has ensured, as far as possible, that the development of an acceptable replacement will follow immediately afterwards. The courts have confirmed that the absence of a suitable redevelopment scheme is an adequate reason for refusing listed building consent for demolition.[2]

1 Planning (Listed Buildings and Conservation Areas) (Scotland) Act 1997, s 15(3).
2 *Davis v Secretary of State for the Environment and Southwark London Borough Council* [1992] JPL 1162.

Appeals

12.46 If an application has been called in, there is no appeal against the Scottish Ministers' decision except on a point of law. Where the decision is made by the planning authority, applicants have a right of appeal to the Scottish Ministers within three months[1] against a refusal or against any conditions attached to an approval. The appellant must certify that they are the sole owner of the property or that they have given notice in the prescribed form to all parties with an ownership interest.[2] The process is similar to that for other planning appeals[3] and governed by the same regulations.[4] The main difference is that an appeal can be made on the ground that the building concerned is not worthy of listing in the first place.[5] In almost all cases decisions are delegated to reporters.

1 Town and Country Planning (Appeals) (Scotland) Regulations 2013, SI 2013/156, reg. 17.
2 Town and Country Planning (Appeals) (Scotland) Regulations 2013, SI 2013/156, reg 18.
3 See Chapter 7.
4 Town and Country Planning (Appeals) (Scotland) Regulations 2013 SI 2013/156.
5 Planning (Listed Buildings and Conservation Areas) (Scotland) Act 1997, s 19(3).

Enforcement of listed building control

12.47 Breaches of listed building control are viewed as a serious matter. Anyone who demolishes or alters a listed building in a way which affects its character, without first obtaining listed building consent, is guilty of an offence which could, in certain circumstances, lead to imprisonment. The only possible ground of defence is that: (1) the work was urgently necessary for health or safety reasons or to preserve the building; (2) it was not practicable to achieve such health and safety or preservation by repair, or temporary support or shelter; (3) the work undertaken was the minimum necessary; and (4) the authority was notified in writing as soon as possible of the requirement to do the work and of the justification for carrying it out.[1]

1 Planning (Listed Buildings and Conservation Areas) (Scotland) Act, s 8(3).

12.48 A person found guilty of a breach of listed building control is liable to a maximum fine of £50,000 and or up to six months imprisonment on summary conviction, or an unlimited fine, and or up to two years in prison on conviction on indictment.[1] In determining the amount of the fine the court has to have particular regard to any financial benefit which has accured or appears likely to accure to the person convicted of the offence.[2]

1 Planning (Listed Buildings and Conservation Areas) (Scotland) Act 1997, s 8(4).
2 Ibid, s 8(5).

Enforcement procedures

12.49 Where unauthorised work has been carried out, the planning authority or Scottish Ministers may refer the case to the procurator fiscal with a view to prosecution[1] and/or serve a listed building enforcement notice.[2] It is the government's view that prosecution for unauthorised works is best confined to extreme cases where action to remedy the situation is unlikely to be feasible eg if an entire building has been demolished.[3]

1 Planning (Listed Buildings and Conservation Areas) (Scotland) Act 1997, s 8(1).
2 Ibid, s 34(1).
3 Historic Scotland 'Intervention by Planning Authorities' extract from 'Memorandum of Guidance on Listed Buildings and Conservation Areas', para 3.2 available as part of the Managing Change in the Historic Environment series at www.historic-scotland.gov.uk/managingchange

12.50 Listed building enforcement notices must be served on the *current* owner, lessee, occupier and on anyone else whom the authority considers has an interest in the property.[1] The procedure involved is similar to that for a breach of normal planning control.[2] Where unauthorised works are currently being carried out and the authority wants these to stop, the notice must specify what these are and state that they are to cease.[3] Where the authority wishes to rectify the damage caused by unauthorised work the notice must specify the steps required to do so, ie either: (1) restoring the property to its former state; (2) carrying out work to bring the building to the state it would have been in if the terms and conditions of a listed building consent had been complied with; or (3) some form of alleviation (falling short of complete restoration) of the effects of the illegal work to the satisfaction of the planning authority.[4] The notice will also specify a final date for compliance and where more than one step or works are required to meet the terms of the notice, the compliance date for each may vary.[5] Listed Building Consent is deemed to have been granted for works which the enforcement notice requires to be carried out.[6] The current owner has a duty to conform with the terms of the enforcement notice, even although that person might not have committed the breach.[7] The current owners can, however, recover their expenses from the person who carried out the unauthorised works.[8] If they fail to meet the terms of the notice by the time specified, they are guilty of an offence. This includes failure to continue to comply after the date for compliance[9] Possible defences are that: (a) they did everything they could be expected to do to secure that all the steps required to comply with the notice were taken; or (b) they were not served with a copy of the notice and were not aware of its existence.[10] In cases where the unauthorised works were carried out before the current owner took title, it may be necessary for the enforcement notice to specify this.[11]

1 Planning (Listed Buildings and Conservation Areas) (Scotland) Act 1997, s 34(6).
2 See Chapter 9.
3 Planning (Listed Buildings and Conservation Areas) (Scotland) Act 1997, s(34)(1A)(a).
4 Ibid, s 34(2).
5 Ibid, s 34(5).
6 Ibid, s 34(4).
7 Ibid, s 39.
8 Ibid, s 38(2).
9 *C&P Reinforcement Ltd v East Hertfordshire DC* [2009] EWHC 3128.
10 Ibid, s 39(4).
11 *Braun v First Secretary of State* [2004] 1 P&CR 15; [2003] 2 PLR 90.

Penalties for failure to comply with Listed Building Enforcement Notice

12.51 On summary conviction an offender can be liable to a fine of up to £20,000, or an unlimited fine on conviction on indictment.[1] In determining the level of fine the court shall take into account any financial benefit to the person convicted as a result of their offence.[2] Alternatively, if the notice is not complied with, the planning authority has the power to serve a fixed penalty notice offering the person the opportunity to discharge any liability to conviction provided they pay the penalty sum specified in the notice within 30 days.[3] The fixed penalty is £2,000 for the breach of a first listed building enforcement notice, increasing to £3,500 for breach of a second listed building enforcement notice and £5,000 for the breach of any subsequent listed building enforcement notice.[4] These sums are reduced by 25% if payment is made with 15 days of receiving the fixed penalty notice.[5] Another enforcement option for a planning authority dealing with a failure to comply with a listed building enforcement notice is for it to carry out the work specified in the notice and charge the expense involved to the current owner, lessee or occupier.[6] As with work required to comply with the notice, the owner or lessee can recover the expenses they have to pay the authority from the person who carried out the illegal works.[7]

1 Planning (Listed Buildings and Conservation Areas) (Scotland) Act 1997, s 39(5).
2 Ibid, s 39(6).
3 Ibid, s 39A
4 Planning (Listed Buildings) (Amount of Fixed Penalty) (Scotland) Regulations 2011/424.
5 Planning (Listed Buildings and Conservation Areas) (Scotland) Act 1997, s 39A(7).
6 Ibid, s 38(1).
7 Ibid, s 38(2).

Appeals against enforcement notices

12.52 Appeals against a listed building enforcement notice have to be made to the Scottish Ministers. There are several grounds of appeal eg that the building is not of special architectural or historic interest, the alleged work has not taken place, or that, if it has, it is not in contravention of listed building control (presumably because it does not affect the architectural or historic character of the building).[1] Where the notice requires works to stop it is legitimate to appeal that the cessation of works required by the notice exceeds what is necessary to remedy the contravention.[2] The appeal should be submitted to the Scottish Ministers before the date specified in the notice for compliance.[3] There are various possible outcomes. The Scottish Ministers may, for example, dismiss the appeal, amend the terms of the notice, remove the building from the list, or grant listed building consent for the works carried out.[4]

1 Planning (Listed Buildings and Conservation Areas) (Scotland) Act 1997, s 35(1).
2 Ibid, s 35(1)(ia).
3 Ibid, s 35(2).
4 Ibid, s 37.

Stop Notices

12.53 Where a planning authority or the Scottish Ministers are concerned about unauthorised works that are being carried out to a listed building, they can use the listed building enforcement notice powers described above to prohibit these. However, a listed building enforcement notice does not come into effect until at least 28 days after it has been served. There can be situations where the authorities want to stop the unauthorised works more quickly than that and in such cases they can also serve a stop notice.[1] This can require the prohibited works to stop within three days or even sooner if the authority can justify that. A stop notice can be served at the same time as a listed building enforcement notice or at any time afterwards up until the date on which the listed building enforcement notice takes effect. The stop notice has to be served on any parties who the planning authority considers have an interest in the building or to be responsible for carrying out the prohibited works. It is an offence not to comply with a stop notice and anyone found guilty of this is liable to a fine of £20,000 on summary conviction and an unlimited fine on indictment.[2] A stop notice remains in force until the listed building enforcement notice to which it relates is withdrawn or quashed, the period for compliance expires, or it is withdrawn by the planning authority; whichever comes first. It also ceases to have effect if the listed building enforcement notice to which it relates is varied in a way which means that relevant works are no longer affected. In certain circumstances, parties affected by a stop notice may be able to claim compensation for any losses arising from it.

1 Planning (Listed Buildings and Conservation Areas) (Scotland) Act 1997 s 41A.
2 Ibid, s 41E.

Temporary Stop Notices[1]

12.54 These notices can be used in situations where no listed building enforcement notice has been issued. A temporary stop notice needs to specify the works concerned, prohibit their execution and give the authority's reasons for this. The notice has to be served on anyone responsible for carrying out the works and anyone with an interest in the building. The notice comes into effect as soon as it is served and remains in force for 28 days (unless it specifies a shorter period). Temporary stop notices are intended to give the authority a chance to stop unauthorised works quickly and then within the 28 day period, use other enforcement measures to secure a permanent solution to the problem. It is an offence not to comply with the notice. As with stop notices, compensation may, in certain circumstances, be payable for losses arising from the service of a temporary stop notice used to require an immediate stop to unauthorised works.

1 Planning (Listed Buildings and Conservation Areas) (Scotland) Act 1997, s 41F.

Emergency Controls

Building preservation notices

12.55 Planning authorities have power to serve a building preservation notice when an as yet unlisted building is threatened with alteration or demolition (a process commonly referred to as 'spot listing').[1] They can use this power if they think that the building is of special interest and, once served, the notice gives the same protection as listed building status for up to six months. During that period the Scottish Ministers have to decide whether or not to list the building. The notice has to be served on the owner, lessee and occupier. If the matter is particularly pressing, or difficulties are being experienced serving notices, the authority may affix the notice conspicuously to some object on the building.[2] In *R v McCarthy & Stone (Developments) Ltd*[3] it was held that a telephone call from the local planning authority was sufficient notice. The notice ceases to be effective if the Scottish Ministers list the building or state that it is not to be listed. If they decide not to list the building, there can be financial consequences for the authority. This is because anyone who had an interest in the building at the time the notice was served may be entitled to compensation for any loss or damage which is directly attributable to the effect of the notice.[4] Compensation can include any penalty sums incurred by the need to cancel or countermand any contracted works.[5] Most authorities will only serve a building preservation notice, therefore, if they are confident that the Scottish Ministers will list the building.

1 Planning (Listed Buildings and Conservation Areas) (Scotland) Act 1997, s 3.
2 Ibid, s 4.
3 [1998] 6 CL 424.
4 Planning (Listed Buildings and Conservation Areas) (Scotland) Act 1997, s 26(2).
5 Ibid, s 26(3).

Certificate that building not intended to be listed

12.56 Spot listing is something that often occurs when proposals are being considered for the redevelopment of a historic or architecturally interesting building that has not yet been listed. There had been concerns that the uncertainty about whether spot listing might occur was an impediment to development. In response to those concerns a new provision was introduced through the Historic Environment (Amendment) (Scotland) Act 2011[1] to remove that uncertainty. Anyone can now apply to the Scottish Minsters for a certificate stating that they do not intend to list a building.[2] The application can be made at any time and need not be linked with an application for planning permission. If issued, the effects of such a certificate are that the Scottish Minsters are prevented from listing the building concerned for five years from the date of issue and the local planning authority is also prevented from spot listing the building during that period.[3] Owners and developers should be aware that the Scottish Ministers response to such an application may be to list the building concerned rather than issue a certificate. However, this at least has the advantage of removing uncertainty at an early stage in the development process.

1 Section 18.
2 Planning (Listed Buildings and Conservation Areas) (Scotland) Act 1997, s 5A(1).
3 Ibid, s 5A(2).

Neglect or damage to a listed building

12.57 Planning authorities and the Scottish Ministers have power to act in cases where a listed building is at risk through neglect or damage.[1] This can include preventative works necessary to limit any deterioration of the building and the provision of temporary support and shelter eg through erection of temporary scaffolding or the placing of a temporary roof over it. The local planning authority or Scottish Ministers may recover the expense involved from the owner.[2] Such action is limited to unoccupied buildings (and unoccupied parts of buildings).[3]

1 Planning (Listed Buildings and Conservation Areas) (Scotland) Act 1997, s 49.
2 Ibid, s 50.
3 Ibid, s 49(4).

Dangerous buildings

12.58 Where a building is in a dangerous condition, local authorities can require that work is carried out to make it safe or have it demolished. This is done through the service of notices under the Building (Scotland) Act 2003.[1] Where the dangerous building concerned is listed, the local authority must, if reasonably practicable, consult with the Scottish Ministers, the local planning authority and any other parties as it thinks fit, before serving the notice.[2] The owners of property on which a dangerous building notice has been served are still bound, however, by the requirement to obtain listed building consent.[3] Anyone who demolishes a dangerous listed building without consent will have to prove that this was urgently necessary in the interests of health and safety and that it was not practicable to secure health and safety (or the preservation of the building) through repairs or other temporary measures (eg shoring).[4] Unless a listed building is so dangerous that it needs to be demolished immediately, the government would prefer the planning authority to serve a repairs notice (see below) rather than allow action to be taken under building legislation. Even when a building has become dangerous, the government expects the local planning authority to take any practicable action to preserve rather than demolish it. The government has been prepared to back this policy with legal action as was shown in 1997 when the then Secretary of State for Scotland successfully sought an interim interdict preventing Highland Council from demolishing a listed school building which was capable of being preserved by the use of shoring.[5] The government points out that, except in the rare instances where a building can suddenly become unsafe (for example because of fire or flood), most buildings only become dangerous after a long period of decline. Planning authorities are, therefore, strongly advised to use the powers available to them to preserve listed buildings before they get into such a dangerous condition.[6]

1 Sections 29 and 30.
2 Ibid, s35
3 Ibid, s 35(4).
4 Planning (Listed Buildings and Conservation Areas) (Scotland) Act 1997, s 8(3).
5 See *Secretary of State for Scotland v Highland Council* 1998 SLT 222; (1997) 63 SPEL 104.
6 Historic Scotland 'Intervention by Planning Authorities' extract from 'Memorandum of Guidance on Listed Buildings and Conservation Areas', para 3.14 available as part of the Managing Change in the Historic Environment series at www.historic-scotland.gov.uk/managingchange

Repairs notice and compulsory acquisition

12.59 Planning authorities and the Scottish Ministers have the power to compulsorily acquire a listed building which they feel is not being properly looked after.[1] They can also acquire any adjoining land needed for amenity, access or management reasons.[2] However, they can only begin the process leading to such acquisition if they first serve a repairs notice.[3]

1 Planning (Listed Buildings and Conservation Areas) (Scotland) Act 1997, s 42(1).
2 Ibid, s 42(7).
3 Ibid, s 43(1).

12.60 A listed building repairs notice[1] must be served on the owner. It has to specify the works reasonably required to preserve the building and point out that if these are not carried out, proceedings may be started to compulsorily acquire the property. Those proceedings may begin two months after the repairs notice has been served. Because it is simply a preliminary step towards compulsory purchase, there is no statutory right of challenge to a repairs notice. An aggrieved owner will only be able to challenge the authority's actions as part of any subsequent compulsory purchase process.[2] The question can arise as to whether the steps required involve strict 'preservation' or in fact amount to 'restoration' and therefore require action more than that specified in the legislation. In *Robbins v Secretary of State for the Environment*[3] the House of Lords took the view that a repairs notice can require work that will return the building to the condition it was in *at the time of listing*. This ensures that a repairs notice can be used to remedy a situation where a listed building has been allowed to deteriorate, possibly deliberately.

1 Planning (Listed Buildings and Conservation Areas) (Scotland) Act 1997, s 43.
2 *Prestige Assets Ltd v Renfrewshire Council* 2003 SC 88; 2003 SLT 679.
3 [1989] 1 All ER 878.

12.61 The proceedings for compulsory purchase in this context are more or less the same as for other compulsory acquisition.[1] Proceedings may be halted by order of the sheriff, if anyone with an interest in the property successfully applies on the ground that reasonable steps have been taken to preserve the building.[2]

1 See Chapter 10.
2 Planning (Listed Buildings and Conservation Areas) (Scotland) Act 1997, s 42(5).

12.62 The amount of compensation payable can be severely limited if the planning authority (or the Scottish Ministers if they are acquiring the building) believes that the building has been deliberately allowed to fall into disrepair in the hope that consent will be granted for its demolition. In such situations, the authority or the Scottish Ministers can make a direction for minimum compensation.[1] In assessing compensation when such a direction has been made; it is assumed that listed building consent and planning permission would only be granted for restoring and maintaining the building in a proper state of repair. This has the effect of excluding all development value. Anyone with an interest in the land can appeal to the sheriff court against such a direction within 28 days of being notified of the draft compulsory purchase order. The sheriff may make an order quashing the direction if he is satisfied that the building has not been deliberately allowed to fall into disrepair. The onus is on the owner to prove that there has not been deliberate neglect.

1 Planning (Listed Buildings and Conservation Areas) (Scotland) Act 1997, s 45(1).

12.63 One problem with these compulsory purchase powers is that, once it has acquired the building, the local authority is then responsible for carrying out the required work. Because of the financial implications of this, many local authorities are inhibited from taking action. One way round this problem is for the planning authority to enter into a 'back-to-back' agreement with a third party (possibly a private developer who specialises in restoring historic buildings) who will take ownership after compulsory acquisition and carry out the required repairs and restoration. However, care must be taken in the drafting of a back-to-back agreement to ensure that the disposal is on the best terms that can reasonably be obtained.[1]

1 *Standard Commercial Property Securities Ltd v Glasgow City Council* 2007 SC (HL) 33; 2006 SLT 1152.

12.64 Repairs notices and compulsory acquisition do not apply to buildings in ecclesiastical use or scheduled ancient monuments.[1] Crown property can only be acquired where it is not currently being held by or on behalf of the Crown and if the appropriate Crown authority consents to the acquisition.[2]

1 Planning (Listed Buildings and Conservation Areas) (Scotland) Act 1997 ss 54 & 55.
2 Ibid, s 42 (6A).

Financial assistance

12.65 Whilst the owners of listed buildings will find that their property is subject to stringent controls, they can at least take some comfort from the fact that grants, loans and other financial assistance can be available. Historic Scotland operates discretionary grant schemes including Building Repair Grants, Repair Grants for Places of Worship, and the Historic Environment Regeneration Fund (for area-based conservation initiatives). Local authorities and City Heritage Trusts also provide grants. Almost inevitably, demand normally exceeds the budgets available. Further information about grant schemes can be found on the Historic Scotland website.[1]

1 www.historic-scotland.gov.uk/index/heritage/grants

12.66 Another potential financial benefit of listed building status from the owner's point of view is that planning permission may be granted for a material change of use which might otherwise have had little prospect of gaining consent. This is because a high value use may play an important role in securing the future of a listed building which is at risk unless a viable use can be found. This would be an important material consideration to balance against other planning policy objections.

2. CONSERVATION AREAS

Introduction

12.67 It is not just single buildings that can be of architectural or historic interest. Whole areas can also be viewed in this way, eg Edinburgh Old Town, or historic villages such as Comrie in Perthshire. Other examples might include attractive groups of unlisted buildings in the form of a town square or (in rural areas) a planned estate. There are over 640 designated conservation areas in Scotland.[1]

1 Historic Scotland 'Scotland's Historic Environment Audit 2010' para 17.

Designation process

12.68 Local planning authorities have a duty to consider 'from time to time' which parts of their district are of such interest that it is desirable to preserve or enhance them,[1] and to designate these as conservation areas.[2] However, they have a broad discretion as to which parts of their area merit designation[3] and it is not necessary for every part of any individual conservation area to contain something of interest. It would be legitimate, for example, to include an area of open space to protect the setting of buildings in the conservation area.[4] However, the justification for designation must be the protection and enhancement of the area and not an ulterior one. In *R (on the application of Arndale Properties Ltd) v Worcester City Council*[5] the court quashed the designation of a conservation area because the purpose had been to prevent the demolition of an unlisted cricket pavilion. The planning authority's justification for designation must also be clear. In *Trillium (Prime) Property GP Ltd v Tower Hamlets LBC*[6] the court quashed conservation area status because the planning authority report recommending designation had been misleading. Once conservation area designation has been made, development is subject to extra controls and initiatives can be taken to improve the area.

1 Planning (Listed Buildings and Conservation Areas) (Scotland) Act 1997, s 61(1)(a).
2 Ibid, s 61(1)(b).
3 *R v Swansea City Council, ex p Elitestone Ltd* [1992] EGCS 72; see also *R v Surrey County Council and Oakimber Ltd* [1995] EGCS 120.
4 See *R v Canterbury Council, ex p Halford* (1992) 64 P&CR 513.
5 [2008] EWHC 678 (Admin); [2008] JPL 1583; see also *Metro Construction Ltd v Barnet LBC* [2009] EWHC 2956 (Admin); [2009] NPC 135.
6 [2011] EWHC 146 (Admin).

12.69 The planning authority can also vary or cancel conservation area status.[1] The Scottish Ministers' approval is not needed for either designation or variation/cancellation, but they must be notified. The Scottish Ministers also have the power to designate conservation areas[2] but this is a reserve power which is used only exceptionally.[3]

1 Planning (Listed Buildings and Conservation Areas) (Scotland) Act 1997, s 62(1).
2 Ibid, s 61(2).
3 Historic Scotland SHEP (20111) para 2.38.

12.70 When considering designation, the planning authority must publish notices in at least one local newspaper and in the Edinburgh Gazette.[1] There is no legal requirement to notify all of the individual owners of property in the area. Local planning authorities are, however, expected to consult with the public if they are thinking of designating an area; a particularly appropriate time for this is during the period of local development plan preparation.[2] Similar procedures have to be followed for variation or cancellation of the designation. As part of the process leading to designation, or when reviewing an existing Conservation Area, planning authorities are encouraged to carry out a full appraisal to ensure that the area's character and appearance are properly understood. Around a third of conservation areas in Scotland have now had an appraisal[3] and they are becoming an important tool in the management and improvement of conservation areas.

1 Planning (Listed Buildings and Conservation Areas) (Scotland) Act 1997, s 62(4).
2 Historic Scotland SHEP (2011), para 2.48.
3 Historic Scotland 'Scotland's Historic Environment Audit' 2010 para 41.

Effects of designation

Article 4 Directions

12.71 Perhaps surprisingly, conservation area designation does not by itself introduce substantial extra controls. Usually the strongest controls are effected by means of Article 4 directions removing permitted development rights (eg regarding window alterations, the erection of fences and the building of house extensions). Around two thirds of conservation areas are covered by an Article 4 direction.[1] These directions require approval by the Scottish Ministers and it is their policy that blanket restrictions are not acceptable, any removal of specific permitted development rights needs to be linked to the character of the particular area as demonstrated through an area appraisal.[2] As a result, the precise effects of Article 4 directions vary from area to area, the aim being to reintroduce control over the particular types of work which might affect each area's character if allowed to go ahead unchecked. As we saw in Chapter 5[3] once an Article 4 direction is in force planning permission is required for any of the types of development affected.

1 Historic Scotland 'Scotland's Historic Environment Audit' 2010 para 41.
2 Historic Scotland 'SHEP' (2011) para 43.
3 Part 5.

Demolition of unlisted buildings

12.72 It is likely that a conservation area will contain many buildings that are individually listed, and these will of course be subject to listed building control, including control over demolition. However, many non-listed buildings may also contribute to the character or appearance of the area and so their demolition normally requires a special permission known as conservation area consent and this is the case whether or not planning permission is also required.[1] Partial demolition does not require conservation area consent. The question of whether what is proposed constitutes the demolition of the whole building is one of fact and degree to be determined in the light of the circumstances in each case.

1 Planning (Listed Buildings and Conservation Areas) (Scotland) Act 1997, s 66(1).

12.73 Exceptions to the need for conservation area consent can be specified in a direction issued by the Scottish Ministers under a power given to them in the Listed Buildings Act 1997.[1] The present direction is the 'Direction on Exemption from Demolition Control in Conservation Areas'[2] which lists 13 exceptions. These include very small buildings (ie not exceeding a *total* of 115 cubic metres), agricultural or forestry buildings built since 1 January 1914, and buildings which are to be demolished as a result of compulsory purchase orders and orders issued under housing legislation prior to designation of the conservation area.

1 Planning (Listed Buildings and Conservation Areas) (Scotland) Act 1997, s 67(2).
2 Issued with SDD Circular 17/1987 'New Provisions and Revised Guidance relating to Listed Buildings and Conservation Areas' (dated 25/9/87).

12.74 The Listed Buildings Act applies listed building controls with modifications to unlisted buildings in conservation areas. As a result, the procedure for obtaining conservation area consent is similar to that for listed building consent.[1] Scottish Government policy[2] is that before considering granting consent, planning authorities should take into account the importance of the building to the character or appearance of the conservation area. If it considers that the building has any value in this context, either on its own or as part of a group, then the authority should always seek to retain the building and, if necessary, promote its restoration. If retention of the building is not considered to be worthy or viable and the site is to be redeveloped, conservation area consent should normally be granted only if the authority is satisfied with the proposed replacement. For example, the authority will want to be satisfied that the nature or appearance of the replacement building or structure preserves or enhances the character of the area.[3] Consequently, in principle planning applications are normally unacceptable in conservation areas where demolition is involved. This can have financial implications for anyone wanting to test the acceptability in principle of a particular proposal. As we saw in Chapter 6, it is common for this to be tested through an application for planning permission in principle, thus avoiding the cost of drawing up detailed plans for a proposal which might not get permission. This may not be possible if the site involved happens to be in a conservation area.

1 Planning (Listed Buildings and Conservation Areas) (Scotland) Act 1997, s 66(3).
2 Historic Scotland SHEP (2011) paras 3.58 & 3.59.
3 *Kent County Council v Secretary of State for the Environment* [1995] P&CR 520.

Tree protection

12.75 Trees in conservation areas which are not already covered by a tree preservation order (TPO) are protected. Advance notice must be given to the local planning authority for any felling or other work to such trees. It is an offence to proceed with such work without the authority's approval or before six weeks have elapsed since notice was given to the authority.[1]

1 Town and Country Planning Scotland (Act) 1997 s 172; see also Chapter 13.

Publicity for planning applications

12.76 An application for any development which the planning authority considers would affect the character or appearance of a conservation area must be advertised in the local press.[1] In addition, a notice must be posted for at least seven days on or near the site. Authorities have to allow 21 days for representations and cannot determine the application until that period has expired and they have taken into account any representations received within that period

1 Planning (Listed Buildings and Conservation Areas) (Scotland) Act 1997, s 65.

Repair of unoccupied buildings

12.77 The Scottish Ministers have the power to direct that urgent repairs are carried out to an unoccupied unlisted building in a conservation area if they consider that its preservation is important for maintaining the character or appearance of the area.[1] It is open to planning authorities and others to suggest to the Scottish Ministers that they use this power. The same procedures and exceptions apply as with similar action in relation to unoccupied listed buildings.[2]

1 Planning (Listed Buildings and Conservation Areas) (Scotland) Act 1997, ss 49, 68.
2 See para 12.57 above.

Permitted development

12.78 We have already pointed out that Article 4 directions are used in conservation areas to give planning authorities control over work which would normally be permitted development. In addition, however, the permitted development order itself differentiates between conservation areas and elsewhere.[1] For example, the following, usually permitted development, would not be so in conservation areas: house extensions; other alterations affected the external appearance of a house; and the creation of a hard surface area in the garden of a house. The maximum size of permitted domestic outbuildings such as garden sheds and garages is lower in conservation areas than elsewhere.

1 Town and Country Planning (General Permitted Development) (Scotland) Order 1992, SI 1992/223 (as amended).

Deemed consent for advertisements

12.79 Deemed consent for the display of some advertisements does not apply in conservation areas.[1] This affects certain illuminated advertisements and advertisements on hoardings surrounding a building site.

1 Town and Country Planning (Control of Advertisements) (Scotland) Regulations 1984, SI 1984/467 (as amended) Sch 4.

Control over standards of new development

12.80 In practice, a major impact of conservation area designation is that a planning authority will exercise stronger control over the standards of any new development than might be applied elsewhere. For example, even planning applications for developments categorised as local developments will normally require the submission of a design statement.[1] Because of the level of detailed required to enable the authority to make a decision, applications in principle will often not be accepted in conservation areas, especially for major proposals. As with listed buildings, there is effectively a presumption in favour of preserving the character and appearance of an area once it has been designated.[2] This presumption applies to the whole conservation area, not just those parts displaying the characteristics which led to its designation.[3] There is also a requirement that authorities take into account the desirability of enhancing conservation areas. There has been debate about what these two obligations mean in practice with suggestions that permission should only be granted for development if it enhances the area. In *Steinberg and Sykes v Secretary of State for the Environment and Camden London Borough Council*[4] for example, the failure of an inspector to consider whether a proposal would enhance the area resulted in planning consent being quashed. It is important to note, however, that the failure here was only a procedural one; the inspector had failed to *consider* the enhancement issue. In other words, the desirability of enhancement is a material consideration that the planning authority should take into account in reaching its decision.[5] It is not therefore the case that an application can only be approved if it would enhance the area, or that it must be refused if it would harm it. As long as the desirability of preservation and enhancement is taken into account, other material considerations may be allowed to outweigh any potential harm.[6] Furthermore, it is now established that a development which has a neutral effect on the character and appearance of an area will meet the test of preserving the area.[7]

1 Town and Country Planning (Development Management Procedure) (Scotland) Regulations 2013, reg 13.

2 Planning (Listed Buildings and Conservation Areas) (Scotland) Act 1997, s 64.
3 *R. (on the application of University College London) v First Secretary of State* [2004] EWHC 2846 (Admin).
4 [1989] JPL 258.
5 See Chapter 6.
6 See *Harrow London Borough Council v Secretary of State for the Environment* (1990) 60 P&CR 525.
7 *South Lakeland District Council v Secretary of State for the Environment and Carlisle Diocesan Parsonages Board* [1992] 2 WLR 204.

12.81 General advice on the standards of design required in conservation areas can be found in 'New Design in Historic Settings' published by Historic Scotland and Architecture and Design Scotland, and in PAN 71.[1] Authorities are also advised to take into account the views of Architecture and Design Scotland where particularly controversial or sensitive proposals are made.

1 SEDD PAN 71 'Conservation Area Management' (2004).

Conservation area enhancement

Enhancement schemes

12.82 Conservation areas are not just about extra controls over development. Planning authorities also have a positive duty to enhance such areas. They are required from time to time to prepare proposals for enhancement[1] (usually known as 'enhancement schemes') and must hold a public meeting to discuss such proposals.[2] Enhancement schemes are often prepared as part of a conservation area appraisal.

1 Planning (Listed Buildings and Conservation Areas) (Scotland) Act 1997, s 63(1).
2 Ibid, s 63(2).

Financial assistance

12.83 It used to be the case that a conservation area had to be designated as 'outstanding' to become eligible for financial assistance from the Scottish Ministers. However, that requirement was removed by the Planning etc (Scotland) Act 2006[1] Local authorities, national park authorities, community groups and other third sector organisations can apply for funding for a Conservation Area Regeneration Scheme (CARS). This provides financial assistance for regeneration and conservation initiatives such as building repairs, small grants for shop front improvements, public realm improvements, training for traditional craftsmen and the appointment of a project officer to coordinate the scheme. Funding from Historic Scotland is pooled with money secured from other sources. For example, the Keith Conservation Area Regeneration Scheme (CARS) was launched in July 2012 with a budget of around £2m made up of contributions from Historic Scotland, the Scottish Government, the Moray LEADER 2007–2013 programme and Moray Council. Funding can also be made available for conservation area enhancement through a Townscape Heritage Initiative (THI) with support from the Heritage Lottery Fund. An example is the Govan Cross THI, a five year programme which began in 2009 and is promoted by Glasgow City Council.

1 Section 55(3).

City HeritageTrusts

12.84 City Heritage Trusts have been established to promote conservation initiatives in Scotland's cities. They also provide information and advice, support research and act as local agents for the distribution of grants.[1]

1 See for example details of the The Stirling City Heritage Trust at www.stirlingcityheritagetrust.org

3. SCHEDULED ANCIENT MONUMENTS[1]

Introduction

12.85 As we have already explained,[2] some buildings and structures which are of historic importance are scheduled as ancient monuments. As well as obvious cases, such as stone circles and ruined castles, scheduled remains can include (for example) ancient field systems, industrial mills and abandoned twentieth-century coastal defence structures. The protection of such artefacts is seen as particularly important since most represent the only opportunity through which we can find out about our past. This opportunity could be lost forever if the monument was damaged or destroyed. There are currently about 8200 scheduled monuments in Scotland.[3] Scheduled ancient monument status is usually separate from listing, although as we have already seen, there can be overlap between the two. Where a structure is both listed and scheduled, the ancient monument provisions apply, as these give greater potential control over any changes.

1 For a brief but very useful guide to this topic, see Historic Scotland 'Scheduled Ancient Monuments: A Guide for Owners, Occupiers and Managers' (2012) available online at www.historic-scotland.org.uk
2 Para 12.25.
3 Historic Scotland 'Works on Ancient Monuments' (2011).

What can be scheduled?

12.86 The present legislation is the Ancient Monuments and Archaeological Areas Act 1979.[1] This defines[2] a monument as any building,[3] structure, work, cave, excavation, or land containing the remains of any of these. A site containing the remains of any vehicle, vessel, aircraft or other moveable structure may also be a monument as can a site containing any other thing, or group of things, that evidences previous human activity. Machinery attached to a monument is regarded as part of that monument unless it can be detached without having to be dismantled. Often, a monument will be partly or entirely below ground and so may not be visible. Land adjacent to a monument can also be included within the area to be scheduled if the Scottish Ministers consider that this is necessary for the monument's support or preservation.

1 As amended by the Historic Environment (Amendment) (Scotland) Act 2011.
2 Ancient Monuments and Archaeological Areas Act 1979 s 61(7).
3 Buildings in ecclesiastical use are excluded (Ancient Monuments and Archaeological Areas Act 1979, s 61(8)).

Scheduling process

12.87 The 1979 Act gives the Scottish Ministers a duty to compile and maintain records of archaeological remains which they consider to be of national importance. They are not obliged, however, to schedule all such archaeological relics. For example in *R v Secretary of State for the Environment, ex parte Rose Theatre Trust Co*[1] the minister, whilst recognising the national importance of the remains of the Rose Theatre (which had been used for the performance of plays by Shakespeare and Marlowe), did not wish to schedule them as this could give rise to a compensation claim and the developer was willing to co-operate in the protection of the remains in any case.

1 [1990] 2 WLR 186.

12.88 Since 2006 Historic Scotland (on behalf of the Scottish Ministers) has used a non-statutory set of criteria for deciding which monuments are of sufficient national importance to be scheduled. This includes factors such as cultural, artistic, archaeological, historic, aesthetic, scientific and social considerations. The criteria can be found in Annex 1 of SHEP.[1]

1 Historic Scotland 'Scottish Historic Environment Policy' (2011).

Effects of scheduling

Scheduled monument consent

12.89 Once a property or remains has been scheduled, consent is needed from the Scottish Ministers for any work to demolish, destroy, damage, repair, alter, add to, flood or cover up the monument.[1] This is known as scheduled monument consent and application for it must be made to Historic Scotland which advises the Scottish Ministers on their decision. A separate consent under s 42 of the 1979 Act is required for any metal detecting activity within the protected area.[2]

1 Ancient Monuments and Archaeological Areas Act 1979, s 2.
2 See the leaflet Historic Scotland 'Metal Detecting Yes or No? Metal Detecting, Scheduled Monuments and the Law' (undated).

Application procedure

12.90 The procedures involved are set out in the Ancient Monuments and Archaeological Areas (Applications for Scheduled Monument Consent) (Scotland) Regulations 2011.[1] Where the proposed works are acceptable to Historic Scotland, an unconditional grant of consent may be given within five weeks. Where Historic Scotland wishes to refuse consent or grant it subject to conditions, they will first issue a provisional view. Where this is not acceptable to the applicant the matter is referred to the Scottish Ministers for a final decision. In such cases the Scottish Ministers will decide the method for determining the application. Whichever method is used, the matter will be considered by a Reporter who will make a recommendation to the Scottish Ministers who will then make the final decision. If scheduled monument consent is refused, compensation may be payable under the 1979 Act. Compensation should be based on the circumstances at the time when consent is refused, not at the date when the property was scheduled.[2] However, if the monument was already scheduled before the application was made, it is unlikely that compensation will be payable. A claim may be successful if the monument is scheduled after the application was submitted and especially if planning permission is granted for the development.[3]

1 SSI 2011 No 375.
2 Currie's Executors v Secretary of State for Scotland 1992 SLT (Lands Tr) 69.
3 Historic Scotland 'Works on Ancient Monuments' (2011), p 9.

12.91 Where works proposed to a scheduled monument are of a type that would need planning permission, both scheduled monument consent and planning permission have to be obtained. While the scheduled monument consent is dealt with by Historic Scotland, the application for planning permission is the responsibility of the local planning authority. The planning authority has to consult with the Scottish Ministers (Historic Scotland in practice) about any planning application that affects a scheduled ancient monument or its setting. In determining the planning application the planning authority has to have regard to the archaeological interest of the monument as an important material consideration,[1] in particular Scottish Government policy that scheduled monuments should be preserved *in situ* and within an appropriate setting. In cases where an authority resolves to grant planning permission but Historic Scotland has advised against this, they must notify the Scottish Ministers first. This notification requirement also applies where Historic Scotland has recommended conditions which the planning authority does not propose to attach to the permission. Notification gives the Scottish Ministers the opportunity to call the planning application in to deal with it themselves. Annex 7 to the Scottish Historic Environment Policy (2011) gives more information on the relationship between scheduled monument consent and planning permission and how the Scottish Government expects this to be handled by the relevant authorities.

1 See eg *Coal Contractors v Secretary of State for the Environment* [1993] EGCS 218.

Cases where consent is not required

12.92 There are nine classes of work for which scheduled monument consent is deemed to have been granted by the Ancient Monuments (Class Consents) (Scotland) Order 1996:[1]

Class I	Certain agricultural, horticultural or forestry works;
Class II	Work carried out more than 10 metres below ground level by the Coal Authority or any holder of a licence granted under Part II of the Coal Industry Act 1994;
Class III	Certain repair and maintenance work to canals by British Waterways (Scottish Canals);
Class IV	Work to repair or maintain machinery not involving a material alteration to the monument;
Class V	Work which is urgently necessary for health and safety purposes;
Class VI	Certain works of archaeological evaluation;
Class VII	Certain works to preserve, maintain or manage a scheduled monument and carried out under the terms of an agreement with the Scottish Ministers;[2]
Class VIII	Certain grant-aided preservation works executed in accordance with an agreement under s 24 of the Ancient Monuments and Archaeological Areas Act 1979; and

Class IX Some survey works carried out by the Royal Commission on the Ancient and Historic Monuments of Scotland.

1 SI 1996/1507.
2 Under the Ancient Monuments and Archaeological Areas Act 1979, s 17.

Enforcement

12.93 The carrying out of any unauthorised work to a scheduled monument is a criminal offence. The law provides similar enforcement measures as those which apply to listed buildings. These include scheduled monument enforcement notices, stop notices, temporary stop notices, compulsory purchase, interdict and reference to the Procurator Fiscal for prosecution. Affected parties have similar rights of appeal, defence and to compensation as apply with listed buildings. A useful summary of enforcement provisions and the penalties that apply on conviction for breaches of control can be found in Historic Scotland 'Works on Ancient Monuments' (2011) pp 6–9.

Financial assistance

12.94 The responsibility for repairing and maintaining a scheduled ancient monument lies with the owner. However, Historic Scotland's monument wardens and heritage management staff are available to provide free advice to owners on how best to manage a scheduled monument and can also give guidance on possible financial assistance. For example, through a management agreement, Historic Scotland can give financial support, normally over five years, towards the capital costs needed to improve the condition of a site and annual payments for management. Ancient Monument Grants can be used to support one-off works to protect a site, such as erecting fencing. Funding for site management may also be available through schemes operating under the Scotland Rural Development Programme. Further information on possible financial support can be found in the Historic Scotland booklet 'Managing Scotland's Archaeological Heritage' (undated) which is available online at www.historic-scotland.org.uk.

Protection of non-scheduled monuments

12.95 All recorded archaeological remains are considered to be 'monuments' but most have not been scheduled (out of the 300,000 recorded monuments in Scotland only about 8,200 have been scheduled as ancient monuments).[1] Local authorities should produce or have access to a local Sites and Monuments Record (SMR)/Historic Environment Record (HER). This is a record of all known monuments and it should be curated by a professional archaeologist on behalf of the local authority or a dedicated heritage body. Whilst these local records have no statutory effect, they should be used by planning authorities in exercising control over development. The local SMR/HER should be used in formulating local development plan policies to protect historic assets. They are also used in determining planning applications affecting any monument. Where a proposed development affects a site in a local record, the planning authority has to have regard to the desirability of preserving the monument and its setting, whether or not it has been scheduled. It is likely that the applicant will be required to provide a survey by a qualified archaeologist assessing the character and extent of any remains and their importance, thus providing an informed basis on which to determine the application.

1 SG PAN 2/2011 Planning and Archaeology (2011), para 3

12.96 It is Scottish Government policy that monuments affected by development should be protected and enhanced through preservation *in situ*. If that is not possible or justifiable, then the monument should the subject of recording and/or excavation followed by analysis and publication of the results.

12.97 It is also possible that previously unknown archaeological remains may be discovered during development. In such cases the Scottish Ministers have the power to schedule remains within a matter of days. Development would then have to stop for an application for scheduled monument consent to be made. If necessary, the Scottish Ministers or the planning authority can use their power to revoke planning permission[1] although in such a case compensation would be payable. It may be good policy for developers to take out insurance against archaeological remains being found during construction work.

1 See Chapter 11.

4. WORLD HERITAGE SITES

12.98 The World Heritage Convention[1] was ratified by the United Kingdom in 1984 and requires the identification, protection and presentation of cultural and natural sites of outstanding universal value. There are currently five inscribed World Heritage Sites (WHS) in Scotland (Edinburgh Old and New Towns, St. Kilda, New Lanark, The Antonine Wall and The Heart of Neolithic Orkney) and twenty eight in the UK as a whole. At the time of writing, the Forth Bridge has been recommended to go forward as a UK Government nomination for world heritage status.[2] This is an extremely prestigious recognition which places inscribed sites on the same footing as the Great Wall of China, the Acropolis and the Taj Mahal. Once inscribed, member states are required to protect this heritage and UNESCO requires them to produce a management plan and monitors their performance.

1 Convention Concerning the Protection of World Culture and Natural Heritage, (UNESCO) 1972.

2 *Planning* 1 June 2012, p 6.

Effects of Inscription

12.99 While inscription does not directly result in additional statutory controls, there are some restrictions on permitted development rights for certain renewable energy and mobile phone operators' equipment works in a WHS.[1] In addition, SPP[2] makes clear that planning authorities should protect a WHS and its settings from inappropriate development. Statutory development plans should include policies setting out the factors that will be taken into account when deciding applications for development which may impact on a WHS. More detailed supplementary guidance may also be prepared.[3] These planning policies will normally include a buffer zone protecting the setting and important views to the WHS and so a wider area is affected than just that within the inscription boundary. Vertical buffer zones are also used to define ground levels below which excavation for new development may not take place in order to avoid damaging undisturbed archaeological remains.

1 Town and Country Planning (General Permitted Development) (Scotland) Order 1992, SI 1992/223, Classes 6I, 6J and 67.

2 Scottish Government 'Scottish Planning Policy' (2010) paras 120–121.

3 See for example 'Frontiers of the Roman Empire (Antonine Wall) World Heritage Site Supplementary Planning Guidance Consultative Draft' Historic Scotland and East Dunbartonshire, Falkirk, Glasgow City, North Lanarkshire and West Dunbartonshire Councils (June 2011).

12.100 Where a proposed development may affect a WHS this will be a significant material consideration for the planning authority dealing with the planning application. An Environmental Impact Assessment is more likely to be required for larger developments[1] and planning permission is unlikely to be granted for any development that would cause harm to a WHS. How planning authorities deal with new development proposals affecting inscribed sites is something that UNESCO closely monitors. In June 2012 it placed the Liverpool Maritime Mercantile City WHS on its list of world heritage at risk because of concerns about the impact of a major proposed redevelopment project called Liverpool Waters.[2] In 2008 the UNESCO World Heritage Committee expressed concern about the potential impact of the proposed Caltongate development on Edinburgh's WHS.[3] This led to press speculation that the city's status was at risk but following a visit by UNESCO inspectors in November 2008 those fears were allayed.[4]

1 A World Heritage Site is defined as a sensitive area in relation to Schedule 2 of the Environmental Impact Assessment (Scotland) Regulations 2011 (SSI 2011 No 139); see Chapter 15.
2 UNESCO News Release 26 June 2012.
3 City of Edinburgh Council 'Old and New Towns World Heritage Scrutiny Process' Report to Planning Committee 2 October 2008.
4 *The Scotsman* 16 November 2008.

5. INVENTORY OF GARDENS AND DESIGNATED LANDSCAPES

12.101 The inventory of gardens and designated landscapes is compiled by Historic Scotland and was first published in 1988. It is a list of ornamental landscapes such as private gardens, public parks, cemeteries, botanical gardens, plant collections and the policies of country estates. Examples include the grounds of Loudoun Castle in East Ayrshire, Gleneagles Hotel in Perthshire and the Necropolis in Glasgow. Whilst originally a non-statutory list, the Scottish Ministers now have a duty to compile and maintain an inventory of all gardens and designed landscapes which appear to them to be of national interest.[1] The 1979 Act (as amended) defines these as '… grounds which have been laid out for artistic effect and, in appropriate cases, include references to any buildings, land, or water on, adjacent, or contiguous to such grounds'.[2] Criteria for the identification of grounds that are of such national importance are contained in Annex 5 of SHEP. There are around 400 in the inventory at present and the Scottish Ministers can add new entries and modify or remove existing ones. In doing so they must notify the owners and occupiers of the affected grounds. They also have to notify any local authorities within whose area the grounds are located.

1 Ancient Monuments and Archaeological Areas Act 1979 s 32A(1).
2 Ibid, s 32A(2).

12.102 The Scottish Government expects planning authorities to include policies protecting inventory grounds in their local development plans. Potential impact on an inventory site will be a major material consideration when dealing with a planning application for development which may affect it. A design statement needs to be submitted with most such applications and the Scottish Ministers need to be notified.[1] There are also some restrictions on permitted development rights for certain renewable energy and mobile phone operators' equipment works.[2]

1 Town and Country Planning (Development Management Procedure) (Scotland) Regulations 2013, SSI 2013 No 155.
2 Town and Country Planning (General Permitted Development) (Scotland) Order 1992, SI 1992/223, Classes 6I, 6J and 67.

6. HISTORIC BATTLEFIELDS

12.103 Scotland has many sites which were the location of battles and these are of considerable historic and cultural importance. In 2011 the Scottish Ministers were given a duty to maintain an inventory of nationally important battlefield sites.[1] The 1979 Act (as amended) defines a battlefield as 'an area of land over which a battle was fought; or an area of land on which any significant activities relating to a battle occurred (whether or not the battle was fought over that area).' Annex 6 of SHEP contains the Scottish Government's criteria for determining which battlefields are of national importance. These include a criterion that it must be possible to identify the battlefield on a modern map. There are currently 28 battlefields in the inventory and examples include: Bannockburn (Stirling 1314); Bothwell Bridge (South Lanarkshire 1679); and, Prestonpans (East Lothian 1745). Other battlefield sites are currently the subject of research which may lead to their being added to the inventory in future.

1 Ancient Monuments and Archaeological Areas Act 1979 s 32B(1).

12.104 As with other elements of the historic environment, the Scottish Government considers that the planning system has a key role in preserving battlefields. Local development plans and supplementary planning guidance should contain policies for their protection, conservation and management. The potential impact of new development affecting them is an important material consideration when determining relevant planning applications. Most planning applications for development affecting a historic battlefield need to be notified to the Scottish Ministers.[1]

1 Town and Country Planning (Development Management Procedure) (Scotland) Regulations 2013 (SSI 2013 No 155), Sch 5, para 5(5).

7. UNDERWATER HERITAGE

12.105 The remains of ship wrecks and other artefacts which lie underwater are an important part of the historic environment. Some of these objects can be protected through the historic environment powers we have already discussed in this chapter. For example, objects on the foreshore and under water can be scheduled under the Ancient Monuments and Archaeological Areas Act 1979 eg the remains of the German warship fleet which was scuttled in Scapa Flow, Orkney in 1919. Also, while the scope of the Planning (Listed Buildings and Conservation Areas) (Scotland) Act 1997 stops at the low water mark, structures such as harbours and lighthouses which are sometimes or partly below the sea can become listed buildings. An example is the Bell Rock Lighthouse. Some historic ship wrecks lying within the seaward limits of Scottish inshore waters (12 nautical miles or 22.2km) have been protected using other powers, for example under the Protection of Wrecks Act 1973. At the time of writing, 8 wreck sites are protected under the 1973 Act, including HMS Campania in the Firth of Forth. A further 7 are protected through scheduled monument status. In future, such historical assets are to be protected through Historic Marine Protection Areas designated under the Marine (Scotland) Act 2010.[1] The act defines historic marine assets as any of the following:

(a) a vessel, vehicle or aircraft (or a part of a vessel, vehicle or aircraft);
(b) the remains of a vessel, vehicle or aircraft (or a part of such remains);
(c) an object contained in, or formerly contained in, a vessel, vehicle or aircraft;
(d) a building or other structure (or a part of a building or structure);
(e) a cave or excavation; or
(f) a deposit or artefact (whether or not formerly part of a cargo of a ship) or any other thing which evidences, or groups of things which evidence, previous human activity.

For a detailed account of how this new protection regime is to operate see Historic Scotland 'Marine Protected Areas in the Seas around Scotland: Guidelines on the selection, designation and management of Historic Marine Protected Areas' (March 2012).

1 Section 67(1)(c).

Chapter 13

The natural environment

1. INTRODUCTION

13.1 Scotland has a rich natural heritage which includes not just many beautiful landscapes but also plants, animals and geology. This heritage can be destroyed very easily and so a range of statutory and other designations exist to protect it. The policy and legislative framework, first established in the UK National Parks and Access to the Countryside Act 1949, has developed significantly in recent years, partly in response to international obligations, but also as a consequence of devolution (eg the establishment of national parks in Scotland).

13.2 Some species, habitats or earth science features are nationally and/or internationally important and there is a series of nature conservation designations at national, European and international levels which seek to protect the best examples. At the time of writing, there are a total of 1,883 protected sites in Scotland (some boundaries overlap) hosting 5,373 designated natural features.[1] Scottish Natural Heritage (see Chapter 2) is a statutory consultee and so has to be consulted about development proposals which might affect natural heritage designations of national importance. In addition to national and international designations, planning authorities designate individual sites of local importance and provide statutory protection to groups of trees and woodlands of importance to local amenity and culture. In this latter respect they work closely with the Forestry Commission.

1 *The Proportion of Scotland's Protected Sites in Favourable Condition 2012: An Official Statistics Publication for Scotland*. Scottish Natural Heritage, May 2013.

13.3 Most of the designations, whether national or international, are not made under planning legislation; however, as they do have important implications for planning law and practice, it is that aspect we concentrate on.

2. THE NATURAL HERITAGE

13.4 National planning policy on landscape and natural heritage is set out in Scottish Planning Policy (SPP), and is supported by Planning Advice Note (PAN) 60 *Planning for Natural Heritage*. Scottish Planning Policy[1] encourages planning authorities to take a broad approach to protecting natural heritage and landscape than just protecting designated sites or species, taking into account eco systems and natural processes in their areas. All public bodies, including planning authorities, have a duty to further the conservation of biodiversity under the Nature Conservation (Scotland) Act 2004, and this should be reflected in development plans and development management decisions.[2] The decision of the European Court of Justice in *Commission of the European Communities v United Kingdom of Great Britain and Northern Ireland*,[3] led to the need for appropriate assessment of development plans as well as individual development proposals (as now required by the Habitats Amendment Regulations 2007, see Chapter 3).

1 Scottish Government, *Scottish Planning Policy*, Edinburgh, February 2010, para 126.
2 Op cit, para 129.
3 Case C 6/04, Second chamber of the European Court of Justice, 20 October 2005.

13.5 There is always potential for conflict between development and natural heritage interests. PAN 60 aims to promote good practice in planning for natural heritage and demonstrate that planning and the development process can be powerful tools for realising natural heritage objectives and creating quality environments for living and working.

International Designations

13.6 Natura 2000 is an EU-wide network of protected areas. These comprise sites classified as Special Protection Areas (SPA) under the Birds Directive[1] and Special Areas of Conservation (SAC) under the Habitats Directive.[2] The government is required to identify and protect such sites of European importance. The Conservation (Natural Habitats etc) Regulations 1994 implement the Habitats Directive and the Birds Directive in the UK. The regulations give all competent authorities (including the Scottish Ministers, SNH, statutory undertakers and local authorities) a duty to have regard to the requirements of the Habitats Directive when exercising any of their functions. Amongst other things, the regulations also provide for management agreements with owners, control over potentially damaging operations, special nature conservation orders, the power for SNH to create bye laws, and powers of compulsory purchase where a management agreement is breached or cannot be concluded.

1 Directive 79/409/EEC on the conservation of wild birds.
2 Directive 92/43/EEC on the conservation of natural habitats, wild flora and fauna.

13.7 The Habitats Directive requires member states to take appropriate steps to avoid deterioration of, or disturbance to, European Sites (including those classified under the Birds Directive). Any plan or project which could have a significant effect on such a site (other than that necessary for its proper management) must undergo an assessment. Because of the sensitivity of many European sites, an assessment may also be required for projects taking place outside the designated site. Any development that would adversely affect the integrity of the site can only be allowed to go ahead under the special circumstances defined in the Directive which are that:

(1) an appropriate assessment has demonstrated that it will not adversely affect the integrity of the site, or
(2) there are no alternative solutions; and
(3) there are imperative reasons of overriding public interest for allowing the development, including those of a social or economic nature.[1]

1 EC Directive 92/43, art 6(4).

13.8 Social or economic matters can only be used to justify a development if the site does not host a priority habitat type and/or a priority species.[1] Where a priority species or habitat is involved, only matters of human health, public safety, benefits of primary importance for the environment, or other overriding considerations specifically approved by the Commission can be used as justification. Where a plan (including a development plan) or project is likely to have a significant effect on a European site, and is not directly connected with or necessary to the management of the site, permission can only be granted if the project will not adversely affect the integrity of the site.[2]

1 As to what constitutes priority habitats and species, see EC Directive 92/43, Annexes I, II.
2 *Skye Windfarm Action Group Ltd v Highland Council* [2008] CSOH 19, included the unsuccessful claim that the appropriate assessment had not been properly undertaken.

13.9 European sites are designated by the Scottish Ministers but only after agreement with the European Commission. Currently, Special Areas of Conservation under the Habitats directive have been designated for 56 habitats and 19 species. At the end of January 2011, there were 239 designated SACs in Scotland.[1]

1 Scottish Natural Heritage, *Natura* (no date). Available at http://www.snh.gov.uk/protecting-scotlands-nature/protected-areas/international-designations/natura-sites/

13.10 Unlike the Habitats Directive, the Birds Directive contains no specific criteria for site selection, so the UK has developed its own guidelines. At the end of January 2011, 153 SPAs had been classified in Scotland, encompassing 81 species.[1]

1 Scottish Natural Heritage, op cit.

13.11 The Natura network in Scotland is now largely complete, though it is possible that a few additional sites may be identified, as a consequence of natural changes and improved knowledge. Work is ongoing to identify sites in the marine environment, and it is anticipated that there will be an increase in the number of marine sites.[1]

1 Ibid.

Adaptation of planning controls

13.12 The 1994 regulations adapt planning controls in three main ways:

(a) by requiring a review of extant planning permissions which are likely to have a significant effect on European sites;
(b) by introducing procedures for dealing with new planning applications for developments which will have a significant effect on such sites; and
(c) by requiring prior written approval for permitted development likely to have a significant effect on such sites.

13.13 It should be noted that a development proposal does not need to be within a European site to come under the ambit of the regulations. The regulations will also apply to proposals affecting land outside designated areas if they could have a significant effect on the natural heritage interest of a European site.

13.14 Extant planning permissions are those that have not yet been implemented or have only been partially implemented. The regulations require planning authorities to review extant planning permissions which, on their own or in combination with other development, are likely to significantly affect a European site. The existence of such permissions will already have become known as a result of the consultations which took place prior to the designation of European sites. If, following consultation with SNH, the planning authority is satisfied that implementation of a permission would adversely affect the integrity of the site in question, it must take steps to remove the harm. However, the steps taken must be the least onerous necessary to avoid damage. If the authority believes that a planning obligation under s75 of the 1997 Act restricting the use and development of the land would be sufficient to achieve this, it is obliged to invite the owner to enter into one. However, if this is not possible, or if the owner begins to implement the permission, the authority may need to serve a revocation order revoking or modifying the permission. Unlike other revocation orders, this may be served prior to confirmation by the Scottish Ministers and will take effect from the date of service, although confirmation will still be required for the order to continue in effect. In contrast to other revocation orders, compensation will not normally be payable, though it may be if the order is not confirmed by the Scottish Ministers.

13.15 Where a planning application is submitted for development that will have a significant effect on a European site, the applicant must provide whatever information the planning authority requires to enable it to carry out an assessment of the likely impact on conservation of the site.[1] The planning authority must also consult with SNH and take into account any representations which that agency makes.[2] In responding, SNH will advise whether, in its opinion, the proposed development would significantly affect the ecological value for which the site was designated. If appropriate, it will also recommend measures that may be taken to avoid damage. Presumably, it will also state whether or not it thinks planning permission should be granted.

1 SI 1994/2716, regs 48(1) and 48(2).
2 Reg 48(3).

13.16 In assessing the likely impact of a development, the government expects local planning authorities to operate the 'precautionary principle'. This means that where there is uncertainty about the likely impact of a proposed development, but grounds exist for believing that it *may* have a damaging impact, the proposal will be treated as if it *will* have a damaging impact. If granting planning permission subject to conditions will prevent an adverse impact, it is government policy that planning authorities should grant conditional permission.[1]

1 SODD Circular 4/1998 'Use of Conditions in Planning Permissions'.

13.17 If the outcome of the assessment is that the development will not have an adverse impact, then the local authority may grant planning permission (unless the Scottish Ministers direct them not to). If the development *will* have an adverse impact, regulation 3 states that the authority may only grant permission in the special circumstances set out in the Habitats Directive. If these special circumstances apply, the authority must first give the Scottish Ministers 21 days notice of its intention to grant permission. Permission may be granted if the Scottish Ministers do not respond within 21 days (or if they notify the council that it may grant permission). The notice period is designed to give the Scottish Ministers the opportunity to call in the application.

Permitted development rights

13.18 The Permitted Development Order (PDO) as amended, grants a general planning permission for a wide range of mainly minor developments. Subject to the limits and other conditions defined in the order, these permitted developments may proceed without an application for planning permission. However, any permitted development which is likely to have a significant effect on a European site, and is not directly related to the management of that site, cannot begin without a special written approval from the planning authority.[1]

1 SI 1994/2716, regs 60–63; see also the *Town and Country Planning (General Permitted Development) (Scotland) (Amendment No 3) Order 1994*, SI 1994/3294.

13.19 If the proposed work will not have a significant effect on a European site, it will still enjoy the normal permitted development rights. However, given the highly technical nature of this issue, it will be difficult for owners to be sure of the effects of proposed work and so they would be well advised to seek advice before carrying it out. To this end, the regulations provide a procedure for obtaining the opinion of SNH. If the agency declares that the proposal will not have a significant effect, then that will be conclusive (ie no special approval will be required). However, if it is confirmed that the proposed development *will* have a significant effect, then the development can only go ahead with the written approval of the planning authority. Furthermore, that approval can only be given if the authority is satisfied (after consulting with SNH) that the development will not adversely affect the integrity of the site.

Ramsar sites

13.20 Ramsar is the name of a town in Iran where the Convention on Wetlands of International Importance was adopted in 1971. The UK Government signed up to the Convention in 1976. The mission of the Convention is 'the conservation and wise use of wetlands by national action and international cooperation as a means to achieving sustainable development throughout the world'.[1] There are currently 51 Ramsar sites designated as internationally important wetlands in Scotland, covering a total area of about 313,500 hectares.

1 See www.ramsar.org.

13.21 All Ramsar sites in Scotland are also either SPAs or SACs (Natura sites), and many are also Sites of Special Scientific Interest (SSSIs), although the boundaries of the different designations are not always exactly the same. It is not surprising that internationally important wetlands are also of European interest for a wide variety of water birds, bogs, lochs, coastal wetlands and other water-dependent habitats and species. Although there is no specific legal framework that safeguards Scottish Ramsar sites, they benefit from the measures required to protect and enhance the Natura sites and SSSIs which overlap them.

National Designations

13.22 There are many types of designation at both local and national level. As stated above, some designations are unique to Scotland (eg National Scenic Areas) while others apply throughout the UK (eg Sites of Special Scientific Interest (SSSIs)). We confine our examination of national designations to those which are more important from a planning law perspective.

National Scenic Areas (NSAs)

13.23 NSAs are areas of 'outstanding scenic value in a national context'.[1] The 40 NSAs were designated in 1980, but not given a statutory basis until the Planning etc (Scotland) Act 2006 introduced s 263A into the 1997 Act.[2] Between them the NSAs cover more than a million hectares of land; 13 per cent of the total land area of Scotland. The Act also states that, within an NSA, 'special attention is to be paid to the desirability of safeguarding or enhancing its character or appearance'.[3]

1 Section 263A(1) of the 1997 Act.
2 Brought into force in December 2010 by the Town and Country Planning (National Scenic Areas) (Scotland) Designation Directions 2010.
3 Section 263A(2).

13.24 Most new developments within an NSA require to be accompanied by a design statement, and there are restrictions on some permitted development rights. Planning authorities also have the power to make Article 7 directions under the 1992 PDO (as amended) restricting permitted development rights for certain mineral operations. Planning authorities should take particular care to ensure that any new development in or adjacent to an NSA does not detract from the quality of its landscape. They should also ensure that development siting and design is of a high standard and appropriate for the area concerned.

National Parks

13.25 Despite powers in the 1949 National Parks and Access to the Countryside Act, no national parks were designated in Scotland under this legislation. NSAs were seen as an alternative until devolution, when the Scottish Parliament passed the National Parks (Scotland) Act 2000. Scotland's two national parks cover 7.2 per cent of the total land area. There are no current proposals for further national parks in Scotland. The aims of national parks[1] are to:

- conserve and enhance the natural and cultural heritage of the area;
- promote sustainable use of the natural resources of the area;
- promote understanding and enjoyment (including enjoyment in the form of recreation) of the special qualities of the area by the public; and
- promote sustainable economic and social development of the area's communities.

1 Scottish Government, *Scottish Planning Policy*, para 138.

13.26 Should conflict arise between any of these objectives in a particular circumstance, the 2000 Act requires that conservation of the natural and cultural heritage should take precedence. The management strategy for each park is set out in the national park plan. To date, two national parks have been designated: Loch Lomond and the Trossachs (established in 2002)[1] and the Cairngorms (established in 2003). A national park authority has been established for each park, responsible for preparing, implementing and keeping under review the national park plan. National park authorities are funded by the Scottish Government and report to Scottish Ministers. National park boards are made up of appointments by Scottish Ministers, local authority ward members and people who live in the area elected by the community. Legislation places an upper limit of the size of the board of the national park authorities of 17 in Loch Lomond and The Trossachs and 19 in the Cairngorms.

1 The Loch Lomond and the Trossachs National Park Designation, Transitional and Consequential Provisions (Scotland) Order 2002 (SSI 2002 No 201).

13.27 The planning responsibilities of the two park Boards are different. While both have responsibility for preparing the development plan (the national park plan), only the Loch Lomond and the Trossachs National Park Authority has responsibility for development management in the park area. In the Cairngorms, the constituent panning authorities must consult the park authority on all planning applications, and the park authority has 21 days within which to decide whether to call in any application which it considers raises a planning issue of general significance to the aims of the park.

13.28 In their joint report *Unfinished Business: A National Parks Strategy for Scotland*,[1] the Scottish Campaign for National Parks and the Association for the Protection of Rural Scotland contend that: Scotland has been relatively slow to recognise the potential for national park designation; there is scope for further designations, given that previous expert reports had suggested the potential for up to five national parks (including one or more Coastal and Marine National Parks) compared with the two designated to date; the Scottish Government should prepare and implement a strategy to designate more National Parks in Scotland.

1 March 2013. Available at www.scnp.org.uk/.

Sites of Special Scientific Interest (SSSIs)

13.29 The ability to identify and protect SSSIs was first provided by the National Parks and Access to the Countryside Act 1949. Today, SSSIs are the main nature conservation designation. As well as being important in their own right, sites which have been designated as SSSIs have been used as the base from which to identify and designate Special Protection Areas (SPAs) and Special Areas of Conservation (SACs) required under European legislation. In Scotland, SSSIs are identified by Scottish Natural Heritage. Section 28 of the 1981 Wildlife and Countryside Act defines SSSIs as 'areas of land or water which are of special interest by reason of their flora, fauna or geological or physiographical features'.

13.30 The Nature Conservation (Scotland) Act 2004 further strengthens SSSI protection. Part 1 of the 2004 Act imposes a wide-ranging duty on Scotland's public bodies to conserve biodiversity and protect the natural heritage. It replaces most of Part 2 of the 1981 Act (which relates to SSSI) and seeks to regulate how land management operations can be carried out on SSSIs, and provides for operations likely to damage an SSSI to be restricted or prevented. This may result in SNH offering a management agreement with associated compensation. Schedule 6 of the Act amends the 1981 Act, strengthening legal protection for threatened species. Part 2 also requires SNH to notify interested parties[1] of any land it considers of special interest due to its natural features, which may include:

- every owner and occupier of the land;
- every local authority in whose area all or part of the land is situated;

- the national park authority where relevant;
- every community council in whose area all or part of the land is situated;
- every relevant regulatory authority likely to have functions related to the land in question;
- every community body which has registered an interest in the land.

1 The notice must be recorded in the Register of Sasines or the Land Register as appropriate.

13.31 Owners, occupiers and local authorities can lodge objections to the notification and SNH is obliged to consider these before it can confirm the SSSI designation. If any objection is made on scientific grounds and SNH is unable to resolve this with the objector, the matter must be referred to the Joint Advisory Committee on SSSIs. This committee is independent of SNH and made up of eminent scientists appointed by the Scottish Ministers. SNH must take the committee's views into account before deciding whether to confirm the designation. This procedure is not extensively used.

13.32 Each SSSI notification must include a site management statement by SNH, setting out guidance to owners and occupiers of land within an SSSI of how the specified natural features should be conserved or enhanced. Public bodies must not carry out operations on an SSSI which is likely to damage any natural feature specified. SNH may give consent to operations subject to conditions. Anyone intentionally or recklessly damaging any specified natural feature in the SSSI is guilty of an offence and liable on summary conviction to a fine up to £40,000, or on an indicted conviction to a fine. Restoration orders can be applied for the purpose of restoring the protected natural feature to its previous condition.

13.33 The Act also provides for Scottish Ministers to establish a Nature Conservation Order, further protecting an SSSI from damaging operations eg use of off-road vehicles, fly-tipping. Proposals by SNH to Scottish Ministers can also lead to a Land Management Order requiring operations to be carried out on land within or contiguous to an SSSI where this is seen as necessary to conserve, restore or enhance a natural feature specified in the SSSI notification. An appeal process is introduced in relation to such Orders.

13.34 SSSIs represent the best of Scotland's natural heritage. They are 'special' because of their plants, animals or habitats, rocks or landforms, or a combination of these. They are designated, following notification of interested parties, by SNH based on scientific (ie not landscape or amenity) criteria. As well as land, they can include freshwater or seawater down to the low water mark of spring tides. At January 2011 there were 1,437 SSSI in Scotland, covering more than 1 million hectares (about 13 per cent of the total land area).[1] The coverage is not static; in recent years SNH has designated new SSSI in response to UK international obligations (eg SPAs, SACs and Ramsar sites) and has removed sites no longer considered to be of special interest. Designation of land as an SSSI does not affect its ownership or occupation.

1 Scottish Natural Heritage *Sites of Special Scientific Interest*, 2011. See http://www.snh.gov.uk/protecting-scotlands-nature/protected-areas/national-designations/sssis/

13.35 The aim of SSSI designation is to control (and if possible prevent) any works that might damage the site. However, rather than impose a regime of statutory controls, the emphasis is on SNH reaching voluntary management agreements with landowners. The three-month period that owners must give before carrying out work is designed to give time for negotiations to take place. Compensation for all pecuniary losses resulting from the restrictions imposed by an agreement may be available as an incentive for owners to negotiate.

13.36 With regard to planning control, there is no ban on planning permission being given, even if the development involved may damage the site. However, the planning authority must consult with SNH when processing the application and it must notify the Scottish Ministers if SNH objects to the grant of permission.[1] An environmental assessment may also be required.

1 The Town and Country Planning (Notification of Applications) (Scotland) Direction 2009. The previous requirement to notify Scottish Ministers of all development proposals affecting SSSIs no longer applies.

13.37 Environmental Impact Assessment (EIA) is a process which identifies the environmental effects of development proposals and seeks to prevent, reduce and offset any adverse effects (see Chapter 15). As part of the process, applicants prepare environmental statements containing information on the potential effects and the mitigation measures proposed. Planning authorities can do much to ensure that environmental statements are of a high quality by working closely with both the applicant's consultants and statutory consultees (including SNH) throughout the assessment process. Where it is concluded that EIA is necessary, it is important to:

- ensure that natural heritage issues are identified at an early stage;
- establish appropriate consultation arrangements;

- determine the scope of the assessment in a systematic manner; and
- agree baseline survey requirements, methods and evaluation criteria with relevant bodies, including non-governmental organisations where they have relevant expertise.

13.38 The requirements for EIA are set out in the Environmental Impact Assessment (Scotland) Regulations 2011. Circular 3/2011 *The Town and Country Planning (Environmental Impact Assessment) (Scotland) Regulations 2011* gives guidance on the application of the Regulations, and Planning Advice Note 58 on *Environmental Impact Assessment* gives advice on best practice in the preparation and scrutiny of environmental statements.

Marine Protected Areas

13.39 Scotland (along with the rest of the UK) has designated a number of Marine Protected Areas (MPAs) which include Special Areas of Conservation (SACs), Special Protection Areas (SPAs), Sites of Special Scientific Interest (SSSIs) and Ramsar sites. The term 'MPA' can be used for several different types of protected areas within the marine environment. The Marine (Scotland) Act 2010 establishes:

- a duty to protect and enhance the marine environment;
- a new statutory marine planning system to sustainably manage the increasing, and often conflicting, demands on the sea around Scotland;
- a new power for Marine Protected Areas, to recognise features of national importance and meet international commitments for developing a network of MPAs, including nature conservation MPAs;[1]
- Marine Scotland, a new directorate of the Scottish Government, responsible for the integrated management of Scotland's seas through a National Marine Plan.

1 This complements the MPA power introduced through the UK Marine and Coastal Access Act 2009 for offshore waters around Scotland.

13.40 MPAs will protect important marine habitats and wildlife, geology and geomorphology, as well as features of cultural importance such as shipwrecks and submerged landscapes. In this respect it complements and extends the established nature conservation network of Natura 2000, Ramsar sites and SSSI. The Act also allows local communities to put forward proposals for Nature Conservation and Demonstration and Research MPAs.

3. TREES AND WOODLANDS

Introduction

13.41 'The Scottish Government's Policy on Control of Woodland Removal'[1] signals a strong presumption in favour of protecting Scotland's woodland resources, especially woodlands of high nature conservation value (such as ancient semi-natural woodland). By 2005, 17 per cent (1.3 million hectares) of Scotland was under woodland, making it one of the least wooded countries in the European Union.[2] The Scottish Forestry Strategy 2006[3] identifies seven key themes for Scotland's woodlands:

- helping to mitigate and adapt to climate change;
- maximising the timber resource;
- supporting sustainable economic growth through business development of the woodland sector;
- supporting community development to improve quality of life and well being;
- improving access to woodlands, to help improve health;
- protecting the environmental quality of Scotland's natural resources;
- helping to conserve and enhance Scotland's biodiversity.

1 Forestry Commission Scotland, 2009. See http://www.forestry.gov.uk/woodlandremoval
2 Forestry Commission Scotland, *The Right Tree in the Right Place*, May 2010, p 6.
3 Available at http://www.forestry.gov.uk/sfs

13.42 The National Planning Framework[1] reiterates the objectives of the Scottish Forestry Strategy and the need to plan proactively for an expansion of woodland cover. It also confirms the protection of existing woodland and that its removal should only be permitted where it will achieve significant and clearly defined additional public benefits. Planning Circular 1/2009 *Development Planning* identifies forestry and woodland strategies as a suitable topic for supplementary guidance in strategic and local development plans.

1 Scottish Government, *National Planning Framework for Scotland 2*, 2009.

13.43 Forestry operations such as planting, felling, lopping or pruning of trees, do not constitute development and so are usually immune from planning control. The Forestry Commission Scotland serves as the forestry directorate of the Scottish Government. It is responsible for the national forest estate in Scotland, provides woodland grants to support new planting and regulates felling through felling licenses. The Commission seeks the views of planning authorities (as well as other key agencies including SNH, SEPA and Historic Scotland) on planting and felling proposals[1] before deciding whether to approve applications and/or call for an environmental impact assessment.

1 The 1967 Forestry Act, as amended, requires landowners to apply to the Forestry Commission for a licence to fell growing trees, although there are certain exemptions.

13.44 The Commission consults planning authorities on applications for new planting of 10 hectares or more (5 hectares in national parks) and may also consult on smaller cases where local protocols exist. Planning authorities have four weeks to consider and respond to such consultations. If there are unresolved objections from a planning authority, the Commission refers the case to its relevant regional Advisory Committee. The Commission also provides guidance on planning for forestry and woodlands.[1]

1 Forestry Commission Scotland, *The right tree in the right place*, Scottish Government. Part 3 replaces Circular 9/1999 on Indicative Forestry Strategies. See also *The Scottish Forestry Strategy,* Scottish Government 2006.

Definition of 'tree'

13.45 Unfortunately, there is no statutory definition of 'tree'. In *Bullock v Secretary of State for the Environment*[1] it was stated that anything which one would normally call a tree *is* a tree. Saplings, for example, might well be very small and yet these are what would often be planted to replace existing trees, and thus fall under tree preservation order protection. There are essentially three ways in which trees are protected under planning legislation: (a) by the imposition of conditions on planning permission; (b) by making a tree preservation order; and (c) through designation of a conservation area. The Statutory procedures for trees comply with the European Convention on Human Rights.[2]

1 (1980) 40 P&CR 246 at 251 per Phillips J.
2 *R (on the application of Brennan) v Bromsgrove DC* [2003] JPL 1444.

Planning conditions

13.46 Under s 159 of the 1997 Act, as amended by the 2006 Act, all planning authorities and Scottish Ministers have a duty to ensure that adequate provision is made in new development for the planting and preservation of trees. They have to do this by imposing conditions on planning permission. However, the government says that planning authorities should be clear that the long term protection of existing and new trees should be secured by the use of Tree Preservation Order (TPO) powers (see below) rather than conditions on the permission.[1] It also suggests that local authorities may find it expedient to use TPO powers to afford temporary protection for existing trees that may be adversely affected by development proposals, until it becomes clear whether there is a need to retain those trees.

1 SODD Circular 4/1998 'The Use of Conditions in Planning Permissions', para 77.

Tree Preservation Orders

13.47 Under s160 of the 1997 Act, planning authorities have the power to make an order for the preservation of existing trees or woodlands in their district, if they consider it expedient in the interests of amenity to do so and/or that the trees, groups of trees or woodlands are of cultural or historical significance. Section 160(3) sets out what a TPO may include. Section 164 empowers Scottish Ministers to vary or revoke a TPO where they consider it expedient to do so. The 2006 Act amends s 159 of the 1997 Act to place a duty on planning authorities to review existing TPOs, and amends s 160 to expand TPO powers to include trees, groups of trees, or woodlands of cultural or historical significance.

Making an order

13.48 The Town and Country Planning (Tree Preservation Order and Trees in Conservation Areas)(Scotland) Regulations 2010[1] make provision for the form of a TPO and the procedure to be followed when making and confirming a TPO. Annex A of Scottish Government Circular 1/2011 *Tree Preservation Orders* sets out the model form of a TPO. Regulation 3 requires that a TPO must define the position of the trees to which it relates by means of a map. A TPO does not need the approval of the Scottish Ministers; it is simply confirmed by the relevant planning authority once it has completed the necessary procedural requirements. Under s 161(2) a confirmed TPO must be recorded in the Register of Sasines or registered in the Land Register of Scotland.

1 SSI 2010 No 434. These regulations replace the Town and Country Planning (Tree Preservation Order and Trees in Conservation Areas) (Scotland) Regulations 1975.

13.49 A TPO takes effect on the date specified in the order, but expires within six months after this date if it is not confirmed by the planning authority within that period. A TPO may also be made for any trees to be planted in compliance with a condition of planning permission, and applies from the date the trees are planted. When it has made an order the planning authority must advertise this fact in a local newspaper, make a copy of the TPO available for public inspection at a convenient place to the locality in which the affected trees are situated, and send a copy to the Forestry Commission. It must also send a copy to all 'interested persons', defined in Regulation 2 as:

- an owner, lessee and occupier of the land on which the trees groups of trees or woodlands to which the TPO relates are situated;
- any other person who to the knowledge of the planning authority, would but for the TPO be entitled to:
  - fell, top, lop, uproot or otherwise damage or destroy any tree to which the TPO relates, or
  - to work by surface working any material in, on or under such land.

13.50 Any person can make a representation on the TPO (reg 5). Any objections to a proposed TPO must be made in writing to the planning authority within 28 days of the service of the notice or advertisement. The authority is required to take into account any objections before deciding whether to confirm the TPO, which it may do with or without modification. Once it decides to confirm an order, the authority must advertise this fact and inform all those who were previously notified that the order was being made, including the Forestry Commission and anyone who made a representation. It should also record the terms of the order in the Register of Sasines or, as the case may be, the Land Register.

13.51 Section 275(8) of the 1997 Act makes it clear that a planning authority may vary and revoke a TPO by making another order. While the courts have declared that the power to make modifications should not be construed narrowly, modifications may be declared *ultra vires* in certain circumstances. In *Evans v Waverley Borough Council* [1] it was held that the modification of an order from one covering 'Trees specified by reference to the Area' to a more general one covering 'Woodland' was *ultra vires*. This was because the modified version was less specific and so would affect all of the trees on the land. As a result, this would create more onerous obligations on the landowner and in particular prevent him from carrying out ordinary management of his land.

1 [1995] 3 PLR 80.

13.52 Under s 171 of the 1997 Act It is an offence for any person in contravention of a TPO to cut down, uproot, willfully destroy a tree or willfully damage, top or lop a tree in such manner as to be likely to destroy it without the consent of the planning authority. The maximum fine on summary conviction is currently £20,000, and on conviction of indictment to a fine. Nothing in a TPO prevents uprooting, felling or lopping of any trees if urgently necessary in the interests of safety, abatement of nuisance, provided written notice is given to the planning authority, or if carried out in compliance with any obligation imposed by/under any Act of Parliament.[1]

1 *Perrin v Northampton BC* [2008] 1, WLR 1307; [2008] JPL 809.

13.53 Where a planning authority decides not to confirm a TPO it must as soon as possible:

- endorse the TPO with a statement to that effect with the date of the decision; and
- give notice of its decision to the Forestry Commission, interested persons, and any person who made a representation.

13.54 Once a TPO is in place, the consent of the local planning authority is required for cutting down, topping, lopping, uprooting, wilful damage or wilful destruction of any trees covered by the order. Regulation 9 of the 2010 Regulations requires that the application must be made to the planning authority specifying the operations for which consent is sought, the reasons for such operations, and must identify by means of a map or plan (of sufficient size and scale) the protected trees that would be affected. Section 28(2)(c) of the 2006 Act provides Scottish Ministers with powers to determine the form and manner of applications for consent under a TPO. Furthermore, the order can require the replanting of any trees which the authority permits to be felled. Such replacement trees are protected by the TPO as if they were the original trees, as are those planted to replace trees felled or uprooted for safety reasons or in contravention of TPO control. Under s167 of the 1997 Act the landowner is under a duty to replace a tree which is removed in contravention of the TPO.

Enforcement

13.55 If it appears to a planning authority that a duty to replace trees or woodlands has not been complied with, it can serve a notice on the landowner (under s 168 of the 1997 Act) requiring the replacement of trees. The notice must be served within two years from the date of the alleged failure to comply with the duty, and specify a period at the end of which it is to take effect (not less than 28 days from the date of service of the notice).

13.56 The planning authority may also serve a notice on the same terms under s 168 requiring the replacement of trees to enforce against any condition of consent granted under a TPO requiring the replacement of trees, since trees planted in accordance with a condition are automatically protected by the original TPO.[1] On failure to comply with a notice, the planning authority may enter the land and plant those trees, and recover any reasonable expenses incurred from the landowner or lessee.[2]

1 Section 168(3A) of the 1997 Act.
2 Section 170(1) of the 1997 Act.

Appeals

13.57 There is no right of appeal to Scottish Ministers against a TPO, either when made or confirmed. However, subject to the provisions of a TPO, an appeal can be made to Scottish Ministers following the refusal of an application to cut down or carry out works to trees. A person on whom a notice is served requiring the replacement of trees may appeal to Scottish Ministers under s 169 on the grounds that:

- the replacement of trees with respect to a TPO or any conditions of consent are either not applicable or have been complied with; or
- the replacement of trees with respect to a TPO should be dispensed with; or
- the requirements of the notice are unreasonable in respect of the period or the size or species of trees specified in it; or
- the planting of a tree or trees in accordance with the notice is not required in the interests of amenity or would be contrary to the practice of good forestry; or
- that the place on which the tree is or trees are required to be planted is unsuitable for that purpose.

13.58 Scottish Ministers may prescribe the procedure to be followed on appeals against notices requiring the replacement of trees.[1] Where an appeal is made it has the effect of suspending the notice pending the outcome of the appeal.

1 SG Circular 4/2013 'Planning Appeals' explains the processes involved in appeals to Scottish Ministers.

Compensation

13.59 Under s 165 of the 1997 Act TPOs make provision for the payment by the planning authority of compensation for loss or damage caused or incurred as a result of either the refusal of any consent under the TPO, or the grant of consent subject to conditions. Any question of disputed compensation will be referred to the Lands Tribunal.[1]

1 Land Compensation (Scotland) Act 1963 ss 9 and 11.

Conservation areas

13.60 Trees in conservation areas which are already protected by a TPO are subject to the normal TPO controls. The 1997 Act also makes special provision for trees in conservation areas which are not the subject of a TPO. Under s 172 anyone proposing to cut down or carry out work on a tree in a conservation area is required to give the planning authority six weeks prior notice. This is to give the planning authority an opportunity to consider whether a TPO should be made in respect of the tree. Any notified works must be carried out within two years from the date of the notice.

13.61 If a tree in a conservation area is removed, uprooted or destroyed in contravention of s172 of the Act, the landowner is under a duty to plant another tree of an appropriate size and species at the same place as soon as he or she reasonably can. The same duty applies if a tree is removed because it is dead, dying or dangerous or because it is causing a nuisance. The duty attaches to subsequent owners of the land, although the planning authority has powers to dispense with the duty.

Exemptions

13.62 There are a number of exemptions to the requirement to give prior notice and these are specified in Regulation 8 of the 2010 Regs.[1] These include:

- cutting down a tree in accordance with a felling licence granted by the Forestry Commission under the Forestry Act 1967;
- work on a tree with a diameter not exceeding 75 millimetres (or where the tree is in a woodland, 100 millimetres where this is done to improve the growth of other trees);
- work on a tree by or on behalf of the Forestry Commission on land placed at its disposal in pursuance of the Forestry Act 1967, or otherwise under its management or supervision;
- work on a tree by or at the request of a statutory undertaker where the land on which the tree is situated is operational land and the work is necessary:

   - in the interests of the safe operation of the undertaking;
   - in connection with the inspection, repair or renewal of any sewers, mains, pipes, cables or other apparatus of the statutory undertaker; or
   - to enable the statutory undertaker to carry out permitted development.
- works on a tree cultivated for the production of fruit in course of a business or trade;
- pruning, in accordance with good horticultural practice, of any tree cultivated for the production of fruit;
- works to a tree where that work is required to enable a person to implement a planning permission other than;
   - an outline planning permission or planning permission in principle; or
   - permitted development rights.
- work on a tree by or at the request of the Scottish Environment Protection Agency to carry out permitted development;
- where the cutting down, topping, lopping or uprooting of a tree if:
   - it is urgently necessary in the interests of safety;
   - it is necessary for the prevention and abatement of a nuisance; or
   - it is in compliance with an obligation imposed by or under any enactment.

1 The Town and Country Planning (Tree Preservation Order and Trees in Conservation Areas (Scotland) Regulations 2010 (SSI 2010 No 434).

13.63 The planning authority can deal with a six-week prior notification by:

- making a TPO if justified in the interests of amenity and/or for cultural or historical significance (the proposal would then have to be the subject of a formal application under the TPO); or
- deciding not to make a TPO and allow the six week period to expire, at which point the proposed work may go ahead as long as it is carried out within two years from the date of the notice; or
- deciding not to make a TPO and inform thc applicant that thc work can go ahead.

13.64 The planning authority cannot refuse consent or grant consent subject to conditions. This is because prior notification is not an application for consent under a TPO (see Chapter 5 for an explanation of prior notification). A number of exemptions apply to the Forestry Commission, and these are set out in s 162 of the 1997 Act (as amended by s 95 of the Planning and Compulsory Purchase Act 2004).

Rights of Entry

13.65 If it appears to a planning authority that a tree, group of trees or woodlands protected by a TPO may be in imminent danger of being cut down, topped, lopped, uprooted, willfully damaged or willfully destroyed, an authorised person may enter the land in question in order to affix a copy of the order to the trees. Any person who willfully obstructs a person acting in the exercise of a right of entry is guilty of an offence and liable on summary conviction to a fine not exceeding level 3 on the standard scale.

13.66 Scottish Planning Policy recognises that ancient and semi-natural woodland is an important natural resource to be protected and enhanced.[1] Other woodlands and individual trees have important biodiversity and landscape value, so should be protected from any adverse impacts as a consequence of development. As well as protecting existing trees and woodland, planning authorities are encouraged by national policy to seek opportunities for the creation of new woodlands and planting of native species. Consequently, planning authorities are given powers to protect existing trees and ensure the planting of new ones where this is seen to be desirable in the interests of amenity. These planning powers run in tandem with the role of the Forestry Commission in tree planting and felling.

1 *Scottish Planning Policy*, para 146.

Chapter 14

Other special controls

1. INTRODUCTION

14.1 Planning and related legislation contains powers to deal with matters of special significance, including activities that do not fall within the definition of 'development'. Such activities raise special issues and environmental impacts, requiring a greater degree of scrutiny and control than would be possible under planning legislation. The required consent procedures are similar to planning permission and so have stimulated periodic debate regarding the scope to rationalise these parallel consent procedures in the interests of reducing demands and costs on applicants, and speeding the permission process.

2. ADVERTISEMENT CONTROL

14.2 We saw in Chapter 4 that the display of advertisements could often qualify as development. For example, under the 1997 Act, the display of an advert on the exterior of a building not normally used for that purpose is a material change of use. The erection of an advertisement hoarding may also be development in the form of a building or other operation.

14.3 Section 182 of the 1997 Act gives Scottish Ministers the power to pass regulations for the control of advertisements. The current regulations are the Town and Country Planning (Control of Advertisements) (Scotland) Regulations 1984,[1] under which adverts are controlled by a self-contained code. This means that normal applications for planning permission will generally be unnecessary; though for some kinds of advert express consent will be required in a manner similar to normal planning permission. If any advert is displayed in a way which affects the character of a listed building, then listed building consent will also be necessary.

1 SI 1984/467 (given effect under the 1997 Act by s 2 of the *Planning (Consequential Provisions) (Scotland) Act* 1997), as amended by the Town and Country Planning (Control of Advertisements) (Scotland) Amendment Regulations 2013 (SSI 2013 No 154 (see below).

14.4 The 1984 Regulations (as amended), complemented by provisions of 1997 Act (as amended by the 2006 Act),provide the basis of advertisement control. It is an offence to display an advertisement in contravention of the regulations. The 1997 Act provides planning authorities with powers to require the removal of any advertisement displayed in contravention of the regulations. Where an offence is proven, fines are applicable. The government has considered review of the 1984 regulations but, at the time of writing, has only implemented limited changes.

14.5 In March 1998 the (then) Scottish Office Planning Minister announced a review of the 1984 provisions,[1] and a consultation paper was produced.[2] This included proposals to add further classes of 'exempted' advertisement in the interests of improving the efficiency of advertisement control, while also seeking to continue to safeguard amenity and public safety. Around the same time the Scottish Executive (as then named) embarked on a major review of the 1997 Town and Country Planning (Scotland) Act. As part of this a 2003 paper[3] identified possible options for inclusion in a draft Planning Bill, including simplifying advertisement control and reducing its impact by reducing the number of adverts requiring express consent and improving the efficiency of the decision making process for those that do. Consideration was also given to the possibility of rationalising planning and related consent procedures. However, the 2006 Act did not include any amendments to the control of advertisements, nor rationalisation of consent procedures generally. The only subsequent change has been introduced by the Town and Country Planning (Control of Advertisements) (Scotland) Amendment Regulations 2013[4] which removes the right of an appellant against the withholding of advertisement consent to appear before and be heard by a person (usually a Reporter) appointed by Scottish Ministers.

1 *Calum McDonald announces review of advertisement control procedures*, Scottish Office news release 0541/98, 18 March 1998.

2 *Review of Advertisement Control in Scotland*, Scottish Office Development Department, March 1998.

3 *Options for Change: research on the content of a possible Planning Bill*, Scottish Executive Development Department, September 2003.

4 Town and Country Planning (Control of Advertisements)(Scotland)Amendment Regulations 2013, (SSI 2013 No 154). These remove the appeal provisions for advertisement consent and replace these by the Town and Country Planning (Appeals) (Scotland) Regulations 2013 (SSI 2013 No 156), which also apply to Listed Building Consent and Conservation Area Consent.

14.6 For the purpose of control under the 1984 Regulations, we can divide adverts into four categories:

1. *Adverts exempt from control.* These are mostly very minor types of advert that do not require consent and are totally outside planning control (unless a listed building is affected).
2. *Adverts with deemed consent.* These are also relatively minor adverts which may be displayed without an application for express consent. However, in certain areas this privilege may be withdrawn by a process similar to the operation of an Article 4 direction, rendering express consent necessary. Also, in any area the planning authority can (probably in a minority of cases) take objection to a particular advert within this category and demand that it be removed. This means that planning authorities will not be flooded with applications for many routine types of advert, but may still exercise selective control over these categories.
3. *Adverts requiring express consent.* All adverts not falling within (1) or (2) above will require an application to the planning authority for consent.
4. *Adverts subject to special control.* In certain areas of special control, only restricted categories of advert may be given consent at all, and more stringent limitations will apply to these than in other areas.

Definition of advertisement

14.7 For the purposes of control, an advertisement is defined as: 'any word, letter, model, sign, placard, board, notice, awning, blind, device or representation, whether illuminated or not, in the nature of, and employed wholly or partly for the purposes of, advertisement, announcement or direction (excluding any such thing employed wholly as a memorial or as a railway signal), and includes any hoarding or similar structure or any balloon used or designed or adapted for use and anything else used, or designed or adapted principally for use, for the display of advertisements, and references to the display of advertisements shall be construed accordingly.'[1]

1 1997 Act, s 277(1).

14.8 It should be noted from this definition that structures such as hoardings used for display are included within the definition of an advertisement. If consent is granted, therefore, for the display of an advertisement involving the erection of a structure which would constitute development (eg a hoarding), planning permission is deemed to be granted for the structure also.[1] Tethered balloons also fall within the definition, and it has been held that it also includes a display of national flags and bunting on flagpoles.[2] On the other hand, beams of light which illuminate signs do not amount to a representation for the purpose of the definition.[3]

1 1997 Act, s 184.
2 *Taylor v Scottish Ministers for Scotland* 1997 SLT 485.
3 *Newport Borough Council v Secretary of State for Wales*; *Great Yarmouth Borough Council v Secretary of State for the Environment* [1996] EGCS 158.

Exemptions from control

14.9 Regulation 3(1) specifies those, mostly minor, types of advertisement that are exempt from control. There is an important qualification to this where the advert is within the curtilage of a listed building, in which case listed building consent *may* be required. Otherwise, for the following categories of advert, no consent is required and so they fall outside the jurisdiction of planning authorities:

(a) *adverts within a building* (unless the main purpose of the building is to display adverts); however, they must not be illuminated or located within a metre of any external door, window or other opening through which the advertisement is visible from outside the building;
(b) *adverts on moving vehicles or vessels* unless the vehicle or vessel is being used primarily for the display of adverts;
(c) *adverts forming part of the fabric of a building* unless they have been fixed or painted on to it or the building is used principally for the display of advertisements;
(d) *adverts displayed on enclosed land* which are not readily visible from outside or from any area within the enclosure over which the public have access;
(e) *certain adverts on tethered balloons*; and
(f) *small (ie not exceeding 0.1 square metres in area) non-illuminated adverts* displayed on articles for sale, or on any container or dispenser from which the articles are sold (such as a petrol pump); such an advert must, however, relate wholly to the article being sold.

All other advertisements can only be displayed if an express consent has been granted, or is deemed to have been granted by the regulations.

Advertisements with deemed consent

14.10 Under Part IV of the 1984 regulations, consent is deemed to be granted for a number of categories of advert. This means that an application for consent is not normally required, but if the advert proves unacceptable, the planning authority may demand that it be removed. The most important adverts of this type are set out in Schedule 4 to the regulations (certain additional categories of advert with deemed consent will be considered later).

Schedule 4 Adverts

14.11 The schedule contains six classes of advert, setting out the maximum permitted height of letters or figures, the maximum permitted height above ground level of the highest part of the advert as well as any other conditions which apply. In addition, most deemed consents are subject to the standard conditions set out in reg 6:

I. *Functional adverts of local authorities, community councils, statutory undertakers and public transport undertakers*. There is no specified maximum height of either the lettering or the advert itself. However, illuminated adverts in this class only have deemed consent if they are warning signs.

II. *Miscellaneous advertisements relating to land on which they are displayed*, ie adverts (a) for identification, direction or warning; (b) for a business operating from the land or building; and (c) relating to religious, educational and certain other institutions, as well as to hotels, pubs, blocks of flats, clubs and boarding houses or hostels. Various limits are set on height, area etc; eg all lettering is limited to a maximum height of 0.75 metres, the maximum height of such adverts above ground level is 4.6 metres, and illumination is only permitted for warning purposes or to indicate that medical services or supplies are available on the premises.

III. *Certain temporary signs*, eg 'for sale' and 'to let' signs, those for the sale of goods or livestock, signs by building contractors on building sites, signs giving publicity for local events, and adverts on hoardings around building sites where the land concerned is designated in a local plan for commercial, industrial or business purposes. In *Wandsworth London Borough Council v Mills & Allen Ltd* [1] it was held that an advertisement displayed on hoardings surrounding land on which a nursing home was being constructed did not have deemed consent because the development was for residential and not commercial purposes. Estate agents boards are limited to one for each sale or letting. In *Porter v Honey* [2] the House of Lords held that deemed consent survived for the first board erected, even if other unauthorised boards were subsequently erected. This is clearly an important issue when more than one agent is instructed to market a property.

1 [1997] NPC 137.
2 [1988] 1 WLR 1420, HL.

IV. *Adverts on business premises, or in the forecourt of such premises*, referring to the nature of the business, the goods sold or services provided, or the name and qualifications of the person carrying out the business. In *Berridge v Vision Posters*[1] it was held to be sufficient that the goods advertised were actually sold on the premises, even though they were unrelated to the principal business carried on there.

1 [1995] 159 JP 218.

V. *Certain internal adverts*. This covers adverts displayed within a building, other than those internal adverts which are totally exempt from control (see above).

VI. *Illuminated adverts on business premises*. These must relate purely to the business undertaken at those premises and give the same types of information granted by class IV.

14.12 The display of an advertisement on a vehicle would not be exempt from the need for planning consent if the principal use of the vehicle at the time of display was for advertising. The usual use of the vehicle at other times was irrelevant. Therefore a business that placed advertising boards on its vehicles at times when it did not need to use them could not benefit from the exemption.[1]

1 *Tile Wise Ltd v South Somerset DC* [2010] EWHC 1618 (Admin).

14.13 Doubling the size of an advertisement amounts to a material increase in the extent of the use of a site for the display of advertisements and therefore requires consent. Therefore deemed consent where an advert had been on display for the preceding 10 years without express consent did not apply.[1]

1 *Wandsworth BC v Adrenalin Advertising Ltd* [2011] EWHC 1040 (Admin).

Other Adverts With Deemed Consent

14.14 Other adverts with deemed consent include:

- election notices, statutory adverts and traffic signs, subject to the conditions specified in reg 12(2);
- adverts on sites which were used for that purpose on 16 August 1948 (reg 13) provided that the use of the site is not substantially altered or increased in extent and subject to the other conditions specified in reg 13(3). If such advertisements subsequently have to be removed, compensation may be payable (reg 30); and
- display of advertisements after an express consent has expired (reg 19) unless it contained a condition to the contrary and subject to the conditions in reg 19(2).

Exclusion of Deemed Consent

14.15 Just as permitted development rights can be removed in certain areas by use of Article 4 directions, deemed consent for the display of advertisements can also be excluded in certain areas. A direction to this effect may be issued by the Scottish Ministers under reg 11 and the procedure is similar to that for Article 4 directions.

Discontinuance Proceedings

14.16 Planning authorities also have power to require the removal of existing advertisements displayed with deemed consent. This can be done by serving a discontinuance notice (reg 14). Such action can be taken if the authority considers that the advert represents a 'substantial injury to the amenity of the locality' or a 'danger to members of the public'. The notice has to be served on the person who is displaying or maintaining the advert (or his agent or servant) and the owner, lessee and occupier of the land on which it is displayed. As well as identifying the advert involved, the notice must specify when the display or use of the site is to discontinue and why. The notice cannot take effect until at least 28 days after it has been served.

14.17 An appeal can be made to the Scottish Ministers against a discontinuance notice (reg 21(2)). It must be lodged within 28 days of service of the notice and is treated as if it were an appeal against refusal of consent to display the advert.

Express consent

14.18 The display of all adverts which are neither excluded from control nor have deemed consent requires an express consent. In deciding whether to grant this, planning authorities have less discretion than in other areas of control. This is because the 1984 regulations make it clear that the decision can be based only on public safety and amenity grounds (reg 4(1)). Furthermore, while other material considerations can be considered, the regulations specify certain factors which must be taken into account in considering amenity and public safety (reg 4(2)). These should include assessment of the general characteristics of the area, including the presence of historic, architectural, cultural or similar features. The authority can disregard the presence of other adverts and so these need not establish a precedent. Public safety grounds largely relate to preventing the view of vehicles being blocked or adverts distracting drivers. There is some evidence from appeal decisions that conventional types of advertisement are unlikely to distract motorists to a dangerous degree, unless they are particularly prominent or near traffic lights.[1] For example, one English appeal confirmed the planning authority's refusal of consent (on traffic safety grounds) for three internally-illuminated adverts on a 16-metre high tower next to a motorway.[2]

1 Young, E 'Advertisement Control Basics' (1988) 23 SPLP 29.
2 *Hounslow London Borough Council v Tie Rack Ltd* (1989) 4 PAD 298.

14.19 Planning authorities cannot take into account whether there is a need for an advert nor its subject matter. No conditions can be imposed on an express consent limiting the subject matter or design unless amenity or public safety is an issue. In other words, planning authorities cannot use their power to censor the content of adverts.

Procedure for Obtaining Express Consent

14.20 In many respects this procedure is similar to an application for planning permission (hence the proposals from time to time for the rationalisation of such consents). Before making its decision, the authority must consult with various parties, notably roads authorities and other transportation bodies, giving them at least 14 days to respond (reg 16). The authority may refuse consent, or grant it subject to the standard conditions specified in the regulations and with or without any other conditions of its own (reg 17).

14.21 Section 7(2) of the Panning etc (Scotland) Act 2006 extends s 182 of the 1997 Act by inserting a new subsection (2A) into the provisions relating to the control of advertisement regulations to specify the form and manner in which an advertisement application must be made.

Duration of Consent

14.22 Unlike decisions on planning permission, advertisement consent can only be granted temporarily. The maximum period allowed under reg 18 is five years, although authorities may give consent for a shorter period, provided they justify their decision. The time limit applies from the date consent is granted. If, however, the advertisement has not yet been displayed, the planning authority may state that consent will run from a future date within six months of its decision. An application to renew a consent may be made at any time during the six months before it is due to expire, in which case the same procedure must be followed as for a new application.

Appeals

14.23 Under reg 21 the applicant has the right to an appeal to the Scottish Ministers if the application is refused or granted subject to conditions. It must be made within six months of the decision or of a deemed refusal and the process is similar to that for an appeal against refusal of planning permission.[1]

1 The *Town and Country Planning (Control of Advertisements) (Scotland) Amendment Regulations* 2013, amend the appeal provisions for advertisement consent in the 1984 regs in respect of the right to be heard. The 2013 regs bring the appeal procedures into line with those for planning permission, allowing the Reporter to decide on the most appropriate process for considering the case.

Revocation and Modification of Express Consent

14.24 Part VI of the 1984 regulations gives planning authorities the power to issue an order revoking or modifying any express consent, provided that any building or similar operations that may be involved are not yet complete. This requires the confirmation of the Scottish Ministers and can only be exercised on amenity or public safety grounds. The procedure involved is similar to that for revocation of planning permission. A compensation claim may be made (reg 23).

Standard conditions

14.25 All adverts for which there is deemed consent, or for which express consent has been granted, are subject to the following standard conditions:[1]

1. all adverts must be kept clean and tidy;
2. hoardings etc must be kept in a safe condition;
3. the removal of an advert, if required, should be carried out to the reasonable satisfaction of the planning authority;
4. prior to the display of an advert, permission must be obtained from the owner, or whoever else is entitled to grant permission; and
5. the advert must not render hazardous any road, railway, waterway or airfield, by obscuring any signal or otherwise.

1 Reg 6, Sch 1.

14.26 Condition 5 only applies to adverts granted by deemed consent, as such matters would be taken into account when granting an express consent. Also, certain of the conditions do not apply to election notices and statutory advertisements.

Special control

14.27 Every planning authority has a duty from time to time to consider whether any part of its district should be defined as an area of special control, and periodically to review the position with regard to such areas.[1] A special control area can only be defined for amenity reasons, and may be either a rural area or any other area which appears to the Scottish Ministers to require special protection. The control is imposed by the planning authority issuing an order, which must be approved by the Scottish Ministers, and (subject to similar approval) may be revoked or varied, by the authority making a subsequent order.

1 1997 Act, s 183; 1984 Regs, reg 8.

14.28 The effect of a special control order is to allow only the types of adverts specified in reg 9 to be displayed. These are mostly advertisements with deemed consent, namely Schedule 4 adverts (in respect of which more stringent limitations apply in special control areas), election notices, statutory notices and traffic signs (as defined in reg 12), as well as adverts for travelling circuses and fairs (reg 27). Planning authorities also have the discretion to grant express consent for certain adverts, namely: (a) hoardings etc publicising local events; (b) announcement or direction signs which, in the view of the planning authority, are reasonably required; (c) public safety notices; and (d) any advertisements which would have had deemed consent but for an infringement of a specified condition. The authority does not have the power to grant consent for any other advertisements in special control areas (reg 9(2)). All this said, special control orders appear to be little used in practice.

Enforcement

14.29 Anyone who displays an advertisement in breach of advertisement control is guilty of an offence under s186(3) of the 1997 Act. This may be either the owner or occupier of the land on which the advert is displayed or the person whose business or goods etc are being advertised. In the latter case it will be a defence if the person concerned can show that the advert was displayed without their knowledge or consent. In *Merton London Borough Council v* Edmonds[1] knowledge of the offence was not taken to mean consent for the display. So although a person may be aware of the illegal display of an advertisement for his business, it may still be a defence that he had not consented to its display.

1 (1993) 157 JP 1129; see also *Wycombe District Council v Michael Shanly Group* [1994] 02 EG 112 (where the owner of the land neither knew of nor consented to the advert).

14.30 If a planning authority is satisfied that an advert is displayed in breach of control, it may take enforcement action; in this case it is not limited to considerations of public safety or amenity.[1] The procedures involved are set out in Part VII of the regulations and are similar in many ways to general enforcement procedures. However, unlawful adverts do not become immune from enforcement by lapse of time under either the 4-year or the 10-year rule (see Chapter 9). Scottish Ministers may quash an Enforcement Notice on appeal or vary its terms in favour of appellant. Issues of amenity or public safety are irrelevant.[2]

1 *Kingsley v Hammersmith and Fulham London Borough Council* [1991] 3 PLR 56 DC.
2 *Site Projects Ltd v The Scottish Ministers* 2008 SLT 445, [2008] CSOH 57.

Fly posting

14.31 The 'fly posting' of placards and posters (ie on other people's sites without consent) is a special problem. Examples can usually be seen advertising pop concerts or political demonstrations on vacant shop windows or hoardings around vacant sites. They often contribute to the derelict appearance of already rundown areas and can also be problematic in specific areas at certain times, eg Edinburgh during the festival. Consequently, planning authorities have special powers to remove or obliterate such adverts under s 187 of the 1997 Act. If the authority can identify the person(s) responsible for the display, it must first give them two days' notice that it intends to exercise its powers. The power does not extend to any placard or poster displayed within a building to which there is no right of public access. Planning Advice Note 80[1] sets out advice to planning authorities on how to effectively control and manage illegal poster advertising in both urban and rural areas.

1 SEDD Planning Advice Note 80 'Control and Management of Fly-Posting'.

3. HAZARDOUS SUBSTANCES

Introduction

14.32 The Planning (Hazardous Substances) (Scotland) Act 1997 confers a duty upon planning authorities, along with the necessary powers, to control a wide range of hazardous substances. This is a technical area of planning responsibility which we only deal with in outline.[1]

1 See SOEnD Circulars 5/1993 'Planning Controls for Hazardous Sunstances: The Town and Country Planning (Hazardous Sunstances) (Scotland) Regulations 1993 and 16/1993 Hazardous Substances Consent: A Guide for Industry.

Hazardous Substances Consent

14.33 Hazardous substances cannot be stored or used above specified quantities unless hazardous substances consent (HSC) has been obtained from the planning authority under s2 (1) of the Act. This could result in HSC being required in situations where no development has occurred that requires planning permission, for example where a hazardous substance, already being used or stored, is sufficiently increased in amount to bring it above the prescribed limit.[1] Like listed building consent, the need for HSC is separate from, and additional to, any requirement for planning permission.

1 The Town and Country Planning (Hazardous Substances) (Scotland Regulations 1993 (SI 1993/323) as amended by Planning (Control of Major-Accident Hazards) (Scotland) Regulations 2009 (SSI 2009 No 378); *Eriden Properties LLP v Falkirk Council* 2007 SLT 966.

Health and Safety Legislation

14.34 The hazardous substances legislation is intended to complement the existing controls under the Health and Safety at Work etc Act 1974. Extra regulation is needed because it is possible for the storage or use of a hazardous substance to conform to health and safety requirements while still representing a residual accident risk. Conversely, any hazardous substances consent will be void if it subsequently appears that it should have been controlled under the health and safety legislation.[1]

1 Planning (Hazardous Substances) (Scotland) Act 1997, s 28.

Substances Controlled

14.35 The Town and Country Planning (Hazardous Substances) (Scotland) Regulations 1993 specify the types of hazardous substance that are subject to control and the quantities at or above which they require hazardous substances consent (Schedule 1). The relevant substances are classified into those which are toxic (eg ammonia), highly reactive and/or explosive (eg hydrogen) and flammable (eg liquefied petroleum gas).

Exemptions from control

14.36 Regulation 4 allows for certain exemptions from control, eg: the temporary storage of hazardous material which is in transit or has been unloaded from a ship during a maritime emergency; where certain substances are contained in aerosols; certain fertilisers. Moreover, some hazardous substances are exempt because they are controlled by other legislation, for example controlled waste (as defined in the Environmental Protection Act 1990) radioactive waste (as defined in the Radioactive Substances Act 1960) explosives (where their location is controlled by the Health and Safety Executive) and substances in pipelines which are controlled by the Pipelines Act 1962. There are other situations where, strictly speaking, there is no exemption but consent is deemed to be granted, for example under emergency powers of the Scottish Ministers,[1] or where use of the substance by a statutory undertaker or local authority has been authorised by a government department (s 10(1)). Deemed consent also exists for some uses that were established prior to 1 May 1993, but only where an application for deemed consent was made at the appropriate time (s 9).

1 *Planning (Hazardous Substances) (Scotland) Act* 1997, s 2.

Applications for consent

14.37 A particular feature of applications for HSC is that the applicant has to publicise the application in a local newspaper before submitting it. Apart from this, the process is similar to an application for planning permission. Before reaching its decision, reg 11 requires the planning authority to consult with a wide range of consultees, including the Health and Safety Executive, Scottish Natural Heritage and the Scottish Environment Protection Agency (SEPA). In the case of an adverse decision, an applicant has the same rights of appeal as an applicant for planning permission. In certain specified circumstances, s 12 empowers a planning authority to revoke or modify a hazardous substances consent. Under s27, every planning authority must keep a register of applications for consent, which should also contain deemed consents, revocations and modifications and any emergency directions.

Enforcement

14.38 Contravention of hazardous substances control is a criminal offence which may lead to a maximum fine of £20,000 on summary conviction, or to an unlimited fine on conviction on indictment (s 21). Alternatively (in less serious cases) the planning authority may issue a hazardous substances contravention notice (regs 18–23), as part of a procedure which is similar to the enforcement proceedings for the breach of other planning controls.

4. MINERALS

Introduction

14.39 Mineral operations are defined as development under s26(1) of the Town and Country Planning (Scotland) Act 1997 (as amended) and so need planning permission, but they are not like other forms of development. They involve the destruction of non-renewable natural resources, often on a very large scale and the manner of their exploitation can cause serious environmental problems if not properly planned and controlled. Mineral extraction is also a temporary use (albeit one which may last for many years) and so thought has to be given as to how the site will be treated and used once operations cease.

14.40 It hardly needs saying that minerals can only be extracted where they exist, but unfortunately this is very often in areas of attractive landscape and environmental sensitivity, or uncomfortably close to where people live. Not surprisingly, therefore, planning applications for major mineral operations are often highly contentious. Another factor to bear in mind when considering mineral development is that operations usually take place over a very long time, sixty years or more in some cases. It is possible; therefore, that the conditions which were attached to mineral consents granted twenty or thirty years ago will not meet today's standards for environmental protection. Equally, standards that we consider sufficient today may not be appropriate in twenty years time. It is necessary, therefore, for mineral operations to be subject to periodic review so that the controls under which they operate can be adjusted to meet modern requirements. The legislation gives planning authorities special duties and powers to carry out such periodic review. This is a highly specialised and complex area of planning law and practice and we only have space to consider a few of the major aspects.[1]

1 For a more detailed general account see Sales, M & Abercrombie I, 'The Extractive Industries', Scottish Planning Encyclopaedia, Vol 1, A2001–A2060; for government advice on particular aspects of mineral operations, see eg SODD Circular 34/1996 'Environment Act 1995: Section 96 Guidance on the Statutory Provisions and Procedures; PAN 50 'Controlling the Environmental Effects of Surface Mineral Workings' (together with Annex A (1996) 'Control of Noise at Surface Mineral Workings' and Annexes B and C (1998) 'Control of Dust at Surface Mineral Workins' and 'Control of Traffic at Surface Mineral Workings' and Annex D (2000) 'Controlling the Environmental Effects of Surface Mineral Workings'; *Opencast Coal – Review of Planning Policy in Scotland* (August 1997); and SODD Circular 25/1998 'Review of Old Minerals Permissions and Environmental Impact Assessment Notes for Guidance.

Definition of minerals

14.41 Before considering the controls which cover mineral operations, it may be useful to clarify what kinds of substances are affected. Section 277 (1) of the 1997 Act gives a wide definition of minerals as 'all substances of a kind ordinarily worked for removal by underground or surface working'. These can include fossil fuels (eg coal, oil and gas), construction materials (eg sandstone, lime, gravel, and sand) precious metals, ores, clay and peat. Certain manufactured materials can also fall within the definition of 'minerals', for example fuel ash, clinker and metallic slag.

Permitted development

14.42 Some (mainly minor or ancillary) kinds of mineral operations enjoy permitted development rights under the Town and Country Planning (General Permitted Development) (Scotland) Order 1992 (as amended). These include:

1. mineral exploration activity (eg drilling or boring of holes) – permitted development classes 53 and 54;
2. works to erect, alter or repair buildings, machinery, plant and other specified infrastructure on land used as a mine – classes 55 and 56;
3. waste tipping at a mine or the removal of material from mineral stockpiles or working deposits – classes 63–66;
4. work required to maintain or make safe a mine, including one that is disused – class 57;
5. certain coal mining operations by the Coal Authority and its Licensees – classes 58–60, 62;
6. winning and working of minerals reasonably required for agricultural purposes within the agricultural unit for which they will be used – class 19;
7. winning and working of peat by any person for the domestic requirements of that person – class 21.

14.43 As with all permitted development rights, these works are subject to a variety of conditions and limitations. For example, mineral exploration activity is not permitted if it is within 50 metres of an occupied residential, hospital or school building. It is also possible for planning authorities to remove these permitted development rights using an Article 4 direction. However, this power cannot be used in relation to mineral works permitted by Classes 54 and 66 (that is certain exploration activities and removal of material from a mineral working deposit).

If it wishes to control these activities, the authority can only do so under the special circumstance outlined in Article 7 of the Permitted Development Order (for example if the site lies within a National Scenic Area).

Planning applications for new mineral development

14.44 Planning applications for mineral development are in general subject to the same legal requirements as applications for any other type of development. However, there are some detailed differences which we now consider.

Notification and Publicity Requirements

14.45 In addition to the normal notification requirements for planning applications, an applicant for permission to carry out mineral operations must place an advertisement in a public newspaper and physically put a public notice in at least one place within the planning authority's district.[1] This is to allow for the fact that mineral rights in the land may be owned by someone other than the landowner and that the identity of the party owning these rights may be unknown.

1 Town and Country Planning (General Development Procedure) (Scotland) Order 1992, SI 1992/224, art 8 (substituted by the Town and Country Planning (General Development Procedure) (Scotland) Amendment (No 2) Order 1994, SI 1994/3293, art 3).

14.46 Planning authorities are required to notify the Scottish Ministers if they receive applications for mineral or opencast coal workings which would occur within 500 metres from the edge of an existing community or sensitive establishment[1] This Direction replaced the previous requirement for a raft of notifications where planning authorities intended to grant permission. Consequently minerals and opencast coal developments are now mostly regarded as being a matter for planning authorities, taking account of local circumstances.

1 Town and Country Planning (Notification of Applications) (Scotland) Direction 2009.

Consultations

14.47 As many mineral proposals are located in areas of attractive landscape or are likely to affect areas of protected natural heritage, Scottish Natural Heritage will normally be an important statutory consultee. The possibility of pollution from mineral operations (eg dust, noise, and contamination of surface or ground water) means that the views of SEPA will also usually be required.

Conditions

14.48 If the authority is minded to grant planning permission, it will want to be sure that the operations are controlled in a way that will minimise any adverse environmental effects. It will also want to take into account that the operations may continue over a long period of time, that the work may be intermittent, and that the land will need to be restored once the operations cease. It is likely, therefore, that a range of conditions covering these, and other matters, will be applied to the consent. These will often be highly technical and aimed at controlling the environmental and other concerns discussed above. They may include, for example, conditions on rates of extraction, noise levels, dust, landscaping, and drainage.[1] It is also normal nowadays for a condition to be imposed requiring operations to begin by a specified date in order to prevent an accumulation of unworked permissions, as this could lead to blight.

1 See SOEnD PAN 50 Controlling the environmental effects of surface mineral working.

14.49 While conditions are subject to the usual general legal requirements relating to planning conditions, Schedule 3 of the 1997 Act makes additional provisions for the attaching of conditions to planning permission for mineral development. These include the duty to impose a condition on the duration of the development (normally not later than 60 years after work commences), and the power to apply such aftercare conditions as the authority thinks fit. Aftercare conditions are designed to ensure that work is carried out to restore the land (or bring it up to a required standard) after work has ceased. They may consist of 'planting, cultivating, fertilising, watering, draining or otherwise treating the land'.[1] An aftercare condition will either specify the steps to be taken or require the developer to submit an aftercare scheme for approval by the authority. The authority may approve the scheme with or without modifications and, once in place, the developer is bound by the scheme. It is also common for planning authorities to use planning obligations including planning agreements to secure restoration and aftercare provisions (see Chapter 7) and they may ask the minerals operator to provide a financial bond to cover the costs of this work.

1 Schedule 3, Part 1, para 2(5).

Review of existing mineral permissions

14.50 As mineral operations may last for decades, the planning conditions under which some older mines are operating may not be up to the standards that society now deems necessary. In addition, with new technology, the nature of mineral operations themselves changes over time. Under provisions originally introduced by the Environment Act 1995 and now incorporated in the 1997 Act,[1] since 1 January 2007 minerals developments have been subject to a review process effectively requiring a fresh application for planning permission so that the conditions applicable to the development can be updated. In so doing, they are also subject to Environmental Impact Assessment.[2] Under these arrangements, planning authorities have a duty to carry out an initial review of all 'old mineral planning permissions' in their area, that is those granted after 30 June 1948 and before 22 February 1982, and periodically review every mineral planning permission granted in their area (except those granted under the Permitted Development Order). Active mineral sites are initially listed by the planning authority; underlying planning permission ceases to have effect if not listed by a certain date. Owners or other interested parties can apply to the planning authority, with conditions then set for renewed planning permissions.

1 1995 Act, s 96, Schs 13, 14; 1997 Act, s 74, Schs 9, 10.
2 *Lafarge Aggregates Ltd v Scottish Ministers* [2004] GWD 2-37.

14.51 Periodic review is an ongoing requirement on planning authorities which, in relation to each permission, must take place every 15 years. The periodic review triggers a requirement for land and minerals owners to submit an application for approval of new conditions. However, when carrying out a periodic review the planning authority has to give at least 12 months advance notice of the date by which the application must be submitted to it. If no application setting out a scheme of new conditions is submitted by the specified date, the existing permission ceases to have effect.

14.52 Lafarge Aggregates appealed against a decision of Scottish Ministers that only certain areas from a 600 hectare (ha) site on Harris in the Western Isles should be included as a dormant stage 1 site in the list of minerals kept by the planning authority under Sch 9 para 3 of the 1997 Act.[1] The issue related to a 1965 permission which included the condition that 'before any work is commenced full details of the proposed operation be submitted for approval'. The developer subsequently submitted a map showing two areas of the site for immediate development and a separate area for future development. Lafarge applied for inclusion at stage 1 their interest in the 600 ha site. The planning authority refused an application by Lafarge in 1997 on the grounds that matters reserved in the original outline permission were never submitted or approved to give any effect to the earlier permission, so that permission was not extant. On appeal, the Reporters recommended the areas identified for immediate development and the one for future development should be included as a dormant stage 1 site. Lafarge appealed, arguing that the 1965 permission was valid for the extraction of minerals within the 600 ha site. The court held that the 1965 permission was valid, but only granted permission in principle within the 600 ha and did not authorise the winning and working of minerals throughout. The effect of the 1965 permission was to authorise the winning and working of minerals only within the three areas identified on the 1965 map. There was nothing to indicate that the 1965 permission left it open to the developer to make successive applications. The 'land to which a relevant planning permission relates' meant the land in respect of which specific minerals development had been authorised, which meant the three areas identified on the 1965 map.

1 *Lafarge Aggregates Ltd v The Scottish Ministers* 2004 SLT 164.

14.53 A 2011 Supreme Court case[1] concerned applications for review of old minerals planning permissions. The original 1965 planning permission gave permission to work the minerals on land in accordance with a plan which had subsequently been lost. The area in which workings had occurred (the green land) was approximately one sixth of a larger area (the red land), and no work had taken place on the land for 20 years. The planning authority, in its statutory review, identified the site (the green land) as dormant due to inadequate evidence of workings. In 2007 the owner applied for approval of a schedule of conditions for the red land, arguing that the green land defined the area covered by the planning permission and therefore it was not within the power of the planning authority to approve the conditions for the red land, arguing that the remainder of the planning permission for the red land had ceased to have effect.

1 *G Hamilton (Tullochgribban Mains) Ltd v Highland Council and another* [2012] UKSC 31 (on appeal from [2011] CSIH 1).

14.54 The Supreme Court unanimously upheld the decision of the lower courts that the listing of a mineral site at stage 1 of the review process was administrative in nature and that it was at stage 2 when conditions were being determined that planning judgment was appropriate to the area of the site. Stage 1 did not permit, nor was the planning authority required to restrict, the underlying planning permission. Hence the extent of existing development rights over a site was to be determined at stage 2. This suggests that, when a planning authority lists a minerals site for the purpose of providing modern working conditions under the review procedure, that listing does not define the extent of the land covered by the old minerals planning permission upon which it relies. This further suggests that, in principle, planning permissions cannot be lost by abandonment.

Other powers

14.55 Planning authorities have the power to make orders revoking, modifying, discontinuing, prohibiting, or suspending mineral working (these powers also applying to the depositing of waste materials or refuse). While the powers relating to revocation, modification and discontinuance are broadly similar to those for other types of planning permission, suspension and prohibition orders are unique to minerals control.

14.56 While the power to ***revoke or modify*** a minerals permission is the same power that applies to all other planning permissions, for minerals permissions it is supplemented by the ability to impose aftercare and restoration conditions on an existing permission.[1] Although in practice ***discontinuance orders*** are similar to any other type of use, those relating to minerals operate under a different part of the Act.[2] The main practical difference is the power given to the planning authority in these circumstances to impose aftercare conditions.

1 1997 Act, s 65(5), Sch 3, Pt II.
2 s 71(8), Sch 8.

14.57 ***Prohibition orders*** (schedule 8 of the 1997 Act, paras 3, 4) may be used where mineral activities have permanently ceased. The planning authority can regard work as having stopped permanently if no winning or working of minerals has taken place to any substantial extent for at least two years and, on the evidence available to it, is unlikely to do so in future. If work has taken place during the two year period, the planning authority will have to indicate why this has not been to 'any substantial extent' if it wishes to serve a prohibition order.[1]

1 *Van Leeuwen v Scottish Ministers for the Environment and Devon County Council* [1995] NPC 157.

14.58 As well as preventing the minerals activity from starting again, the prohibition order may require the owner to remove plant or machinery, take steps to remove or alleviate any harm to amenity, and meet any conditions of the original consent. It can also impose restoration and aftercare conditions. Once an order is in force, the original planning permission for the site it relates to ceases to have effect.

14.59 The planning authority must serve a notice on the owner or occupier of the land and any other person who may be affected by the prohibition order. Those notified have 28 days to object to the Scottish Ministers. The order has to be confirmed by the Scottish Ministers who can take into account any evidence of work restarting after the planning authority served the notice. If Ministers conclude that work has restarted, they may decline to confirm the order on the ground that work has not ceased permanently.[1] In other words all an operator has to do to prevent the order taking effect is to restart work before it is confirmed. The order cannot take effect until it has been recorded in the Register of Sasines or, as the case may be, registered in the Land Register (1997 Act, Schedule 8 para 8).

1 *R v Secretary of State for Wales, ex p Mid Glamorgan County Council* (1995) Times, 10 February, CA.

Suspension Orders

14.60 Suspension Orders (Sch 8, para 5(2)) are used where the planning authority is of the view that mineral activities have stopped temporarily. This can be assumed to be the case where there has been no work for 12 months but it appears that resumption is likely. A suspension order is designed to ensure that specified 'steps for the protection of the environment'[1] are carried out. Such steps must be designed to preserve the amenities of the area around the site, protect the site itself from damage, or prevent deterioration in its condition. Appropriate steps might include the removal of machinery, erection of fences, or disposal of stock piles or waste heaps. Where a suspension order is already in place, the planning authority may also issue a supplementary suspension order which can either require additional or alternative action to be taken or can cancel an existing suspension order.

1 1997 Act, Sch 8, para 5(1).

14.61 As with prohibition orders, suspension and supplementary suspension orders need to be confirmed by the Scottish Ministers (Sch 8, para 7). The only exception to this requirement is where a supplementary suspension order revokes a previous suspension order without requiring that any 'fresh step shall be taken to protect the environment'. All suspension orders (including supplementary ones) have to be recorded in the Register of Sasines or registered in the Land Register. Under para 9 of Schedule 8, planning authorities have a duty to review all suspension orders every five years in order to consider whether a prohibition order or supplementary suspension order should be issued. A suspension order cannot prevent work starting again. All the owner or other interested party has to do is give notice of the intended date to restart work. Once work has recommenced to a substantial extent the planning authority (or the Scottish Ministers if necessary) has to revoke the suspension order. Compensation may be payable where the planning authority takes any of these actions, but this may be abated by the amounts specified in the Town and Country Planning (Compensation for Restrictions on Mineral Working and Mineral Waste Depositing) (Scotland) Regulations 1998.

14.62 Finally, 'winning' and 'working' of minerals are regularly used as if they are inseparable. However in 2009 the Court of Appeal established that 'winning and working' are distinct operations and a minerals planning permission should be construed accordingly.[1] The decision related to a site in the Peak District National Park and a 1952 planning permission for the 'winning and working of fluorspar and the working of limestone won in the course of working the fluorspar'. In 2006 the National Park Authority served an enforcement notice on the owner and operator of the site alleging that limestone was being worked and sold in breach of the permission because it had not been won in the course of working the fluorspar. An appeal against the notice was dismissed but a subsequent High Court appeal succeeded on the basis that it was inevitable that significant quantities of limestone would be won in the winning and working of fluorspar (the main purpose of the permission). The High Court had no need to consider the precise meaning of 'winning' and 'working' and whether or not they are part of the same operation or have separate meanings. However it concluded that both were general, interchangeable terms meaning mineral extraction. On appeal by the Secretary of State and the minerals planning authority, the Court of Appeal approved earlier common law definitions[2] that distinguish between 'winning' and 'working' and held that there was no reason not to apply those definitions to the wording of the 1952 permission. To 'win' a mineral is to make it available or accessible to be removed from the land; to 'work' a mineral is (at least initially) to remove it from its position in the land.

1 *Bleaklow Industries Ltd v Sec of State for Communities and Local Government and another* [2009] EWCA Civ 206.
2 *English Clays Lovering Pochin Ltd v Plymouth Corporation* [1974] 27 P&CR 447.

14.63 The Court of Appeal therefore concluded that the planning inspector (England) had been right to dismiss the enforcement appeal and allowed the appeal by the Secretary of State and the minerals planning authority against the decision of the High Court. The planning permission only permitted the working of limestone won from the working of fluorspar and not the limestone removed in the winning of the fluorspar. This means that, unless there is ambiguity, a planning permission is to be interpreted in accordance with the particular meanings of the words used in the description. It also means that 'winning' and 'working' are separate terms with distinct meanings and, when used together, imply two operations that may be separated for planning purposes.

These have implications for the words used in the description, or in the conditions, of a planning permission.

5. LAND ADVERSELY AFFECTING THE AMENITY OF A NEIGHBOURHOOD

14.64 Where the condition of a property or land is causing adverse effects on local amenity (eg a dilapidated building or vacant land which is becoming unsightly through 'fly tipping') planning authorities have the power to take action to remedy the situation under ss 179–181 of the 1997 Act. Occupied land or buildings can also be subject to such action. Ancient monuments are, however, exempt from the waste land provisions (s 179(5)).

Amenity notices

14.65 A notice has to be served on the owner, lessee and occupier specifying what steps are required to abate the amenity problem and the date (not less than 28 days after service of the notice) by which the work should be carried out. If the work is not carried out by then, the authority can enter the land to carry out the work itself and recover its expense in doing so (1997 Act, ss 135, 179(6)).

Appeals

14.66 The person on whom the notice has been served, or anyone else with an interest in the land, can appeal against it to the Scottish Ministers at any time before the date when it is due to take effect (s 180(1)). Under s 180(3) there are five grounds of appeal:

(a) the amenity of the area is not adversely affected;
(b) the steps required are more than what is necessary to remedy the problem;
(c) insufficient time has been given to comply with the notice;
(d) the condition of the land results from what might normally be expected from its lawful use; or
(e) that the notice has not been served correctly. The process is similar to that for an appeal against an enforcement notice.

Chapter 15

Environmental impact assessment

1. GENERAL

15.1 Environmental impact assessment (EIA) is a procedure through which new development projects which might have an adverse effect on the environment can be identified and assessed at an early stage. It originated in a directive of the then European Community,[1] which came into force in July 1988 and required each of the member states to pass legislation implementing the directive's provisions.

1 Directive 85/337/EEC (now Directive 2011/92/EU which codifies Directive 85/337/EEC and its three subsequent amendments, ie Directives 97/11/EC, 2003/35/EC and 2009/31/EC).

15.2 The preamble of the original directive, explaining its rationale, stressed that:

> '...the best environmental policy consists in preventing the creation of pollution or nuisances at source, rather than subsequently trying to counteract their effects ... (which creates a need to) take effects on the environment into account at the earliest possible stage in all the technical planning and decision-making processes.'

To this end, the directive resolved that:

> '...general principles for the assessment of environmental effects should be introduced with a view to supplementing and coordinating development consent procedures governing public and private projects likely to have a major effect on the environment.'

15.3 This area of law has been subject to regular change. The original directive was implemented in Scotland by regulations in 1988[1] which were then replaced in 1999[2] to reflect the provisions of an EC amending Directive in 1997.[3] However, due to further amendments to the directive as well as changes to the 1999 regulations and several important court decisions, the Scottish Government decided that it was necessary to produce a new set of consolidated regulations in 2011. These are the Environmental Impact Assessment (Scotland) Regulations 2011 (the 2011 Regulations).[4] Useful advice on the practical operation of these is contained in Scottish Government Circular 3/2011[5] and in a brief users guide[6] also published by the Scottish Government. Further statutory amendments are likely in future not least because the European Commission is proposing more changes to the EIA Directive.[7]

1 Environmental Assessment (Scotland) Regulations 1988 (SI 1988/1221).
2 Environmental Assessment (Scotland) Regulations 1999 (SSI 1999 No 1).
3 EC Directive 97/11.
4 Environmental Impact Assessment (Scotland) Regulations 2011 (SSI 2011 No 139).
5 SG Circular 3/2011 'The Town and Country Planning (Environmental Impact Assessment) (Scotland) Regulations 2011'.
6 Scottish Government *A Users Guide to the Environmental Impact Assessment (Scotland) Regulations 2011* (undated); see also the Scottish Government Planning EIA webpage.
7 European Commission 'Proposal for a Directive of the European Parliament and of the Council amending Directive 2011/92/EU on the assessment of the effects of certain public and private projects on the environment' (2012).

15.4 More often than not, the sort of project or activity likely to have an effect on the environment will also fall within the definition of 'development' and will therefore be subject to planning control. In these cases environmental impact assessment has conveniently been incorporated into the procedure for obtaining planning permission. However, it may also be required for activities that do not require planning permission in the usual way (because they are not development or are permitted development). In some cases, eg Forestry works; there are separate regulations which deal with EIA. It should be noted, however, that the Courts have held that decisions on whether or not proposed works fall within the definition of development can, and should be, broadly interpreted so as to include, wherever possible, projects which require an EIA (see paragraph 4.4 above). We will mainly be concerned with those projects and activities that *are* subject to normal planning control.

15.5 Environmental impact assessment (EIA) is initially the responsibility of the would-be developer who is required, in those cases where EIA is necessary, to collect and assess information about the likely environmental effects of their project. This can include information that the competent authority (normally the planning authority) has advised the developer needs to be included. The findings will be embodied in an environmental statement (ES) which will normally be submitted along with the planning application so that the planning authority can take it into account when reaching its decision. The ES also needs to be made available to consultation bodies and the public so that these parties can provide comments on it and the planning authority also has to take these into account. If the ES contains satisfactory proposals for minimising any adverse environmental effects, then the planning authority may see fit to grant permission; otherwise, it may refuse consent, or grant it subject to conditions designed to deal with any environmental problems.

15.6 It was already within the remit of planning authorities to consider environmental issues when making decisions, as these are material considerations which they have a duty to take account of.[1] However, the regulations on EIA further formalised that process for some large projects, making it mandatory in certain cases.

1 See Chapter 6.

Meaning of 'environment'

15.7 Before proceeding further, we should perhaps be clearer about precisely what it is that the regulations are designed to protect. This can be found in the prescribed information for an ES, which *inter alia* must describe 'the aspects of the environment likely to be significantly affected by the proposed development, including, in particular, population, fauna, flora, soil, water, air, climatic factors, material assets, including the architectural and archaeological heritage, landscape and the interrelationship between the above factors.'[1]

1 The Town and Country Planning (Environmental Impact Assessment) (Scotland) Regulations 2011, (SSI 2011 No 139) Sch. 4, Part 1.

15.8 It will be noted that the provisions are designed to protcct not just the natural environment, but also the man-made environment where that is considered sufficiently worthwhile to merit preservation.

2. PROJECTS REQUIRING ASSESSMENT

15.9 The EU directive (as codified) identifies two categories of project that may be subject to EIA. These are embodied in Annexes 1 and 2 of the directive. Annex 1 projects are major developments in respect of which EIA is *mandatory* in all cases. In the case of Annex 2 projects, EIA is normally only required where it is considered that the particular project is likely to give rise to significant environmental effects (see below). These requirements are repeated in Schedules 1 and 2 to the 2011 Regulations[1] and the criteria for determining whether an EIA will be required for specific proposals are contained in Schedule 3 to those Regulations. Project works subject to EIA can include demolition.[2]

1 The Town and Country Planning (Environmental Impact Assessment) (Scotland) Regulations 2011 (SSI 2011 No 139).

2 *Commission v Ireland* (C-50/09).

Schedule 1 projects (assessment mandatory)

15.10 Schedule 1 projects may be summarised as developments which involve the following:

Crude Oil Refining.
Coal and shale gasification and liquification.
Power (including nuclear power) generation.
The production, processing, reprocessing, storage or disposal of nuclear fuel or radioactive waste.
Iron and steel works and other metallurgical processes.
Asbestos processing.
Integrated chemical installations.
Railways and airports.
Motorways and other large roads; the realignment or widening of some roads.
Ports, canals and piers.
Hazardous waste disposal through incineration, chemical treatment or landfill.
Non-hazardous waste disposal through chemical treatment or incineration.
Abstraction of groundwater, artificial groundwater recharge schemes, transfer of water resources, and treatment of wastewater.
Works involving oil-related, gas or chemical products, including extraction, pipeline construction and storage.
Intensive rearing of poultry or pigs.
Production of pulp, paper and board.
Quarries.
Carbon dioxide capture and storage.

15.11 Most (though not all) of the Schedule 1 definitions contain quantitative limits, for example non-nuclear power stations are only included if they have a heat output of 300 megawatts or more. As a result, it is generally only major projects in the above categories that fall within Schedule 1, though smaller projects of the same type may be caught up within Schedule 2. In addition, if an increase in an existing use takes it over one of the thresholds then that will trigger the need for an EIA.

Schedule 2 projects (assessment may be required following screening)

15.12 The list is too extensive to reproduce in detail, but is classified under the following main headings:

Agriculture, silviculture and aquaculture.
Extractive industry.
Energy industry.
Production and processing of metals.
Mineral industry.
Chemical industry.
Food Industry.
Textile, leather, wood and paper industries.
Rubber industry.
Infrastructure projects.
Other projects (eg motor racing tracks and sludge deposition sites).
Tourism and leisure.

15.13 Care has to be exercised when considering whether a proposed development falls within one of the categories defined in Schedule 2. For example, 'Infrastructure' does not just include projects that would normally be regarded as such (eg roads, pipelines and dams); it also includes urban development projects, such as shopping centres, sports stadiums and industrial estates.[1] The Scottish Ministers have the power to add to or alter the categories of project that fall under both Schedules 1 and 2.[2]

1 See for example *R (on the application of Goodman and another) v Lewisham Borough Council* [2003] EWCA Civ 140.
2 1997 Act, s 40.

Schedule 2 projects requiring assessment

15.14 It is for the planning authority (or, in some cases, the Scottish Ministers) to determine whether an EIA is required in respect of any particular Schedule 2 project. An EIA will only be required for development that the decision maker considers is likely to have significant effects on the environment by virtue, *inter alia*, of its nature, size or location. This is determined through what is known as a screening opinion. If the authority adopts a screening opinion that the development is likely to have significant effects on the environment then it becomes what is known as an 'EIA development' and an assessment is required.

15.15 When considering the types of project that will require EIA, it is natural to think of those that fall within the first strand of the definition of development, ie building, engineering, mining or other operations. However, it should be noted that an activity that qualifies as development merely by virtue of being a material change of use may also require EIA in some cases. For example, an industrial unit, without any external alterations, could come to be used for a purpose falling within Schedule 1 or Schedule 2, for example, a change from assembly of computers to the processing of rubber materials.

3. PLANNING CONTROL

15.16 In cases where EIA is required, the developer will apply for planning permission in the usual way, except that the procedure is likely to take longer and be slightly more complex. In particular, a planning authority is absolutely prohibited from granting planning permission for an EIA development (ie a Schedule 1 project or a qualifying Schedule 2 project) without first taking the necessary environmental information into consideration. This does not just apply to applications for planning permission; EIA may also apply to the following types of planning applications/consents:

- Permitted development rights, including some cases where an application for the prior approval of the planning authority is required (see Chapter 5).
- Permission granted by a simplified planning zone scheme or enterprise zone order (see Chapter 5).
- Applications to review mineral permissions under ss 8, 9 or 10 of the 1997 Act, often referred to as ROMP applications (see Chapter 14).
- Urgent applications to the Scottish Ministers for development by the Crown under s 242A of the 1997 Act.

Multi-stage consents

15.17 Normally an EIA will be required only once and this will be at the point where the principle of a proposed development is being considered, eg in connection with an application for a full or an in principle planning permission. However, following the case *Commission v UK* (C508/03) it has been established that the need for an EIA may arise at later stages in the process. This might be because an adverse environmental impact only becomes apparent once an application is submitted for the approval of the detailed design of a project that already has planning permission in principle. It could even happen where an EIA was conducted at the in principle stage but the full environmental impact was not identifiable at that point. Multi stage consent includes the need to obtain written approval of detailed matters relating to a full planning permission.

15.18 Where later stage applications are submitted for a proposal that has already been treated as an EIA development, the authority must take into account any previous EIA for that proposal. If the applicant chooses to submit a revised or updated ES with the later stage application then that triggers the same publicity and consultation requirements which applied to the original EIA. As a result, applicants are only likely to do this in exceptional circumstances. However, whether or not the applicant chooses to do so, it is open to the planning authority to request further information if it feels it needs that to properly asses the environmental impact of the proposal then before it to be determined.

15.19 In multi stage cases where an EIA has not previously been required, if it becomes clear at a later stage that an EIA is needed after all, the planning authority will adopt a new screening opinion which supersedes any earlier opinion. This will trigger the need for the applicant to prepare an ES and for the authority to carry out the necessary consultations and publicity. The authority then has to take the results of the EIA into account when determining the later stage application. Understandably, a developer may be concerned that a scheme of theirs which already has planning permission in principle might suddenly be treated as an EIA development because of a detailed submission they are planning to lodge. Where this is the case, the developer can first request a screening opinion from the planning authority in the usual manner (see below).

Screening

15.20 Where a developer proposes a project which falls within Schedule 2 they can decide to prepare and submit an ES with their planning application in which case the proposal automatically becomes an EIA development. However, the professional fees involved in producing an ES can be considerable. As a result, the developer may wish to establish that this cost is truly necessary before commissioning an ES. They can do this by seeking a screening opinion from the planning authority. Such a request has to identify the site concerned and briefly describe the proposed development and its potential environmental impact. If the authority needs more information in order to reach an opinion it has to notify the applicant of this making clear what that other information is. The authority has three weeks (or any longer period agreed with the applicant) in which to adopt a screening opinion and issue this to the applicant.

15.21 If the authority fails to issue a screening opinion within the required period or adopts an opinion which the applicant is unhappy with, the latter can then apply to the Scottish Ministers for a screening direction and the procedure involved is broadly the same as that for a screening opinion.

15.22 If the planning authority receives a planning application for a development falling within Schedule 2 which is not accompanied with an ES then that authority must adopt a screening opinion anyway. Also, as we have already seen, the planning authority has to consider the need for an EIA at each stage of a multi-consent process. It is also possible that due to new evidence or some other changes, the authority will have to adopt a new screening opinion during the processing of an application for consent through a single stage process. This might also happen if the proposal goes to the Local Review Body (see Chapter 7) or is passed to the Scottish Ministers through a call in (see Chapter 6) or appeal (see Chapter 7).

15.23 Whenever an authority's screening opinion is negative (ie that an EIA is not needed) then reasons need to be given for this and a copy made publicly available in Part 1 of the planning register (see Chapter 6).The authority can then proceed to determine the application without an EIA. On the other hand, if following screening it decides that the proposal **is** an EIA development then, as we have already seen, the planning application cannot be determined until an ES has been submitted by the applicant. The applicant has to be notified of this and, if they do not provide an ES the planning application will be refused. The Scottish Ministers also have the power to issue a screening direction indicating whether for any particular development an EIA will be required.

15.24 The criteria to be used for screening are set out in Schedule 3 of the 2011 Regulations. They are grouped into three main considerations which are the characteristics of the proposed development, where it is located and its potential impact. Not surprisingly the size of the proposed development is an important consideration as is its use of natural resources, its potential for nuisance, waste or pollution generation and accident risk. The cumulative impact of the proposal with other developments also has to be considered. With regard to location it is more likely that an EIA will be required in sensitive areas such as those subject to designations to protect the natural or historic environment. Population density is also significant. Important characteristics of development impact include its magnitude and complexity, the probability of it occurring and its duration, frequency and reversibility. When screening a proposal the authority should not normally take into account any proposed mitigation measures even if these would be likely to remove an adverse environmental impact and could be secured through conditions on a planning permission.[1] The safe route is to require the proposal to go through the EIA process in such circumstances because it may not be assumed that the mitigation measures would be successfully implemented and also the environmental impact of the construction process itself needs to be considered.[2] Where a proposed development ought properly to be regarded as an integral part of a much more substantial project then the need for an EIA should be considered in that wider context rather than in isolation.[3]

1 *Roao Lebus v South Cambridgeshire DC* [2002] EWHC 2009 Admin.
2 *Urban Renewal Southern v John Gillespie* [2003] EWCA Civ 400.
3 *R v Swale BC ex parte RSPB* (1991) 1 PLR 6 and *BAA Plc v Secretary of State for Transport, Local Government and Regions* [2002] EWHC 1920 Admin.

Scoping

15.25 As we have already discussed, when a developer proposes an EIA development they have to prepare an Environmental Statement (ES) and usually submit this to the planning authority at the same time as their application for planning permission. To help with the preparation of the ES, the EIA regulations allow the developer to formally apply for the opinion of the planning authority and statutory consultation bodies about the information that will need to be included in the ES. This is known as a scoping opinion and the process involved is similar to that which we saw above for screening opinions. The planning authority has five weeks (or any other period agreed with the applicant) in which to provide a scoping opinion. Before doing so, the authority has to consult with the applicant and all of the relevant statutory consultation bodies (see para 15.30 below). It must also take account of: (a) the specific characteristics of the particular development; (b) the specific characteristics of development of the type concerned; and (c) the environmental features likely to be affected by the development. If the planning authority fails to provide a scoping opinion within the required period the applicant can apply to the Scottish Ministers for a scoping direction and the process involved is similar to that for seeking a scoping opinion.

Gathering environmental information

15.26 An applicant intending to prepare an ES is entitled to receive reasonable access to information held by the consultation bodies which may help them to prepare it. To obtain this the applicant has to serve a notice on the planning authority under reg 16 of the 2011 Regulations.

The authority then has to notify the consultation bodies of this and remind them of their duty to consult with the applicant and to make available any information they hold that may be needed for the ES. However, the statutory bodies' obligation is only to disclose information already in their possession and they do not have to undertake research, nor need they disclose information which they have a duty to keep confidential. They are also entitled to make a reasonable charge for providing the information.

Environmental Statement (ES)

15.27 When an applicant submits a planning application for an EIA development they will normally submit an Environmental Statement (ES) at the same time. The 2011 Regulations (Schedule 4) prescribe the content of an ES in 2 parts and these are as follows:

Part 1

- Description of the development, including in particular—(a) a description of the physical characteristics of the whole development and the land-use requirements during the construction and operational phases; (b) a description of the main characteristics of the production processes, for instance, nature and quantity of the materials used; and (c) an estimate, by type and quantity, of expected residues and emissions (water, air and soil pollution, noise, vibration, light, heat, radiation, etc.) resulting from the operation of the development.
- An outline of the main alternatives studied by the applicant and an indication of the main reasons for the choice made, taking into account the environmental effects.
- A description of the aspects of the environment likely to be significantly affected by the development, including, in particular, population, fauna, flora, soil, water, air, climatic factors, material assets, including the architectural and archaeological heritage, landscape and the interrelationship between the above factors.
- A description of the likely significant effects of the development on the environment, which should cover the direct effects and any indirect, secondary, cumulative, short, medium and long-term, permanent and temporary, positive and negative effects of the development, resulting from: (a) the existence of the development; (b) the use of natural resources; (c) the emission of pollutants, the creation of nuisances and the elimination of waste, and the description by the applicant or appellant of the forecasting methods used to assess the effects on the environment.

- A description of the measures envisaged to prevent, reduce and where possible offset any significant adverse effects on the environment.
- A non-technical summary of the information provided in Part 1 (applicants are encouraged to publish this separately from the main ES).
- An indication of any difficulties (technical deficiencies or lack of know-how) encountered by the applicant or appellant in compiling the required information.

Part 2

- A description of the development comprising information on the site, design and size of the development.
- A description of the measures envisaged in order to avoid, reduce and, if possible, remedy significant adverse effects.
- The data required to identify and assess the main effects which the development is likely to have on the environment.
- An outline of the main alternatives studied by the applicant or appellant and an indication of the main reasons for the choice made, taking into account the environmental effects.
- A non-technical summary of the information provided in Part 2 (again applicants are encouraged to publish this separately).

Adequacy of the ES

15.28 The planning authority has to ensure that the ES is adequate and contains all of the environmental information required to make a decision on the proposal. For example, if further tests and surveys are required these must be completed and the information made available to the public and consultation bodies and then taken into account by the authority before a decision is made on the application.[1]

1 *R v Cornwall CC ex parte Hardy* [2001] JPL 786.

Notification and publicity

15.29 In addition to the normal notification connected with the planning application (see Chapter 6), the planning authority has to carry out notification about the ES using the form set out in Schedule 5 of the 2011 regulations. The notices have to identify the location of the proposed development, give information about where copies of the ES can be inspected (without charge) or purchased (and at what price), and set out how representations can be made. The notices should be served on neighbours (as defined in the Development Management Regulations;

see Chapter 6). Press notices giving similar information have to be placed in a local newspaper and also the Edinburgh Gazette and the applicant has to meet the costs of this. Copies of the ES and all related documents have to be available at the planning authority's offices for at least 4 weeks from the date of notification.

Consultation

15.30 The planning authority has to send three copies of the ES, the planning application and all related documents to the Scottish Ministers. It also has to send a copy to each consultation body and, in certain circumstances, the Health and Safety Executive. The 2011 Regulations define consultation bodies as follows: any adjoining planning authority where the proposed development is likely to affect land in their area; Scottish Natural Heritage; Scottish Water; the Scottish Environment Protection Agency (SEPA); the Scottish Ministers; and, any other bodies designated by statutory provision as having specific environmental responsibilities and which the planning authority or the Scottish Ministers, as the case may be, considers are likely to have an interest in the application. In certain cases the Health and Safety Executive has to be consulted. The relevant district salmon fishery board is a consultation body for marine fish farm developments. Non-statutory bodies may also be consulted where their expertise would be useful, eg the Royal Society for the Protection of Birds.

15.31 The consultation bodies are to be advised by the planning authority that they may make representations. The applicant has to give the planning authority enough copies of the ES to meet these statutory requirements plus an additional 5 copies. A reasonable number of copies also have to be made available for members of the public, although the applicant can charge for these. The planning authority cannot begin to consider the ES until after it has given all consultees time to make representations and this should be a period of at least 4 weeks.

Additional information

15.32 If the planning authority considers that the applicant should provide more information to meet the requirements for an ES as set out in Schedule 4 to the 2011 Regulations, they can write to the applicant requiring them to produce this. Once it has received this information from the applicant the authority has to publicise it in the same way as the original ES (see para 15.30 above) and provide copies to consultees.

Post decision requirements

15.33 Where planning permission is to be granted for an EIA development this is likely to be subject to conditions (see Chapter 6) or a planning obligation under s75 of the 1997 Act (see Chapter 8) to ensure that any necessary mitigation measures are implemented. In multi-stage consent processes, it is possible for the planning authority to impose conditions on the permission as a whole not just the later stage approval.[1]

1 Town and Country Planning (Environmental Impact Assessment) (Scotland) Regulations 2011 (SSI 2011 No 139), reg 4(2).

15.34 Once an EIA development application has been determined, the planning authority has to write to the Scottish Ministers and consultation bodies advising them of the outcome. It must also advertise the outcome in a local newspaper or by other reasonable means. A statement also has to be placed in the authority's planning register (see Chapter 6) containing: the content of the decision and any conditions attached to it; information about public participation; the main reasons and considerations on which the decision was based; a description of the main mitigation measures (if relevant); and information about the right to challenge the validity of the decision and the process for doing so.

15.35 Whether or not an EIA is required is a quite separate issue from the planning merits of the development. A decision not to require assessment in a particular case carries no implication that planning permission will or should be granted for the development. Equally, planning permission will not automatically be refused because the EIA for a development shows that it will have an adverse environmental impact. The decision on planning permission will still be based on the provisions of the development plan and all other material considerations of which environmental impact is just one.[1]

1 SG Circular 3/2011 'The Town and Country Planning (Environmental Impact Assessment) (Scotland) Regulations 2011', para 14.

Permitted development

15.36 In Chapter 5 we looked at the range of developments which can normally be carried out without an application for planning permission because planning consent has been granted in advance by the Town and Country Planning (General Permitted Development) (Scotland) Order 1992. However, where a proposed permitted development falls within Schedule 1 EIA is mandatory and so, with some exceptions, there can be no permitted development rights. In the case of Schedule 2 developments, if the authority adopts a screening opinion that the proposed permitted development is an EIA development then again, with some limited exceptions, there will be no permitted development rights. The onus is therefore on the developer to find out in advance whether their proposal will enjoy permitted development status or whether they will be required to submit a planning application accompanied by an ES.

Appendix 1

Town and Country Planning (Scotland) Act 1997

s 26 Meaning of 'development'

(1) Subject to the following provisions of this section and to section 26AB, in this Act, except where the context otherwise requires, 'development' means the carrying out of building, engineering, mining or other operations in, on, over or under land, or the making of any material change in the use of any buildings or other land or the operation of a marine fish farm in the circumstances specified in section 26AA.

(2) The following operations or uses of land shall not be taken for the purposes of this Act to involve development of the land –

(a) the carrying out of works for the maintenance, improvement or other alteration of any building being works which –
  (i) affect only the interior of the building, or
  (ii) do not materially affect the external appearance of the building,

  and are not works for making good war damage within the meaning of the War Damage Act 1943 or works begun after 7 December, 1969 for the alteration of a building by providing additional space in it underground;

(b) the carrying out by a roads authority (as defined by section 151(1) of the Roads (Scotland) Act 1984) on land within the boundaries of a road of any works required for the maintenance or improvement of the road but, in the case of any such works which are not exclusively for the maintenance of the road, not including any works which may have significant adverse effects on the environment;

(c) the carrying out by a local authority or statutory undertakers of any works for the purpose of inspecting, repairing or renewing any sewers, mains, pipes, cables or other apparatus, including the breaking open of any road or other land for that purpose;

(d) the use of any buildings or other land within the curtilage of a dwellinghouse for any purpose incidental to the enjoyment of the dwellinghouse as such;

(e) subject to subsection (2A) the use of any land for the purposes of agriculture or forestry (including afforestation) and the use for any of those purposes of any building occupied together with land so used;
(f) in the case of buildings or other land which are used for a purpose of any class specified in an order made by the Secretary of State under this section, the use of the buildings or other land or, subject to the provisions of the order, of any part of the buildings or the other land, for any other purpose of the same class;
(g) the demolition of any description of building specified in a direction given by the Secretary of State to planning authorities generally or to a particular planning authority.

(2AA) The Scottish Ministers may in a development order specify any circumstances, or description of circumstances, in which subsection (2) does not apply to operations mentioned in paragraph (a) of that subsection which have the effect of increasing the gross floor space of the building by such amount or percentage as is so specified.

(2AB) The development order may make different provision for different purposes.

(2A) Development includes the carrying out of drainage for agriculture or of any other water management project for that purpose, but does not include the carrying out of irrigation work.

(3) For the avoidance of doubt it is hereby declared that for the purposes of this section –

(a) the use as two or more separate dwellinghouses of any building previously used as a single dwellinghouse involves a material change in the use of the building and of each part of it which is so used;
(b) the deposit of refuse or waste materials on land involves a material change in its use, notwithstanding that the land is comprised in a site already used for that purpose, if –
    (i) the superficial area of the deposit is extended, or
    (ii) the height of the deposit is extended and exceeds the level of the land adjoining the site.

(4) For the purposes of this Act building operations include –

(a) demolition of buildings,
(b) rebuilding,
(c) structural alterations of or additions to buildings, and
(d) other operations normally undertaken by a person carrying on business as a builder.

(5) For the purposes of this Act mining operations include –

(a) the removal of material of any description –
 (i) from a mineral-working deposit,
 (ii) from a deposit of pulverised fuel ash or other furnace ash or clinker, or
 (iii) from a deposit of iron, steel or other metallic slags, and
(b) the extraction of minerals from a disused railway embankment.

(6) Where the placing or assembly of any equipment in any part of any waters which –

(a) are inland waters,
(b) not being inland waters, are landward of the baselines from which the breadth of the territorial sea adjacent to Scotland is measured, or
(c) are seaward of those baselines up to a distance of 12 nautical miles,

for the purpose of fish farming there would not, apart from this subsection, involve development of the land below, this Act shall have effect as if the equipment resulted from carrying out engineering operations over that land; and in this section –

'equipment' includes any tank, cage or other structure, or long-line, for use in fish farming;
'fish farming' means the breeding, rearing or keeping of fish or shellfish (which includes any kind of sea urchin, crustacean or mollusc);
'inland waters' means waters which do not form part of the sea or of any creek, bay or estuary or of any river as far as the tide flows; and
'nautical miles' means international nautical miles of 1,852 metres; and

(6AA) Where the making of any material change in the use of equipment so placed or assembled for that purpose would not, apart from this subsection, involve development of the land below, this Act shall have effect as if the making of any such material change was development of that land.

(6A) The Scottish Ministers may by order made by statutory instrument make such modifications as they consider necessary or expedient to the definitions of 'equipment' and 'fish farming' in subsection (6); and an order under this subsection may make different provision for different purposes and different areas.

(6B) In subsection (6A), 'modifications' includes amendments and repeals.

(6C) The Scottish Ministers may by order make such provision as they consider necessary or expedient for the purpose of, or in connection with, the application of this Act to –

(a) any such placing or assembly as is mentioned in subsection (6) in waters described in paragraph (b) or (c) of that subsection; or
(b) any material change in the use of equipment placed or assembled in those waters.

(6D) Any order under subsection (6C) may in particular provide that a planning authority specified in the order is to be the planning authority for the purposes of such an application of this Act despite the placing or assembly being something done, or the material change of use being made, outwith the district of the authority.

(6E) But in the application of subsections (6C) and (6D) to a case where, by virtue of paragraph (a) of section 10(1) of the National Parks (Scotland) Act 2000 (asp 10) the planning authority is a National Park authority, the reference in subsection (6D) to the district of the authority is to be construed as a reference to the National Park.

(6F) And the Scottish Ministers may direct that subsections (6C) and (6D) are to apply to a case where –

(a) by virtue of paragraph (b) of that section 10(1), a National Park authority is to be treated as the planning authority, or
(b) by virtue of paragraph (c) of that section 10(1), a National Park authority is to have certain functions in relation to planning.

(6G) For the purposes of any such application as is provided for in –

(a) paragraph (a) of subsection (6F), the reference in subsection (6D) to the district of the authority is to be construed as mentioned in subsection (6E) and for the words 'planning authority specified in the order is to be' in subsection (6D) there is to be substituted 'National Park authority specified in the order is to be treated as',
(b) paragraph (b) of subsection (6F), the reference in subsection (6D) to the district of the authority is to be construed as mentioned in subsection (6E) and for the words 'planning authority specified in the order is to be the planning authority' in subsection (6D) there is to be substituted 'National Park authority specified in the order is to have functions in relation to planning'.

(6H) Before making an order under subsection (6C), the Scottish Ministers –

(a) must consult –
  (i) every planning authority, and
  (ii) the Scottish Environment Protection Agency, and
(b) may consult such other persons as they think fit.

(6I) An order under subsection (6C) may (without prejudice to the generality of that subsection) –

(a) modify any enactment, instrument or document,
(b) make such incidental, supplemental, consequential, transitional, transitory or saving provision as the Scottish Ministers think necessary or expedient,
(c) provide for the delegation of functions,
(d) make different provision for different purposes and different areas.

(6J) For the purposes of the exercise by a National Park authority of any planning functions which it has by virtue of subsections (6C) and (6D) in respect of waters described in paragraph (b) or (c) of subsection (6), any reference in section 9 of the National Parks (Scotland) Act 2000 (asp 10) (general purposes and functions of National Park authority) to the National Park itself is to be construed as including a reference to those waters.

(7) Without prejudice to any regulations under this Act relating to the control of advertisements, the use for the display of advertisements of any external part of a building which is not normally used for that purpose shall be treated for the purposes of this section as involving a material change in the use of that part of the building.

26AA Marine fish farms: circumstances referred to in section 26(1)

(1) The circumstances to which section 26(1) refers are –

(a) that the marine fish farm is being operated after –
  (i) the date which is the appropriate date in respect of that fish farm, or
  (ii) if earlier than that date, the date on which planning permission is granted, or an application for planning permission is refused, under section 31A, and
(b) that the operation involves the use of equipment which was placed or assembled in waters at a time when that placing or assembly did not constitute development under this Act.

(2) For the purposes of subsection (1)(a), the appropriate date in respect of a fish farm is whichever is the later of –

(a) a date prescribed by the Scottish Ministers for the purposes of this subsection, and
(b) the date on which any authorisation which –
 (i) relates to the operation of that fish farm, and
 (ii) is in effect at the date of commencement of section 4 of the Planning etc. (Scotland) Act 2006 (asp 17), ceases to have effect.

(3) In this section and in section 31A –

'authorisation' means –

(a) a consent for fish farming issued by the Crown Estate Commissioners,
(b) a licence granted under section 11 of the Orkney County Council Act 1974 (c.xxx), or
(c) a licence granted under section 11 of the Zetland County Council Act 1974 (c.viii),

'equipment' has the same meaning as in section 26(6), and

'marine fish farm' means a fish farm situated in any part of any waters referred to in paragraphs (b) and (c) of section 26(6).

26AB Power by order to provide marine fish farming is not 'development'

(1) The Scottish Ministers may by order provide that –

(a) section 26(6) does not apply as respects the placing or assembly of equipment for the purpose of fish farming in waters identified in the order (the 'relevant waters'),
(b) section 26(6AA) does not apply as respects any material change in the use of equipment so placed or assembled for that purpose, and
(c) the operation of a marine fish farm in the relevant waters in the circumstances specified in section 26AA is not 'development' for the purposes of this Act.

(2) An order under subsection (1) may be made only with the agreement of the planning authority (or planning authorities) for the relevant waters; and in this subsection the 'planning authority' means the planning authority specified in an order under section 26(6D).

Appendix 2

The Town and Country Planning (Use Classes) (Scotland) Order 1997

(SI 1997/3061)

1. Citation and commencement

This Order may be cited as the Town and Country Planning (Use Classes) (Scotland) Order 1997 and shall come into force on 2nd February 1998.

2. Interpretation

In this Order, the following expressions have the meanings assigned to them:

'care' means personal care including the provision of appropriate help with physical and social needs or support; and in class 8 (residential institutions) includes medical care and treatment;

'class' means a class specified in the Schedule to this Order;

'day centre' means non-residential premises which are used for social purposes, recreation, rehabilitation or occupational training and at which care is also provided;

'industrial process' means a process, other than a process carried out in or adjacent to, a mine or quarry, for or incidental to:

(a) the making of any article or part of any article including a ship or vessel or a film, video or sound recording;

(b) the altering, repairing, maintaining, ornamenting, finishing, cleaning, washing, packing, canning, adapting for sale, breaking up or demolition of any article; or

(c) the getting, dressing or treatment of minerals;

in the course of any use other than agriculture;

'site' means the whole area of land within a single unit of occupation;

'support' means counselling or other help provided as part of a planned programme of care.

3. Use classes

(1) Subject to the provisions of this Order, where a building or other land is used for a purpose in any class specified in the Schedule to this

Order, the use of that building or that other land for any other purpose in the same class shall not be taken to involve development of the land.

(2) References in paragraph (1) to a building include references to land occupied with the building and used for the same purposes.

(3) A use included in and ordinarily incidental to any use in a class shall not be precluded from that use by virtue of being specified in another class.

(4) Where land on a single site or on adjacent sites used as parts of a single undertaking comprises uses within both class 4 (business) and class 5 (general industrial), those uses may be treated as if they were in a single class in considering the use of that land for the purposes of this Order, provided that the area used for a purpose falling within class 5 (general industrial) shall not be substantially increased as a result.

(5) Nothing in any class shall include any use –

(a) as a theatre;
(b) as an amusement arcade or centre, or funfair;
(c) for the sale of fuel for motor vehicles;
(d) for the sale or display for sale of motor vehicles;
(e) for a taxi business or for the hire of motor vehicles;
(f) as a scrapyard, or a yard for the breaking of motor vehicles;
(g) for the storage or distribution of minerals;
(h) as a public house;
(i) for any work registrable under the Alkali, etc Works Regulation Act 1906;
(j) for the sale of hot food for consumption off the premises;
(k) as a waste disposal installation for the incineration, chemical treatment (as defined in Annex IIA to Directive75/442/EEC) under heading D9), or landfill of waste to which Directive 91/689/EEC applies.

NOTE to Article 3(5)

Paragraph (k) introduced by The Environmental Impact Assessment (Scotland) Regulations 1999 (SSI 1999 No 1)

4. Change of use of part of building or land

In the case of a building used for a purpose within class 9 (houses) the use as a separate house of any part of the building or of any land occupied with and used for the same purposes as the building shall not, by virtue of this Order, be taken as not amounting to development.

5. Revocation

The Town and Country Planning (Use Classes) (Scotland) Order 1989 and the Town and Country Planning (Use Classes) (Scotland) Amendment Order 1993 are hereby revoked.

ARTICLE 3

SCHEDULE

Class 1. Shops

Use –

(a) for the retail sale of goods other than hot food;
(b) as a post office;
(c) for the sale of tickets;
(d) as a travel agency;
(e) for the sale of cold food for consumption off the premises;
(f) for hairdressing;
(g) for the direction of funerals;
(h) for the display of goods for sale;
(i) for the hiring out of domestic or personal goods or articles;
(j) as a launderette or dry cleaners; or
(k) for the reception of goods to be washed, cleaned or repaired;

where the sale, display or service is principally to visiting members of the public.

Class 2. Financial, professional and other services

Use for the provision of –

(a) financial services;
(b) professional services; or
(c) any other services (including use as a betting office);

which it is appropriate to provide in a shopping area and where the services are provided principally to visiting members of the public.

Class 3. Food and drink

Use for the sale of food or drink for consumption on the premises.

Class 4. Business

Use –

(a) as an office, other than a use within class 2 (financial, professional and other services);
(b) for research and development of products or processes; or
(c) for any industrial process;

being a use which can be carried on in any residential area without detriment to the amenity of that area by reason of noise, vibration, smell, fumes, smoke, soot, ash, dust or grit.

Class 5. General industrial

Use for the carrying on of an industrial process other than one falling within class 4 (business).

Class 6. Storage or distribution

Use for storage or as a distribution centre.

Class 7. Hotels and hostels

Use as a hotel, boarding house, guest house or hostel where no significant element of care is provided, other than premises where alcohol (within the meaning given by section 2 of the Licensing (Scotland) Act 2005) is sold, pursuant to a premises licence issued under that Act, to persons other than persons consuming meals on the premises and other than a use within class 9 (houses).

NOTE to Class 7

Changes introduced by The Licensing (Scotland) Act 2005 (Consequential Provisions) Order 2009 (SSI 2009 No 248).

Class 8. Residential institutions

Use –

(a) for the provision of residential accommodation and care to people in need of care other than a use within class 9 (houses);
(b) as a hospital or nursing home; or
(c) as a residential school, college or training centre.

Class 8A. Secure residential institutions

Use for the provision of secure residential accommodation, including use as a prison, young offenders institution, detention centre, secure training centre, custody centre, short-term holding centre, secure hospital, secure local authority accommodation or use as military barracks.

NOTE about Class 8A

Introduced by the Town and Country Planning (Application of Subordinate Legislation to the Crown) (Scotland) Order 2006 (SSI 2006 No 270).

Class 9. Houses

Use for –

(a) as a house, other than a flat, whether or not as a sole or main residence, by –
  (i) a single person or by people living together as a family; or
  (ii) not more than 5 residents living together including a household where care is provided for residents;

(b) as a bed and breakfast establishment or guesthouse [(not in either case being carried out in a flat)] where at any one time not more than 2 bedrooms are, or in the case of premises having less than 4 bedrooms 1 bedroom is, used for that purpose.

NOTE to Class 9

In paragraph (b) words in square brackets added by the Town and Country Planning (Use Classes) (Scotland) Amendment Order 1998, SI 1998/1196.

Class 10. Non-residential institutions

Use, not including residential use –

(a) as a crêche, day nursery or day centre;
(b) for the provision of education;
(c) for the display of works of art (otherwise than for sale or hire);
(d) as a museum;
(e) as a public library or public reading room;
(f) as a public hall or exhibition hall;
(g) for, or in connection with, public worship or religious instruction, or the social or recreational activities of a religious body; or
(h) as a law court.

Note to Class 10

Paragraph (h) introduced by the Town and Country Planning (Application of Subordinate Legislation to the Crown) (Scotland) Order 2006 (SSI 2006 No 270).

Class 11. Assembly and leisure

Use as a –

(a) cinema;
(b) concert hall;
(c) bingo hall or casino:
(d) dance hall or discotheque; or
(e) swimming bath, skating rink, gymnasium or area for other indoor or outdoor sports or recreation, not involving motorised vehicles or firearms.

Appendix 3

The Town and Country Planning (General Permitted Development) (Scotland) Order 1992

(for development initiated on or after 6 February 2013 see SI 1992/ 223 as amended by secondary legislation including the Town and Country Planning (General Permitted Development) (Scotland) Amendment Order 2011 (SSI 2011 No 357) – including the following provisions)

SCHEDULE

PART 1

DEVELOPMENT WITHIN THE CURTILAGE OF A DWELLINGHOUSE

Enlargement of a dwellinghouse

Class 1A.—(1) Any enlargement of a dwellinghouse by way of a single storey ground floor extension, including any alteration to the roof required for the purpose of the enlargement.

(2) Development is not permitted by this class if—

(a) any part of the development would be forward of a wall forming part of the principal elevation or side elevation where that elevation fronts a road;

(b) any part of the development would be within 1 metre of the boundary of the curtilage of the dwellinghouse and it would extend beyond the line of the wall forming part of the rear elevation that is nearest that boundary by more than—

(i) 3 metres in the case of a terrace house; or

(ii) 4 metres in any other case;

(c) the height of the eaves of the development would exceed 3 metres;

(d) any part of the development would exceed 4 metres in height;

(e) as a result of the development the area of ground covered by the resulting dwellinghouse would be more than twice the area of ground covered by the original dwellinghouse;
(f) as a result of the development the area of ground covered by development within the front or rear curtilage of the dwelling-house (excluding the original dwellinghouse and any hard surface or deck) would exceed 50% of the area of the front or rear curtilage respectively (excluding the ground area of the original dwellinghouse and any hard surface or deck); or
(g) it would be within a conservation area.

Class 1B.—(1) Any enlargement of a dwellinghouse by way of a ground floor extension consisting of more than one storey, including any alteration to the roof required for the purpose of the enlargement.

(2) Development is not permitted by this class if—

(a) any part of the development would be forward of a wall forming part of the principal elevation or side elevation where that elevation fronts a road;
(b) any part of the development would be within 10 metres of the boundary of the curtilage of the dwellinghouse;
(c) as a result of the development the height of the dwellinghouse would exceed the height of the existing dwellinghouse, when measured at the highest part of the roof and excluding any chimney;
(d) as a result of the development the area of ground covered by the resulting dwellinghouse would be more than twice the area of ground covered by the original dwellinghouse;
(e) as a result of the development the area of ground covered by development within the front or rear curtilage of the dwelling-house (excluding the original dwellinghouse and any hard surface or deck) would exceed 50% of the area of the front or rear curtilage respectively (excluding the ground area of the original dwellinghouse and any hard surface or deck); or
(f) it would be within a conservation area.

Class 1C.—(1) The erection, construction or alteration of any porch outside any external door of a dwellinghouse.

(2) Development is not permitted by this class if—

(a) its footprint would exceed 3 square metres;
(b) any part of it would be within 2 metres of a boundary between the curtilage of the dwellinghouse and a road;
(c) any part of the development would exceed 3 metres in height; or
(d) it would be within a conservation area.

Class 1D.—(1) Any enlargement of a dwellinghouse by way of an addition or alteration to its roof.

(2) Development is not permitted by this class if—

(a) it would be on a roof plane forming part of the principal elevation or side elevation where that elevation fronts a road;
(b) it would be on a roof plane and would be within 10 metres of the boundary of the cartilage of the dwellinghouse which that roof plane fronts;
(c) as a result of the development the height of the dwellinghouse would exceed the height of the existing dwellinghouse, when measured at the highest part of the roof and excluding any chimney;
(d) its width would exceed half the total width of the roof plane, measured at the eaves line, of the dwellinghouse;
(e) any part of the development would be within 0.3 metres of any edge of the roof plane of the dwellinghouse; or
(f) it would be within a conservation area.

Improvements or alterations to a dwellinghouse which are not enlargements

Class 2A.—(1) The erection, construction or alteration of any access ramp outside an external door of a dwellinghouse.

(2) Development is not permitted by this class if—

(a) the combined length of all flights forming part of the access ramp would exceed 5 metres;
(b) the combined length of all flights and landings forming part of the access ramp would exceed 9 metres;
(c) any part of the ramp would exceed 0.4 metres in height;
(d) the combined height of the ramp and any wall (excluding any external wall of the dwellinghouse), fence, balustrade, handrail or other structure attached to it would exceed 1.5 metres; or
(e) it would be within a conservation area or within the curtilage of a listed building.

Class 2B.—(1) Any improvement, addition or other alteration to the external appearance of a dwellinghouse that is not an enlargement.

(2) Development is not permitted by this class if—

(a) it would protrude more than 1 metre from the outer surface of an external wall, roof plane, roof ridge or chimney of the dwellinghouse;

(b) it would be a wind turbine;
(c) it would be a balcony;
(d) it would be on the roof and would result in a raised platform or terrace;
(e) it would be within a conservation area; or
(f) it would be development described in class 2A(1), 3B(1), 6C(1), 6F(1), 6H(1) or 72(1).

(3) Development is permitted by this class subject to the condition that the materials used for any roof covering must be as similar in appearance to the existing roof covering as is reasonably practicable.

Other development within the curtilage of a dwellinghouse

Class 3A.—(1) The provision within the curtilage of a dwellinghouse of a building for any purpose incidental to the enjoyment of that dwellinghouse or the alteration, maintenance or improvement of such a building.

(2) Development is not permitted by this class if—

(a) it consists of a dwelling;
(b) any part of the development would be forward of a wall forming part of the principal elevation or side elevation where that elevation fronts a road;
(c) the height of the eaves would exceed 3 metres;
(d) any part of the development would exceed 4 metres in height;
(e) any part of the development within 1 metre of the boundary of the curtilage of the dwellinghouse would exceed 2.5 metres in height;
(f) as a result of the development the area of ground covered by development within the front or rear curtilage of the dwellinghouse (excluding the original dwellinghouse and any hard surface or deck) would exceed 50% of the area of the front or rear curtilage respectively (excluding the ground area of the original dwellinghouse and any hard surface or deck); or
(g) in the case of land in a conservation area or within the curtilage of a listed building, the resulting building would have a footprint exceeding 4 square metres.

Class 3B.—(1) The carrying out of any building, engineering, installation or other operation within the curtilage of a dwellinghouse for any purpose incidental to the enjoyment of that dwellinghouse.

(2) Development is not permitted by this class if—

(a) any part of the development would be forward of a wall forming part of the principal elevation or side elevation where that elevation fronts a road;
(b) any resulting structure would exceed 3 metres in height;
(c) as a result of the development the area of ground covered by development within the front or rear curtilage of the dwellinghouse (excluding the original dwellinghouse and any hard surface or deck) would exceed 50% of the area of the front or rear curtilage respectively (excluding the ground area of the original dwellinghouse and any hard surface or deck);
(d) it would be within a conservation area or within the curtilage of a listed building; or
(e) it would be development described in class 3A(1), 3C(1), 3D(1), 3E(1), 6D, 6E, 6G(1), 6H(1) or 8.

Class 3C.—(1) The provision within the curtilage of a dwellinghouse of a hard surface for any purpose incidental to the enjoyment of that dwellinghouse or the replacement in whole or in part of such a surface.

(2) Development is not permitted by this class if it would be within a conservation area or within the curtilage of a listed building.

(3) Development is permitted by this class subject to the condition that where the hard surface would be located between the dwellinghouse and a road bounding the curtilage of the dwellinghouse—

(a) the hard surface must be made of porous materials; or
(b) provision must be made to direct run off water from the hard surface to a permeable or porous area or surface within the curtilage of the dwellinghouse.

Class 3D.—(1) The erection, construction, maintenance, improvement or alteration of any deck or other raised platform within the curtilage of a dwellinghouse for any purpose incidental to the enjoyment of that dwellinghouse.

(2) Development is not permitted by this class if—

(a) any part of the development would be forward of a wall forming part of the principal elevation or side elevation where that elevation fronts a road;
(b) the floor level of any part of the deck or platform would exceed 0.5 metres in height;
(c) the combined height of the deck and any wall, fence, balustrade, handrail or other structure attached to it, would exceed 2.5 metres; or

(d) in the case of land within a conservation area or within the curtilage of a listed building the deck or platform would have a footprint exceeding 4 square metres.

Class 3E.—(1) The erection, construction, maintenance, improvement or alteration of any gate, fence, wall or other means of enclosure any part of which would be within or would bound the curtilage of a dwellinghouse.

(2) Development is not permitted by this class if—

(a) any part of the resulting gate, fence, wall or other means of enclosure would exceed 2 metres in height;
(b) any part of the resulting gate, fence, wall or other means of enclosure would exceed one metre in height where it—
  (i) fronts a road; or
  (ii) extends beyond the line of the wall of the principal elevation or side elevation that is nearest a road;
(c) it replaces or alters an existing gate, fence, wall or other means of enclosure and exceeds whichever is the greater of the original height or the heights described in sub-paragraphs (a) and (b);
(d) it would be within a conservation area; or
(e) it would be within, or bound, the curtilage of a listed building.

Interpretation of Part 1

For the purposes of Part 1—

'balcony' means a platform, enclosed by a wall or balustrade, projecting outward from the external wall of a building, with access from an upper floor window or door;
'bound' means to share a common boundary, and 'bounding' is to be construed accordingly;
'enlargement' means any development that increases the internal volume of the original dwellinghouse, and includes a canopy or roof, with or without walls, which is attached to the dwellinghouse, but does not include a balcony;
'footprint' means an area of ground covered by development;
'front curtilage' means that part of the curtilage of the original dwellinghouse forward of the principal elevation;
'rear curtilage' means that part of the curtilage of the original dwellinghouse which is not the front curtilage;
'rear elevation' means the elevation of the original dwellinghouse that is opposite its principal elevation;
'resulting dwellinghouse' means the dwellinghouse as enlarged, taking into account any previous enlargement;

'side elevation' means the elevation of the original dwellinghouse linking the principal elevation with the rear elevation; and

'terrace house' means a dwellinghouse—

(a) situated in a row of three or more buildings used, or designed for use, as single dwellinghouses; and

(b) having a mutual wall with, or having a main wall adjoining the main wall of, the dwellinghouse (or building designed for use as a dwellinghouse) on either side of it, but includes the dwellinghouses at each end of such a row of buildings as is referred to.

Any reference in Part 1 to—

(a) height is a reference to height when measured from ground level, and ground level means the level of the surface of the ground immediately adjacent to the building or structure or, where the level of the surface of the ground is not uniform, the level of the lowest part of the surface of the ground adjacent to it;

(b) the measurement of a dimension is a reference to the measurement of external dimensions; and

(c) 'the principal elevation' is a reference to the elevation of the original dwellinghouse which by virtue of its design or setting, or both, is the principal elevation.

PART 1ZA

DEVELOPMENT TO A BUILDING CONTAINING A FLAT

Class 4A.—(1) Any improvement or other alteration to the external appearance of a dwelling situated within a building containing one or more flats.

(2) Development is not permitted by this class if—

(a) it would be an enlargement;

(b) it would protrude more than 1 metre from the outer surface of an external wall, roof plane, roof ridge or chimney;

(c) the dimensions of an existing window or door opening would be altered;

(d) it would be a balcony;

(e) it would be on the roof and would result in a raised platform or terrace;

(f) it would be a wind turbine;

(g) it would be within a conservation area or within the curtilage of a listed building; or

(h) it would be development described in class 6C(1), 6F(1) or 6H(1) or 72(1).

(3) For the purposes of this class—

'balcony' means a platform, enclosed by a wall or balustrade, projecting outward from the external wall of a building, with access from an upper floor window or door;

'enlargement' means any development that increases the internal volume of the original building, and includes a canopy or roof, with or without walls, which is attached to the building but does not include a balcony;

a 'window' or 'door' includes its frame; and

the measurement of a dimension is a reference to the measurement of external dimensions.

PART 1A

INSTALLATION OF DOMESTIC MICROGENERATION EQUIPMENT

Class 6C.—(1) The installation, alteration or replacement of a flue, forming part of a biomass heating system, on a dwellinghouse or building containing a flat.

(2) Development is not permitted by this class if–

(a) the height of the flue would protrude more than one metre above the highest part of the roof (excluding any chimney) on which the flue is fixed;

(b) in the case of land within a conservation area or a World Heritage Site, the flue would be installed on the principal elevation of the dwellinghouse or building containing a flat; or

(c) the flue would be within an Air Quality Management Area.

Class 6D.—The installation, alteration or replacement of a ground source heat pump within the curtilage of a dwellinghouse or building containing a flat.

Class 6E.—The installation, alteration or replacement of a water source heat pump within the cartilage of a dwellinghouse or building containing a flat.

Class 6F.—(1) The installation, alteration or replacement of a flue, forming part of a combined heat and power system, on a dwellinghouse or building containing a flat.

(2) Development is not permitted by this class if–

(a) the height of the flue would protrude more than 1 metre above the highest part of the roof (excluding any chimney) on which the flue is fixed;
(b) in the case of land within a conservation area or World Heritage Site, the flue would be installed on the principal elevation of the dwellinghouse, or building containing a flat; or
(c) in the case of a combined heat and power system fuelled by biomass sources, the flue would be within an Air Quality Management Area.

Class 6G.—(1) The installation, alteration or replacement of a free-standing wind turbine within the curtilage of a dwelling.

(2) Development is not permitted by this class if—

(a) it would result in the presence within the curtilage of a dwelling of more than one free standing wind turbine; or
(b) the wind turbine would be situated less than 100 metres from the curtilage of another dwelling.

(3) Development is not permitted by this class in the case of land within—

(a) a conservation area;
(b) a World Heritage Site;
(c) a site of special scientific interest; or
(d) a site of archaeological interest.

(4) Development is not permitted by this class if the wind turbine would be within the curtilage of a listed building.

(5) Development is permitted by this class subject to the following conditions—

(a) the developer must before beginning the development apply to the planning authority for—
    (i) the approval of the authority in respect of the design and size of the proposed wind turbine; and
    (ii) a determination as to whether the prior approval of the authority will be required in respect of the siting and external appearance of the proposed wind turbine;
(b) the application is to be accompanied by—
    (i) a written description of the proposed development, including details of the design and size of the proposed wind turbine; and
    (ii) a plan indicating the site;

(c) the development is not to be commenced before—
  (i) the applicant has received written approval from the planning authority in respect of the size and design of the wind turbine; and
  (ii) the occurrence of one of the following—
    (aa) the receipt by the applicant from the planning authority of a written notice of their determination that prior approval in respect of the siting and external appearance of the proposed wind turbine is not required;
    (bb) the expiry of a period of 28 days following the date on which the application was received by the planning authority without the planning authority giving notice of their determination that such approval is required; or
    (cc) where the planning authority gives the applicant notice within a period of 28 days following the date of receiving the application of their determination that such prior approval is required, the giving of such approval;
(d) the development must, except to the extent that the planning authority otherwise agree in writing, be carried out—
  (i) to the extent to which prior approval is required, in accordance with the details approved;
  (ii) to the extent to which prior approval is not required, in accordance with the details submitted with the application;
(e) the development is to be carried out within a period of three years from the date on which all approvals required in accordance with this paragraph have been given.

(6) Development is permitted by this class subject to the conditions that a free-standing wind turbine—

(a) must, so far as reasonably practicable, be sited so as to minimise its effect on the amenity of the area; and
(b) is used only for the purposes of domestic microgeneration; and
(c) that is no longer needed for or capable of domestic microgeneration must be removed as soon as reasonably practicable.

Class 6H—(1) The installation, alteration or replacement of an air source heat pump within the curtilage of a dwelling.

(2) Development is not permitted by this class if—

(a) it would result in the presence within the curtilage of a dwelling of more than one air source heat pump; or
(b) the air source heat pump would be situated less than 100 metres from the curtilage of another dwelling.

(3) Development is not permitted by this class in the case of land within a conservation area if the air source heat pump would be visible from a road.

(4) Development is not permitted by this class if the air source heat pump would be within—

(a) a World Heritage Site; or
(b) the curtilage of a listed building.

(5) Development is permitted by this class subject to the following conditions—

(a) the developer must before beginning the development apply to the planning authority for a determination as to whether the prior approval of the authority will be required to the siting and external appearance of the air source heat pump;
(b) the application is to be accompanied by a written description of the proposed development and a plan indicating the site;
(c) the development is not to be commenced before the occurrence of one of the following—
    (i) the receipt by the applicant from the planning authority of a written notice of their determination that such prior approval is not required;
    (ii) the expiry of a period of 28 days following the date on which the application was received by the planning authority without the planning authority giving notice of their determination that such approval is required; or
    (iii) where the planning authority gives the applicant notice within a period of 28 days following the date of receiving the application of their determination that such prior approval is required, the giving of such approval;
(d) the development must, except to the extent that the planning authority otherwise agree in writing, be carried out—
    (i) where prior approval is required, in accordance with the details approved;
    (ii) where prior approval is not required, in accordance with the details submitted with the application;
(e) the development is to be carried out—
    (i) where approval has been given by the planning authority, within a period of three years from the date on which approval was given; or
    (ii) in any other case, within a period of three years from the date on which the application under paragraph (a) above was made.

(6) Development is permitted by this class subject to the conditions that an air source heat pump—

(a) must, so far as reasonably practicable, be sited so as to minimise its effect on the amenity of the area;
(b) is used only for the purposes of domestic microgeneration; and
(c) that is no longer needed for or capable of domestic microgeneration must be removed as soon as reasonably practicable.

Interpretation of Part 1A

For the purposes of Part 1A–

'Air Quality Management Area', has the meaning given in section 83(1) of the Environment Act 1995;
'dwelling' means a dwellinghouse, a building containing one or more flats or a flat contained within such a building;
'free standing wind turbine' means a wind turbine which is not installed on a building;
'microgeneration' has the meaning given in section 82(6) of the Energy Act 2004;
'domestic microgeneration' means the production of electricity or heat for domestic consumption using microgeneration equipment; and
'World Heritage Site' means land appearing on the World Heritage List kept under article 11(2) of the 1972 UNESCO Convention for the Protection of the World Cultural and Natural Heritage.

PART 2

SUNDRY MINOR OPERATIONS

Class 7.—(1) The erection, construction, maintenance, improvement or alteration of a gate, fence, wall or other means of enclosure.

(2) Development is not permitted by this class if—

(a) the height of any gate, fence, wall or other means of enclosure to be erected or constructed within 20 metres of a road would, after the carrying out of the development, exceed one metre above ground level;
(b) the height of any other gate, fence, wall or other means of enclosure to be erected or constructed would exceed two metres above ground level;
(c) the height of any existing gate, fence, wall or other means of enclosure maintained, improved or altered would, as a result of the development, exceed its former height or the height referred to

in sub-paragraph (a) or (b) as the height appropriate to it if erected or constructed, whichever is the greater; or

(d) it would involve development within the curtilage of, or in respect of a gate, fence, wall or other means of enclosure surrounding, a listed building. or

(e) it would be development described in class 3E(1).

PART 25

CLOSED CIRCUIT TELEVISION CAMERAS

Class 72.—(1) The installation, alteration or replacement on any building or other structure of a closed circuit television camera for security purposes.

(2) Development is not permitted by this class if—

(a) the development is in a conservation area or a national scenic area;

(b) the dimensions of the camera including its housing exceed 75 centimetres by 25 centimetres by 25 centimetres;

(c) any part of the camera would, when installed, altered or replaced, be less than 250 centimetres above ground level;

(d) any part of the camera would, when installed, altered or replaced, protrude from the surface of the building or structure by more than one metre when measured from the surface of the building or structure;

(e) any part of the camera would, when installed, altered or replaced, be in contact with the surface of the building or structure at a point which is more than one metre from any other point of contact;

(f) any part of the camera would be less than 10 metres from any part of another camera installed on a building or structure;

(g) the development would result in the presence of more than four cameras on the same side of the building or structure; or

(h) the development would result in the presence of more than 16 cameras on the building or structure.

(3) Development is permitted by this class subject to the following conditions:—

(a) the camera shall, so far as practicable, be sited so as to minimise its effect on the external appearance of the building or structure on which it is situated;

(b) the camera shall be removed as soon as reasonably practicable after it is no longer required for security purposes;

(c) the field of vision of the camera shall, so far as practicable, not extend beyond the boundaries of the land upon which the building or structure is erected or of any area which adjoins that land and to which the public have access.

(4) For the purposes of this class–

'camera', except in paragraph (2)(b), includes its housing, pan and tilt mechanism, infra red illuminator, receiver, mountings and brackets.

Appendix 4

The Town and Country Planning (Development Management Procedure) (Scotland) Regulations 2013

(SSI 2013 NO 155)

SCHEDULE 3

Classes of development – regulations 20(2)(c) and 41(1)(b)

The following are the classes of development specified for the purposes of regulations 20(2)(c) and 41(1)(b)—

(1) the construction or installation of buildings for use as a public convenience;

(2) the construction of buildings or other operations, or use of land—

(a) for the disposal of refuse or waste materials or for the storage or recovery of reusable metal;
(b) for the retention, treatment or disposal of sewage, trade-waste, or effluent other than—
  (i) the construction of pumphouses in a line of sewers;
  (ii) the construction of septic tanks and cesspools serving single dwellinghouses, single caravans or single buildings in which not more than 10 people will normally reside, work or congregate;
  (iii) the laying of sewers; or
  (iv) works ancillary to those described in sub-paragraphs (i) to (iii);
(c) as a scrap yard or coal yard; or
(d) for the winning or working of minerals, including management of extractive waste.

(3) the construction of buildings or use of land or buildings for the purpose of slaughtering animals (including fish and poultry) or the

processing of animal carcasses for final disposal or as part of the production of other goods;

(4) the construction or use of buildings for any of the following purposes—

(a) building for indoor games
(b) cinema
(c) dancing
(d) fun fair
(e) gymnasium (not forming part of a school, college or university)
(f) hot food shop
(g) licensed premises
(h) music hall
(i) skating rink
(j) swimming pool or
(k) theatre;

(5) the construction of buildings for or the use of buildings or land as—

(a) a crematorium or a cemetery;
(b) a zoo or wildlife park or for the business of boarding or breeding animals;

(6) the construction of buildings and use of buildings or land for motor racing;

(7) the construction of a building to a height exceeding 20 metres;

(8) the construction of buildings, operations and use of buildings or land which will—

(a) affect residential property by reason of fumes, noise, vibration, smoke, artificial lighting, or discharge of any solid or liquid substance;
(b) alter the character of an area of established amenity;
(c) bring crowds into a generally quiet area; 31
(d) cause activity and noise between the hours of 8 pm and 8 am; or
(e) introduce significant change into a homogeneous area.

Index

[References are to paragraph number and appendices]